The Stories of My Life

Hilarious, Heartwarming, Harrowing, and Heartbreaking

Tales From a Common Man

By B. R. Allen

The Stories of My Life

Hilarious, Heartwarming, Harrowing, and Heartbreaking Tales From a Common Man

© Copyright B. R. Allen Publishing, 2025

All rights reserved

This book or any part thereof may not be reproduced in any form, stored in a retrieval system, or transmitted in any form by any means – electronic, mechanical, photocopy, recording or otherwise – without prior written permission of the publisher, except as provided by USA copyright law.

brallenpublishing@gmail.com

First Edition

Paperback ISBN 978-1-7342363-2-3

E Book ISBN 978-1-7342363-3-0

Table of Contents

Introduction	1
Section I – The Younger Years	
Chapter 1 In the Beginning…	7
Chapter 2 California Dreaming	10
Chapter 3 The Nightmare: Leaving California	28
Section II – Travails of Travel	
Chapter 4 Unfair Share	58
Chapter 5 My History with Long Beach Airport	70
Chapter 6 Honeymoon Delayed But Not Denied	77
Chapter 7 The Longest Travel Days	97
Chapter 8 More Mishaps and Misery	105
Section III – Music is my Muse	
Chapter 9 Musical and Spiritual Experiences	114
Chapter 10 The Grand US Tour of 1969	121
Chapter 11 The College and Teaching Years	131
Chapter 12 The Twists and Turns of the Music Biz	135
Chapter 13 Combining Business and Pleasure	150
Section IV – My Sometimes Wacky World of Business	
Chapter 14 German-American Cultural Relations	176
Chapter 15 Trade Show Tales	180
Section V – Close Encounters of the Famous Kind	
Chapter 16 A Night With Les Paul	192
Chapter 17 Bigwigs in Buffalo	197
Chapter 18 Hangin' With a Hall of Famer	202
Chapter 19 A Hero's Welcome	213
Chapter 20 Other Notable Chance Meetings	218
Section VI – Close Encounters of the Animal Kind	
Chapter 21 The Dog Days	233
Chapter 22 Birds of a Feather	237
Chapter 23 Uninvited Guests	241
Section VII – Tales From the Hood	
Chapter 24 Big Black Cat	247
Chapter 25 Annual Race Ritual	250
Chapter 26 Home Invasion	252
Section VIII – This Is Personal	
Chapter 27 Dredging up the Past	255
Chapter 28 From Rags to Riches to Ruin	268
Chapter 29 Medical Errors, Irreversible Damage	274
Section IX – It's a Wrap	
Chapter 30 The Beginning of the End	283
Pictures	287
Acknowledgements	295
About the Author	296

Introduction

After I retired from working in the world of marketing, mostly in the IT sector, and since I didn't have anything else to do, I sat down one day and reflected on all the life experiences and the people I encountered. It only took a few minutes before my mind wandered off and I started thinking about how nice a nap would be. After all those long days that turned into long nights and all those hours of sleep I lost working and raising a family, I thought of how I've got a lot of napping to do to catch up on my sleep in retirement.

After waking up from my first nap of the day, I reboarded my train of thought and got back into deep contemplation about my life. For some random reason, I got to thinking about how my dad loved to tell old stories, as most of us Allen's do. I have shared many of my famous stories with friends and family in various social settings, sometimes driving my audience to sudden sleepiness better than an Ambien.

After lunch and my second nap of the day, I was again pondering my life's history, and I recalled our oldest daughter, Adrian, who had challenged me to write down many of the stories she had heard me tell over the years. I then decided that I should capture those memories and interesting tales before my brain's hard drive started losing megabytes of data. I also reflected on how many of those stories taught me valuable lessons and how I succeeded or failed in applying lessons I was supposed to have learned. Thus, the uncommonly brilliant and novel idea of documenting some of my experiences duly motivated me to get to work.

The First Struggle

The next thing I thought about was what title would be appropriate and catchy – something that would grab everyone's attention and have people fighting like Walmart shoppers at a Black Friday sale to buy my book.

Since marketing was my chosen profession, one would think that it would be a fairly simple task. However, I seemed to struggle with what title I should give to this future literary masterpiece. Perhaps my creative marketing skills had subsided like an old baseball player who can't catch up to a fastball at the end of his career. The more I thought about it, the more I'd swing and miss.

My struggle for a title continued for several weeks and countless naps, and I was further losing confidence that my creative genius had been tapped out like a keg at a frat party. Maybe I just didn't have it anymore. But I kept thinking that someday it would hit me. Maybe during the middle of the night I would suddenly wake up and have an epiphany. Or maybe it might miraculously come to me as I was walking in the forest – oh wait, we don't have forests around here. Perhaps it might mysteriously reveal itself as I was nodding off prior to another nap.

How I could encapsulate in a book title all the life experiences I have had and all the great relationships I developed over the years was becoming an increasingly difficult challenge. It kept turning out to be an insurmountable mountain that I was beginning to think I could not climb – either out of laziness or sheer stupidity. I continued to ask myself, "Self, how can you write a book if you can't even come up with a simple title?" That conversation was brief when I answered myself saying, "Good question."

Quite often, as I have learned the hard way, marketers can get too bent on being overly clever or cutesy – sometimes even outsmarting themselves (New Coke and Bud Lite come to mind). One day, it dawned on me that sometimes brilliance is in simplicity, so I decided that the best course of action was to follow the KISS principle – keep it simple, stupid – just call it what it is. So, in a momentary absence of creative brilliance, the title magically revealed itself to me: **The Stories of My Life**. It may not be pure genius, but it'll work.

A Common Man

I then decided that I needed a subtitle to further pique people's interest should they accidentally gaze at the book cover while wandering the aisles of a bookstore or happen to stumble on it while online. My first thought was that readers might actually find some of my stories **hilarious**. OK, that's a start. My next thought was that a few of the tales I can tell might be **heartwarming** to some people. OK, that works, too. I then decided that some of my stories were a bit **harrowing** – yeah, that's true. I also concluded that I, like most people, have had several **heartbreaking** experiences I could painfully retell. Yes, at least those four words are getting me somewhere.

My final thought was that I am just an ordinary guy, having never done anything extraordinary that would make me famous – an obviously true statement. But then again, not everyone can be eminently renowned – and that's OK . I recalled the lyrics in a country song by John Conlee that said:

> I'm a Common Man, I drive a common van, my dog ain't got no pedigree.
> If I have to say I'm gonna stay that way, 'cause high-browed people lose their sanity,
> And a Common Man is what I'll be.

I then put all those observations together, and voila, I had created the brilliantly compelling subtitle, **Hilarious, Heartwarming, Harrowing, and Heartbreaking Tales from a Common Man**. Admittedly, it might not be Shakespearean, but it was good enough for me.

The Times of My Life

Some of the stories in this book may bring tears to your eyes, while others may bore you to tears. Most certainly, I probably won't be able to tell a story that is so funny that it makes people cry from laughter. For me, a hearty chuckle will suffice. As an aside, have you ever wondered why when we are sad, we cry, yet we can laugh until we cry? God must have a twisted sense of humor.

In any case, some of my stories may be enthralling, while others may be found to be overly tedious and mind-numbing. For me personally, some stories are fun to re-live, while others are sad and painful to remember.

I will carefully stick to the truth of how the tales are told, and I will promise to only embellish details when it's selfishly expedient to do so. Most of the names of people mentioned are innocent and true, but I sometimes change the names of those who are guilty of some wrongdoing or were simply being a jerk. My intent is to not incriminate anyone – I will only do that if it's completely necessary and they fully deserve it.

Like everyone else, I have experienced elation while also enduring devastation. My life has been more mundane than magical, and more normal than abnormal. I will state that I am somewhat famous, yet with one caveat—my fame only extends to my family and friends, but it seems that some of the people I called friends don't even remember who I am. Sad but true.

Some may think that writing this book is a waste of my time – which certainly could be true – but at least it gives me something productive to do besides taking a nap. Yes, it will mean fewer naps and less time watching stupid YouTube videos, but this lofty creative effort requires sacrifice which I am unselfishly willing to make.

Remembering and reliving the happy times is fun. At times it's exhilarating, although probably only to me. It often brings back a sliver of the original feeling of elation that causes my eyes to well up as I recapture the feeling of that rush of dopamine that surges through my body. Then I realize I am exhausted and it's time for another nap.

And then there's the other side when I recall those times when heartbreaking news hit me like a gut punch from Mike Tyson. Those times are not easy to relive but sometimes recalling them can be a valuable tool for us to recalibrate or reset ourselves. Yes, it might even be cathartic – or even a liberating feeling that we survived when we thought our world had ended.

Quite often, reflecting on periods of adversity causes us to be thankful that we actually lived through those tough times or harrowing experiences. Consider the old saying, "Hard times create strong men, strong men create easy times, easy times create weak men, and weak men end up on psych meds and in many years of therapy." Well, something like that…

I have made miraculous comebacks from injuries – well maybe not so miraculous after all, because several of them have come back to haunt me today. I now realize that's what old age does. I have also come to learn that aging is not for the faint of heart – it sometimes is challenging work just to roll out of bed in the morning and get this achy bag of bones moving. I finally figured out why old people like me are called grown-ups. It's because every time we get out of bed or get up from a chair, we groan!

If I do make it out of bed and manage to gather the strength to make a pot of coffee, catch up on the daily news, and eat breakfast, I start looking forward to when I can take my first nap of the day.

Strange Phenomenon

Let me whet your appetite with a quick retelling of the most recent memorable event. I promise that I am not making up what was a highly unusual episode. Observing what transpired right in front of my eyes ranks as the strangest thing I have ever witnessed.

This experience actually involves two separate but similar incidents that caused me to have goose bumps along with a feeling of intrigue and amazement. In addition, I must say that I was spooked. Yes, I have experienced various serendipitous encounters and unusual events, but this tale is just plain weird. And I swear I was not under any type of hallucinogenic drug nor was I dreaming during one of my many naps. These two separate events occurred on February 23, 2024, and November 6, 2024.

As was customary, I took our little chihuahua Rowdy outside for his pre-bedtime potty ritual. I was standing on the front porch while he took care of his business. It was a cloudless night with very few stars faintly visible, mostly due to the light pollution at my location. I happened to notice some strange-looking white lights in the western sky that were randomly spaced and brighter than a star. I was baffled by what I was seeing. There were originally three lights that were moving strangely. I watched to make sure they were not airplanes and realized these lights were moving in a manner that would eliminate any type of aircraft. I then went back inside to retrieve my phone and capture a recording of the lights. I took a still photo showing the street and neighboring houses as a reference. I began recording on my phone at 12:53am.

The three lights in the sky began pulsating, quickly shape-shifting from a small speck to a larger ball-like orb. They would arbitrarily dart back and forth while staying in the same section of the sky. They were behaving like nothing I had ever seen before. At first, I thought someone was playing with some type of laser, but I didn't think these bizarre lights were at all reminiscent of various laser shows I had seen. There were no beams of light, just bright lights bouncing around in the sky. I was completely mystified.

When the lights moved rapidly, they would leave a short tail that would quickly evaporate. Sometimes when they moved, they would squeeze into a tight oval shape and move in a squiggly fashion. It was indeed a highly unusual sight to behold. And then it got even more weird.

The white lights disappeared for a few seconds and then I saw a lime green orb of light appear. It exhibited the same moving behaviors as the white lights. Whenever it stopped moving, it would enlarge and take on a semi-transparent appearance. When I zoomed in, I was even more enthralled. The only way I can describe it would be to think of a small petri dish with tiny living organisms rapidly scurrying around inside the dish. There were also fuzzy little dots within the orb that would pulsate and disappear. Then the orb quickly transformed from green to purple, and then to orange, and then back to white. At one point when the orb was green, it came down close to the ground near a streetlight about 150 feet from where I was standing. It quickly darted higher in the sky where it continued to zip back and forth, all the while pulsating. The single orb was then joined by two other colored orbs that were darting across the sky.

After about ten minutes of recording, the lights whizzed to my right and then disappeared into the night sky. I remained outside for several minutes to see if the lights would return, but they did not. When I went to bed, I tried to process what I had witnessed. I was puzzled and amazed, dazed and confused. It was the strangest phenomenon I had ever witnessed.

The following morning, I decided to download the files from my phone to my desktop computer and open them in my video production software program. I was able to zoom in and further observe how the lights behaved. I was even further captivated by what I had captured on video. I watched the video in slow motion which was eye-popping.

I decided to investigate how I might report the incident. I found the National UFO Reporting Center and uploaded an incident report and the video. Come to find out, there were numerous similar incidents that spanned many parts of the world over the past several years. It was comforting to know that I was not the only crazy person in the world.

It Happened Again

Experiencing a strange phenomenon once is unusual; seeing it twice is beyond crazy. The following November, it happened again. As before, I stepped outside to let Rowdy go potty and noticed a strange blue orb, this time in the southeastern sky. I ran back into the house to retrieve my phone to record it. The light stayed stationary while slowly pulsating for a few minutes, and then it began movements and behaviors similar to the previous orbs. This one did not change colors; it stayed blue for the entire six minutes, and then it rapidly zoomed to the right and disappeared. Again, I was perplexed.

As my further research found, these strange lights are called plasma orbs (or plasmoids) and are classified as unidentified aerial phenomenon (UAPs). No one really knows what they are or what causes them. I am not a hoaxer, and I can assure everyone that these two incidents absolutely happened. I can vouch for the fact that I was not on some exotic illicit drug, and my proof is the video recordings.

I am curious about alien life forms and have invested probably far too many hours watching *Ancient Aliens*. Many folks have bought into aliens visiting our planet. However, I am not fully convinced that other non-human beings have come to our beautiful blue planet, but I haven't ruled it out either. Having witnessed two incidents of strange and unknown phenomenon, I am convinced, nevertheless, there is still much we don't know and understand about our world and our universe. And that's OK because curiosity and intrigue fuel us to achieve enlightenment.

Maybe aliens are just jerking us around by giving us a strange light show, or maybe they are tormenting us. I don't know what's going on, but I do know that those bizarre lights rank at the top of the list as the weirdest thing I have ever seen.

Stuff Happens

I will close this long-winded introduction with a final observation. Woven into every event and every encounter in this book is some kind of serendipity (such a musical word – love it!). My own definition of serendipity is: "Finding or experiencing things not sought or planned that happen out of pure luck, through coincidence, by accident, a mere fluke, an unintended happenstance, or lastly, because of providential fate." Seeing orbs flying in the sky was certainly not planned nor was it on my bucket list – it just happened. So it is with the stories in this book. Stuff just happened.

Call it right place, right time, or in some cases, wrong place, wrong time. I have truly racked up many unusual and memorable experiences that I can't explain why they happened to me – they just did. I have been blessed, and yes, in some cases, I have been cursed with these out-of-the-ordinary experiences.

We do have some control over how things transpire, but how the plot and each chapter in life ultimately unfolds is mostly unpredictable, as is this book. Life is full of surprising twists and turns, plus ups and downs. After all, that's what makes our lives a random journey that can occasionally be boring, sometimes entertaining, oftentimes interesting, and mostly unexpected. Such are ***The Stories of My Life***. Now, let's get on with the show before I begin nodding off again.

Section I

The Younger Years

Chapter 1

In The Beginning…

I suppose the best place to start telling one's life story is at the very beginning, but strangely, I don't have any memories of that fateful day in 1950 when I was brought into this world in Dallas, Texas. Probably because I spent most of my early years napping much like I do nowadays. Isn't it interesting how life is a circle? We build up stamina in our early years by taking frequent naps to get ready for living, and then when we get old, we nap a lot because we are exhausted from all the living we had to do.

I don't recall much during my early years, but the first of two vivid memories I have were rather traumatic events. Both occurred in 1957.

On April 2nd (yes, I had to look it up as my memory is not that good), an estimated F3 or F4 tornado hit the Oak Cliff and West Dallas areas. We lived near the Love Field airport, and I remember playing in the front yard with my brothers and a few neighbors. It started raining softly, and we could see lightning and hear thunder in the distance. It looked like a typical thunderstorm was brewing. No big deal – it's Texas.

Back in those days, we didn't have extensive storm warning systems that blasted alarm notifications through cell phones and televisions – we barely had radios! The civil defense warning system was a guy with a megaphone shouting from a rooftop. The standard warning he shouted was, "A tornado is coming! Please take cover then put your head between your legs and kiss your ass good-bye!"

We stopped whatever game we were playing when my mom came outside to check out the rain. I vividly remember us all gazing to the southwest where we saw an enormous tornado that was leisurely moving through Oak Cliff. The view we had was from about five miles as the crow flies, and since the rain had stopped, visibility was clear. There were no buildings to obstruct our view back then. The color of the funnel was a very dark gray, and we could vividly see debris swirling around – even from several miles away. We all just stood there in silence, awed by what we were witnessing.

The tornado stayed on the ground for 16 miles, wreaking havoc as it slowly moved through Oak Cliff and into West Dallas. Ten people lost their lives, more than 200 were injured, and 540 houses and businesses were damaged or destroyed. Interestingly, it was the most photographed and filmed tornado for many years. Meteorologists were able to study the behavior of the tornado in terms of wind speed and debris impact. Again, no cell phones with cameras existed, and there weren't any crazy storm trackers clamoring to get as close as they could in their make-shift cars or vans that pretend to be tanks. But what data the meteorologists were able to gather set somewhat of a baseline for development of the "F" rating system used today. It was an important tornado for meteorologists, but not so much for the people and their structures that were affected.

I also recall us driving through some of the devastation a few days later because our church was in Oak Cliff. I was amazed yet horrified at the severity of Mother Nature's wrath. It was my first realization that she doesn't mess around. It's like Mother Nature wreaking havoc in her own rage room.

Sweet Taffy

The next traumatic event occurred a few months later when my aunt Marianna, who I adored, was visiting. We had dogs around pretty much my entire childhood, and at the time, we had a beautiful blond cocker spaniel who was the sweetest dog ever. Her name was Taffy. Everybody loved her and she loved everybody.

When it was time for Marianna to leave, she gathered up my two cousins Donna and Sharon and headed out the door. A few minutes later, Marianna came flying through the front door in tears and said, "I didn't see Taffy when I was backing out of the driveway, and I ran over her." We all went outside and saw Taffy lying there. It was devastating to not only my family, but poor Marianna was mortified. I can only imagine how horrible she felt. I remember being sick to my stomach and shedding a lot of tears. That's the first time I ever felt overwhelming sadness. I really didn't like that feeling and did not want to ever feel that again. Much to my chagrin, as life happens, it would be the first time but not the last time I would experience such painful sadness.

Well, that wore me out emotionally. Glad I've gotten that out of the way. I think I'll move on…but maybe the remedy is a nice long nap.

Chapter 2

California Dreaming

My father came home from work one day in the spring of 1957 and broke the news that he had received a great new job offer from his company, Purex Corporation. He had started working with them eight or so years earlier by performing the most important task in the manufacturing plant – he was screwing bottle caps on bleach bottles as they came off the production line. In his early years of employment, and because of his high-level performance in executing such an essential task, he received a promotion into a production management position. His bosses saw star potential. Later, he was promoted to a sales position covering the southwest and knocking sales numbers out of the park. Again, his star potential was shining brighter.

At that time, Purex had grown from a garage operation in 1922 with a single production facility headquartered in South Gate, California to eight production plants, with the newest one having been built in Dallas. A dry laundry detergent was added to the product mix in 1946, and the company was making acquisitions starting with the Old Dutch Cleanser brand, then acquiring Brillo and other household cleaning products. The company was on the rise as was Dad's business career when he accepted the position of Special Assistant to the President of the corporation at the new headquarters in Lakewood, California. Our move from Texas to California was completed in the summer of 1957.

As an aside, Dad never went to college. After serving in the Navy during WWII, he came back home, started his career with Purex, and spent 35 years with the company as a production and management troubleshooter. He was tasked with turning around failing or under-performing manufacturing facilities across the country which required frequent travel and a subsequent five relocations. More on that later. Ultimately, Dad worked his way to the position of Vice President and General Manager of one of Purex's largest divisions. He was the only member of the upper-management team without a college education. Not bad for a guy who started out screwing bottle caps on bleach bottles.

California Here We Come

The move to California was somewhat traumatic because we were leaving behind a large extended family with lots of aunts, uncles, cousins, and a very close-knit group of church friends. However, moving to California in 1957 was far better than most other locales our family could have been sentenced to – more on that later. Dad got rid of the old Chevy rattletrap, mostly because it probably would have died before we got out of Dallas. So, Mom and Dad loaded me and my two older brothers Rick and Gary into a shiny new Buick, and off we went on a new family adventure.

Southern California was an idyllic place for kids to grow up during this time period – great weather with lots of sunshine and so many things to do for entertainment. We settled in Long Beach where we were a 10-to-15-minute drive from the beach and an hour's drive from the mountains.

There were around 4 million people in the sprawling Los Angeles County in 1957, and Orange County had 500,000. Today, there are more than 12 million people in the city of LA alone, and OC is around 3.5 million. Population density was a fraction of what it is today which meant traffic and overall crowding was miniscule compared to today. We loved living in something close to paradise.

Not surprisingly, we had a steady stream of friends and family we left behind visiting us from Texas. At times during summers, it would seem like we were hosting a boarding house. We went to Disneyland so many times during those first few summers that Mickey Mouse knew us on a first name basis, as did all the cowboys of the old west at Knott's Berry Farm. We went to Marine Land so many times, the dolphins and whales would turn backflips when we showed up. The lifeguards at Huntington Beach knew us well and would greet us with a wave and a smile – especially if our guests included those from the female gender. And I must say, our female visitors enjoyed ogling at those handsome hulks with magnificently sculpted and tanned lifeguard bodies. We were always happy to host our visitors to our little piece of paradise.

A Splinter of a Saga

Rick and Gary started playing Little League baseball the following Spring of 1958. I was too young to play at the time, but I was a great assistant to my mom who was the league's loudest and best cheerleader. Dad became involved in helping run the league as a member of the board of directors. He later was elected president and served for many years until I moved up to Pony league at age 13. We essentially lived at the ball field and repeatedly enjoyed the fine dining offered by the concession stand. No telling how many hot dogs, Fritos, Snickers, and Twizzlers I consumed during those years. Those were dietary staples.

The ball field was about a mile from our house. One day, I decided to walk to the field to watch my friends play – with Mom's permission, of course. It was a straight shot but required crossing a very busy street. I had become rather adept at the art of busy street-crossing – almost a sport unto itself. There were no crosswalks back then – it was every man (or kid) for himself. I learned to dodge cars with the agility of a gazelle.

I was watching my friend's game while sitting on the weather-worn and ragged wood plank bleacher benches and munching on concession stand delicacies. I scooted across the bleacher plank to move closer to a friend I was talking to. As I slid over, I felt something penetrate my right hip through my pants. It definitely felt like I had just been stabbed by a Samurai sword. It really hurt. I limped to the restroom to look at my hip, expecting to see blood gushing from the wound. There was no blood, but there was a puncture wound with a large slinter of wood visible. I immediately decided I needed to get home, so I started the one-mile trek, limping along with the pain getting worse with each step. In today's world, I would have used my cell phone and called my mom or dad to come pick me up and take me to the doctor. That option was obviously not available because we were still living in the stone age when it came to personal communications.

I toughed it out and made it home, bursting through the door with tears in my eyes. I had never endured so much pain, and it seemed like I would never make it through as each step was met with more pain and more tears. It was my own "trail of tears." I told my mom what had happened, and she looked at my wound and could not see a splinter – only a small puncture wound. She asked me if I was sure there was a splinter, and I told her something was in there. By that time, it felt like I had a two by four jammed into my hip, not a splinter. Gladly, mom loaded me up and we went to the emergency room. The doctor examined my wound and when he pressed on the area, I thought he had just jammed another two by four into my leg. At that point, he believed me that something was in there.

His strategy was to x-ray my hip to see if they could see something. Sure enough, there it was. I was relieved that I wasn't crazy or hallucinating from the dire pain and encouraged that he would be able to extricate what was beginning to feel like a mortal wound. At that point, I would have been happy for him to just cut off my leg if it relieved the pain. The next stage of his strategy was to numb my hip and dig around to find the two by four. After the numbing shots, he made an incision to start the search for the painful culprit. Sorry if this whole saga is causing uncomfortable feelings when reading this, but trust me, that is nothing compared to what I was enduring.

The doctor kept digging around. It felt like he was using a shovel to find the buried two by four. He was now an inch deep, which felt more like a mile. The doctor kept asking me if I was sure I had a splinter and I said, "The x-ray shows it, I feel it, and I would really appreciate it if you would please find it and get it out!" After a few more minutes of mining for wood in my hip, he gleefully said he found it. The joy he felt for finally finding it paled in comparison to mine. He was proud of himself – I was ecstatic.

He gently pulled out the splinter and showed it to me. It measured an eighth of an inch in diameter and 2 ¾ inches long. He told my mom and me that the splinter had worked itself further into my hip because of my long walk home. The nurse took my splinter, placed it on a four-by-four gauze pad, and then taped it up nicely as a souvenir. I said to myself, "Gee, thanks!" I didn't even get a sticker or a sucker either.

The doctor stitched me back up and gave me a few pain pills and sent us on our way. I did keep the splinter for a few months as a badge of courage and perseverance. I then decided to gain my revenge, so I ceremoniously burned it in effigy. This ordeal was my first encounter with excruciating pain, and I vowed to never sit on a wooden bleacher seat again. Every time I see a wooden bleacher, I am reminded of this horrible experience. No thanks, I'd rather stand. Thank God for today's aluminum bleachers!

Schwinning Around the Block

Like most people who learned to ride a bicycle, I had my share of scrapes, bumps, and bruises. We didn't have training wheels back then. All I had was my brother's single gear Schwinn bike. I clearly recall the first attempt. The only "training" I got was my brothers putting me on the bicycle, holding me up, and then pushing me while they were running behind the bicycle. Then they would let go and I was on my own. That's how most kids learned back then. After I was launched, I was good for the first few feet and then the front wheel started shaking. It was probably me shaking the handlebar because I was scared to death. I was trying to pedal and steer the bike – the wheels were shaking, and I steered right into the curb.

Fortunately, my body flew onto the grass. Whew. I escaped catastrophic injury. My brothers were adamant about me learning how to ride a bike – mostly because they were tired of hauling me wherever they went, so they picked me up, stuck me back on the bike and off we went again. This time I made it past the neighbor's yard and was doing great until it was time to turn. I rotated the handlebar so far to the right that the bike made an abrupt stop, and I went flying through the air. This time, the concrete won. I was sprawled out in the street and could feel the burn on my knees and elbows from the painful scrapes—we called them strawberries.

My brothers came running over and said, "You almost had it!" I said to myself, "Yes, I have had it with this alright." I got up, went into the house, and fell into the arms of my sympathetic mother. Mom then cleaned off my scrapes with Mercurochrome which was not supposed to burn. But boy, did it ever. I thought I was going to pass out. I didn't know any curse words at the time, but they probably would have come in handy had I known a few. But then again, I might have had another affliction after my mouth was washed out with soap. As it turned out, my lack of a vile vocabulary was actually beneficial at the time. After I regained my composure and my mom wiped away my tears, I made an adult-type decision that I would try it another day when my wounds and my pride had healed.

After a few days of bearing the pain of those diabolical strawberries, my brothers encouraged me to give it another try. I put on several layers of long pants and long-sleeved shirts thinking that this strategy would help if I failed miserably again. Nowadays, we buy training wheels, a helmet, knee pads, and elbow pads for kids to learn how to ride a bike. I'm sure some parents would wrap their kids in bubble-wrap if they could. Not so much back in the old days. It's funny how that protective equipment is quickly shed by most kids because they think it's demeaning and stupid.

After extensive in-depth instruction and guidance from my brothers, I reluctantly agreed to try it again. I gathered up as much bravery as I could muster. I mounted the bike with my brothers holding on, put my feet on the pedals, put on the most determined look on my face, and then off we went with the launch. As they let go, I held the handlebar steady, pedaled nice and easy, and got past the neighbor's house with my brothers running alongside cheering me on. It was working. I was riding like a champ. My brothers stopped running and I was on my own. I felt like I was in the zone, intently focusing, then I realized I was coming to the street corner, and I was going to have to execute a right turn. I slowed down, eased into the turn, and was elated that I made it through the turn. I would have patted myself on the back, but I had a deadly vice grip on the handlebar.

That elation didn't last long as I realized another right turn was coming. But this time, my confidence was rising, and I executed another perfect turn. As I traveled down the rest of the block, I told myself, "I got this!" The next turn came and again it was flawlessly executed. I was rounding the bend now headed for home, totally juiced at my accomplishment. Then it dawned on me. How do I stop? Yikes, I hadn't prepared for that, and my big brothers forgot that part of their detailed instructions. Perhaps they didn't think I'd make it that far. I screamed, "How do I stop?" Back in the stone age, bicycles did not have sophisticated handlebar breaks that you squeeze to stop – the brake was engaged when the rider back-pedaled.

Fortunately, they ran along with me as I slowed down and caught me before I fell. I got off the bike, got lots of hugs, and did my best celebration dance that would make every NFL player proud. I did it! I made it around the entire block. Woo hoo!

I got my own three-gear Schwinn for Christmas the following winter. It was one of the best presents ever. I was now able to explore the world on two wheels.

A Stinging Surprise

After I turned twelve years old, I was allowed to ride my bike to the beach that summer with my brother Gary and a few of our neighborhood friends. We would pack a sack lunch and head out for a day of body surfing and fun in the sun and building castles in the sand. Unlike today, the beaches were not crowded and there were no homeless people camped out. The beaches were clean and well-kept.

A new genre of music blared from everyone's radios on the beach (yes, we even had battery-operated portable radios back then). We listened to the music of Dick Dale and the Del Tones, The Surfaris, Jan and Dean, The Ventures, and of course, the kings of them all, a little group called The Beach Boys. The music was iconic and fun. It was a critically important part of how much joy we found at the beach. Today, whenever I hear one of the great oldies of that era, I am transported back in time, smelling (and tasting) the salt water, feeling the sand between my toes, and absorbing the warm rays of the sun (we didn't know much about skin cancer back then and sunscreen had not been invented). Surf music was a huge part of my early teen life.

We would trek to the beach two or three times a week – sometimes even more. We had a blast (to use an old phrase from back then). One of our friends got a surfboard and a mini trailer that hooked on to the back of a bicycle for his birthday. We took turns transporting the surfboard to the beach and sharing it. I was not a great surfer, and I had a lot of crashes before learning the artform enough to at least ride a good-sized wave successfully. It was a lot of fun.

One eventful day, we were enjoying a day of surfing, but things went south quickly. Everyone feared jellyfish, sting rays, and of course, sharks. I was sitting on the sand when our friend Bobby came running out of the water with a jellyfish attached to his stomach. He was tearing it to pieces as he was ripping it off his body and screaming as you can imagine. A lifeguard came running over to help extract the jellyfish from his body. He then took Bobby to the lifeguard station and rinsed his stomach with vinegar. That, too, was not a pleasant experience. We decided to end our day at the beach, hop on our bikes, and get Bobby home ASAP. By the time we got home, blisters had appeared on his stomach. Fortunately, he recovered a few days later. The only scars left were very nasty memories of his jellyfish encounter.

On another eventful day at the beach, yours truly was the victim. We were body surfing, and it felt like I had stepped on a sharp piece of a seashell. It felt like a bad pin prick, but it was nothing that would deter me from continuing my bodysurfing. After all, I was a tough kid that endured the mostly good-natured abuse and aggravation from two older brothers.

After a few minutes, my foot started aching, and within another few minutes, it was getting noticeably worse. I told my friends I was getting out of the water to rest. I limped to where my towel was. I dried off, laid my towel down, and sat down to look at the bottom of my foot. There was a decent-sized round puncture wound in the extremely sensitive upper arch of my foot, and to my astonishment, it was spitting out blood. I looked back at the tracks I made in the sand and saw my right foot had deposited bloody footprints in the sand.

I limped to the lifeguard station and told him I had hurt my foot on a sharp seashell. He climbed down off his perch to check it out, looked at my wound, and perfunctorily told me a big bad stingray had stung me. He said I needed to get to a doctor ASAP. I explained that I had ridden my bike to the beach and that my leg was now hurting so badly, there was no way I could make it home. The pain had traveled from my foot to my calf and all the way up my thigh. He asked if one of parents could come and pick me up, and I told him they were both at work. My dad's office was about 45 minutes away, and my mom was about 20 minutes away. He then told me he would call his supervisor on his two-way radio (yes, fortunately we had those back in the old days) and would have him call my mom.

The lifeguard then put me on a wagon and transported me to the supervisor's building. No, they didn't have three-wheelers back then – he manually pulled me on the wagon. My mom showed up after about 20 minutes It seemed like an eternity since my entire appendage felt like there were a thousand needles stuck in my leg. We had to get my bike, and my mom had to fit it in the trunk without my help – which was an interesting activity. We were about 20 minutes away from the doctor's office and I told my mom that I didn't know if I would make it, and if I didn't, I wanted her to know that I loved her. I said this pain was way worse than the splinter episode.

I, like most kids, hated going to the doctor. It was never a pleasant experience and always involved shots (which I hated). But this time, I didn't care how many shots he had to give me as long as he put me out of my misery. And if that included putting me down like an old dog, I was OK with that.

I was still alive when we pulled up to the doctor's office, although I was sure death's door was about to open. Somehow, Mom managed to get me out of the car and into the doctor's office. I was thrilled that the doctor was able to see me right away. With my last gasps of breath, I was able to tell him a stingray had stung me, and I thought I could hear God calling my name. The doctor assured me that the sting was not fatal, and that he knew just what to do.

He grabbed a syringe, filled it with some magic liquid and stuck it in my butt. The shot was a piece of cake compared to the pain I was feeling. He told my mom to take me home and put me to bed because I was about to take a long nap. He assured me that I'd feel much better when I woke up. Thankfully, back in 1946, a new wonder drug was developed called diphenhydramine (Benadryl). The doctor helped load me back into the car and we headed home.

Fortunately, we lived close by because when we got home and Mom helped me to bed, I was out like a light. It was about 2:00pm when I hit the bed, and Mom came in to wake up about six hours later. When I opened my eyes, my first thought was, "Wow, that was a good nap." See, even back then I knew the value of a good nap. Mom asked me how I was feeling, and as I gathered my senses, I felt to see if my right leg was still attached because I couldn't feel any pain. Sure enough, it was still there. I was still a bit groggy, but I realized I had miraculously escaped the clutches of death. I sat up on the side of the bed, then stood up, and like most growing boys, I said to my mom, "I am starving. Can I eat dinner now?"

The Big Guy in the Little League

At my team's first practice prior to my last year in Little League (I was twelve years old), our coach had drafted a few new kids. One of them looked like a man amongst us boys. He was huge. Our coach introduced this new player to the team. He was appropriately named Greg Sampson. I recalled the stories of Sampson in the bible, and I immediately thought this must have been what he looked like at age twelve. Greg had blond hair, was a head taller, and weighed at least sixty or seventy pounds more than any of us.

The coach asked us to play a little catch to warm up our arms. I went over to Greg to introduce myself and asked if he'd like to play catch. That was my first mistake. I was the starting catcher and prided myself in being able to catch anything and everything.

We started tossing the ball back and forth, and as the intensity grew, I knew I was in trouble. I had no idea that a kid could throw the ball that fast. I was a huge LA Dodgers fan, and my favorite pitcher was Sandy Koufax who could throw a 100-mile per hour fastball. I thought to myself that this new kid was a future Koufax. I asked him to hold on a minute while I got my catcher's mitt because it was killing my hand to catch the ball with my regular glove. The coach quickly noticed what Greg was capable of and his eyes grew bigger and bigger as Greg kept throwing harder and harder. He was a little wild with some of his throws, but the speed was eye-popping. It was obvious that he would be our best pitcher.

Next on the practice agenda was batting practice. I put my catcher's gear on, and the coach started pitching batting practice. Several of our players were fairly good hitters, and then Greg came to bat. He struggled with the first few pitches, and then he launched a fly ball that was so high, I thought it would bring rain from the cloudy skies. Then he hit a ground ball to our all-star shortstop who had the good sense to not even try to catch the ball. It was smoked. After a few more swings and misses, Greg got one on the sweet spot of the bat that cleared the outfield wall by a good 25 feet. Wow. No one in our entire league could hit a ball that far. Behind my catcher's mask, I cracked a huge smile and said to myself, "Man, am I glad he's on our team."

The more I got to know Greg, the more I realized how quiet, shy, and kind he was. He was a gentle giant. I could also tell he was a bit insecure, especially about his baseball talents. As the season wore on, his confidence grew as did his league-wide reputation.

After the first game he pitched, I told the coach I needed a new catcher's mitt because my hand was numb from catching Greg's fastball. The next game, the coach gave me a sponge to put inside my old mitt which helped a little bit, but still my hand was numb after the game. I blame Greg for giving me permanent nerve damage right below my index finger. I think of him every time my hand gets really cold because that spot unfailingly gets numb. I always think of Greg when that happens. Thanks, Greg!

I am not joking when I say that there were kids on other teams that were scared to death as they stepped into the batter's box when Greg was pitching. Not only was his size intimidating, but the speed of his fastball was also scary. Kids would stand as far away from the plate as possible and not even try to swing the bat. I remember one kid who actually refused to come to bat despite his coach's encouragement – he didn't want any part of what Greg was throwing.

Whenever Greg came to bat and hit the ball, the opposing team's players would take cover rather than try and catch the ball. He hit some home runs that Barry Bonds on steroids would have been proud of. He developed into an amazing player, and fortunately for me, an amazing best friend. Sadly, we only had two years together before my family moved away (more on that move later).

Greg Versus the Tree

One Saturday when we were in seventh grade, we were at our junior high school playing flag football with some of our friends. I was playing quarterback and Greg was my wide receiver – and I do mean WIDE receiver. I don't mean obese-wide – I mean broad-shouldered wide. I dropped back to pass and threw it in Greg's direction. He caught it and went out of bounds at full speed. That's where it got interesting.

The school had planted some new, small trees several yards out of bounds. Greg didn't see an oncoming tree because he was looking back at me after catching the ball. I thought to myself, "Oh no, he's going to run into that tree." Sure enough, he did. We all started laughing hysterically because the tree was uprooted and lying flat on the ground. Greg was unfazed and still standing. He started laughing, too. It was him against the tree, and Greg won that battle. It still makes me laugh today.

Greg was so worried he was going to get in trouble for leveling that tree. That's the kind of young man he was. We all swore ourselves to secrecy – the long laugh we enjoyed was well worth it. So, we all pitched in and tried our best to put the tree back in its place. Needless to say, it was a fruitless effort – the tree was a lost cause. I walked to school every day past the place where that tree should have been and always chuckled.

Greg and I lost contact with each other after my family moved away. The next time I saw Greg was in 1972. I didn't see him in person; I saw him on television. My dad and I were watching the Rose Bowl which featured Stanford and Michigan. Undefeated Michigan was a heavy favorite over Stanford. During the game, Michigan was marching down the field when number 91 made a touchdown-saving tackle for Stanford. The announcer said, "Greg Sampson makes a great tackle." I looked at Dad and said, "Did he just say Greg Sampson?" Dad said, "He sure did." I was amazed and excited for my good buddy.

As it turns out, Greg was a stud defensive lineman standing 6 feet 6 inches and weighing 265 pounds. Amazingly, after graduating from Stanford, he was the sixth pick in the NFL draft in 1972. For those that are not familiar with the NFL football draft, being picked in the first round is a huge honor, and being the sixth pick is an enormous honor. The Houston Oilers drafted not only a talented player, but a great young man. After two years as a defensive lineman, the Oiler's coaching staff convinced him to convert to an offensive tackle. He quickly learned the new position and excelled, having been selected to the All-Pro second team in 1978.

Sadly, Greg's football career ended abruptly at the beginning of training camp in September of 1978. He was involved in a frightening head-on collision during a morning drill with center Carl Mauck, Elvin Bethea, and Curly Culp. We old-school football junkies are very familiar with those names. After a violent collision, Greg said all he remembered was seeing "a galaxy of stars for a few seconds." He got up and continued with practice. The NFL did not have a concussion protocol back then – players were supposed to just tough it out.

After a break for lunch, Greg became nauseous and was seeing a bright light that gave him a severe headache. He continued playing in training camp for the next twelve days, but the headaches never went away. Finally, he was flown back to Houston to get a CT scan. The doctor looked at the results and told Greg, "You are an extremely sick man. I'm taking you to the ER right now. I don't know how you are alive today."

As it turns out, Greg had suffered a subdural hematoma – a serious brain injury that could have killed him. Immediate surgery was necessary to remove the damage. Several of his teammates, including Earl Campbell and Dan Pastorini, were regular visitors to the hospital. After a long recovery, it was obvious that Greg would never play football again. He subsequently suffered epileptic seizures and was put on some heavy meds that he said made him feel like a zombie. That lasted seven years.

Every 18 months, Greg would get a CT scan to check and see if the hematoma had returned or if the scar tissue had grown. Fortunately, all previous scans showed that the scar tissue and the hematoma had not grown. In 1986, something miraculous happened. The CT scan showed the scar tissue and the hematoma inside his brain had somehow disappeared. The doctors were mystified and told him he could stop taking his medications – he has been fine since then. When asked what happened and why, Greg said, "Divine intervention, that's all I can think of."

I caught up with him again in 2018 and found out that Greg is happily retired, although he stays busy as the owner and manager of a beautiful seaside resort property in Southern California. Thankfully, the good-natured, quiet, gentle giant from my childhood was doing great.

Boxing, BB's, and Big Brother

It was a pleasure and an honor to grow up in such a great home atmosphere where we all loved each other. Mom and Dad were happily married and we brothers loved each other and got along great – except for the typical and occasional spat. We were truly a middle-class family that had just about everything we needed, from a black-and-white television and a washing machine to two cars and a small but decent house. It was 1200 square feet of coziness that housed Mom, Dad, we three brothers, and my grandmother. The house also had a nice backyard and a two-car garage in the back. I'm not sure how much my dad paid for the house back then, but in today's market, it is worth around a million dollars. So, I guess I could say we grew up in a million-dollar house. It sure didn't seem like that back in the day.

One Christmas, I guess I was eight or nine years old, Dad decided it would be a good idea to buy us boys two pairs of boxing gloves. We didn't fight much as brothers, but perhaps he thought it might help solve some of the disagreements we had with each other. Maybe he thought we needed to learn self-defense, or maybe he thought we could settle disagreements by just duking it out. Although, by being the youngest, I was certainly at a severe disadvantage in any kind of physical altercation. My best defense was that I could run fast.

Boxing was a big sport at the time with legends such as Sugar Ray Robinson, Floyd Patterson, Emile Griffith, Sonny Liston, and a young kid named Cassius Clay (later known as Muhammed Ali). We regularly watched "Friday Night Fights" on our small black and white TV. It was the highlight of our week. Remember, there was no ESPN or Fox Sports. We didn't have cable TV or streaming services with 1000 channels to choose from. We had the three major networks; CBS, NBC, and ABC, plus we could get a UHF station if you had the rabbit ears embellished with aluminum foil and turned in just the right direction. TV entertainment choices were certainly not what they are today.

One beautiful summer day, we three boys were out in the back yard goofing off and sparring with each other with the boxing gloves. My oldest brother Rick told me to stand still so we could see how close he could get to hitting me in the face without hitting me. Being the trusting soul that I am, I willingly and innocently stood there to let him accomplish his experiment.

He started by taking a mighty swing with a right cross and missed me by a few inches. No big deal, I was brave. He then took a roundhouse left hook that came a bit closer but still missed me. He then reared back with a right jab, and he came a little too close. I remember feeling like my nose had hit the back of my skull. I saw stars and little birdies flying around just like I had seen in many cartoons. I went down on the grass like a telephone pole in a hurricane.

The next thing I remember, the stars were gone, and the little birdies had flown away. I could hear a faint voice saying something, then I realized it was Rick trying to wake me up and asking me if I was OK. I could feel a warm liquid flowing down my cheeks as I lay on the ground. I wiped my hand across my nose and cheek and saw blood on my hand which almost made me pass out again. I don't like seeing blood – never have, never will – especially since it was my own!

Gary and Rick helped me up and took me inside. My sweet grandmother nearly passed out when she saw all the blood but maintained enough composure to grab a towel. She laid me down on the linoleum lined kitchen floor so I wouldn't bleed on the carpet, and then grabbed an ice pack – because, as we all know, boys will be boys, and you better always have an icepack handy. Grandma asked me what happened. My brain was still scrambled, but I still had the sense to realize I had to tell her something that would keep peace amongst us brothers. So, I told her Rick was trying a boxing experiment and he accidentally hit me in the nose. It was a noble thing for me to do, but still a bit self-serving because I didn't want to rat out my brother and then have to deal with the aftermath.

I quickly recovered from the near mortal wound, and as I laid down on my bed to rest and recover, upon reflection of my short experience with boxing, I hastily came to the realization that it was most certainly not going to be my choice for an athletic career. Even football seemed a lot tamer because at least the players got to wear helmets and pads for some semblance of protection. Not so much in the boxing ring.

Another incident involving my dear, sweet older brother was when he got a BB rifle for Christmas. I never thought it was a bad idea – I thought it would be cool and maybe I could shoot it as well. Not long after Christmas, I remember being in Rick's bedroom, I'm sure I was being an annoying little brother, and he told me to get out. It was not a good decision for me to stick around because he was armed with a weapon.

I often thought about what it might feel like to be shot with a BB gun. How much would it hurt? Would it just sting? Well, my curiosity was about to be fulfilled. He pointed the rifle at me and told me one more time to get out. I take full responsibility for my own bad judgement, and I did not heed his warning. He warned me again. I didn't budge until he raised the BB gun and aimed it at me. I got up and started running for the door when suddenly, I heard the rifle go off and I felt a burning sting in the small of my shirtless back. I fell to the ground thinking I had just received a fatal wound.

I started crying and thought my life was over. I reached back to see how much I was bleeding and to see how long I had to live before I bled out. I could see the tragic headline in the newspaper: "Young Boy Shot and Killed by His Brother." The subheadline would read: "Choice of weapon was a BB rifle."

Unexpectedly, I could not feel any blood, nor did I see any on the carpet. I stopped crying and went to the bathroom to check in the mirror and see how big the hole in my back was. Much to my surprise, all I could see was a tiny red spot about the size of a BB. The pain was gone. I realized I would survive after all. I started laughing. Rick started laughing. Little did I know then that it would be just another story I would live to tell about in a book someday.

One other quick story about Rick. As an older brother, he was always the more adventurous one. There were a few times when he set a good example of what not to do. He had a few friends that didn't always make the right decisions.

One Saturday night, he was with some of his buddies, and they decided to drive around in LA for the night. One of the teens had bought some cherry bombs from a fireworks stand. They are pretty much what the name describes – round, red, about an inch in diameter with the fuse sticking out on top, and they pack quite a large and loud explosion. So much so, they were outlawed in the US in 1966.

As boys do sometimes, they were evidently feeling a bit mischievous that night, so they started tossing cherry bombs under cars at stop lights to watch the passengers' reaction when the bomb went off. I am fairly sure all the drivers and their passengers were not amused. I'm surprised the boys didn't cause several heart attacks that night. Unfortunately for these playful boys, an LA police officer saw one of the teens in the car toss one of the cherry bombs. It was the last one they would toss that night.

The phone rang about 10:00PM and my dad answered – it was the LAPD. The boys were being held at the police station and my dad had to go pick up Rick. Needless to say, Dad was not happy. He had to drive all the way into LA, which was about a 30 or 40-minute drive. Although I was not in the car that night, I'm sure that the drive home was not pleasant. Perhaps that incident is what prompted Rick to eventually become an attorney and serve as a distinguished state judge for 30+ years.

Road Tripping

After a few years in Long Beach, dad and mom announced we were going on vacation and heading back to Dallas to visit friends and family. The plan was to stop along the way and take in some of the sights we missed on the trip when we moved to California. It was summertime, and fortunately, we had air conditioning in our beautiful Buick because traveling through the desert without air conditioning was a brutal test of endurance – if not stupidity. Travelers also had to plan their gas supply carefully because sometimes there was a hundred miles or more between gas stations back then.

One day while traveling through the desert on the famous Route 66, our family escaped death by about two feet. We were on a two-lane portion of the road that was flat. There wasn't a nice 4-lane interstate back then. It was a windy day with sand blowing and sometimes visibility was not good. I recall seeing a car in front of us with a spare tire on the roof. We were about fifty feet behind it. The wind was blowing hard, and the tire was not securely fastened to the roof. Suddenly, the tire came flying off the roof as it was levitated by the wind, and we could see the tire hit the pavement and bounced once, then twice, heading right towards us. We were traveling about 60 or 65 mph and on a horrible collision course with the tire. It would not have been pretty. It surely would have caused a major wreck and most likely killed us all had it come through the windshield. It was like it was happening in slow motion as I remember it.

Very fortunately for us, there was no on-coming traffic in the other lane. A car had just passed us in the opposite direction and dad swerved left into the on-coming traffic lane. The tire whizzed past our car, missing by just a couple of feet on the passenger side. It was so close you could read Goodyear on the side of the tire. It would have been a terrible head-on collision had a car been heading towards us. Dad quickly swerved back into the right-hand lane. Whew. Disaster avoided. We were all shaking. Dad pulled over on the shoulder to gather himself. He was also so angry that the tire was not securely tied down. That was the angriest I had ever seen my dad. He was livid and shaken at the same time. After we all changed into a new pair of underwear, we continued with our journey.

That evening, we stopped at a motel and decided to have Mexican food for dinner. We boys loved Mexican food, especially bean burritos. We stuffed ourselves and went to bed. After breakfast the next morning, we headed back out across the desert. It was boiling hot outside, and the air conditioning was having trouble keeping up. I'm not sure which one of us started it, but the bean burritos were coming back to haunt us. There were smelly farts flying and the odor was beginning to overwhelm all of us.

We boys started laughing, but Dad did not find it humorous. There we were, out in the middle of the desert, and the option was to either deal with the smell or deal with the heat. As Dad rolled down his window, he hollered, "You boys know better than that. Haven't you had any raisin's?" – meaning haven't we been raised better than that? We thought he meant haven't we had any raisins? I said, "No, it was the bean burritos – we didn't have raisins." Mom and we boys were laughing hysterically – Dad, not so much.

Dad finally found some amusement in the situation and started laughing as well. Most of us have been there where you just can't stop laughing – it's just overwhelming. After several minutes, we all got our composure back. And then, like one of those situations where you think you've got yourself under control, I couldn't help it and started laughing again. Everyone else chimed in with a few more minutes of belly laughing and crying. It was exhausting and exhilarating at the same time. I still chuckle when I think about it. It's funny how the hilarity of a situation can last a lifetime.

Who doesn't love to laugh? Laughter is such a wonderful thing. I am so glad God gave us a sense of humor. We should try using this valuable tool a lot more to help maintain our sanity – we would all be a lot better off!

The trip back to Texas was one of the best vacations ever. We got to renew friendships, see family, and enjoy the wonderful Texas-style hospitality. We saw the Grand Canyon, the Painted Desert, and many more beautiful sights. It was a vacation worthy of life-long memories – including one of the hardest and longest laughs of my life.

We made other road trips, most of which were short trips within California. One of the cool things about living in SoCal was we could drive for two hours to the mountains, have a day's worth of fun in the snow, and then drive back to sunshine. There are few places where one can play at the beach one day, then play in the snow the next day. It was great.

A Famously Infamous Photo

My poor mom. Raising three boys was an entirely new adventure for her since she grew up with her sister and her mother who was a single mom. Granted, girls present their own set of challenges, but boys...well, boys will be boys. When you have no experience in dealing with young boys as they grow up, you don't know what to expect. Surprises are a regular occurrence.

I recall one incident that is famous within our family. It was late summer in 1961, and my dad bought electric hair clippers to save money on our haircuts. They had yet to be used, but us brothers decided to put them to good use. Rick was starting football practice, and since it was still summertime, the usual tradition was to shave your head so your head wouldn't get so hot while wearing a helmet during practice. Makes sense. So, under Rick's instructions, we moved a chair into the bathtub, he sat down, Gary took the clippers, and then he proceeded to shave Rick's head. All went well. Gary and I thought it looked quite stylish. I'm not sure who brought up the idea – I suppose it was a group effort – we decided it would be a good idea for Gary and me to have a shaved head as well. So, Rick shaved our heads. After all, it was a wonderful expression of brotherhood and solidarity. We all had beautiful, thick hair back then – not so much these days, but that's another story.

When our mother got home from work, we met her at the front door to show off our new hair style, or should I say lack thereof. Mom was a vivacious, spunky, and sometimes excitable person. When she saw what we had done, she almost fainted.

She was shocked. Dumbfounded. Speechless. But then it really hit her. We were scheduled to have family portrait pictures taken that evening. She became even more appalled at what we had done. She wasn't quite distraught, but close to it. It was probably enough that she wanted to pull her own hair out, but thankfully, she refrained.

We kept the appointment, much to my mother's chagrin and reluctance. I could tell the photographer was highly amused with what his photographic subjects looked like. There we were, three boys with shaved heads, a father who was mostly bald, and an extremely attractive mother who in fact had a full and beautifully coiffed head of hair. The photo remains a classic and elicits smiles and laughter from all who see it. It shall forever be famous – or live in infamy – within the family archives. It also served as a stark reminder to our mother and to all that have seen the photo that yes, boys will be boys.

Public Apology

Gary, my middle brother, was always in a strange position. He had an adventuresome older brother in Rick who was three years older, and he had to deal with his baby brother, me, who was about three years younger. Sometimes, unfortunately for him, he was stuck in the middle. In most families, the oldest sibling always has it tougher because their parents are learning the challenging and sometimes impossible task of good parenting. Middle siblings have it a bit easier because most parents learn from their mistakes, but there's always that "middle child syndrome" that middies must deal with. And then there's us younger siblings. We get a bit more of a pass from our parents because they have mellowed out. But there is a downside for the youngest, in that we always must deal with those pesky older siblings that can mete out all kinds of torment and torture on us babies of the family. I endured my share of both.

Youngest siblings do get left out of things that the older kids can do – that's just a fact of life and a cross we must bear. I recall my brothers taking off on their bikes for a fishing expedition to Bachman Lake with some of their friends when we lived in Dallas. It was a short bike ride near our first home, but I couldn't ride a bike, nor did I have one even if I knew how. My poor little heart was broken that I was left out. I was out in the front yard crying as they departed on their adventure. My mother took me into the house and tried to comfort me as I shed an abundance of crocodile tears. My life was ruined. There was no television to distract me. No video games to play. Remember, it was the dark ages.

Within a few minutes, Gary walked in the front door. He was such a softie – he felt bad for leaving little brother behind. Mother told him to get back out there and go to the lake, but he told her it was OK and that he would go another time. That was Gary's first mistake in dealing with me – he should have gone and enjoyed himself, but he just couldn't. I played that card a few more times as we grew up, and unfortunately for him, he would usually fall for it. He showed what a sweet person he was.

Now, I would like to publicly apologize to Gary for being a sometimes bratty, manipulative, and inconsiderate little brother – he didn't deserve it, and I didn't deserve his kindness.

I could follow that up with an excuse such as, "My brain wasn't fully formed, and I didn't know what I was doing." Or "I hadn't found my moral compass yet." But as Ben Franklin said, "Never ruin an apology with an excuse." So, Gary, I apologize—no excuses.

Adventures in Riverside

After my brother Rick graduated from high school, he attended the University of California at Riverside and played football there. At that time, UCR was a small school, and the City of Riverside had a population of about 80,000 residents. It was mostly a farming community in the Mojave Desert known for growing citrus crops. It is fifty miles east of Los Angeles and was fairly isolated from the big metro area back then – not so much today.

Virtually every Saturday during football season, we would pile in the car and make the 60-mile drive to watch Rick play football. They were good times, and never once do I recall having any issues with bean burritos or flatulence with my brother Gary or myself during the car treks. That certainly made my dad happy. Perhaps it was because we were not allowed to eat bean burritos ever again.

We ventured to other cities where UCR was playing in 1964, including another small city of around 100,000 residents in the middle of the desert called Las Vegas. I had heard it was known for gambling and other debaucheries, so I was especially curious as a fourteen-year-old kid to see what interesting sights we might encounter. When we arrived, I was expecting the city to be like the Dodge City we saw in the TV series *Gunsmoke* – saloons, gambling halls, drunk men all over, and ladies walking the streets. Nope, I didn't see any of that.

The only "major" casino was The Sands, and it looked more like a motel than anything else. I do recall seeing my first one-armed bandit when we checked into our hotel. The whole city was nothing like I had envisioned, and most certainly not anything like Las Vegas is today. The University of Nevada Las Vegas was a tiny school cómpared to what it is today. I went to Las Vegas some twenty years later for a trade show and the difference was mind-boggling.

The other stark memory I have of my brother's time at UCR was when he informed us that he had decided to play rugby during the football off-season and invited us up for one of his games. None of us had any idea what rugby was. I don't think any of us knew it was even a sport. So, we launched off on another trek to Riverside to take in our first rugby game. I was intrigued to learn about this sport.

We all had watched many football games because all three of us boys played. I was on a Pop Warner league team and was playing flag football in junior high (they did not allow full contact football in California junior high schools at the time). My middle brother Gary was starring on his high school team, and Rick had a successful football career in high school and college.

Rick had told us rugby was like football but with some different rules. We got to the stadium and sat down. The first thing I noticed was that none of the players were wearing pads or helmets, which I thought was strange since he said it was a game similar to football. The teams lined up and the game began. A few minutes into the game, I thought to myself that it was more akin to unorganized chaos than football. Here were these grown men running, tackling, and assembling in what we learned was called a "scrum." We had no idea what was going on except we could see players limping on and off the field, some were bloodied, a few were spitting out teeth, and one large lad had to be carried off the field by his teammates – only to return to the game a few minutes later.

My poor mother was in shock to see her first-born son out there playing amongst this chaos and human carnage. My dad was jaw-dropped. Gary and I looked at each other trying to figure out why in God's name would our brother submit to this type of physical abuse – all in the name of a crazy game. We were all appalled. It was pure torture for my mom, although she did her best to cheer on her son – you could see the fear and worry on her face.

They say that rugby is truly a man's game. I submit that it is undoubtedly a madman's game. Fortunately, Rick survived the game with only a few bumps and bruises. The rest of us survived without suffering a heart attack or getting too nauseous from the broken bones and bloodshed. I thought my brother had lost his sanity, and fortunately, he survived a full three seasons of rugby. How he made it through that many rugby games without a severe injury was absolutely miraculous. He did go down in history at UCR for having been the only athlete to have lettered in baseball (1 year), football (3 years), and rugby (3 years). He hung up his spikes because of a series of concussions and other injuries, and I'm pretty sure his future wife had some influence on his decision.

Chapter 3

The Nightmare: Leaving California

A momentous year for our family was 1964. Big brother Rick graduated from UCR – the first college graduate of our branch of the Allen family.

The next major event was when Dad came home from work one day in late November and told us he had accepted a job promotion which included a very nice pay raise and a lot more responsibility. We all thought that was great until he got to the part where he informed us that we were moving to Chicago. My thoughts were, "What? Chicago? No! We can't leave California for Chicago, especially in the middle of the school year. I can't leave all my friends." He told us his new job was plant manager at one of Purex's largest manufacturing facilities in East Chicago, Indiana, just outside of Chicago.

I mentioned earlier that Dad became the company's troubleshooter. The East Chicago plant had union problems, after all it was Chicago, a heavily unionized area. The plant was also underperforming in its production output. Dad was taking on a huge challenge and a lot larger set of business problems to solve.

The original move from Dallas to Long Beach affected Gary and Rick far more than me because I was only seven years old. Seven years later, the move to Chicago had a major impact on the entire family. We were well established in our social circles, firmly rooted in, and loving life in California. Now, we had to relinquish relationships, pull up our roots, and move to an unfamiliar part of the world.

I have no doubt that it was an exceedingly difficult decision for my dad to accept his new position and move his family – he also had carved out his own place in the California community. I am also firmly convinced that it was also a very difficult decision for my mother, and it took a lot of courage and trust that this was the best thing for the family.

Leaving behind close neighborhood friends, our church family, and our school buddies was very difficult. Sure, we could move to a new house, but relationships are and always will be the most heart wrenching and soul crushing part of a relocation. Physical things can be replaced, but developing new relationships takes time. I was scared. I was sad. I was nervous. I was confused. I had anxiety. I was a mess. I was in denial that this was truly happening.

Then one day reality set in. Shortly after Christmas, the movers showed up. That's when it hit me hard as I watched our stuff being loaded onto the moving van. It was happening. I was fourteen but I couldn't hold back the tears. As the moving van pulled away, I thought maybe I should have laid down in the driveway in protest so it couldn't leave, but I don't think that would have worked. I suppose it was fortunate that we didn't have to make that long drive from Long Beach to Chicago – that would have been even more painful. Instead, we boarded a flight from LAX and we headed out to our new home. More tears flowed as the plane took off. That chapter of my life had ended, and a new chapter had begun.

I had no idea what was in store for us from a weather perspective. Yes, I had heard that it was called the windy city, and it was cold in the winter, but boy, none of us were prepared for what we were about to experience. When we landed, it was brutally cold with snow everywhere. Mind you, our experience with snow was to play in it for a day and then go home to warmth and sunshine.

We didn't have heavy coats, gloves, hats, or boots. "Not to worry," Dad says, "We'll go to the store tomorrow and get everything." We had to stay in a hotel for a week until all our belongings came. We went by to see our new house. It was nice, but I would have preferred that it be located in Long Beach – NOT in Indiana!

We finally got settled into the house. Gary and I started attending our new schools, which we both initially hated. After a few weeks, the sadness and depression had only gotten worse. To add insult to injury, it was one of the worst winters with tons of snow and really cold temperatures – and it just wouldn't go away. I was so sick of seeing snow and having to wear heavy coats, gloves, hats, and boots every time we went outside. Shorts, t-shirts, and barefoot sounded so much better.

I wished that I would wake up in the morning and we would all be back in Long Beach. Much to my chagrin, my dreams just weren't going to come true. I prayed every day, "Please God, wake me up from this horrible nightmare."

Obviously, I quickly learned to hate snow and freezing weather and promised myself that I would NEVER live anywhere like this again. I learned how to shovel snow and scrape ice off windshields – I hated both. I kept asking myself, "Why on God's green earth would anyone in their right mind live in a frozen tundra like this?" Why would people intentionally choose to punish themselves by living in a freezer? "Yes," I thought to myself, "Hell has frozen over!"

It was a very rough time for the Allen family. Lucky for big brother Rick, he stayed behind in sunny California to start his new life while we were sentenced to live in Siberia. Mom had a tough time with it all, as did Gary and me. Dad tried his best to make the best of the situation, but to no avail. The family was struggling to adapt. No one was really happy. It was not a fun time, and it led to strife and discontent amongst the troops. I know I thought about organizing a mutiny, but that wouldn't do anybody any good. We all blamed Dad for the mess we were in – he's the one that caused all this. It was unfair, and as I look back on it, he was just trying to make a better life for us – which, to his credit, he did.

Gary and I grew closer through all the chaos. We were always close brothers but given the situation we were in with no friends in a foreign land, we needed each other. I will say he was far more helpful to me than I was to him. He was my sanctuary when I was distraught. He kept me from losing what little sanity I had left. It was a long and emotionally painful winter.

Sometime in early April, I realized we even had grass in our front and back yards – all I had ever seen was white snow. We finally got to meet a few of our neighbors, who like us, emerged from hibernation because the temperature had gladly made it above freezing. They were nice and they welcomed us, but they weren't our long-time close neighbors from California. As the weather warmed up and we began to settle into our new world, things started getting better. Gary and I were getting used to our new school and started making new friends. We started getting involved in basketball and baseball. We found a new church and made additional friends there. I had started learning how to play guitar and sing back in Long Beach, and I came to learn that it was a great expressive outlet for me. It helped me a lot in getting through the tough times. Music was a major healing force for me.

By summertime, I finally gave in and decided to make the best of the situation – I realized I had no other choice because running away and hitchhiking back to Long Beach was not a viable option – although I did seriously consider it. The warm weather certainly helped a lot. Dad took us to Cubs and White Sox games, but neither of those sad-sack teams even came close to my Dodgers. Gary and I started playing football in late summer. He was on the high school team, and I was on the junior high team.

Life had finally turned around for the family, and I no longer had the urge to call for a mutiny. Our house had a full basement, and it became Gary's and my sanctuary. Dad fixed it up nicely and bought us a ping-pong table and a pool table. We had a couch and chairs down there – it was pretty cool. It was quite a task to move all that stuff down into the basement, but Dad made it work. We had a nice place where friends wanted to come over and hang out. Dad did us right – he had worked his way fully off the naughty list.

Wasco Wedding

When we left California, big brother Rick met and fell in love with a pretty nursing student named Wendy. I suppose he had the good sense to realize that moving to the frozen tundra of Chicago was not his best option. Smartly, he chose to stay behind.

Rick and Wendy decided to get married in August of 1965. We made the trek back to California for this momentous event and we took the opportunity to visit many of our old friends as well. The wedding was held in Wasco, which was (and still is) a small town in the central valley of California. We arrived a few days ahead of the wedding and we stayed in a very small motel. It was predominantly a farming community, so there was not much to do in terms of restaurants and entertainment.

Prior to the ceremony, I recall attempting to put on my first tuxedo. I did require a bit of help with the assembly. The starched white shirt did not have buttons – it had little things called studs, and I had no idea how they worked. I also had no idea what that thing was that I was supposed to put around my waist. I learned it was called a cummerbund. Where they came up with that name and why anyone would choose to wear one is still a mystery to me. I'm glad my dad knew how all the tuxedo stuff worked, otherwise I would have given up and worn shorts and a T-shirt. As events played out, that probably would have been a better choice.

It was a beautiful blue-sky day with only one problem – it was scorching hot. Mind you, the central valley of California can get as hot as the Mohave desert – especially in mid-August. While standing outside in front of the church, I was sweating profusely and didn't even have my tuxedo jacket on. I couldn't wait to get into the church where there was air conditioning. When we walked into the church, it was just as hot inside as it was outside. Much to my chagrin, the air conditioning consisted of open windows on both sides of the sanctuary. It had to be 110 degrees inside and not even the slightest breeze.

It was time to line up for the wedding. We groomsmen and Rick walked in, lined up, and the wedding began. Wendy's father was the minister of the church, so he performed the ceremony. It was a beautiful ceremony, but because of the heat, it felt like we were in hell. As the wedding progressed, sweat was rolling down my face, I could feel my shirt as it became increasingly saturated. For some reason, I sweat a lot anyway, and with a tuxedo on and a scorching hot temperature with no breeze whatsoever, the cards were stacked against me.

I did not know I was in trouble until the singer's voice started fading away. It was like someone was slowly turning down the volume. At the same time, my vision was beginning to fade slowly. I kept telling myself I was going to be fine – I had to just hang in there for a few more minutes. I had never experienced anything like that, and I was confident it would just go away – hopefully soon! I do recall the words, "I now pronounce you man and wife." I thought, OK, I'm going to make it. Rick and Wendy then kissed for what seemed like an eternity. I was fading fast and was thinking, "Come on you two, the honeymoon starts later, let's get this thing over with right now."

I vaguely remember hearing the recessional music start, and I knew I was supposed to turn and follow Gary down the aisle with a bridesmaid on my arm. I was to escort Wendy's older sister, Judy, who happened to be a nurse. I have a hazy memory of her grabbing my arm, and then we proceeded to walk up the aisle. She knew I was fading fast because I was whiter than Casper the friendly ghost. I could no longer hear anything, and my vision was just a big blur. I have a slight recollection of making it to the last row of pews and then there was a total blackout. Judy knew what was about to happen and when I collapsed, she just let me down easily.

The next thing I remember was waking up with a bunch of beautiful women fanning me with anything they could find while I was lying on a couch. They had stripped off my jacket and un-studded my shirt. I doubt they were enjoying the view and getting all excited about seeing a skinny kid's chest. They then propped me up and started pouring water in my mouth. I started coming around. I was as dehydrated as a dry riverbed in Death Valley. It seemed as though I couldn't get enough water. I remember they gave me some watermelon and it was a heavenly tasting treat – it had never tasted that good before.

I soon gathered myself, got dressed again, and went back into the sanctuary for the customary picture-taking. Everyone was glad to see that I had been resurrected from the dead. Rick was giving me a hard time for passing out at his wedding, and I proudly exclaimed how I had made it through the whole thing. He should've been happy – it would have made for a far worse scene had I passed out DURING the ceremony. I was proud of myself for making it through. I learned a hard lesson about what dehydration can do.

The day after the wedding, we began our trip back to Chicago. At least we had escaped the devil's grasp and the heat of hell. I never thought I would long for a wintery day…

Benny and the Cage

At Highland High School, Gary quickly established himself as an excellent athlete. He was an outstanding baseball player who played in a semi-professional league. He was a cornerstone of the football team. I started high school the year after Gary had graduated. As a sophomore, I walked into summer football practice and was greeted by the coach, Ken Sypult. He was a former NFL lineman and later became an Indiana High School Football Hall of Fame inductee as a coach.

Coach Sypult was old-school and came across a bit gruff. He sauntered over to greet me as I was at my locker getting ready for the first practice. He kind of growled and with his gravelly voice said, "So you're Gary's brother, huh? Are you any good? You better be 'cause you got big shoes to fill." I was just a shy, skinny kid and I meekly said, "I don't know, sir." He then said, "Well, get your butt out there and show us what you can do." All I could muster was, "Yes, sir."

One day during summer practice, the coaches introduced us to a new drill that featured a cage they built with 4x4's and chicken wire. It was open on two sides, and it was about four feet tall, six feet wide and six feet deep. Two players would get down in their football stance on opposing sides of the cage and the idea was to develop playing skills with man-to-man contact. One side was offense, one side was defense. Some of the contests were epic – it was survival of the fittest.

I recall my first encounter with the cage. I was a measly 150 pounds and six feet tall. I was not an interior lineman, but everybody had to do battle in the cage. I remember standing in line and counting bodies on the other side to see who I would be doing combat against. A bit of fright came over me when I saw that Benny, an all-conference, All State honorable mention senior linebacker was who I would be matched against. He was known as a bad ass that nobody messed with. I tried to change places with the guy in front and behind me in line, but I had no takers.

My brain was racing with thoughts about how I was going to stay alive in this battle. Then I thought, what on earth are these coaches doing by pitting a skinny little sophomore against a known assassin of a football player who outweighed me by nearly a hundred pounds? It was cruel and unusual punishment. I wondered if these coaches got some sick, perverse enjoyment in seeing the slaughter of an innocent kid. I had to quickly develop a strategy for survival.

The time had come. I was the blocker on offense and Benny was going to be the defender. With a dogged determination, I got down in my stance to face my destiny. Just before the whistle blew to start the bone-jarring encounter, I had decided to use my quickness and keenly crafted cunningness to take Benny out. The whistle blew and I aimed my left shoulder directly at his knees. My strategy was to go low and go hard. With bullet-fast speed and all the explosive energy I could muster out of my 150 pounds, I launched myself and then felt the collision.

Benny went down and ended up on top of me. My strategy worked like a charm – my speed and shrewdness paid off. I successfully executed my block. There was a moment of silence, and then the coach said, "Great job, Allen!" Some of the players were whispering among themselves about what had happened. I got up, dusted myself off, and felt exceedingly proud. I breathed a huge sigh of relief. Benny, on the other hand, was not happy about the skinny little sophomore taking him down.

After we each served as offensive blockers, we had to reverse the roll and get back in line to play defense. I got back in line on the defensive side, relieved that I had survived. Whew, that was over. I looked over at the line on the opposing side, and there was Benny counting to see how many guys were in line in front of me. I counted the players in my line in front of me – there were seven. Benny also counted out seven and placed himself in line. I thought my encounter with him was over, but to no avail.

I knew he would be out for revenge, and I was the sitting duck target. As the line dwindled down and the time for the second battle approached, I had to come up with another strategy. As I learned in the first clash with Benny, it was not a matter of the survival of the fittest, it was the battle of the smartest. So, I had to develop another brilliant strategy, but it had to be perfect, otherwise, Benny was going to annihilate me.

The time had come again. All the players and coaches were anxiously awaiting Battle Royale 2.0. We lined up on opposite sides of the cage. Everyone was standing around in silence and anticipation – perhaps rehearsing for the moment of silence that would be necessary after I was slaughtered by Benny.

We got down into our stances – him on offense and me on defense. Benny's eyes got very large and I'm pretty sure they were not sending love messages to me – quite the contrary. He reminded me of a mad bull that had steam blowing out his nostrils. He was ready to extract his revenge.

The whistle blew, and in a lightning-fast motion I faked to the left, then quickly twisted my body to the right. Shockingly, I was still standing. I felt no pain and there was no major collision. Benny had completely missed me. He whiffed. He ended up lying face down on the ground. My first reaction was that of victory and relief. Then I said to myself, "Oh no, you have really made him angry – I'm a goner." There was another long moment of silence, and then everybody including the coaches started laughing – except for Benny. He jumped up and took off his helmet. He was livid. I knew I was a dead boy walking.

I was the fastest kid on the team, and I was ready to hit the road, counting on my adrenaline to kick in like a second stage rocket boost. I felt confident I could escape. To my utter shock and surprise, and to everyone else watching, he started laughing too. My body shuddered and I almost collapsed with a sense of relief. I bent over and put my hands on my knees and didn't know if I should laugh or cry. Cautiously, I chose to laugh.

Thankfully, Benny and I got along fine after that. Maybe he learned to respect a skinny little sophomore kid a tiny bit. I played safety behind him while he was playing linebacker. I'm not sure if our little incident made him a better player – perhaps it did. Maybe he learned to play smarter. Who knows. He went on to play college football after he graduated.

My lesson learned is it's not the size of the man in the fight that matters, it's a matter of developing the right strategy because you're scared to death of getting hurt…or something like that.

Leaving Me Breathless

Highland High School was never a powerhouse football team during the five years we lived there. During my sophomore year, our record was two wins, six losses and one tie. We had a pretty good team, although our record certainly did not reflect it.

Along with playing wide receiver on offense and safety on defense, I also served as the punter and placekicker – although most of the time I was not sure which place my kicks would end up. During one game, I set myself up for a punt. I caught the snap from our center, gave the ball a good solid hit, and watched it soar mightily in the air. As soon as my feet landed on the ground, an opposing player planted his helmet smack dab into my chest. I hit the ground as hard as that kid hit me. Out of the corner of my eye, I saw the referee throw the penalty flag and he and the offending player took off running down the field. I thought it was great that we were getting the ball back because of the penalty.

When I gathered my senses, I had an inkling that something was terribly wrong – I realized I couldn't breathe. I remember laying there thinking about what I should do. I picked my head up and looked down the field and realized everyone was fifty yards away and I was about to die. I'll never forget that empty feeling of seeing everybody what seemed to be a mile away. My mom and dad were likely the only two people in the stadium who were looking at me. It was a lonely feeling. Time was moving very slowly. I had no idea what to do – I couldn't get up, so I just laid there.

What seemed like an eternity passed when suddenly, I heard a voice say, "Son, are you ok?" It was the referee. I said to myself, "Now, that's a stupid question to ask as I lay here dying and unable to speak." I managed to shake my head no, and then he asked me what was wrong. I obviously could not answer his question, and then he asked me again. I remember playing the game called Charades, so I thought maybe the ref would play that game with me. I pointed to my mouth thinking he would get the hint. Then he asked me, "Did you get hit in the mouth?" I shook my head and thought, "No, you idiot, I CAN'T BREATHE!" I then opened my mouth and pointed my finger into my mouth. He then asked me if there was something wrong with my throat.

At that point, I was losing hope in ever winning this game of Charades and was resigned that I truly was going to die. Desperately, I thought I would give it one more try and pointed to my chest. He then asked me if I could breathe. I said to myself, "Finally – we have a winner!" and shook my head no. He then grabbed me by the belt and lifted me up, arching my back. I then took a huge gasping breath and realized I was miraculously going to live. With perseverance and tenacity, I won this round of Charades with the ref, and I gladly lived to tell about it.

The Blizzard of '67

We were in our third winter since our move from Long Beach. I had gotten begrudgingly used to scraping ice and shoveling snow – mind you, I still hated it. It was normal to take ten minutes putting on layers of clothes along with a heavy coat, a hat, gloves, and boots just to go the store – or anywhere for that matter. I still thought there was nothing normal about it, but it was a matter of survival in the frozen tundra of Chicago.

January 26th in 1967 shall forever live in infamy in my life. When I went to school that Thursday morning, it was snowing lightly. It was just another winter day. Around 10:00am, we got word that heavy snow was on its way, and school was closing because of a blizzard warning. We all had to go home. Snow was now falling heavily, and the wind started blowing – nothing too uncommon for a winter day in Chicago. But this was different. It was bordering on white-out conditions. It took a good while for the bus to get Gary and me home, but we made it. Snow was starting to pile up quickly. I called my mom who was at work in a neighboring city's school district office. She said she was heading home, and we should get the driveway shoveled so she could get the car in the garage.

Gary and I put on all our winter survival gear and began shoveling. We were both slinging snow as fast as we could because we knew Mom would be home in ten or fifteen minutes. There was no way we could clear the entire driveway, so we started shoveling two tracks. The snow was now absolutely pouring out of the sky. The wind was howling and blowing the snow around. When I got to the end of the driveway, I was exhausted. Much to my chagrin, I turned around and saw that there was already another four or five inches of snow filling up the two tracks Gary and I had just shoveled. I stopped and thought to myself, "So this is what they call a blizzard." Unbeknownst to me, the worst was yet to come.

We started re-shoveling the driveway tracks, and then we saw that Mom was pulling in the driveway. The car stopped making progress because there was so much snow. We put our shovels down and got behind the car to try and help push it into the garage. The tires were not getting enough traction. I was so angry and disgusted with the situation that I guess my adrenaline kicked in, and with superhuman strength, from Gary and I, the car started moving with enough momentum that it finally made it into the garage. I screamed, "I want to move back to Long Beach!"

At around noon, there was already well over a foot of snow on the ground. Around 1:00pm, Mom called Dad who was still at work. He said all the roads were closed and there was no way to get home. All the workers in the plant were stuck there. Nobody was allowed to leave. There were about a hundred workers snowed in. And the snow kept falling, and falling, and falling.

At around 7:00pm, Mom called to check on Dad. Sadly, he explained that there was no food except for what was contained in several vending machines. They ran out of change, so Dad ordered the maintenance supervisor to get a hammer and crowbar and bust all the machines open. They rationed out the food and had to settle in for the night. They had no television. All they had for entertainment was a few decks of playing cards and two sets of dominoes. More troubling, there was no place for anyone to sleep.

The snow kept coming and the wind was gusting more than fifty mph. Mom, Gary, and I felt terrible that we were tucked in warm and comfy with plenty of food. I'm sure that every employee in the plant never forgot how they spent the blizzard of '67.

O'Hare airport had never closed – the crews were accustomed to dealing with snow and ice conditions. But this time, Mother Nature had taken over control. Everything in northern Indiana where we lived and all of Chicago was completely shut down. And the snow kept piling up. Mom and I watched the ten o'clock news. There were more than twenty thousand cars and hundreds of buses stranded on streets and highways. Snow drifts were already up to fifteen feet in some places. The entire area was fully paralyzed. The snow kept falling and the wind kept blowing.

It was now Friday morning, and we made it through the night. I will never forget what I saw when I opened the living room curtains the following morning. To my utter shock, the front of our house was literally buried in snow from the ground to the roof. It was an eerie feeling. I went into the kitchen and looked out at the back yard. It was covered in what seemed like four to five feet of snow. And it was STILL snowing, although thankfully, not as heavy.

We checked in with my dad and he said he spoke with the city about getting the employees out of there. They told him the main street where they were located was expected to be plowed sometime later that morning. Every snowplow and every first responder in the Chicago area were frantically working to get stranded people home. Snowplows from all parts of Illinois, Wisconsin, and Indiana were being brought in to help dig out the city.

Around noon, Dad called and said they got the road cleared off enough to try and make it home. He said he was bringing three other employees with him because they lived too far away to attempt a return home. The drive from the Purex plant to our house was normally no more than ten or fifteen minutes with traffic. Around four o'clock, we heard the back door open. Dad and his workers had made it. The main roads were mostly passable, but the trip was slow and treacherous. None of the neighborhood streets were plowed. Dad had to park his car at a gas station, and they had to hike through knee-deep snow for about a mile. Dad's production manager was an older guy who had heart problems. It was a miracle that he made it without having a heart attack.

Mom managed to rig everybody up with some dry clothes and quickly threw together a yummy meal for the starving victims. I'm sure food never tasted so good, and a warm, comfy home never felt so cozy. The visitors ended up staying with us until Sunday. Dad loaded them up in the car and took them home. It took him all day because many of the roads had yet to be plowed.

The final snowfall total in our area of the blizzard was 26 inches in a 36-hour period. Sixteen inches fell in the first twelve hours. Wind gusts topped 55 mph. Lightning and thunder were widely reported, and several funnel clouds were spotted. Twenty-six people died. It was the worst blizzard the area had ever seen. Needless to say, it took months for all the snow to slowly melt away. It was a storm for the ages. Ironically, two days prior to the storm, a record high of 65 degrees was recorded in Chicago. I thought perhaps we had been transported back to Long Beach. Boy was I wrong.

Track Tales

As a sophomore, I was the fastest player on the football team. The team always ended practice with the dreaded drill – wind sprints, which consisted of 50-yard dashes. The team would line up across the field and race to the 50-yard line. We'd get about a minute's breather, and off we'd go again. I tried my best to not expend too much energy early on because after five or six sprints, Coach Sypult would decree that the winner of the next sprint would get to hit the showers. That's when I put on the speed and beat everybody else.

Unfortunately for me, Coach Sypult quickly figured out my strategy. If I came in second or third during the first few sprints, he started yelling, "Allen, you are loafing!" We would run wind sprints over and over until exhaustion set in. Whenever I won the race for the showers after he figured out what I was doing, he would make me run at least two more, and he'd let the second-place kid hit the showers instead of me. I had to change my strategy, so I would run just hard enough to win the early sprints and then hit it just hard enough to win the race for the showers. Sometimes, he would still make me run extra sprints. He could be a tough coach, but now I know he was trying to push me and make me a better player.

One day while leaving the football field after practice, the new track coach, Mike Poehline, jogged over to me and said, "I need you on my track team next Spring." I told him I had never run on a track team before, but I would think about it. Over the next few weeks, every time I'd see him in the school hallway, in the gym, or in the locker room, he'd ask me if I had made up my mind.

I kept putting him off, and then at the end of football season, coach Sypult called me into his office and in his gruff voice said, "Boy, you need to join Coach Poehline's team – he'll make you a better runner. If you want to make the football team next year, you better do it." I was a bit shocked that he would say that since I was already a starter on both offense and defense as a sophomore. Out of shear fear and not wanting to go against his orders, I found coach Poehline the next day and told him I would try out for the track team.

When track season rolled around, I went to the first practice. Coach P's specialty was cross country and distance running – which I had absolutely no interest in. He was an avowed long-distance runner himself. He started the practice off with a brief introduction, and his goal was to put together a good team and compete for the conference championship. I thought that was a noble goal.

The next thing on the agenda was some "warm-up" running. We ran four 220-yard sprints with only a minute to catch our breath (yes, we had yards – not meters back then). After that, I was exhausted and thought that was a good enough workout for the day. He then said it was time to run four 440's and then we would do two 880's. He also said we would close the practice with a mile run after we worked on our individual events. I asked Coach P if I could talk to him privately for a second. He obliged.

I told him there was no way I was going to make it through all that running. I explained that I came to run sprints, not long distance. I promised him I would work very hard on short distances, but I was not built for long distance racing. Surprisingly, he said, "OK, we got a deal." I guess he was desperate since he had very few runners interested in sprints.

He had already sized me up and said, "Allen you've got pretty good speed, you're tall, and you've got long legs. I think you should try running hurdles." I glanced over to the high hurdles and thought there's no way I can run and jump over those things – why would I try such a thing? It looks somewhat dangerous trying to jump over something that's 39 inches high. There's no way I can do that. He convinced me to give it a try and lowered the hurdle to 30 inches. I thought maybe that was a bit more manageable.

He told me all I had to do was figure out which leg would be my lead leg, and which one would be my trail leg. He then jogged off to coach the other runners. Mind you, we didn't have YouTube back then where you could watch videos and learn how to do almost anything.

It then dawned on me that I had seen hurdlers in the Olympics lift their left leg up as they approached the hurdle, and they tucked their right leg up underneath as they went over. So, I ran toward the hurdle and tried that strategy, and much to my surprise, I didn't kill myself – I actually made it over the hurdle. I tried it several more times and was successful, so I set another hurdle up to try two in a row. It worked. I thought I was getting it down pretty well.

Coach P then trotted over and said I was doing great. He then informed me that the hurdles needed to be thirty feet apart and that I needed to take three steps between them. I'm not a math genius, but I quickly calculated that each step would have to be roughly 10 feet. I certainly agreed that I had long legs, but there was absolutely no way I could jump a hurdle and then take three steps and jump another – and then do that ten times in a row. I was sure that was not possible – even with my long legs. I thought five steps was more logical and tried that. It was very clumsy, but I did it. He said I'd never win any races doing five steps – it had to be three. He set up the hurdles at 30 feet apart and told me to think of it as a rhythm – jump-one-two-three, jump-one-two-three, jump-one-two-three.

With the hurdles at their lowest setting because I didn't have the guts to try it with them on the high setting, I bolted out of the starting blocks and was determined to do the three-step rhythm. I had my doubts, but miraculously, it worked. It felt like it was a real stretch taking those giant steps, but I got into the rhythm and cleared all 10 hurdles. Coach P yelled from across the track, "Way to go, Allen, now raise the hurdles up and do it again." The guy didn't even give me a minute to bask in the glory of my success, but that's what good coaches do.

I raised the hurdles and got loaded up in the starting blocks to give it the old college try. I burst out of the starting blocks and about halfway to the first hurdle, doubt set in. I was caught in no-man's land where if I tried to stop, I'd crash into the hurdle, and if I kept going, well, I probably crash into the hurdle. Either way, I thought I was doomed. I made the decision to just keep going, full steam ahead, torpedoes be damned. I jumped and somehow made it over the first hurdle. I had a very brief sigh of relief, and then I realized another hurdle was on the horizon.

I quickly got it together and remembered "jump-one-two-three." I stretched those long legs of mine as far as they could go and leapt into the air. I cleared the next hurdle. Then it really hit me. I had a full head of steam and was afraid I couldn't stop, but I was also afraid I couldn't keep going. Eight more hurdles were staring me in the face. I decided to just keep going, and if I crashed, I'd probably survive—perhaps with less than a fatal injury.

The good news was that I made it all the way to the end and didn't crash. The bad news is that it took me about twenty seconds which would have placed me dead last in any high school track meet on the planet. At least I didn't suffer any injuries – especially a catastrophic one. Coach P congratulated me for making it to the end and said, "At least that time gives you a lot of room to improve."

I kept on working hard to improve over the next few weeks, and my times gradually came down. When it came time for our first track meet, I was ready to see how I stacked up against some competition. My times kept improving, and I was the fastest on our team. Actually, I was also the only one on our team that ran the high hurdles.

The day of our first track meet was in mid-April. Chicago weather can be iffy at best during the early spring. A storm blew through that day – it was winter's last gasp. It was cold and there was snow and ice on the ground. I recall getting "warmed up" for my race, and I noticed there were icicles hanging on the hurdles. We all know how I hate cold weather, and I thought it was highly insulting to have to run a race in these conditions. My sweatsuit gave me a little warmth and comfort, and Coach P laughed at me when I asked if I could run the race with my sweats on. I didn't think it was an outrageous request, but he did.

I called over one of our team managers as I was getting ready to get in the starting blocks. I told him to stand next to me so that when the starter said, "On your mark," I could strip off my sweats and instructed the manager to take them and meet me at the finish line. He thought I was joking. I was not. Running a race in tiny shorts and a tank top in the freezing cold was not my idea of a fun activity. Then came, "On your mark." I quickly stripped down, handed the sweats to the manager, and said, "Hurry, get to the finish line." He obliged and took off. Then came, "Get set." I loaded myself into the starting blocks, and the gun went off.

I will never forget the sight of running over those hurdles with icicles hanging off them. I finished the race in second place. I was shocked that it went that well since it was my first race, and yes, there were more than two people in the race – there were six. I credit my motivation and speed solely to the cold. Getting to the finish line as quickly as possible so I could put my sweats back on was all the incentive I needed. When I got to the finish line, I grabbed my sweats and put them on in record time. The manager was laughing. I was not. I was just glad I didn't freeze to death while in mid-air going over a hurdle and then hitting the ground and shattering like a glass at a Jewish wedding.

In my first season, I won a couple of races and got to run in the conference finals in the high hurdles. I also ran the 180-yard low hurdles and qualified for the conference finals. In addition, I competed in the long jump and won a few meets with my best jump being twenty feet, six inches. I did well for a skinny sophomore who had never competed in track. Coach P was pleased and proud of me. I was proud of myself.

Incidentally, Coach Mike Poehline went on to become head track coach at Purdue University where he earned Big Ten coach of the year five times and coached 31 athletes who earned All-American honors. He later served as a staff coach at the US Olympic training center. He was a valuable coach and mentor to many long-distance runners who competed and won medals in the Olympics.

The Junior Year Curse

My junior year in 1968 was destined to be a breakout year in both football and track. Our football team started off well. Through five games, I caught 5 touchdowns, had 4 interceptions (one for a touchdown), and was kicking extra points. I even did fairly well during one game where I had to play quarterback since our starter was injured. Things were going great until early in the sixth game.

I was playing wide receiver and was blocking downfield for our running back. I went to throw a block, and the defender hauled off and kneed me on my right side. It was an intentional act of unnecessary roughness, but he was not penalized. I tried to get up but the pain in my ride side was burning. Even taking a breath was painful. I made it to the sidelines and one of the assistant coaches asked me what was wrong. I told him what happened and said it was hard to breathe.

Back in the old days, the cure for any football injury was to just tape it up and get back in the game. So, assistant coach Evans grabbed a roll of athletic tape, I lifted my jersey, and he then began wrapping the tape around my entire torso, literally from right below my chest all the way to my belt line. He finished up and said, "All right, get back in the game – we need you." I bent over to try and get into an offensive down position, but I couldn't even bend over because the tape was so tight, and the pain was excruciating. Coach Sypult came over to check on me and I told him I couldn't play – I was in too much pain and the tape was making it even harder to catch what little breath I could take.

Half-time came and I went to the locker room with the team. I told the coaches I needed to go to the emergency room because it felt like someone was stabbing me every time I took a breath. One of the coaches went and found my dad and then brought him to the locker room. He helped me get my pads off, which was a chore in and of itself because every movement caused the stabbing pain. After getting all my pads off, there was one more challenge ahead.

I will never forgive coach Evans for taping up my entire torso. Removing the tape literally added insult to injury. I didn't have a lot of hair on my torso, but there was certainly enough to cause me to scream while each and every inch of tape was being ripped off. I do believe that this type of torture would be a good technique for the CIA to use when trying to extract information from a terrorist – it might even be more effective than waterboarding. At the time, I might even have opted for waterboarding. I know I would have sung like a canary if I were a terrorist. Even some Medieval torture techniques paled in comparison.

To make matters worse, with each rip of the tape, I would gasp which exacerbated the stabbing pain in my side. My dad and one of the coaches had gotten most of the tape off, and it was time to rip it off my injured side. They gave it one last big rip which felt like a huge spear was plunged into my side. I thought I was going to pass out. The good news was that it was done. I asked them if I could just lie still for a few minutes while I gathered what little sanity and bravery I had left. Dad helped me get dressed and off we went to the ER.

Getting in and out of the car caused more excruciating pain, but I managed to make it into the ER without succumbing to death. The x-rays showed I had two broken ribs, and when I gave them a urine sample, there was blood in my urine. I had a contused kidney as well. The doctor said there was not much they could do other than give me some pain medication. At that point, I was ready to be put out of my misery. I gladly took the pain meds, and we headed home.

The next morning, it felt like I had been run over by a train. It was hard to breathe and hard to get into any comfortable position. Every little movement caused piercing pain. More pain meds, please. I managed to make it through the weekend, but there was no way I could go to school and sit in those horribly uncomfortable desks all day. I missed a week of school and playing football was out of the question. My recovery took a good while. I did learn that broken ribs are no joke – especially since medicine was still in the dark ages back then. There were no muscle relaxers or any other type of magic meds. Aspirin was the go-to pain medicine. I did recover with no long-term ill-effects but was unable to play the rest of the season.

Disaster Strikes Again – The Junior Year Curse Part 2

Historically, track workouts started in early April, but to get a head start on the season, Coach Poehline decided to introduce an indoor track season starting in February. There were very few schools in the area who had indoor track facilities, but Coach P thought it would be advantageous to introduce this innovation at our school.

The gym was not built for track, but we made do with what we had to work with. Runners could always just run around in the gym with no problem. He brought in whatever equipment was useful, including some hurdles for me to work with. Conditions were not optimal, but Coach P was trying to make it work. It was a far better idea than trying to run outdoors with a foot of snow on the track and temperatures well below freezing every day.

The gym was not long enough for me to set up more than a few hurdles, so I had the brilliant idea of using a very long hallway in the school building. That way, I could run almost the equivalent of a 60-yard race. It was functional since it was after school hours, although many of the teachers thought it was a bit crazy. I worked hard and felt like the head start would give me an ultimate advantage when the outdoor meets started. My first year in track was surprisingly good, but I wanted to kill it as a junior.

One day at practice, Coach P announced we would be competing in an indoor track event at a major Catholic high school in the area. The team was excited that we would be the first one from our school to compete in an indoor track meet. When the day arrived, we boarded the bus and off we went. I had seen a few indoor events on TV, so I thought it was going to be really cool to compete in one.

The high hurdles was one of the first events, so I started warming up by doing a little jogging and stretching. I noticed that the hurdles were far different than the ones we used. Ours were a much different design that had a rounded bottom, so if and when you hit the hurdle, it would just rock forward – it was no big deal. I was used to grazing the top of the hurdle and it didn't throw me off. Upon close inspection of the hurdles at this facility, I noticed they had a squared off bottom portion and were weighted – theirs were old-school, we had the new-school type.

I then decided to practice a few starts and go over the first hurdle or two to get a feel for the track. I got myself in the starting blocks, got set, and then headed for the first hurdle. My lead leg heal skimmed the top of the hurdle and caused me to twist a bit, and then disaster struck.

My trail leg hit the hurdle squarely and twisted me even more. That weighted hurdle had won, and I had lost. I was way off balance, and I knew trouble was coming. When my lead leg hit the ground, my body was still twisting in the air. The whole weight of my body came down on my lead leg. When my foot hit the ground, my body was twisted, and my leg was straight. My hip absorbed all the weight in a jamming, twisting motion. I hit the ground hard. My leg hyperextended backwards. It felt like my hip and leg were both broken. The pain was excruciating, and then my leg became completely numb.

Coach P was across the track, but he saw what happened. He came running over and asked if I was OK. I said, "No, my leg is either broken or it has been ripped off my body – I can't feel a thing." He felt my leg to see if anything was broken and then told me he didn't think anything was broken. He then said he was going to bend my leg and to let him know where it hurt. He bent my left leg at the knee, and I literally could not feel anything – it was still totally numb.

I told him I needed to just lay there for a few more minutes. Coach P told me the race was about to start and asked if I was still going to run the race (he was joking). I lifted my head up and gave him the dirtiest look I could muster. He then said he needed to get me off the track so they could run the race and asked me if I could walk. I asked him, "How can I walk when I can't feel a thing in my left leg?" He then called over some teammates and they lifted me up, carried me off the track, and sat me in a chair.

My mom showed up about the time they sat me in the chair. I was glad she didn't see the accident. Coach P told her what had happened and suggested she take me to the ER to get x-rays to see if anything was broken. My teammates helped me to the car and off we went.

By the time we got to the ER, I had gotten some feeling back in my leg and was able to limp in. Remember, the only tool they had was x-rays – the CT scan and MRI machines had yet to make it on the drawing board. Fortunately, the x-rays did not find any broken bones. They gave me a few pain pills and told me to stay off my leg for a few days. I told them that certainly would not be a problem.

The more the numbness in my leg wore off, the more pain I felt in my hip area. That was where the pain stayed for a month. I was able to walk with a limp, but there was no way I could even think about running, let alone jumping over hurdles. My track season came to an abrupt halt that day before the very first race.

About eight weeks after the tragic accident (yes, it was tragic to a junior in high school who had lofty ambitions), I was able to start jogging. FYI – there were no rehab facilities back then, and physical therapy science was still in the dark ages. The end of track season was approaching, and I had run out of time.

My left hip has never been the same. Sadly, those types of injuries may heal when we are young, but they tend to come back and haunt us when old age hits. I was thinking I had a slight dislocation of my hip and did some damage to the joint and surrounding ligaments – at least that's what the current pain was saying back then. Decades later, an MRI showed I was correct. The orthopedist said I most likely suffered a partially dislocated hip and had a stress fracture that ran down my femur several inches.

During the following summer, I was able to start running again, but I knew it was going to take a lot of hard work to get back to where I was in terms of speed and agility. I was heading into my senior year, and I wanted to have great seasons with football and track and perhaps earn a scholarship for one or both sports. Since I had lost half a season with my football injury and the entire track season, I knew how important it was that I do well in the upcoming year.

Senior Year

It had been more than four years since we left paradise behind. I was the only son left at home because Gary had gone off to college. We had settled into the community. Life in Long Beach was a distant memory. It was the summer of 1968.

My senior year started off well. I was chosen to be captain of the football team. I started dating Sally, our homecoming queen. I was elected president of the Letterman's Club. I was captain of the track team. I was student director of the choir. I was the lead singer in a garage band. My high school life could not have been better. I would never have believed it would turn out that way the day we got off the plane in January of 1964.

Football practice started in late August. I spent the summer working hard to recover from my track injury. My hip was doing much better, and I regained most of my speed and agility. I say most because I could tell I had lost a step or two. I was encouraged because it looked like we were going to have a good team.

A Bell-ringing Disaster

Coach Sypult had convinced the school board to purchase a victory bell that we could ring after each win. It was mounted on a trailer and was a very large bell. To ring the bell, the captains had to mount the trailer and turn the wheel on each side of the bell, rocking it back and forth. Coach Sypult wanted to begin a new tradition, but ringing the bell had an ignominious start.

Maybe the bell was going to bring us good luck because we won our first game. It was time for breaking in the new tradition. The team and all the fans gathered around the trailer to celebrate the victory. Jim, nicknamed "Bear," was the other captain. I went to one side of the trailer and Bear went to the other. I reached up and grabbed the wheel of the bell to help me get up on the trailer. Just as I grabbed it, Jim gave the wheel a big turn. My hand got caught between the wheel and the iron support holding the bell.

I felt horrific pain, but I climbed up and we rang the bell. Everyone cheered. It was a great moment until I looked down at my blood-soaked left hand. My fingers had gotten smashed. The tip of my middle finger was gushing blood. My fingernail was ripped off. I did not use foul language as mentioned earlier, but this would have been another good opportunity to let loose a long string of expletives.

I jumped down off the trailer and grabbed a towel from one of my teammates and ran over to my mom and dad. As one might expect, we took another trip to the emergency room. The doctor removed what little I had left of my middle finger's nail. He then stitched up my finger and put an enormous bandage on it. He gave me some pain medication and said to go home, keep it elevated, and keep ice on it off and on for the next couple of days. Fortunately for me, according to the x-ray, no fingers were broken – they were just badly smashed.

I went home, took a pain pill, and then crashed for the night. As I was going to sleep, I thought about how the victory bell tradition was christened with the blood of one of the team's captains. What a way to start a new tradition. And what a way to start my senior year. I was desperately hoping this was not the beginning of another disastrous year in my athletic career.

The next morning, I woke up and it felt like either an elephant stepped on my fingers, or someone took a hammer and smashed them. I took another pain pill and went back to sleep.

I made it through the rest of the weekend, and on Monday, I returned to school. One of my elective classes was typing class (yes, that was actually a class back then). I walked into class with my hand wrapped and showed the teacher the huge bandage on my middle finger. She asked me what happened, and I relayed the story. She then asked me how long the doctor told me I had to wear the bandage. I told her it would probably be at least two weeks. She suggested that I go to the counselor's office and change classes because I could not properly do all the exercises with my hand wrapped and an enormous bandage on my middle finger. I was then transferred into a business accounting class which was the only other option.

When I showed up for football practice that day, I showed coach Sypult my wrapped hand and bandage and said I don't think I can practice. He growled at me and said, "Get suited up and get your butt out there to practice." I knew I was a critical part of the team, so I dutifully obliged – mostly out of fear of the coach. I practiced the rest of the week and got clearance from the doctor to play in the game – as long as I wore a heavily-padded bandage to keep my middle finger protected.

The game began with me catching a long touchdown pass. Things were going fine, and the large bandage was not causing me any problems catching passes. In the second quarter, I was on defense playing safety. The opposing quarterback went back to pass, and I saw their wide receiver crossing the field. I ran in his direction. Their quarterback threw the pass high and far. I hustled over to break up the pass. The receiver and I jumped. We both caught the ball simultaneously. As it turned out, I ended up with the ball, and he ended up with my bandage. Fair exchange I would say. I took the ball and ran up the field for about 50 yards and was tackled.

As I got up, I realized my bandage was gone. I looked back up the field and saw it lying on about the twenty-yard line, so I started trotting back to retrieve it. As I was running back to get it, coach Sypult became exasperated and started yelling at me to get in the huddle for the next play. I turned to him and said, "I gotta get my bandage!" He looked at me like I was crazy, and when I reached down to pick it up and put it back on, he just hung his head and laughed. The ref also thought I was crazy, and I'm sure everyone in the stadium was questioning my sanity as I ran to the other end of the field. But the doctor said I could play as long as I used the padded bandage, so I was the only one not crazy! I played the rest of the game, and we won.

As I got over to the victory bell after the game, I was very careful not to reach up and grab the wheel as I was getting up on the trailer. I successfully climbed up and we rang the victory bell without any further blood or injuries. My finger didn't fully heal until the end of the season. Highland High School was never known as a powerhouse football program, so it was considered a good season when we ended up with five wins and four losses.

Senior Year Track

Track season rolled around, and I had lofty expectations for myself, as did Coach Poehline. I worked up the courage to see if I could still run and jump over the high hurdles. I survived the initial trial, and I felt fairly good. However, my speed and jumping abilities just weren't what they used to be. Coach P suggested I try the long jump since I did so well as a sophomore while jumping better than twenty feet.

My first jump was terrible, so I tried it again. It was also a paltry fifteen feet or so. I tried it again. Same result. My left leg (the one that was injured) was my take-off leg, and there just wasn't any power. Coach P encouraged me to keep working at it by trying to use my right leg as my take-off leg. I just couldn't make it happen. I kept practicing over the next few weeks, but to no avail, so I threw in the towel and gave up on the long jump which was very disappointing.

My times on the hurdles were getting better, but as the season started, I had plateaued slightly below my sophomore times. I had lost some speed. I worked harder, trying to strengthen my left (lead) leg. My technique had improved according to Coach P. He said to keep working on a faster turnover rate in my steps which would improve my speed.

Side note: I know many readers will think all I have to talk about is injuries and mishaps, but as I got older, thankfully, bad physical events began to subside. All we must deal with as we age are the memories and the discomfort that inevitably rear their ugly heads, sometimes decades after an incident. It's funny how we remember details about accidents and ailments – probably because they had a major effect on our lives in one way or another.

We all know that our brain "forgets" the physical pain so that we don't feel it again. However, the gory details of the preceding moments and the painful aftermath become firmly implanted into our memories. As we matriculate from youth to adulthood, most of us live and learn and we learn to live. As they say, with age and experience comes wisdom. I know for myself, I endured enough of those painful ailments to not place myself in circumstances where I might suffer the same maladies that I experienced in my youth.

If we play a sport of virtually any kind involving physical activities that challenge the body, there will always be muscle aches and pains along with injuries – it's the nature of the beast. As previously outlined, I've certainly had my share. The ultimate problem is that those injuries can come back to haunt us in our twilight years – and as I have mentioned, mine certainly have.

Back to my senior year of track. I started making progress as the season wore on. My times continued to get better, and I started winning some races. My goal was to win the conference title. It was a reasonable goal, one that I thought I could achieve. Sure, it would be nice to win the state championship, but given the circumstances of my prior injury, I knew that might be too lofty of a goal to accomplish.

I kept working hard and was gradually getting back to where I wanted to be. However, there was one competitor (I'll call him John) that I had run against many times, and he always beat me. He was from a cross-town rival school, so always losing to him was especially irritating. He was kind of a jerk, and that made it even more frustrating. In the conference finals, I was up against him. He was being his typical cocky, self-absorbed guy talking trash before the race, and I really wanted to beat him just once. This was possibly the last time I would have the opportunity unless we both qualified for the regional meet.

I felt really strong and determined that day. I decided to just give it everything I had and run the best race I could. He was in the lane next to me, so I could constantly see how I was doing against him during the race. We loaded into the starting blocks. When the starting gun went off, I burst out as fast as I could – it felt like one of my best starts. As we approached the first hurdle, he was slightly ahead of me. I didn't panic – I became more determined.

Unexpectedly, a feeling of peace and freedom came over me. I'm not sure where it came from, but I remember it distinctively. Suddenly, it felt like I had traveled to a different level of consciousness. It felt like I was flying. The race was playing out in slow motion. By the fourth hurdle, I had edged slightly ahead of my nemesis. By the next to last hurdle, I was a full step ahead and still gaining speed. I crossed the last hurdle and headed for the finish line. I glanced to my left and saw John about two steps behind me as I crossed the finish line. In an instant, I came back to earth and reality set in. I beat him. I had run the race of my life. It was a glorious victory. It was exhilarating.

Coach P came running over and gave me a big hug. We were jumping up and down. My teammates ran over and were celebrating with me. It was a great moment. I had beaten my best time by over a second, and I was going to the state regional finals. My time of 14.9 seconds was the fifth fastest time in the state that year. I achieved my goal – mission accomplished.

In all the ruckus of the jubilation, I recall glancing over and seeing John staring at me with his hands on his hips. He looked like he was in shock. He turned and walked away without saying a word. I wanted to go rub it in, but my mom and dad taught me to be better than that.

It was a huge accomplishment for me. I was high on victory for the rest of the week. I felt vindicated and rewarded for all the hard work I had put in to come back from a significant injury. As an 18-year-old kid, I learned the valuable lesson that hard work and determination do pay off. Or maybe it was a sudden burst of adrenaline.

The following Saturday was the regional meet. I won my qualifying heat and was headed to the finals. I was running against some amazingly fast hurdlers. I loaded into the starting blocks, and then the starting gun went off. I didn't get a good start, but I headed for the first hurdle. My lead leg cleared the hurdle, but my trail leg nicked the hurdle which threw me off a bit – at least I didn't go sprawling on the track like my previous incident.

I cleared the next few hurdles and was making up some time on the other competitors. I knew I had to get it going. I was in a good position and optimistic until the last hurdle. My lead leg just didn't get up high enough and my foot hit the hurdle hard which threw my steps off. I gave it all I had to the finish line and ended up placing fourth. Unfortunately for me, only the top three advanced to the state meet.

I was disappointed, but not distraught. I knew from my own experience that sometimes unplanned things can occur in races. We can't run perfect races all the time – even Olympians know that. Stuff happens. The results were not what I wanted, but I was OK with it.

So, that brought an end to my high school athletic career. I had experienced the thrill of victory and the agony of defeat. I had suffered painful injuries and came back to achieve some successes. I was a better person because of my athletic adventures. Granted, it would have been far easier without the injuries, but the accomplishments and team comradery made it all worthwhile. The life lessons I learned were invaluable.

The Viet Nam Years

When 1966 rolled around, our country was experiencing a tumultuous time. The United States was experiencing something we had never seen since the civil war – an agonizingly divided populace. The war pitting South Viet Nam and North Viet Nam had been ongoing since 1960 as turmoil continued to spread through both countries. I won't go into a detailed history of the war simply because there are far more knowledgeable historians that can better tell the story, and it would take an entire separate book to do it justice. What I will talk about is how the war affected the lives of Rick, my oldest brother, and our entire family.

Rather than waiting to be officially drafted for military service, Rick voluntarily enlisted in the Marine Corps in April of 1966. He knew that he would serve in the war in some capacity. It was a noble act – a call of duty. During that time, around 35,000 of America's finest young men were being drafted or volunteering for military service in order to feed the need in our ever-growing involvement in the war. Rick graduated from University of California-Riverside in June of 1966 and reported for duty at Officer's Candidate School in Quantico, VA in August. He was commissioned as a first lieutenant and eventually achieved the rank of captain in the Marine Corps.

From there, he transferred to Pensacola, FL for flight school where he graduated and received his wings. It was a seminally important moment for our family, so we loaded into the car and drove from Chicago to Pensacola for the ceremony. I remember my eyes welling up with tears as those golden wings were pinned on his beautiful white Marine uniform. I still treasure the picture of that moment. I was so proud of my brother, as was our whole family.

Rick continued his flight training, transitioning to fly UH-1E helicopters – otherwise known as "Huey" gunships. Huey's became a versatile workhorse for the Marines, flying medical evacuation missions, transporting troops into battle, while also serving as an air assault helicopter in support of troops on the ground.

After receiving his orders for deployment to Viet Nam, Rick was able to travel to Chicago to visit his family. It was a consequential trip, in that, the troublesome possibility existed that it was the last time we would see him alive. The undertone of that potential was there, although it was hard to fully grasp it. It was like a nagging nervousness that sat in the pit of everyone's stomach. I know I felt it as a brother, and it was all the more difficult for Mom and Dad. It was excruciating for them – I felt it.

For Dad, having served in World War II, he knew of the evils and the ugly side of war as he was in the midst of battles in the Pacific Region when the US waged war against Japan. I know it was a painful thing for Dad to see his oldest son depart into an uncertain future and go through the horrific experiences that most likely lay ahead for Rick. Dad knew what it was like to say good-bye and leave his pregnant wife behind as he left to do his duty and serve his country. But Dad knew what the call of duty entailed, and he proudly bid his son farewell.

On the other hand, Mom was a mess. Being the strong woman she was, she wore the mantle of being a brave and supportive parent, but deep inside she was torn up. I can only imagine how it felt to give her son that last hug and kiss. She had done the same thing when she agonizingly said goodbye to her husband as he went off to war. She was pregnant with Rick at the time. Now, she was having to do it all over again with her son. She also felt great empathy for Rick's wife, Wendy, since Mom had been in the same position.

I can only imagine the agony of leaving your loved ones behind as Dad and Rick did. Seeing my parents experience the anxiety of Rick's departure was painful. It was gut-wrenching for all of us. There were lots of tears shed in our family in the subsequent days, weeks, and months. To make matters worse for Mom, she was in the middle of some difficult health issues, ultimately resulting in having a hysterectomy.

Back then, the medical world did not have the extensive set of hormone therapies they have now, so basically, she had to go through that process virtually cold turkey. The transition was tough for her. She was one of the sweetest, kindest, most caring people anyone could ever meet, but for several months, she became a different person. She not only was battling an internal hormonal war, but her son was also in the middle of a war in Viet Nam.

To further add to her miseries, Mom began having terrible migraine headaches that were debilitating for her. I recall her coming home from work many times sick to her stomach with pain. The doctor's recommended remedy was to take aspirin, put a cool rag on her head, and lie still in a dark, quiet room. I felt so bad for her. It was painful for us to watch her suffer through those headaches, and I can only imagine what she was going through. The headaches continued for many months, although they gradually subsided in frequency.

The level of tension and anxiety within our household was at an all-time high. As a family, we had never experienced stress like that before. I could tell Mom was struggling trying to deal with not only her health, but also having a son go off to war. Her and Dad's relationship was seemingly being torn apart. I recall hearing them fight like they never had before. I was fifteen years old at the time, and I had never witnessed my parents behaving like this before. I would get that sick, sinking feeling of butterflies in my stomach, and I felt sheer anxiety like I never had before. Mom's health issues, the relationship difficulties between my parents, and our constant worries about Rick were all agonizing.

Gary, being the sweet brother he was, would hug me and wipe away my tears during those times of upheaval. He was incredibly supportive and helped me immensely. I felt angst when we moved from Long Beach to Chicago, but these emotions were far beyond that.

Dad was doing his dead-level best to keep things together, and to his credit, he was a compassionate and understanding husband and father. Poor Mom didn't know what was happening to her. She didn't like herself and was at a loss as to what to do. It's the first time I saw my mother depressed. She was always a bundle of energy and living a life of joy. Mom's faith in God helped her through these physically traumatic months, and thankfully, the difficult times began to gradually subside as her body adjusted to life after a hysterectomy. It was certainly difficult at times as a family, but we all hung together for each other.

While Rick was in Viet Nam, we would get a check-in call from him every week or two. It was always a thrill for us to hear his voice and know that he was doing OK. On the first few calls, he would go into intimate details as to what he was doing, describing war stories that made us all very scared for him. These calls made Mom extremely uncomfortable and would send her into depression and result in lots of tears. I felt bad for her and knew what she was going through both physically and emotionally. It was also very upsetting for Dad to hear, and I'm sure it brought back very uncomfortable memories for him.

One day, I had just gotten home from school when the phone rang. It was Rick checking in. I told him Mom and Dad weren't home. We exchanged pleasantries. It was always good to hear from him, but I felt like I had to let him know that describing all the events he was experiencing in gory detail was very upsetting to us, especially for Mom. I explained how great it was to hear from him, but I suggested he tone it down a bit in terms of his description of the war. He fully understood, and from then on, the calls were far more bearable. Mom would shed lots of tears after those calls – she always felt a sense of thankfulness and relief, but the anxiety was also hard for her to bear.

During all the chaos of the war, Rick's wife Wendy informed him he was going to be a father. Imagine the angst they both were feeling at the time. Wendy had to live through a pregnancy and give birth by herself, while Rick was wondering if he would ever see or know his son. Their son Tim was born in April of '69 while Rick was still deployed – just like Rick was born while Dad was at war.

Rick had flown hundreds of missions after his deployment to Da Nang in August of 1968. Flying Huey gunships was definitely risky business. These helicopters were always smack dab in the middle of the action. Quite often, the missions included landing and extracting troops in very treacherous battle zones or staving off enemy attacks from the air to protect troops on the ground. According to several sources, about half of all Huey's used in the Viet Nam war were shot down in battle. Unfortunately, Rick was part of those statistics.

On a mission in July of 1969, Rick's helicopter was hit by a ground-to-air rocket and his helicopter went down in an active battle zone in the middle of the jungle. Sadly, his young gunner died in the crash. Rick was briefly knocked unconscious. His head hit so hard that it cracked his helmet. His left leg was severely damaged, and he sustained broken ribs. As he tried to extract himself from the helicopter, he could hear Viet Cong soldiers yelling and talking in the distance. Rick succeeded to find a rescue flare and managed to climb on top of the downed aircraft.

He could hear other Huey's in the area and was hoping one of them would see his distress signal. He managed to get the attention of one of the pilots who landed and helped extract Rick and the body of his gunner. They successfully made it out of the battle zone and returned to their base. Rick was then medevacked from the base to a hospital in Yokosuka, Japan where he spent two months recovering from his injuries. Eventually he returned to the El Toro Naval Air Station near Irvine, CA where he served until he received an honorable discharge from the Marine Corps in 1971.

During the summer of '69, I was performing with a national touring group called Continental Singers. As destiny would have it, we happened to be performing in Northern Indiana at the time, and I happened to be home when Mom and Dad received the call that Rick had been shot down but had survived. There were a lot of tears shed out of thankfulness that although he was injured, he managed to make it through that horrific event alive.

I will never know, and it's hard to comprehend the personal courage and bravery it took for Rick to climb into that helicopter and head off into battle, not knowing if he would make it through another mission alive. Pause for a moment and fully absorb that thought...

I can only imagine what Rick and every other soldier that has served our country experienced, and so many did not make it back to their loved ones alive. War is ugly. War is painful. War is deadly. For those brave souls that live through war, it leaves physical and emotional wounds. For many soldiers, the physical wounds are the easiest to live through. The emotional wounds take far longer to heal, and unfortunately, in some cases they never heal. Terrible things that brave soldiers see and experience are difficult to unsee. Things that are experienced are not easily forgotten. Horrific memories of catastrophic events cannot be erased.

The aftermath of the Viet Nam war was the first time we, as a community, fully realized there was literally a living nightmare that soldiers lived through when they returned from war. We began to recognize there was a problem, but the medical community, including psychiatrists and psychologists, did not realize what was happening to so many veterans, nor were they prepared to deal with it.

The after-effects were devastating to so many returning soldiers, and it was absolutely frightening for both the soldiers and their families. It's heartbreaking that far too many families experienced such devastating upheaval in the aftermath of the war that tens of thousands of marriages collapsed. Further, it is even more discouraging to realize and admit how we, as a country, failed to help the more than 22,000 Viet Nam veterans that ended up taking their own life. The failed marriages and suicides are not counted as casualties of the war, but they certainly should be.

How does a soldier process all of what they witnessed? How do they manage their thoughts? It would be nice to simply erase those horrific memories, but unfortunately, those vivid images keep coming back to haunt them. It was not until 1980 that Post Traumatic Stress Syndrome was coined as a diagnosis. Identifying it was one thing. Finding the expertise to provide adequate tools and resources was an enormous challenge – and it will continue to be as long as there is the trauma of war.

Imagine what it would be like being awakened in the middle of the night when your spouse or father is screaming and convulsing in a cold sweat. It would be frightening to say the least. That is not the only thing that can happen. PTSD symptoms can include severe depression, irritability, hostility, unrestrained anger, hypervigilance, social isolation, self-destructive behavior, traumatic flashbacks, uncontrolled fear, severe anxiety, mistrust, guilt, loneliness, insomnia, nightmares, emotional detachment, unwanted thoughts and desires, and the list goes on. It's a devastating illness that can ruin individual lives and families when not treated.

Rick is my hero. Despite his challenges and difficulties after the war, he went on to be a successful attorney and a state judge in California for almost forty years until he retired. He transcended the horror, violence, loss of friends, and betrayal he experienced. I have the utmost admiration for him, and I am proud to call him my brother.

Other combatants who returned were not so fortunate. PTSD is a common diagnosis for these men and women. Without help, many often turn to drugs, alcohol, and suicide to cope with the trauma. They experienced wounds to the mind and spirit as an invisible wound that will never heal. The lucky ones get treatment and learn to manage the illness over a lifetime. The most salient point is that PTSD is not cured, it's managed.

Far too many brave men and women survived the bullets and shells but were destroyed by the war. Like so many thousands of brave soldiers, it's a constant battle in working through the travails of PTSD.

Those of us that have never served in battle can never fully comprehend the ravages of war. We can think about it. We can read about it. We can see it in movies. We can wonder about it. Unless we have lived it, we can never completely understand the effects it has on the person who served.

As I have written these words and recalled these memories, I have shed many tears. These are painful memories, and the tears I have shed are for my brother and so many other noble soldiers who have suffered through so much pain. My tears are also for those that didn't make it home and for their families that must endure the everlasting pain of losing a loved one. Lastly, the tears are for those family members who stood tall and supported soldiers in need as they worked through dealing with the painful and horrible aftermath of war. The soldiers that have served are recognized heroes. Spouses and children of soldiers are all too often not recognized – they are unsung heroes.

I fully admire Rick and all the others who have sacrificed themselves in service to our country. My biggest fear is that subsequent generations will forget about or take lightly what it has taken to defend our nation. It is our duty to them and our eternal responsibility to never take for granted the sacrifices that have been made for us. Every student should emerge from our educational system knowing and fully understanding why they enjoy their freedoms. Sadly, far too many of us, including many educators themselves, don't understand, appreciate, or hold in reverence what others have sacrificed for our country.

Read this number: 30,177. According to research concluded in 2021, that is the number of soldiers and veterans that have committed suicide since 2001 – and that number continues to grow. It is heartbreaking. It is devastating to families and friends that must endure that kind of pain. Many, if not most of those lives could have and should have been saved with the proper recognition and intervention. We need to do more. In fact, I say we are morally obligated to do more to honor those that have served their country. They are worth every second of time and every penny of money that we can invest – it's the least we can do.

To close out this chapter, allow me to extract a portion from my first book, *I Know We Are Better Than This*. It is specifically about the Viet Nam war and how those brave soldiers like Rick were mistakenly disrespected. They did not start the war. They did not seek out the war. They bravely responded to the call of duty when their country asked them to.

> The 60's and 70's were a strange time in our country that was challenging on many fronts, from the controversy over the Viet Nam War to racial division. The youth of America were lost and confused (including myself), and college campuses went from a place of learning to becoming a cultural battleground.
>
> When the veterans returned from the Viet Nam War, the country was in bad shape, and as we all know, these brave and noble veterans were unceremoniously greeted with disdain and contempt. It should never have happened that way. There were no parades of celebration. These soldiers, along with having to deal with the horrors of war, had to deal with hostilities in their own country for which they served. The way they were treated was despicable, undeserving, and disrespectful. It was a dark day for our country, not to mention a dark day for those who answered the call of duty and put their lives on the line for us and the lives of strangers thousands of miles away.
>
> Another forgotten and under-appreciated group that was dishonored was the wives, mothers, fathers, sisters, and brothers that lost a loved one or had to deal with the recovery and on-going problems that the after-effects of the Viet Nam war brought. All those family members paid their own price, and for many, the cost was dear. Sadly, they still live with it today. We honor the soldiers that have served, and deservedly so. Unfortunately, we forget to honor the unsung heroes who had to deal with the consequences of the aftermath of war. I have often thought we should have the day after Veterans Day as the Unsung Heroes Day. The families of soldiers deserve their own recognition because of the sacrifices they made. They deserve to be honored because they served our nation in a different way, and their lives were irrevocably altered.
>
> Here's a quote from John Sorenson, former president of the Viet Nam Helicopter Pilots Association: "...I submit that the men and women who served in the Viet Nam War are the Greatest Generation of our Generation [Baby Boomers]. We lined up when others didn't. We took an oath where

others didn't. We served when others didn't. Then we were despised and ridiculed when others weren't. We stuck together and supported each other when others didn't. We are without any doubt the 'Greatest Generation of Our Generation.'"

Well said Mr. Sorenson.

There is no more noble thing to do than to be willing to sacrifice one's life for others, and our Viet Nam veterans were robbed of the acclaim they deserved. They followed orders. They risked their lives – many lost their lives. They still live with the pain of war and nightmares that followed, and we, as a country, dishonored not only them, but their families as well. It obviously was not a popular war, but every one of those soldiers and their families deserve our full honor, our respect, and our unending gratitude for their nobility and service to EVERY one of us that lives free today. I will humbly say, "Thank you to every Viet Nam veteran for your service, thank you to the families for their service, and I humbly apologize to you on behalf of our country. We failed you, and for that, we are deeply sorry." *"I Know We Are Better Than This."*

May God place his powerful hand on those brave soldiers and their families who struggle to find peace and solace still today. May every person who enjoys the freedoms brought to us by the sacrifices of our service members forever remember and hold those brave souls in the highest regard. All our freedom fighters answered the call of duty. It is therefore our duty to continually honor and revere them. It's absolutely the least we can do.

Section II

Travails of Travel

Chapter 4

Unfair Share

As I look back on all the traveling I have done, it's hard to believe so many weird things actually happened to me, but they did. Most people have had strange, fascinating, and undoubtably frustrating tales to tell while traveling – it's the nature of the beast. However, I am convinced that I have had my unfair share of unique and unusual stories to tell during my journeys to many parts of the world.

Combining my business travels, a summer musical tour, and on various vacations, I have been fortunate to visit 42 states and 16 countries. I have spent innumerable hours on an airplane, having logged more than 1.7 million miles in the air. By my rough calculations, I have spent more than six months of my life sitting in an uncomfortable seat on an airplane, although on rare occasions, when I was fortunate enough, I did spend some of that time in business or first class. Add to that another six months getting to and from the airport, plus waiting to board, along with the many delays and layovers that are an unfortunate part of travel. It boggles my mind that I spent approximately one year of my life just getting to and from all the destinations, whether it be for business or pleasure.

Painful Lesson Learned

The first memorable travel tale occurred when I was sixteen. It was the first time I traveled by myself, so I was a bit apprehensive, but confident that I could manage. Mom and Dad were kind enough to send me to visit my brother Rick for a week during a summer break. He was in flight school at the Naval Air Station in Pensacola, FL. I was so excited.

My itinerary involved flying from Chicago to Atlanta and then taking a connecting flight to Pensacola. I had a layover in Atlanta and decided to eat dinner prior to my flight. I looked at my watch and saw it was a little after 6:00pm and my flight was scheduled for 7:30pm, so I had plenty of time. I had a nice, casual dinner and decided to head for my gate since it was around 7:00pm.

When I got to the gate, there was no one there getting ready to board. That was my first clue that something was wrong. I approached a gate agent and asked when my flight was going to board. She asked what flight I was on, and I told her the one to Pensacola. To my utter shock and dismay, she told me the flight had taken off thirty minutes ago. My heart sank.

I was puzzled and asked why it had left before the departure time. She gave a little chuckle and answered that it had taken off on time. I was even more confused. I looked at my watch and it was a little after seven. I thought maybe I was in an episode of The Twilight Zone. I could hear that haunting theme music. Those of you who are too young won't remember that great TV show (Google it). I had no idea what was going on until I looked at a clock on the wall behind the ticket counter and it said 8:05. My mind was blown. How could that be?

I told her my watch said 7:05. The ticket agent then informed me that Atlanta was on eastern time, and I then realized my watch was on central time. It never dawned on me that there was a time zone change. My mind was racing, my stomach was churning, and I was in pure panic mode.

The gate agent informed me that the next flight to Pensacola was the following morning at 10:00am. Recall that there were no cell phones or text messaging back in the dark ages of 1967. I made my way to a pay phone and had to make a collect call back home because I did not know Rick's phone number – I had to let him know I missed my flight. Only old folks like me actually know what a pay phone or a collect call is. I won't explain that to the youngsters – just Google it.

My parents were baffled as to how I could miss my flight, and I explained to them the time zone issue. They felt bad for me and were worried. Dad was a veteran traveler and said he would try and find a place for me to stay. I told him I would be fine and would find a place to sleep at the airport and take the morning flight to Pensacola. It was my bad, and I would just deal with it. I got Rick's phone number from Mom and had to place another collect call to him.

Rick's wife Wendy answered the phone and accepted the collect call. I explained to her what happened, and she also felt bad for me having to spend the night at the Atlanta airport. I assured her I would be fine and gave her my flight information for the following morning.

My first thought after hanging up was what am I going to do for the next fourteen hours. Mind you, the Atlanta airport back then was tiny compared to what it is today. Needless to say, I was in for a long, boring night. I couldn't entertain myself by watching a movie or stupid YouTube clips on my phone because there were no cell phones. I can imagine the youngsters reading this having sweaty palms and going through an anxiety attack at the shear horror of not having a cell phone in their grasp while having to endure a traumatic episode like this. Back then, we had no electronic security blanket. I was too young to go to the bar to try and ease the pain. That's what I would do now – after all, a few beers would have certainly helped!

After 10:00pm, everything in the airport was shut down. I did manage to buy a few snacks to get me through the night. I explored the entire airport. There was no one there except a security guard and a few other poor souls that had to suffer through the same ignominious predicament I was in.

My main mission in exploring the airport was to find a bench or somewhere I could lay down. There were no cots or blankets as they now have at most airports so that weary travelers can at least attempt to get some sleep. Unfortunately, all they had were uncomfortable seats with arms which prevented me from at least lying down. I tried using the clothes in my suitcase to make some sort of bed on the hard tile floor, but that was a futile tactic. So, I explored the airport some more. I did ask the security guard if he had any suggestions on where I could find a place to sleep. All he said was, "Good luck!" That was immensely helpful.

Obviously, it was a long night. I was so bored being bored because being bored is really boring. I tried to get some sleep while sitting in a rather uncomfortable chair, but I finally gave up. Have you ever tried to kill fourteen hours with nothing to do? It was excruciatingly tedious. It seemed like my watch was moving in slow motion. Every minute seemed to last an hour, and every hour seemed like a day. I found out what sleep deprivation torture was like, and I did not particularly like it. I fully understood why they consider it an effective torture technique.

The next morning, I got some breakfast and gave a lengthy sigh of relief that the longest night I had ever spent finally came to an end. It goes without saying that I was the first passenger waiting at the gate. Had I known what a "happy dance" was back then, I certainly would have been executing it joyfully as I walked across the tarmac and boarded the plane. No, we didn't have fancy boarding bridges to walk through back then. Passengers just walked on the tarmac and walked up the stairs to get on the plane. I sat down in my seat and thought if the flight was delayed or cancelled, my head would explode. Fortunately for the rest of the passengers and crew, they did not have to witness the spectacle of my brain exploding all over them.

The plane took off and I was on my way to Pensacola. Happily, I was able to gather what little sanity I still had left. I was never able to sleep on a plane, but I was out like a light soon after the pilot said, "Welcome aboard." It was only an hour and a half flight. I slept the whole time, but it seemed like I had slept for days. The next thing I knew, I felt the bump as the tires touched the runway in Pensacola. At last, the longest fourteen hours of my first sixteen years came to an end.

My visit to Pensacola to see Rick and Wendy was great. They lived on a bayou with a small dock in the backyard extending out into the water for about twenty feet. They had a dog that was an interesting character. He was a very happy and sweet dog. I was quite amused to see that Sammy was an excellent "fisher-dog." He would stand on the edge of the dock and watch for fish to stray close. If they came too close, Sammy would dive into the water and snag the fish in his mouth.

It was hilarious to see him swim back to shore with the fish in his mouth, seemingly smiling ear-to-ear from the artful acquisition of his prey. He would then feast on his prize and then leave the smelly carcass for someone else to clean up. I thought the least he could do was to throw the carcass back in the bayou, but evidently, he thought differently. Some of the fish were pretty impressive in size and it was highly entertaining to watch him fish since I had never seen a more talented, resourceful, and determined dog.

The Steak Chase

If Sammy had one character flaw, it was that he loved to eat. His voracious appetite got him in big trouble one day while I was visiting. Rick had bought some steaks for dinner, and we were sitting in the backyard with the beautiful steaks on the grill. As we were talking, I happened to notice that Sammy was stalking around the grill scheming on how to acquire one of the delicious steaks. Rick yelled at him to get away and Sammy sauntered off for a few minutes. He sat down about ten feet away and was staring at the grill. I'm sure he was working out a strategy.

He slowly and stealthily eased his way closer to the grill. Much to our surprise, Sammy stood up on his hind legs and delicately snatched what he thought would be a gourmet meal right off the grill. I assume he liked his steak rare because Rick had just put the steaks on the grill a few minutes earlier. Sammy then made a fast exit with his prized prime steak in his drooling mouth. I'm sure he was looking forward to enjoying his dinner. Rick jumped up and ran after him, yelling for Sammy to stop and come back.

Sammy had other ideas and started running like a scared racehorse down the street. Rick took off right behind him, using his lightning-fast speed trying to catch Sammy, screaming at him with words and phrases I shall not repeat here. The race was on, and both were highly determined to win.

Down the block they ran. I couldn't help but laugh at the situation, but for Rick it was no laughing matter. Rick was about to catch him, but Sammy made a strategic decision to turn around at the end of the street and head back home. Both were still in a full-speed gallop. As they approached the house, I assume Sammy finally realized that Rick was not going to be deterred from retrieving the steak.

When Sammy got to the front yard, he dropped the steak. I suppose he decided that his life was in danger, and he should relinquish his gourmet meal, cut his losses, and head for the hills. Out of breath and sweating from the all-out sprint, Rick grabbed the steak off the ground while still using some very choice words and then marched over to the trash can, lifted the lid, and threw the steak in. I jokingly told Rick he should just let Sammy have it because it was ruined. He disgustingly said, "I'll be damned if I'm going to let him eat that steak. If I can't enjoy it, neither can he."

As might be expected, Sammy was nowhere to be found for the rest of the evening. We were able to split up the remaining two steaks and enjoyed a nice meal. Poor Sammy, on the other hand, had to settle for fish that night instead of a delicious steak. But at least he could take solace in the fact that he was still alive.

The rest of my stay in Pensacola was a lot of fun. I had gotten my driver's license about six months prior, and Rick had purchased a shiny new Pontiac GTO. For those of you who are not familiar with GTO's, they were the first muscle cars ever built. They had a powerful engine and were built for racing with a four-speed transmission. It was a really cool car that even had a famous song written about it. He let me drive it several times—it was quite a thrill to get behind the wheel with so much horsepower.

Rick had also bought another toy – a Ducati 250CC dirt bike. There was a dirt bike trail not too far from his house and he took me there to show me how it was done. I had never driven or even ridden on a motorcycle, let alone riding a powerhouse dirt bike. I was an expert bicycle rider and surely this would be a piece of cake. But when I mounted up for my first ride, I turned the throttle a bit too much. When I released the clutch control, the Ducati just jumped right out from under me, and I ended up with a mouthful of dirt. I quickly assumed that's why they fittingly call it a dirt bike. Rick had a good laugh and told me to barely turn the throttle and release the clutch slowly.

My second try was a success – I got the bike going and managed to stay on until it was time to hit the first little mound. I didn't have enough momentum to make it up the mound and fell sideways. Rick had another laugh and ran over to get the bike off me. I got up, dusted myself off, spit out another mouthful of dirt, and was determined to try again. He suggested I try riding around the parking lot to get used to the bike.

After circling around the parking lot, I was gaining enough confidence to try the course again. I made it up the first hill, then the next one, and then there was a jump ahead. I decided to just go for it and soared through the air. It was an exhilarating feeling until the bike and I hit the ground. I had accidentally turned the handlebar to the left. When the bike and I landed, the bike came to a screeching halt while I went flying forward. As I was about to hit the ground, I could tell another mouthful of dirt was in my immediate future. Sure enough, it was.

Rick had another laugh, but he ran over to see if I was OK. I got up and dusted myself off once again. He then advised me to keep the handlebar straight when I landed. I thought to myself, "If you could have told me that sooner, I could have avoided another mouthful of dirt." He then jumped on the bike and told me to watch how it's done. I carefully observed how he was riding.

Like getting bucked off or falling off a horse, they say the best thing is to get back on and try it again. As an adventurous sixteen-year-old kid, or should I say a glutton for punishment, I decided to hop back on that Ducati horse and give it another try. Evidently, I had learned my painful lessons well and was able to make my way through the entire course without falling off and chewing more dirt. Rick and I took turns riding the rest of the day and it ended up being a fun time.

In the subsequent days while Rick was attending flight school and Wendy was working as a nurse, I would ride down to the dirt bike track virtually every day and buzz around. I enjoyed it, and fortunately, I didn't have any major falls or wounds, nor did I have to eat more dirt.

After an eventful week with big brother Rick, it was time to fly home. I made sure to be aware of the time change on my connecting flight through Atlanta. In fact, after I landed in Atlanta, I picked up a snack and went straight to the gate. I dared not leave the gate area for any reason. There was no way I was going to chance another night in the Atlanta airport. Luckily, I made it back home with no other incidents – I made it through my first solo travel experience and certainly learned to pay attention to time zones whenever I travelled. It's funny how one bad experience can vividly stay with us for the rest of our lives. Painful lesson learned.

An Eventful Trip From Chicago to Dallas

My tour with the music group Continental Singers ended in late August of 1969 (more on that later). I flew back home from Los Angeles to Chicago for a few days and immediately had to leave for college at Dallas Baptist University. I had to be there a few days early before school started because I had never taken the ACT test which was a requirement for admission. I had taken the SAT, but DBU required the ACT test. I had been accepted, but the test was the last box to check. DBU allowed incoming freshmen to take the test at their campus a few days before the school year began, so I loaded up my stuff and headed to Dallas.

It was a bit painful for my parents to see their youngest son leave for college – especially for Mom. They carted me off to O'Hare airport for a 9:00pm flight, and it was hard for me to say goodbye mostly because I had spent the entire summer on the road with Continental Singers. Still, leaving home and being 1,000 miles away was a bit traumatic, but off I went. The plane departed on time, and we were scheduled to land in Dallas at 11:15pm. My uncle George was picking me up and I was going to stay with his family until school started.

The flight was proceeding as usual until around 9:45 when suddenly the plane went into a nosedive. This was not turbulence – it was truly a nosedive. The flight attendants were serving beverages, and they were fighting to keep the cart from mowing down anyone in its path. They frantically fought and eventually got the cart stowed safely. It seemed like we were going straight down. The plane was shaking wildly and speeding toward what felt like surely a crash landing. The pilot came on the intercom and was shouting some kind of message but the noise of the rapid descent and with the plane creaking and shaking, no one could understand a thing he was saying. We were all in the dark, both literally and figuratively speaking.

People were panicking and some were screaming. The woman sitting beside me was crying, as were several others around me. It was starting to set in with me that the end of my life was near. I had lived eighteen and a half years, and this was it. I noticed that the oxygen masks did not pop down, so I figured the pilot thought there was really no need for them since we were all doomed.

We were a religious family, and I started praying for God to intervene and save us from the impending crash – I wasn't ready to die, and from their reactions, neither was anyone else on the plane. I figured that when we crashed, it would not be a painful death, so there was no need to pray that it be quick and painless.

It seemed like things started moving in slow motion, and time was being stretched. The plane was still shaking, and the noise was nearly deafening. I was sitting in a window seat, and I could see we had cleared the clouds, and I noticed some city lights below. I was resigned that the end was near. I offered to hold the hand of the lady sitting next to me and she gladly grabbed it and gave me a half smile and a firm squeeze.

As we got closer to the ground, I spotted airport lights, and I figured the pilot was going to crash us in an area where minimal damage would be done. I thought it was a noble and considerate decision on his part. If we were going to die, there was no need in taking a bunch of other people with us as we transitioned to our eternal destiny.

The ground grew closer and closer very rapidly. We were probably at about 3,000 feet when the pilot quickly levelled off the plane. I wasn't sure what that meant, but I, like all the other passengers, was desperately hoping for some good news. Only about two minutes had passed since all the chaos began, although it seemed like an hour. It was now 9:50. The airport lights were approaching fast, and I noticed a bunch of red lights blinking off and on. I realized they were from fire trucks and ambulances. I thought that was definitely NOT a good sign.

I felt the landing gear go down, so I thought maybe that was either a good sign or the pilot was optimistic enough that he could at least try to cushion our crash somehow. I saw the ground was right below us and I braced myself for the impending doom. I felt the landing gear lock into place and was encouraged that we might actually be able to land.

The plane's tires hit the runway hard – there was a big jolt. There were lots of screams, but I thought to myself we were at least on the ground, and we had not crashed. The pilot then literally slammed on the brakes. Had everyone not had their seat belts on, people would have been catapulted all over the plane. The tires were squealing, the plane was shaking, and as I looked out the window, I saw smoke billowing around the airplane as we were still speeding down the runway. I then assumed an engine was on fire and we were all about to explode into oblivion.

We finally came to a screeching halt in the middle of the runway. The emergency exit doors flew open, and the flight attendants were shouting to leave everything behind and head toward the emergency exits. I was near the exit, and jumped out of my seat. I saw that they had deployed the emergency exit slide, and we were instructed to jump on the inflatable slide and slide down, so I did. When I got to the bottom, I saw that people were tumbling down the slide out of control. I noticed one of the flight attendants was trying to catch passengers as many of them hurtled down the slide. I knew she could not catch them all, so I pitched in to help her. She was shouting for everyone to run away from the plane as fast as they could.

Out of the corner of my eye, I noticed the tires were still billowing smoke, but the engines didn't seem to be on fire. I thought that was comforting because I was catching people coming down the slide with the jet engine about fifteen feet away.

Finally, the captain and the rest of the crew came down the slide and we all took off running. As we were running, I asked the flight attendant I was helping, "What is going on?" She said there was a bomb on our plane, and it was supposed to go off at 10:00. I looked at my watch and it was 9:56. We stopped running when we were about a hundred yards from the plane. Several buses were on their way to transport everyone to the terminal. It was 9:59. We all stood on the tarmac staring at the plane, anticipating a huge explosion.

At 10:00, nothing happened. We waited. 10:05 hit and the plane was still sitting there. At 10:15, we loaded into our buses and started heading for the terminal. When we arrived at the terminal everyone unloaded from the buses. We all stood inside the terminal watching through the window, still expecting an explosion. By 10:30, nothing had happened. I spoke to the pilot and asked what was going on. He explained that a phone call was made to American Airlines from someone in Chicago after we took off that said they had planted a bomb on our flight. The caller said the bomb was programmed to go off at 10:00, so the pilot called a "Mayday" emergency, and the closest airport was St. Louis, which is where we landed.

I immediately called Uncle George (yes, another collect call) and luckily caught him before he left for the airport. I explained what had happened and told him I would call him when we were leaving St. Louis.

We all sat around waiting, and around 11:00, we could see the bomb squad carefully approaching the plane. We were told that all carry-on items and checked baggage would have to be searched by the bomb squad and that we should be prepared to sit it out until everything passed inspection. They also told us that we would be taking a different plane to Dallas, and I was certainly happy about that.

So, we waited. And waited. We were also told not to stray too far from the gate because as soon as all the luggage was checked, we would re-board the new plane and depart.

After all the checked bags and carry-ons were searched, nothing suspicious was found. Around 5:30am, they announced that we would be departing, and everyone could board the plane. I quickly called George (another collect call). Of course, I woke him up, but he was happy to hear all was well and we were heading for Dallas. At long last, we departed at 6:00am and landed just around 8:00. After getting my bags (yes, I had two bags because I was moving to Dallas and there were no baggage fees back then), we left the airport. George kindly took me to get some breakfast and then we headed to DBU so I could take my ACT test. I arrived just in time.

As one might assume, it was a battle to even stay awake during the test, let alone trying to ace the test. The room was quiet and seemed like a pretty good place to take a nap in between test sessions. It was also painfully hard to keep my eyes open because of all the reading the test required. I would have far rather been sleeping in a bed than sitting at an uncomfortable desk for three hours struggling mightily to merely stay awake. I did the best I could on the test, which was not very good, but I was still able to meet their minimum standards for admission. If my score was good enough for them, it was certainly good enough for me.

During the late 60's, there were numerous bomb threats instigated by crazy nut-jobs that would occasionally wreak havoc on travelers like me. Unfortunately, it was sort of a fad, and I, along with all the other passengers on my plane, were victims of life-disrupting, villainous antics perpetrated by an idiotic hoaxer. Back then there was no caller-ID – not to mention all these pranksters had to do was to place a call from a random pay phone and no one could trace their call. Perhaps these twits should have been eternally damned to suffer the terror and anxiety my fellow passengers and I had to endure. Sadly, I'm sure the perpetrator was never caught. Perhaps the upside to this incident was that I survived and got to tell this story in my book.

Yes, One More Night

As has been previously shown, the airline gods can be unkind – or perhaps they have a perverse sense of humor. Maybe they think torturing us must be funny.

I have one more tale to tell from my college years. It involves a trip in 1971 to California to visit Rick and Wendy and see my first nephew, Tim, who was almost two years old. I had not seen him yet, and I had not seen Rick and Wendy since he returned from Viet Nam. Mom and Dad were kind enough to send me to visit them during spring break.

When I got to Love Field airport in Dallas, I found out that due to inclement weather, my early afternoon direct flight on United Airlines to LAX was cancelled. The ticket agent told me the only flight she could book me on was a flight to Lubbock and then connect to LAX. I called Rick (still another collect call) and gave him my new arrival time. We joked that if I didn't have any bad luck in visiting with him, I wouldn't have had any luck at all.

I boarded the flight with my bag and my cherished Framus 12-string guitar which they allowed me to carry on, and we headed for Lubbock. Quite unfortunately, and as my bad luck would have it, Lubbock was experiencing inclement weather as well. We had to circle the airport until the weather cleared. Yes, you guessed it – I missed my connection to LAX. I had to make another collect call to Rick after we finally landed in Lubbock to give him the bad news. This was getting ridiculous, but it got worse.

The only way United could get me to LAX was to fly from Lubbock to Albuquerque that evening, then spend the night at the airport, and take an early flight to LAX. Since I was experienced in spending the night at the airport, I was a bit more prepared to absorb this insanity without actually going insane – although it was touch and go.

I took off from Lubbock and landed in Albuquerque around 10:00pm. Their airport was far tinier than Atlanta's, so there was no exploration, and again, absolutely nothing to do but wait for my 8:00am flight the following morning. It was another long night, but at least I had my guitar to provide some sort of entertainment. I played and sang until my fingers were raw. A few poor souls that were also stranded enjoyed the entertainment I was providing, and then I decided to try and get some sleep. I had gathered enough experience in learning how to sleep upright that I surprisingly got a few hours of shut-eye.

The sun came up – it was a beautiful sunrise. I managed to eat an early breakfast, and we boarded the flight to LAX. As I was boarding, the flight attendant said I could not carry on my guitar. I tried my best to convince her that I did not want it to be checked as baggage because it might get damaged. I explained that I was allowed to carry it on for the flights from DFW to Lubbock, and from Lubbock to Albuquerque. She wasn't having it and was adamant that I could not carry it on. I did not want to cause a scene, so reluctantly, I ended up checking it. She guaranteed it would be safe and handled with care.

Thankfully, the plane took off and it was a smooth flight to LAX. After we landed, I met Wendy at the baggage claim area and my suitcase came. We waited for my guitar, but it was a no-show. My stomach was churning, and my temper was beginning to flare. After waiting half an hour, the baggage claim attendant told me they could not find it and took my name, and I then gave them Rick and Wendy's address and phone number. He said they would call when they located it. I was mortified that my guitar was lost, and I was not a happy camper. I would have liked to have vented to that evil flight attendant, but I'm sure it would have done absolutely no good.

The following morning, I got a phone call from the baggage supervisor who explained to me that my guitar had been damaged, but they were going to repair it. He said it fell off the baggage truck, but he would see to it that it would be repaired to its original condition. I told him there was no way they could restore it to its original form and that they needed to replace it. He explained that they had previously worked with a guitar repair person that was excellent at restoring damaged guitars. I thought to myself, "Great, that's encouraging – you've had to do this before?" He guaranteed that it would be nicely repaired and delivered to me in three days. I was still very skeptical.

I was crushed by all of this. I loved that guitar. I paid $200 for it with my own money I earned while working at the gas station my dad owned. That was a lot of money for me back then. The equivalent in 2025 dollars would have been around $1,600. It had a beautiful sunburst finish and sounded great.

Three days later, there was a knock at the door. I opened the door and there was a delivery driver standing with my guitar. The first thing I noticed as he handed it to me was that the case was cracked. I told him not to leave yet because if the guitar was not fully restored to its original condition, I was going to refuse it and demand that United reimburse me for the original cost of the guitar.

When I opened the case, I was horrified. That beautiful sunburst finish looked like a third grader had tried to re-color it. I took the guitar out of the case and looked at the bottom of the guitar. It looked like they had put wood filler in the eight-inch crack and varnished over it. There was also a gouge out of the face of the guitar where they had also used wood filler. I was disgusted and told the driver there was no way I was going to accept it, and he could just take it back to United. He told me he could not do that and said I should just keep it and take it up with United. I did not want to give him a hard time because he had nothing to do with this, so I signed for it, and he went on his way.

I immediately called the baggage claim person I had spoken to and told him I was livid and disappointed that they thought my guitar was fully restored. I informed him that I wanted a new guitar, and he said there was nothing he could do because they considered the guitar repaired and restored. I then vented my anger and said I wanted to speak with his boss or whoever else I could talk to. He said, "Sorry, but this case is closed," then he hung up. I thought my head was going to explode. I vowed revenge and was determined to never fly United again, which still to this day, I have not. I changed my return flight from LAX to American Airlines.

When I got back to Dallas, I wrote a lengthy letter and addressed it to the vice president of customer relations at United's corporate headquarters. I included pictures of the "restored" guitar and mentioned its original cost. I didn't have a person's name, but I was hoping it would at least find its way to someone. Recall that it was virtually impossible to find out who to contact – there wasn't a Google or email back then. I had little hope that anything would ever be done when I mailed the letter.

I used my home address where Mom and Dad lived because I was still in school in Dallas. About two weeks later, Mom called and said I had gotten a letter from United, and included in the letter was a check for $200. I thought I was going to faint. I couldn't believe they actually sent me a check. I was blown away and finally felt fully vindicated. I wrote him a letter of thanks and told him how much I appreciated his response.

The story gets even better. Mom and Dad added some money to my $200, and I was able to buy a brand new Martin 12-string guitar, which was a huge upgrade from my Framus 12-string. I still own and love that wonderful Martin guitar. The beauty of the sound is unmatched, and its value has grown substantially – it is now a collector's item and worth a lot of money. It's more than 55 years old. In the end, things turned out OK for me. All's well that ends well. However, I fully intend to keep my vow to never fly United again due to my pain and suffering!

Chapter 5

My History with Long Beach Airport

As mentioned earlier, I spent ages seven to fourteen growing up in Long Beach, CA. It occupies a special place in my heart for being the place where I spent my formative years. In 1957, the same year we moved there, Douglas Aircraft opened a manufacturing plant adjacent to the Long Beach airport to produce their newest aircraft innovation, the DC-8 Jetliner. Competitor McDonnell Aircraft also built an adjacent manufacturing facility.

Mind you, the Long Beach airport, although very small, had a long history in aviation beginning in 1919. It became a favorite location for many of Amelia Earhart's famous flights and was where she initially caught the bug to become a pilot. It also became the first illuminated airport in the country in 1928, allowing take-offs and landings at night. The airport also played an important role in the manufacturing and testing of military aircraft during World War II. It was surprising how such a small airport had an important historic influence on the aircraft industry.

It was a relatively short bike ride from our house to the airport, and we would occasionally go there to watch planes take off and land. At that time, American, TWA, and United all had commercial flights in and out of Long Beach, but it was not a major hub like LAX. Prior to their merger, McDonnell and Douglas would fly their experimental airplanes in and out of the airport as well.

I recall one occasion when we witnessed a historic flight. One of our friends at church worked for Douglas and told my dad that he should take us boys to the airport to witness the maiden take-off and landing of the first passenger jet, the DC-8. On May 30, 1958 (yes, I had to look it up), we loaded up in the car and headed for the airport. There were many cars and people surrounding the airport to watch what back then was an extraordinary event.

After Dad parked the car, we got out and sat on the hood. Within a few minutes, we saw an enormous plane taxiing to the end of the runway. It was much bigger than what we were used to seeing. After another few minutes, we heard the four jet engines begin to rev up. They got louder and louder and almost reached a near deafening point (there were no noise restrictions on planes back then). The giant bird began to roll forward. It barreled down the runway, rapidly gaining speed, and the noise was increasing even more. I had never heard anything so loud in my life – I thought my eardrums were about to burst. The nose of the plane tipped up and off it sailed into the wild blue yonder (yes, youngsters, that's a cultural reference from my generation).

It was a cloudless, beautiful day as the big bird took flight, soaring skyward in a majestic fashion. I sat there in awe of what I had just witnessed. I remember seeing the jet tip its wings and bank to the left as it gained altitude. It continued out over the ocean, and about ten minutes later, it headed back to the airport for landing. It was amazing to see the big bird approaching the airport. It was huge compared to the commercial planes I had flown on. The landing gear popped down, and it descended gracefully toward the runway. The wheels touched down with a cloud of smoke and it was safely back on the ground. The engines gave out another big roar as the jet slowed down, and then it taxied back to the Douglas hanger. It was exciting to see a new era in air travel begin.

A Different Boomer Generation

I was also a witness to another interesting tidbit in the development of the airline industry in Southern California. While playing inside one day, I heard a large boom that rattled the windows and shook the house. It was really loud – I thought a huge bomb had exploded. My first thought was that the Russians had dropped an atomic bomb on Los Angeles. Tensions between the Russians and the US were very high back in those days, so I thought it was a natural reaction on my part. I went outside and looked around, but I did not see a mushroom cloud or any type of large fire. I asked my Grandmother Bennett, who was living with us at the time, what had happened, and she had no idea. It startled her as well.

Later that evening, we were watching the news, and the reporters explained that a sonic boom had occurred over Los Angeles as a result of an experimental aircraft breaching the sound barrier. Eventually, it became a somewhat regular occurrence since many military and commercial aircraft were being tested by McDonnell and Douglas over the Southern California skies. We quickly learned to live with these alarming booms that rattled the windows and shook the walls. Propeller-driven planes are not able to exceed the speed of sound, but the new jets obviously could. As a young, inquisitive boy, it was very fascinating to imagine anything going faster that the speed of sound at 760 mph (Mach 1). Now, we have aircraft that travel at Mach six and beyond. Amazing.

Long Beach Airport Craziness

During my business career, I made many trips to Southern California, and if at all possible, I would try to fly in and out of the Long Beach airport. LAX had become a major hassle for getting in and out of the airport – not to mention, most of my business was in and around the Long Beach, Anaheim, and Irvine area. Any opportunity to avoid LA traffic was high on my list of things to not have to deal with – been there done that far too many times. The Long Beach airport was still a small, quaint place, and was very easy to get in and out of quickly and painlessly.

I'm not sure what it was – or why – but there were three interesting incidents that occurred on trips to and from Long Beach.

The first one happened before we even took off from Dallas and headed for Long Beach. I had boarded the plane and was sitting in a window seat on the left side. I was reading my newspaper and waiting for all the other passengers to board. The plane was filling up and I happened to look out the window and was astonished to see my checked bag sitting upright on the tarmac about fifty feet away from the plane. I rarely checked my bag, always preferring to use a carry-on, except this was going to be a long trip and required more clothing than normal. I knew it was my bag because it was black with silver stripes on the side – it was easily identifiable, even at fifty feet. I thought it was a bit crazy to see my bag sitting on the tarmac all by itself. It was as if some jokester had placed it there. I wondered if anyone was going to notice it and put it on our flight.

I watched it for a few minutes and then decided I needed to get into action – I certainly did not want to arrive in California while my bag was still sitting on the tarmac in Dallas. I pushed the flight attendant call button because I was beginning to panic. The plane was almost fully loaded. The flight attendant weaved her way through the passengers that were still boarding and was slightly annoyed with me. I told her my bag was sitting in the middle of the tarmac and someone needed to retrieve it. She said, "Sir, I find that hard to believe." I told her to lean down and look out the window. She did, and she was surprised to see a lonely bag sitting out in the middle of nowhere. She asked me, "Are you sure that's your bag?" I said I was absolutely sure it was my bag.

She headed to the front of the plane, and since passengers were still boarding, it reminded me of a salmon trying to swim upstream. A few minutes later, and after everyone had boarded, here came the pilot. He stopped and asked me what the problem was, and I explained to him that my bag was sitting on the tarmac and pointed to it. He kind of chuckled and said, "That can't be your bag – are you sure?" I emphatically said, "YES, THAT IS MY BAG!"

He could tell I was getting exacerbated, so he looked out the window and said, "Well, I'll be damned, how did it get there?" I asked him, "How would I know? But I sure would appreciate it if someone would retrieve it and get it on the plane." I told him I was a platinum American Airlines member and there was an ID tag on the handle with my name on it. He asked my name and then told me he would personally go check it out. He then headed toward the front of the plane.

Everyone had boarded by this time, and the co-pilot announced, "We will be getting on our way soon, but we have an issue we need to take care of." I'm sure the other passengers were not pleased to hear that, but as Clark Gable said in *Gone With The Wind*, "Frankly my dear, I don't give a damn." I just wanted my bag when I arrived in Long Beach.

I watched out the window as the captain walked down the stairs and across the tarmac. When he got to my bag, he reached down, looked at the ID tag, shook his head, and then laughed. He walked the bag back to the plane and had one of the ground crew members open the baggage compartment, and he put my bag inside.

The captain then climbed the stairs and got back on the plane. He walked down the aisle to me and said, "I'm glad you noticed it – it must have fallen off the baggage cart." I then said, "Yes, that has actually happened to me before." He inquisitively looked at me and said, "Huh?" I then said, "Never mind, it's a long story – let's just be on our way to Long Beach. Thanks for retrieving my bag." He then gave me a thumbs up, returned to the cabin, and off we went with just a few minutes of delay.

The second incident strangely involves baggage as well, but in a different way.

Again, I reluctantly checked my bag on the return trip to Dallas because it was too big for carry-on. We successfully boarded the plane, and the pilot and flight attendants were going through their last-minute routines. The doors to the baggage compartments were closed and we were ready to go. I was sitting in a window seat in the next to the last row with no one sitting beside me. Suddenly, I felt and heard a loud banging right below my feet. I thought it was a bit strange, but I ignored it. Several seconds later, I heard bang, bang, bang, bang a little louder below my feet.

We were now taxiing down the runway getting ready for take-off. The banging started again. The flight attendant put her head around the corner as she was getting everything locked down for take-off and said, "Sir, would you please stop banging on the floor?" I laughed and said, "I'm not doing that!" We both heard the banging again, so she stepped around the corner and stood there. We had reached the end of the runway, and the pilot was waiting for the go-ahead for take-off. The banging got louder and louder and more persistent. The flight attendant then frantically got on the phone to the pilot and told him, "Stop the take-off, something is wrong – there's banging in the baggage compartment."

I heard the engines slow down, and the pilot came on the intercom and said, "Ladies and gentlemen, we are going to return to the gate to check something out. Please be patient while we investigate." The plane taxied back to the gate and the engines were turned off. The pilot got off the plane and called the ground crew over. I could see them talking to the pilot.

They walked to the rear baggage compartment below me and opened it. Much to their surprise (mine, too!), a young man, most likely a baggage handler, climbed out from inside the compartment. I could see there was a heated conversation going on between what looked like a ground supervisor and the young man. The supervisor was obviously very annoyed, and the young man was hanging his head in shame. The ground crew closed the compartment, and the pilot got back on the plane and announced that they had cleared up the problem, and we would be on our way.

After about a half hour's delay for our flight to be re-slotted and cleared for takeoff, the flight attendant came up to me while we were taxiing back out and said, "I've never seen anything like that before." I said, "Perhaps someone played a nasty prank on the poor guy, or he just chose an inconvenient time and location to take a nap. Either way, someone is probably going to get fired." She laughed and agreed. Had the plane taken off and the flight continued, the poor fool in the compartment would have been dead when we landed. The flight successfully took off and we returned to Dallas. Thank God this incident didn't require spending another night in an airport!

Disaster Averted at 35,000 Feet

Several months after the baggage compartment debacle, a third incident occurred while departing from Long Beach. It was another beautiful day to fly as the plane took off from the Long Beach airport. Our vice president of sales and I had finished a successful business trip, and we were headed back home. After my previous experience with the baggage stowaway event, I was ready for smooth sailing – or should I say an uneventful flight out of Long Beach.

When we took off, the pilot steered the usual course out over the water and banked left over Catalina Island. I settled comfortably into my window seat while reading the newspaper. I always preferred a window seat for two reasons. First, I enjoy watching the scenery below, and secondly, I can lay my head against the side of the plane to take a nap. As we turned back toward the California shoreline over the San Diego area, I looked out the window and saw what I thought to be condensation spewing out from under one of the wing flaps – or more precisely, one of the ailerons. I thought nothing of it – it was a clear liquid that just looked like water, and I went back to reading my newspaper.

After twenty minutes or so, we continued our flight eastward, and the pilot announced that we were climbing to our cruising altitude of 35,000 feet and he expected a smooth flight. I finished reading my newspaper as we reached our cruising altitude and decided to take a nap. I reached up to close the window shade and happened to notice that the clear liquid was still spewing from the wing. I had seen condensation blow from a wing before, but not for more than a few minutes. We were about twenty minutes into the flight, and I thought it was rather unusual.

I sat and watched it for a few more minutes and decided I needed to say something. I pushed the flight attendant call button. She walked up the aisle and asked how she could help. I told her, "I think something is wrong because there was a liquid spewing out of one of the ailerons." She said, "It's probably just condensation," and then turned to walk away. I said, "Ma'am, I also figured it was condensation, but it has been spewing continuously like this since we took off from Long Beach – shouldn't someone have a look?" She then bent over and looked out the window to see what I was talking about and said, "Oh I see it. Let me go speak with the captain about it and see what he says – I'm sure it's OK." I thought to myself that if it was fuel, we could become a giant fireball any second.

By that time, several passengers around me overheard my conversation with the flight attendant and were a bit alarmed. Others started looking out the window, noticing the same thing. One gentleman behind me looked out and said, "I'm a private commercial pilot and if it's hydraulic fluid, which it looks like it is, that is really bad news – the pilot may not be able to control the plane." He added, "If it's fuel, that's also not a good thing." His comments caused a lot of stir among the passengers around me and everyone, including me, thought we were in trouble.

A few minutes later, the captain came walking down the aisle and asked, "What's going on?" I told him a liquid was spewing out of the wing and suggested he should have a look. The other passengers in my row got up along with me, and the captain sat down in my seat to have a closer look. He peered out the window for several seconds and said, "Well, you are sure right – there is something going on. Let me look it up in the flight manual and I'll get back to you Thanks for letting us know."

After about five minutes, the captain came on the intercom and announced, "Ladies and gentlemen, one of our eagle-eyed fellow passengers noticed a possible mechanical problem. We are going to divert our flight and land in Phoenix shortly. Please fasten your seat belts." I was expecting another nosedive descent so we could get on the ground as quickly as possible before the plane exploded into a fire ball. It wasn't quite as fast a descent as the bomb scare flight, but the captain certainly didn't waste any time getting us down on the ground. As we landed and began taxiing, I could see fire trucks accompanying us on both sides of the plane and two were following behind. It certainly brought back unfond memories of my bomb scare incident.

We pulled up to the gate and were instructed to gather our belongings and deboard the plane. As the passengers were unloading, I saw five or six ground crew members gathering around below the wing. They were trying to see where the leak was coming from. They got a ladder out, and one of them climbed up to check out the wing. He shook his head, and I could read his lips when he said, "No, I don't see any problem." I thought about yelling, "Yes, you moron, something WAS spewing out of the wing!" However, I decided it would be fruitless since he would not be able to hear me. I said to myself, "There's no way I am getting back on this plane."

As I reached the exit of the plane, the captain met me, pulled me aside, and asked if he could get some information from me. I said, "Sure, no problem, what do you need to know?" He said he had to file an FAA incident report, and he needed my contact information in case they wanted to interview me. I gave him my business card and my cell phone number.

I asked him if he knew what was causing the spewing and he explained it was a leak from one of the fuel lines. I thought, "Great, we WERE about to be disintegrated in a fireball." I then asked him if we were in any danger. He then nonchalantly said, "Naw, kerosene jet fuel has a very high flash point temperature, so we were not in that much danger." I thought, "Much danger? At 35,000 feet? Now that was somewhat reassuring!" He then added, "You can actually throw a lighted match into a bucket of jet fuel, and it would not ignite – the match would just extinguish as it hit the liquid." He added, "Jet fuel is certainly not like gasoline that can ignite with just a small spark." I thought, "Thank God – if not, we wouldn't be having this conversation!"

The captain then told me he truly appreciated my awareness and said I was a good passenger to bring this issue to his attention, although he did add, "We would have had enough fuel to make it to Dallas, but you still did the right thing." The flight attendant then thanked me profusely for speaking up and handed me a bottle of champagne and two drink vouchers. Before I left the plane, I turned and asked the captain if we were going to take the same plane to Dallas. I was reassured when he said, "No, this plane is required to go out of service to repair the fuel line." I said, "Thanks for telling me that because there was no way I was flying back to Dallas on this plane." He laughed and said, "If I was you, I wouldn't either!"

When I got to the lobby after exiting the plane, I was expecting a hero's welcome from all the passengers. Not so much. Our VP of sales greeted me, not knowing I was the one who spotted the issue and caused us to land in Phoenix. He said, "I wonder who the dumb ass was that caused this mess." We were close friends, and I jokingly said, "I am that dumb ass you dumb ass, and I just saved you from being incinerated in a fireball. I spotted a fuel leak that could have killed us all." I jokingly said that to make him feel bad, even though the captain said we were not in much danger. He looked at me and said, "Well, I'm sorry, I must be the dumb ass." I then replied, "If the shoe fits…now let's go get a beer to celebrate my heroism!"

American Airlines found us a new plane within an hour, and we reboarded to head back to Dallas. As I boarded, I asked the flight attendant who gave me the champagne if I could pop the cork so I could share it. She said, "No, you'll have to wait until you get home, but I hope you'll enjoy it with your wife." I said, "She doesn't drink alcohol unless the label says Jack Daniels, so unfortunately, I suppose I'll have to drink it all myself." She then smiled and replied, "Well, I hope you enjoy it." As might be expected, I did.

Chapter 6

Honeymoon Delayed But Not Denied

When my beautiful bride Linda (I do mean that literally) and I got married in 1979, we didn't have a pot to...well you know the saying. We couldn't afford to pay attention, let alone pay for an extravagant wedding or to go on a fancy honeymoon. We spent our wedding night in our tiny little apartment with a cheap bottle of champagne, but we were happy and deeply in love. I promised that someday we would go on a honeymoon, and God bless her, that was good enough for Linda. It took me five years, but I finally was able to deliver on my promise.

A month prior to us getting married, I went to work for a very small professional audio manufacturer, MICMIX Audio Products (pronounced mike-mix). I saw a small ad in the newspaper employment want-ads section — yes, that was the main source when looking for a job back then. I called and set up an interview, and much to my surprise, the president and owner of the company hired me on the spot. Perhaps he was desperate, or maybe I was the only one that responded to the ad. In any case, I was thrilled that I got the job.

I was hired to be the sales and marketing manager. It was my first real job in the business world after teaching high school music for five years and working at a talent agency where I met Linda. I had never worked in sales or marketing, and I'm not sure why the owner hired me. Most likely, it was because I came cheap and had a background in the music business with some experience in concert sound reinforcement, and a little bit of recording studio experience.

I loved my job and put my heart and soul into that tiny little company. I got to travel a little, meet lots of really cool people, and I began cutting my teeth on learning about marketing and sales. I eventually ended up being president and part owner of the company. More on that in another chapter.

After five years on the job, MICMIX was going to open a new European distributor, and I was tasked with traveling to London to get the new distributor trained and set up to sell our products. I thought maybe I could make good on the promise of a honeymoon and take Linda with me to London. I figured while we were that close to other parts of Europe, we might as well take in as much as we could.

I went to the library (yes, there was no internet) and researched it thoroughly. Linda and I had always been interested in German castles, so I sent a letter to the German visitor's office. They mailed me several brochures, maps, and information on historic sights to see.

It was quite a daunting task to plan a two-week trip with very few resources back in the dark ages of 1984, but I was determined to make it a memorable trip for us. I tediously researched and planned our itinerary which took us from London, to Switzerland, through Germany, then Amsterdam, back to London, and then home.

In shopping for flights with our company travel agent, she told me that American Airlines had expanded the number of flights to London out of DFW and they were promoting a "spouse flies free" program when a business class ticket was purchased. I worked it out with my company that I would pay the difference between an economy fare and a business class fare, so our total airfare cost was only $300 for both of us to fly business class. Such a deal! Back then, business class was not nearly as expensive as it is today.

Our three girls, Adrian, Dusty, and Ashley were 8, 7, and 2 years old at the time. Fortunately, my mom and dad were absolute saints for agreeing to babysit them for the two weeks we would be gone, so we delivered the kids to them the day before our departure. We were then all set for our adventure. Mom and Dad owned a farm at the time, and the kids would have a great time following Grandpa around as he tended to the cattle, mended fences, and they would even get to ride on the tractor. The girls could help Grandma tend to the garden, can foods, chase the chickens around, and cook tasty fresh foods.

As we headed to the airport, there was much trepidation on my part because I was scared to death that all my logistical planning would crash and burn. One delayed flight, one missed connection, one mistake in my planning could be disastrous. I spent innumerable hours getting everything lined up, making sure I thought of every little detail.

Unpleasant Seating Experience

The trip to the airport went smoothly. The baggage check went smoothly. We started boarding on time. I recall how excited I was that Linda and I were flying business class – I thought that was so cool – and she was thoroughly impressed as we sat down in those big, comfortable seats while those poor souls in economy were settling into their small, uncomfortable seats. Linda wanted the window seat, so I sat down in the aisle seat.

As I sat down and watched all the other passengers board, I immediately smelled something that was awful. It smelled like vomit. It was an undeniably putrid smell. Linda leaned over and smelled it too. I checked our shoes to make sure we hadn't stepped in something but couldn't see anything on our shoes. I looked on the floor of the plane and didn't see anything. We both were becoming overcome by the highly unpleasant smell, so I called one of the flight attendants over and told her we had a problem. I explained that it smelled like someone had vomited in our seats. She leaned over and said, "Yes, I do smell something. Hold on, I'll be right back."

Linda and I both got out of our seats and were standing in the aisle because we could no longer tolerate the smell. Everyone knows that vomit is one of the most, if not the most terrible smell there is – not only because it's an obnoxious odor, but what it represents!

To my utter horror and shock, the flight attendant came back with a can of air freshener. She said she always carried some in her suitcase if she ever had a hotel room that smelled bad. She proceeded to spray our seats and everywhere around. She then said, "There, that ought to take care of the problem."

Linda and I were rather doubtful, but we were trying to be accommodating. We sat back down, and as soon as the noxious perfume wore off, the smell came rushing back like a… well, you get the picture. We were getting increasingly frustrated. My plans for a perfect trip were already in jeopardy before we even got off the ground. We both were getting sick to our stomachs from the smell of the air freshener combined with the smell of vomit. (I find it interesting that the horrific smell of vomit actually makes us want to VOMIT!).

We were sitting in bulkhead seats with the tray tables in the armrest. In trying to locate the source of the pungently offensive smell, I reached over and opened my armrest. I was horrified and further disgusted because the compartment was full of vomit.

OK, that was it – enough of this smell-induced torture. We both got up and I called the flight attendant over again. I could tell she was getting a bit annoyed, but not nearly as upset as we were. I told her we had to move to different seats. It was either that or we could sit where she was sitting, and she could sit in one of our seats. She said, "Sir, we are about to start taxiing out for takeoff, can you and your wife please take your seats." I reached down and opened that tray table and said, "Would YOU sit in this seat?" She bent over and looked inside and said, "Oh, dear God, no sir, I would not." I said, "Well that's great, I'm glad we finally agree on something."

She looked around and saw the business class section was full and then excused herself and told us she'd be right back. A few minutes later, the crew supervisor came over to us and said, "We are truly sorry for this inconvenience, and we would like for you to gather up your belongings and join us in first class for our trip tonight. Please follow me."

I felt vindicated and glad I didn't have to throw a tantrum and get us thrown off the flight. They did the right thing. Disaster averted, and we got to soak up all the luxuries of first-class travel. Neither one of us had ever flown first class before, so it was especially enjoyable. We had our own little pods, our own TV with various movies to choose from, along with lay-flat seats for sleeping. That's not to mention gourmet meals (at least for airline standards), unlimited booze, plus noise-cancelling headphones. What a great way to start our trip, although we did pay for it in terms of nauseatingly odoriferous trauma. It was tough, but we endured the painfully luxurious flight. We landed in London the following morning.

Linda Gets Punked

We took a taxi to our hotel, checked in, and then I headed off for all-day meetings with our new distributor while Linda went sightseeing on her own, taking in London's Museum of Natural History (lucky her, poor me). That evening, Linda and I were to have dinner with Tim, our customer's lead audio engineer, as well as Fiona, their office administrator. Tim was a fairly quiet guy, whereas Fiona was far more outgoing. Our first stop for the evening was to go to a very old English pub in Old London and have a beer.

We walked to the pub from our hotel. As we approached the entrance, we noticed some rather dicey-looking ladies and gents sitting outside on the ground up against the outside wall. Upon closer inspection, we realized they were full-blown punks with an abundance of tattoos, piercings everywhere, crazy hairdos with wild colors, and all six of them looked as if they were as thoroughly stoned as Keith Richards. Mind you, this was years before the punk phenomenon hit the US. We had never seen anything like that before. We had heard of the punk movement emanating out of the UK, but we had never before seen a real group of punks literally in living color.

As we casually strolled by, my adventuresome wife stopped and said to the punks in her Texas drawl, "Hi, how are y'all doing?" Three of the them awakened from their stupor and squinted as they looked up to see what kind of strange alien was speaking to them in a southern American accent. Tim was trying to shuffle us into the pub, and I was trying to pry my wife away from the scene I thought was about to turn ugly. No telling what these crazy animals would do. Then it dawned on me that they were most likely very harmless, given their highly intoxicated level of unconsciousness.

My fearless, undaunted wife then bursts out and says, "Can I get my picture taken with you guys?" One of them says, "Sure, if you give us a few pounds for a beer." Linda turned and said to me, "Give me some money, please." I was thinking that she had lost her mind, and Tim was standing there in shock. Fiona was in full support of Linda's escapade and encouraged her to sit right in the middle of them.

Linda was dressed nicely and looked sophisticatedly beautiful as always. She sat down in the middle of the punks and said, "OK take my picture!" Reluctantly, but like a good husband, I obliged. Linda was beaming and the punks were trying hard to just open their eyes. I took the picture and then helped her up. She handed them three pounds (about six dollars back then), blew them a kiss and said, "Thank y'all – have a good night!"

I'm sure when they sobered up, (well, if they ever did) they were wondering exactly what had happened, and why that drop-dead gorgeous angel had visited and wanted a picture taken with them. Tim, being the soft-spoken, quiet engineer, was wondering the same thing. I was thinking, "That's just Linda being Linda." The picture turned out great and has a special place in our memories of London.

The Bimbo and Buckingham Palace

After my two days of training and collaborating with my company's new distributor, Linda and I had two free days scheduled so we could do some sightseeing around London prior to departing to continental Europe. I got up early and went down to get coffee and breakfast. Linda was always prone to easing into the morning. In fact, she always said mornings would be far better if they began later in the day – like around noon.

Surprisingly, when I went back to the room, she was dressed and ready to venture out. Our first stop was going to be Buckingham Palace since Linda always found that the history surrounding the royals was fascinating. We visited the throne room, the ballroom, the royal portrait gallery, admired the many ornate crowns on display, and then we heard that the changing of the guards was about to take place. We went outside and managed to find a good spot from which to watch. We both found it interesting, although I must say it was forty-five minutes of a less-than-exciting ceremony. At least we could cross that one off the bucket list.

Our next stop was Westminster Abbey. We were standing in front of Buckingham Palace trying to hail a taxi. There were many tourists trying to do the same thing, so it was a bit of a chaotic mess trying to find a taxi. Finally, a taxi pulled up with a passenger who was climbing out of the car. I thought, "Great, we'll grab that one." I was rather surprised to see a buxom blond bimbo (literally) hop out, and she asked if I could take her picture in front of Buckingham Palace. I politely told her yes, and then I asked the taxi driver to wait for a minute, which he did. The bimbo was scantily clothed in a tight-fitting dress and her large breasts were proudly and profoundly on display.

She gave me her camera, readied herself, and smiled. As I took the picture, I noticed she was wearing a ribbon sash that contestants wear in beauty pageants. Most appropriately, I suppose, it said, "Miss Body Beautiful-USA." Now it all made sense. I took a few pictures of her as she posed in several positions. Linda was quite amused with it all, and she asked Miss Bimbo to pose with me so she could capture this randomly bizarre moment. Sure enough, Miss Bimbo was happy to oblige, so Linda took the picture – which is another unique and famous memory from our adventures. But that was not the end of our encounter with Miss Bimbo.

She was thrilled to meet some Americans and wanted to have a nice chat, but I told her we were on our way to visit Westminster Abbey. The taxi driver was kind enough to wait while all the pictures were taken – I am pretty sure he found the whole incident rather funny. Linda and I climbed into the taxi, and before I could shut the door, Miss Bimbo said, "I'll just ride with you if you don't mind," as she plopped herself virtually halfway onto my lap. When the taxi took off, she asked, "What is Westminster Abbey? Is it someplace where we can eat lunch?"

I courteously explained that it was one of the most revered churches in the world. She then replied, "Well, maybe they will still have something to eat." I could see the taxi driver chuckling and enjoying the deep conversation we were having. Thankfully, it was a short ride. I paid the driver and then we exited the taxi in front of the church. Linda and I headed for the entrance with Miss Bimbo happily tagging along with her Miss Body Beautiful-USA sash still proudly displayed. There were numerous women who were scowling at Miss Bimbo, mostly because their husbands or boyfriends were ogling at her well-endowed, curvaceous body. I was somewhat embarrassed, but Linda continued to think it was rather amusing—but it got worse.

Linda and I, along with Miss Bimbo, entered the beautiful, ornate cathedral where kings and queens were crowned or married, and many famous people are buried. I could feel the history just oozing from the walls of this gorgeous place. The quietness and solitude of this beautiful church was awe-inspiring. I was humbled seeing the names of so many famous figures in British history and imagining the many momentous events that took place there. We were standing and gazing at the various grave markers embedded in the floor of Westminster Abbey that included so many famous British history-makers. Suddenly, I hear Miss Bimbo's New York-accented voice loudly ask, "Who was Sir Isaac Newton?" Her voice reverberated through the entire cathedral. It stopped people in their tracks, and they turned to see who had uttered that poignantly inquisitive question. Then she blurted out, "He must have been famous since he's buried here."

Linda and I were mortified and did our best to disappear ourselves, but to no avail. I whispered to Miss Bimbo that he was a famous scientist, and then I explained that we should be using our quiet voice since we were in a very holy place. She then, in her loud New York voice said, "Oh, I'm so sorry." Once again, it reverberated throughout the entire cathedral. I was horrified and started plotting how Linda and I could fade into the woodwork or magically melt into the floor.

We quietly departed from the main part of the cathedral to seek refuge from Miss Bimbo. However, she faithfully followed us into The Poet's Corner where literary giants like Geoffrey Chaucer, Robert Browning, Alfred Lord Tennyson, and Rudyard

Kipling (among others) are buried. This time she tried to ask a question in her quiet voice, but it was obvious she didn't have a volume knob and blurted out, "Who are these people? I don't know any of them."

Feigning the temptation to say what I really wanted to say, I simply told her they were famous British poets, which is why they call this part of the Abbey "The Poet's Corner." Amazingly, the light went on and she nodded and said, "Oh, I get it." I was pleased that she finally understood something. She then told us she was hungry and asked if it was time for lunch.

I had been looking forward to slowly and peacefully taking in the experience of Westminster Abbey, and Miss Bimbo was just ruining things for me. Linda was a bit more understanding, but I was unable to take it all in the way I wanted to with Miss Bimbo continuously disturbing my experience.

I quietly convinced Linda that we needed to let Miss Bimbo go her own way. We told her we were going to the restroom, which we did. I'm a pretty good guy with a lot of patience, but parading around Westminster Abbey with a scantily dressed dizzy blonde with a Miss Body Beautiful-USA sash draped across her unnaturally enlarged chest was a tiny bit more than I could tolerate. Not to mention her annoying, boisterous voice asking inane questions. It just seemed sacrilegious and was beyond the pale of what I could endure.

As Linda and I exited the restrooms, we took a side hallway and went downstairs to see the royal tombs. Sadly, we got separated from Miss Bimbo and did not see her again. Perhaps she's still there waiting for us, but I'm thinking she bailed out to find someplace to eat lunch. At last, we were finally able to fully take in the Westminster Abbey experience.

The French vs. the American War

When our stay in London came to an end, it was time to venture off to continental Europe. Linda and I took a train out of London to Dover, England where we would cross the English Channel. The Chunnel did not exist back then where someone could drive their car onto a train and be in France in thirty minutes. The predominant means of traversing the English Channel was by boat, which had been the standard means of transportation across the channel for far more than a thousand years. During the past century, sea-worthy ferries were able to carry cars and passengers across the channel at a very reasonable cost.

In the mid-70's, a new means for ferrying cars and passengers came along called a hovercraft which became increasingly popular. The hovercraft was driven by giant fans on the bottom of the ferry that provided an aircushion, allowing it to literally skim over the top of the water at up to 70 mph which was far faster than the typical ferry.

There were also giant fans in the rear that provided the hovercraft's propulsion. It was an innovative means of transportation, but eventually, hovercrafts succumbed to the fact that the English Channel was fraught with rough seas, and the hovercraft did not work well in those conditions. Many scheduled trips were cancelled and delayed, and eventually passengers opted for old-school ferries even though the trip may have taken an hour more than the hovercraft. The market spoke and hovercrafts were eventually phased out in the late 80's.

We boarded the hovercraft and headed for Boulogne, France. It was an interesting experience to hear all those giant fans kick in and feel the hovercraft rise. It then slowly gained momentum and took off across the water. Fortunately for us, the waves were quiet that day, and we skimmed our way to Boulogne where we boarded a train headed for our next stop, Zurich, Switzerland.

We departed from Boulogne, and about an hour into the train ride, Linda and I were getting hungry since it was around lunchtime. We made our way to the dining car and checked out the very limited menu. It was more like a snack car than a dining car, but there were a few cooked options. I opted for a piece of pizza, and Linda chose the Croque Monsieur which is essentially a fancy name for a grilled cheese sandwich. There was only one person tending to the diners – he was the cook and the cashier and was about as friendly as a grumpy prison guard. He was French and spoke very little English, so it was difficult to communicate, mostly because he obviously hated his job and displayed a bad attitude toward us lowly Americans.

But seriously, how hard is it to understand the words pizza and Croque Monsieur? We were able to successfully order our food, and I paid for it with my credit card. We sat down and waited for our food. He was snooty from the outset, and as it turned out, he was a lousy cook as well. When he laid our order on the counter, the small pizza I ordered was overcooked and Linda's grilled cheese was literally burnt on both sides. I picked up our food, walked to our table and sat down. Despite the fact that the pizza was over-cooked, I was starving and took my first bite. Linda, on the other hand, looked at her charred sandwich and was not very happy. She said she wanted another one because that one was burnt.

I picked up her sandwich and went back to the counter and explained as best I could that she wanted him to make her another sandwich that was not burnt to a crisp. The inept cook yelled (imagine a heavy French accent), "No, eeze good, you eat." I tried explaining that it was unacceptable, and to please make her another one, to which he replied, "No, eeze good, you eat." Overhearing the conversation, Linda got up from her seat, came over to the counter, and in no uncertain terms told the cook he was a jerk (well, that's not exactly the words she used) and she demanded another sandwich. Again, Frenchy shouted, "No, eeze good, you eat." I said to myself, "Oh boy, the battle was about to commence."

Evidently, Frenchy was not schooled in the art of managing a dissatisfied customer, especially a feisty, hangry Americano. Linda then told him he could put the sandwich where the sun don't shine (to put it nicely) and then again demanded a new sandwich. Frenchy then lost his mind and started screaming obscenities in French. We didn't know what he was saying, but it couldn't have been very nice. Linda then unleashed a verbal counter offensive that was equally and appropriately offensive.

I intervened and gave my colorful opinion of Frenchy's behavior, and he started screaming and cursing at me. Although I wanted to jump over the counter and deck this obstipant idiot, I figured it was not worth going to jail in France – it would certainly ruin our vacation and completely disrupt my meticulously planned itinerary. I told Linda we should just leave, but I could tell I was not making a very convincing argument. She wasn't quite finished telling Frenchy about his mother and his heritage, along with reiterating what he could do with the sandwich. I was aware of the stories about how French people were rude to Americans, but I couldn't believe we were fully experiencing it ourselves.

In a final act of assuring that Frenchy knew exactly how she felt, Linda grabbed the charred sandwich and turned it upside down along with the paper plate. She defiantly began smearing it all over the counter. It was most certainly an effective final statement to Frenchy, and I grabbed my pizza and Linda's hand so we could begin our exit. As we exited the dining car, there were additional parting words from both of us that were pointedly directed to Frenchy. There was enough steam coming from Linda's head to power the train the rest of the way to Zurich.

When we made it back to our seats, we both sat there quietly trying to calm down, and I ate my over-cooked pizza, mostly because I was starving. I suggested we read our books and just wait to get something to eat when we change trains in Basil, Switzerland. Linda sat there quietly for 15 or 20 minutes and then she said, "I'm starving, can you please go back and get me a piece of pizza?" My first thought was, "Are you kidding me? Not only no, but hell no!"

However, being the loving husband that I am and not wanting my wife to suffer starvation, I got up and marched back to the dining car and asked Frenchy for another piece of pizza, and I told him to please not burn it unless he wanted to further feel the wrath of two crazy Americanos. He growled a bit, cooked the pizza correctly, and as I was leaving, I could not help myself, I had to share with him my own parting thoughts. As I left the dining car laughing, I could hear him screaming more obscenities.

I got back to my seat and handed Linda a perfectly cooked pizza which she devoured in a matter of seconds. After all, she had expended a lot of energy and had worked up quite an appetite. She smiled and thanked me. I smiled back at her as I recalled that venerable saying, "Happy wife, happy life."

We enjoyed the remaining portion of our train ride as it wound its way through the beautiful Swiss Alps. We spent the next day and a half enjoying Zurich – it truly is a beautiful city. We then rented a car and loaded up our suitcases. We were sitting in a parking lot while it was drizzling rain. I had my trusty map out charting how to navigate to our next destination. I wasn't quite sure of the exact route. Remember, GPS for lowly peasants was not available at the time, nor was Google Maps – I had to rely on maps printed on paper that I never could figure out how to re-fold properly.

After a few minutes, I saw a man that was getting into his car parked next to us, and he noticed I was looking intently at my large, unfolded map. He got back out of his car, knocked on my window, and asked if I needed help. It was still drizzling rain, and I opened my window to tell him we were headed to Schaffhausen. He spoke good English and pointed out the best route we should take. I thanked him and he said, "No problem – happy to help." The Swiss people had certainly made a better impression than Frenchy.

The Rhine Falls and the Autobahn

Based on the gentleman's detailed directions, we successfully navigated to Schaffhausen, Switzerland, a small, quaint Swiss town featuring Baroque and Renaissance architecture. It sits on the Rhine River just outside of Germany near Rhine Falls, the "largest waterfall" in Europe. The city was founded around 1,000 AD. After we arrived at the downtown hotel, we took a walk and found a very nice restaurant for dinner. There weren't many customers, but it looked nice, and the menu looked good. We were escorted to our table by a lovely young lady who was our waitress. She started off speaking German, so I asked if she spoke English. She was very friendly and started speaking perfectly good English with a distinctively British accent.

Come to find out, she was Italian, and along with English, she also spoke Romanian, German, and French. I told her it was unusual to hear her speak with a British accent, yet she was from Italy. Her English was perfectly British with no hint of an Italian accent. She then explained that Italian was her native language, but she learned to speak English from her husband who was British. I told her that it was amazing that a full-blooded Italian spoke perfect British English.

We had a short but very nice one night stay in Schaffhausen, and as we headed for Germany the following day, we stopped by to visit the Rhine Falls. I was expecting something akin to Niagara Falls since Rhine Falls were billed as the largest falls in Europe. We were a little disappointed because rather than being high falls with water crashing down, these falls were very long and cascading through multiple levels. It certainly was beautiful, but nothing compared to Niagara.

We crossed into Germany and hit the autobahn. I had read and heard that the autobahn was more like a NASCAR race than our typical US freeway. Outside of cities, there were no speed limits. After twenty minutes or so, I recall cruising along about 75 mph, windows down, just enjoying the cool air. From out of nowhere, I heard and felt a car scream past us with a whoosh. It startled me enough to jump and wonder what just happened, but at least it wasn't bad enough for me to stop and have to change my underwear. But it was close.

I had been to a NASCAR event and stood right next to the wall as the cars screamed by, so I realized what had just happened. I looked up and saw a red Porsche disappear quickly (and noisily) into the horizon. The driver had to be going 130 or 140 mph. The car was literally out of sight in less than ten seconds.

After recovering from that shock, we continued cruising on down the autobahn. Linda didn't like me driving fast and kept telling me to slow down. She decided to take a nap because we still had more than two hours before we arrived at our next destination. While she was asleep, I began to wonder what it was like to drive more than 100 mph. I had never driven faster than about 80 mph – mostly because I had never owned a car that could go that fast. The car we rented was a very nice Renault large sedan (full-sized by European standards), and I mischievously thought about taking advantage of a nice, flat road with no traffic while Linda was snoozing.

I slowly accelerated (don't tell Linda I did this) and before I knew it, I was speeding along a little over 100 mph. Then 110. Then 120. I cruised along for about a minute or so, then decided I would cut back the speed to around 90. I had achieved my devious goal of smashing my personal speed record. Mission accomplished. I'm all about safety over speed when driving, but by briefly zipping down the German autobahn, I did get to check that box off my bucket list.

The Castle Experience

Linda and I were excitedly looking forward to our next stop on the grand European tour. As mentioned earlier, I had gathered information on German castles that also served as hotels. I had corresponded by letter and made a reservation for two nights at Hirschhorn Castle, located on a hillside above the Neckar River near Heidelberg. The brochure stated their best room was the bridal suite, so since we were on our belated honeymoon, I requested the suite in my letter. I did receive a return letter confirming our reservation. As a reminder, snail mail was the optimum form of long-distant communication – this was in the days of old before the internet and email, plus making a phone call to Germany was very expensive back then.

We travelled on a road along the Neckar River, and then we spotted the castle perched beautifully on a steep hillside – just as it was pictured in the brochure. We wound our way up the driveway and pulled into the parking area. We were so excited to actually spend the night in the bridal suite of a castle. We unloaded our bags and made our way to the front desk to check in. The young lady at the front desk greeted us with a smile and spoke fluent English.

She gave us a very warm welcome and provided a brief history of the castle. The first section was originally constructed around 1250 AD which blew us away. Additional portions were built in the mid-1500's. She then took us outside and pointed out the various areas of the castle. After that, she accompanied us to our bridal suite on the top floor. The accommodations were absolutely fabulous.

As we entered the room, to the left was a canopied bed with tall wooden bedposts that was sitting on an elevated platform. Straight ahead was a couch and love seat along a wall of windows that overlooked the Neckar River valley – the view was fantastic. On the right was a small sitting area with a table and two chairs in a rounded alcove that served as a balcony. The entire room was ornately decorated with antique furnishings. The bathroom featured an antique clawfoot bathtub, a shower area, and a beautiful marble sink. It was by far the nicest room we had ever stayed in. Score one for me!

The castle was on the smallish side compared to other gargantuan castles. Nonetheless, it was steeped in history and filled with character. The grounds featured tall castle walls, three defensive turrets, various internal buildings, several garden areas, and a tall tower. We explored all sections of the castle, imagining the history of each area and taking in the castle's aura.

One of the most unique features was the tower. It stood about 100 feet tall and had a circular cascading stairway leading to the top observation area. What was so interesting was that the stone stairs had significant indentations that were worn from the thousands of footsteps going up and down the tower. We also have a famous picture of Linda posing as a damsel in distress and her white knight (me) coming to save her. Fortunately, it was a successful rescue with a fairy tale ending. We lived happily ever after.

We had happy hour on a huge stone deck area while watching river barges navigate up and down the river. The food in the restaurant was excellent, and the castle staff was friendly and attentive. Our stay could not have been better. It was such a great experience that we returned to Germany 20 years later and again stayed at the castle and enjoyed the same beautiful suite.

Anholt, Germany

In the packet I received from the German tourist agency prior to our trip, there was a brochure from a castle in Anholt, Germany that caught my eye. It happened to be on our way as we were ending our continental European tour in Amsterdam, so I made the reservation (again, by mail) for one night.

As we approached the castle, it was definitely far different than the Hirschhorn castle. It was a large structure in a flat, open space. It looked more like an exquisite enormous mansion, but it had turrets and a tower, so it did have typical castle traits. The first thing we noticed was a wide moat which was home to a large flock of swans – including a big beautiful black swan. We crossed over the drawbridge to the hotel part of the castle to check in. They have 33 rooms that were converted for hotel guests.

The rest of the castle included a residence occupied by members of the family that owns the property, an extensive library that includes a collection of books from the 1600's, a knight's room (including antique suits of armor), an impressive museum, a large hall for entertaining, and a dungeon – yes, a very real dungeon that was dark and musty. It didn't look like a pleasant place to spend any more time than just passing through with a tour guide. There was also a very nice (and pricey) restaurant.

The history of the castle was fascinating. In 1347, the land was given to a local prince who was the original owner, and he immediately began building the first castle structures. The property went through many phases of construction and a very complex string of owners through the 1700's. It had been invaded on numerous occasions and taken over by various hooligans. Each time the castle structures were damaged in battles, they were rebuilt.

World War II was not kind to Anholt Castle. This small area on the border between Germany and The Netherlands was ravaged during the war. Around 70% of the castle was damaged or destroyed. Several years after the war, the owners of the property got a group of architects and engineers together and began restoration back to the original structures as much as possible. Interestingly, they left a small part of one area of the castle untouched that was damaged in the war because that was part of the history of the castle.

After taking in the castle museum, knight's room, and of course, the dungeon, Linda and I decided to have a nice dinner at the fancy restaurant. We sat down and the waiter came over and handed us our menus. Upon opening them, we noticed everything was in German. I didn't think there would be a problem because I had taken German in high school and could speak a little of the language, although it had been nearly twenty years ago.

I recognized several words like beef, pork, fish, and chicken, but outside of that, I had no idea what the rest of the menu said. After a few minutes, the waiter came back over to take our order. We were a bit embarrassed that we could not read the menu. I asked him if he could help translate the menu for us since all the entrees had fancy names that I could not translate. He admitted that he spoke very little English, and as he was straining to do a translation, I could tell we were getting nowhere. I asked if there was someone who could help translate the menu. He then said, "Eine moment, bitte." I did recognize what that meant – one moment, please.

The waiter came back a few minutes later with the hotel manager in tow. She said she spoke a little English and would try to help. I knew we were in trouble because I noticed she was carrying a German to English dictionary. She picked up the menu and started looking up words. Mind you, this was a gourmet restaurant, and she was struggling to find many of the words. We were still getting absolutely nowhere, and we were all at a loss as to what to do.

An older lady who was sitting with her husband at a nearby table overheard the conversation and the struggle we were having. She got up from her table, came over, and kindly said with a German accent, "Can I help? I speak English." I said, "Yes, please, we have no idea about what to order." She then sat down at our table and went through the menu with us, explaining what each item was. She had been to the restaurant on many occasions and gave an informative commentary on each entrée. We picked out what we wanted to order. The waiter came back over to our table, and the kind lady gave him our order. What a relief!

She said in her German accent, "My name is Katrina and that is my husband Lothar. We frequently stay here at the castle." I told her how much we appreciated her help. She got up and then said, "No problem, enjoy your dinner."

As we were finishing our delicious gourmet dinner, Linda suggested we send over a bottle of wine for the couple to enjoy. Good idea. I was able to communicate enough with our waiter to order a reasonably priced bottle of a German Reisling and instructed him to deliver it to Katrina and Lothar. The waiter delivered the wine as they were finishing their dinner. They smiled and thanked us.

Katrina and Lothar then got up from their table and asked if they could join us in order to share the wine and visit with us. Of course, we said yes. Within our conversation, we found out they spent spring, summer and fall at their home in northern Germany and spent their winters in Palm Springs, CA. We also found out they were a part of and rubbed elbows with the upper echelon of aristocrats and royals within Germany and other parts of Europe. In other words, they were loaded. However, they seemed to be very down-to-earth. We had a lengthy and enjoyable conversation with them.

We finished the bottle of wine about the time the restaurant was closing. As we all got up to leave, Lothar handed me a business card. It was a very simple card that had his name, address, phone number and business name. He said to contact them if we were ever in northern Germany again. I looked at the card and his full name was Lothar Diesel. Come to find out, he was the grandson of the inventor of the diesel engine. Now it all made sense – no wonder they were rather well-to-do. We said our good nights and went to bed.

The following morning, we went down to have breakfast. Katrina and Lothar were also having breakfast, and they invited us to join them. Again, we had more lovely conversations. They were so nice to lowly peasants like Linda and me. We finished our breakfast, and as we were all leaving, they wished us safe travels and again invited us to visit them.

Searching for Windmills

Off we went to our final destination, Amsterdam. As we were driving through The Netherlands (back then it was known as Holland), we were on the lookout for those famous windmills. Surprisingly, during our two-hour drive, we saw a grand total of zero windmills. None. Nada. It was disappointing since Holland was so famous for its windmills.

We had a brief but good two-day stay in Amsterdam. I did have some business to deal with at my company's distributor there. The president of the distributor was very kind to host us for a dinner at his house. He picked us up at our hotel, and because I had commented that we had yet to see a windmill in Holland, he made sure to drive us by to see a windmill that was not far from his house. Mission accomplished – we finally saw a windmill. He was also kind enough to provide us with a sightseeing tour of Amsterdam the following day.

The next morning, we flew back to London, spent the night there, and then took an early morning flight back to DFW. We didn't get upgraded to first class, although it dawned on me that I knew a possible way of getting that accomplished. Rather than go down that pathway, I decided we should just enjoy the business class seats.

It was great to be back home after more than two weeks on the road, and it was good to see the kids again. The girls had a great time, and I'm sure mom and dad were exhausted at the end of two weeks – I certainly would have been! It was a fun-filled trip that provided Linda and me with many great memories. Our delayed honeymoon was certainly worth the wait. And to my utter shock and surprise, all my research and careful planning paid dividends – the trip went off without a hitch. Thanks to my handy-dandy maps, we didn't get lost once.

The Venetian Palace

With all the travel I have done, I accumulated a lot of airline miles and hotel points. They did come in handy on numerous occasions. For example, on one of our subsequent trips to Europe, I cashed in Hilton or Sheraton points for all our hotel stays. In Paris, we stayed at the Paris Hilton (not the person, she obviously would not tolerate peasants such as us staying with her). We definitely could not afford to eat at any of the hotel's fancy restaurants. We ate meals in our room that we bought from local eateries. We literally roamed all over Europe scavenging for inexpensive food while staying in very fancy hotels. In Munich, it was the Hilton. In Rome and Milan, it was Sheratons.

In Venice, we stayed at a Hilton property called the Hotel Danieli located right on the Venetian lagoon, and it was two buildings down from St. Mark's square. This hotel was formerly a palace that was originally built in the 1500's by a very wealthy family. The lobby featured exquisite woodwork paneling on the walls, gorgeous furniture, antique paintings, handmade chandeliers featuring crystal and blown glass, along with a stunning circular stairway. We were in high cotton, living it up like we belonged there (which we certainly did not).

Our room was very spacious and elegantly decorated, featuring a multi-colored glass-blown chandelier. There was a small balcony that overlooked the Venetian lagoon. When we checked into the hotel, we were given an old-style skeleton key (Google it) that was about six inches long. It had a loop on one end with a velvety cord and tassel dangling from it. It was a rather unique key. The usual custom for older hotels was to leave the key at the front desk whenever you exited the hotel. That was fine, because I didn't want to haul that enormous key around with a tassel hanging out of my pocket.

After dinner, Linda and I settled into bed, enjoying the very expensive cotton sheets and a down comforter. We were lying in the lap of luxury. Unlike our sheets and comforter back home, I don't think Wal-Mart was the hotel's supplier. The following morning, Linda couldn't be pried out of the comfy bed, so I decided to explore Venice and find some breakfast. I walked down the beautiful stairway heading for the lobby, and as I approached the bottom, to my shock and horror, the entire lobby was flooded with about a foot of water. I stopped in my tracks and thought, "Holy crap, what kind of disaster has struck this elite and ornate hotel? What about all the antique furniture?"

As I surveyed the lobby, I noticed that the furniture was elevated and sitting on cinder blocks. I thought, "OK, at least all the furniture is not ruined." I then asked myself, "How in the world am I going to be able to get some breakfast?" I was not prepared to wade through a foot of water. I then noticed there were wooden planks placed on cinder blocks that led to the front desk and then out the front door.

I carefully transversed my way to the front desk and asked what was going on. The gentleman at the front desk explained that Venice experiences "acqua alta" during the winter months, which is caused by high tides. Because the hotel is directly on the lagoon, he said it was a common occurrence, and they were fully prepared for it. I certainly wasn't. I had heard that Venice was gradually sinking, but this was ridiculous. The thought came into my head how suddenly and unexpectedly it was happening. That led me to think we had better pack our bags and get out while the gettin' was good – but maybe I still had time to grab some breakfast.

I told the front-desk clerk I was looking for a place to eat, and since the hotel's restaurant was closed, I asked where I might go. He then told me to walk to St. Mark's square on the planks outside, turn right, walk on more planks to an area that was on higher ground, and I could find a restaurant there. I said to myself, "OK, this is an adventure I wasn't expecting, but I am very hungry, and I desperately need a cup of coffee." Off I went walking the planks. It was fascinating to see Venetians sloshing through the water with their knee-high rubber boots in St. Mark's square. It certainly was an interesting experience, and I did accomplish my mission to find some breakfast and coffee.

After breakfast, I made my way back to the hotel to roust Linda out of bed. The water had started to subside, and by 10:00am or so, the staff of the hotel was diligently using squeegees to clear the remaining water off the stone and tile floors. The furniture was being removed from the cinder blocks, and the hotel was getting back to its original beautiful place.

Linda and I then took in some of the beautiful sights in Venice. We also took a boat ride across the bay and visited a glass blowing and crystal factory on the island of Murano. The showroom where their products were displayed featured amazing glass-blown works of art, including one enormous chandelier that was created for Audrey Hepburn. It was selling for $100,000. The salesperson told us that when Hepburn saw it, evidently it was a little too big for her taste, so she said, "Thanks, but no thanks." It was stunningly exquisite, and we would have loved to hang in our dining room. The only drawback was that it was a wee bit out of our price range.

Venice was certainly one of the most interesting and unique places we had ever visited. We did manage to take a gondola ride on the canals. Since the gondola driver didn't sing, I was forced into serenading my wife with my version of "O Sole Mio" (which means "My Sunshine"). Perhaps it was not quite as romantic as a scene out of a movie, but at least we got to check the gondola ride and our visit to Venice off our bucket lists.

We then travelled to Rome for three days. It was amazing to see The Coliseum, Trevi Fountain, and the Vatican. Another thrill was to walk amongst the ruins and feel the aura of an ancient civilization. We even stood at the exact spot where Marcus Brutus stabbed Julius Caesar. As Linda and I stood there, we imagined the intrigue. We envisioned the conspirators encircling Caesar, and we could almost hear Caesar say, "Et tu Brute?" as he was stabbed. Rome was a real highlight of our trip. Linda and I always wanted to visit Rome, and it was great to check that off our bucket list.

Frozen on Pike's Peak

Many years later after all the kids had grown up and moved out, Linda and I decided to venture off to Colorado for a rare vacation and a mountain escape. We wanted to find a nice cozy house or cabin in a quiet place. I found several possibilities in my research – mind you, this was before the existence of AirB&B or VRBO. Since we didn't really have a lot of money to spend on luxurious accommodations, I decided to reach out directly to several property owners to see if any other them would be interested in trading an American Airlines round trip ticket in exchange for a four day stay. Again, I had lots of miles in my AA account, so I was hoping someone would bite on the offer. Sure enough, one owner contacted me back, and said he was interested. We worked out all the details and off we went to the mountains of Colorado.

We flew into Colorado Springs (of course, on AA miles), rented a nice 4-wheel Nissan Murano SUV (on Avis points), and then headed to our cozy destination. It was a very large farmhouse that had five bedrooms – it was far larger and nicer than we expected. It definitely was a bargain exchange. It was nestled in a small valley and the views were spectacular.

The following morning, we decided to drive through the mountains and venture up to Pike's Peak. Linda nor I had ever been to the top of a mountain with an elevation of 14,000 feet, so it sounded like a fun adventure. Little did we know what was coming.

As we started our journey up the mountain, the road was a nice four lane highway that was easily navigable. However, the higher we climbed, the more the road narrowed. It went from four lanes to two narrow lanes. The road was so narrow I could reach out and high-five the drivers coming down the mountain. Along with becoming narrower, the road became more treacherous with the mountain on one side of the road and a thousand-foot drop on the other. What made it more frightening was that there were no guard rails. If we happened to drive off the edge, we probably would have tumbled and rolled all the way to downtown Denver. It would have been ugly, not to mention fatal. I was white-knuckling the steering wheel while Linda was becoming more and more uncomfortable the higher we ascended.

It's hard for me to imagine anyone in their right mind competing in the famous Pike's Peak race up and down this treacherous road. Those people either have a death wish or they are undoubtedly insane. It's a 19-mile trek with 156 turns, some of them being very tight. Except for those idiots who race up the mountain, the usual trip is 2 to 3 hours round trip.

When Linda and I got about two-thirds of the way up the mountain, she suddenly said, "Stop the car I want to get out." I said, "What do you mean?" She said, "I'm done, I don't want to go any further – let me out now!" I said, "You can't just get out and stand there." She spunkily said, "Oh, yes I can – I'm getting out." I stopped the car and she carefully exited. She then put her back up against the side of the mountain. I then said, "There's no way I am going to try and turn this SUV around on this narrow road." She then told me, "Go to the top and pick me up on your way back down – I'm not going anywhere."

I then decided I would try and find a safe place to turn around up ahead. As I pulled away, I felt bad about leaving my poor wife behind, but I had to do what I had to do. I rounded the corner and saw a full-sized sleeper van blocking the road. I pulled up behind the van, and as I did, a young boy jumped out of the passenger side and trotted up to my car. I rolled down the window and he said, "Mister, can you help my mom? She is scared to death and can't drive anymore." I got out of the car and approached the van on the passenger side. When I looked in, I noticed the poor lady was frozen with fear and she had a vice grip on the steering wheel. I said, "Ma'am, are you OK?" She tearfully said, "No, I am not OK, I am scared to death and can't go any further."

My first thought was, "OK, now I have two frightened women to deal with – what am I going to do?" There was no cell service, and I was not about to try and turn that van around – let alone my SUV. I was at a complete loss as to what I could do. Of all the things I had been through, I had never encountered such a predicament. After a few minutes of pondering a strategy, I saw a truck pull around the corner and park behind us. A park ranger got out of the truck. I thought, "God has sent an angel to rescue us!"

The ranger walked up to me and asked what was going on. I said, "The lady driving that van is scared stiff and won't even got out of her car." He chuckled a bit and said, "It happens pretty often up here. By the way, is that your wife standing on the side of the road back there?" I said, "Sure is, she couldn't go any further either." He then said, "Well, we've gotta get both vehicles turned around, can you help me out?" I told him, "Sure, as long as I don't have to do it, I'll guide you." He said, "That's fine, just stand over there on the edge and guide me while I turn this van around." Mind you, I am somewhat scared of heights, especially when there's a thousand-foot drop awaiting. My stomach churns and my palms get sweaty just watching movies involving height-related escapades. Then again, maybe I'm not afraid of heights – perhaps I'm just afraid of what happens upon impact with the ground.

I nervously made my way to the edge and stood there, making sure I didn't look down as the ranger was getting into the van. He had to pry the lady's hands off the steering wheel and help her out of the van. He then carefully executed about a 20-point U-turn as I kept him from backing off the edge of the cliff. He eventually got the van turned around. We then repeated the same strategy and got my SUV turned around.

The ranger asked the lady if she was OK to drive down. She was hesitant, but she agreed after I told her she could just slowly follow me back down the mountain with one caveat – I had to stop and pick up my wife who was standing around the corner. I profusely thanked the ranger for his assistance and off we went.

I picked up Linda and we eventually made it down to safety. We stopped at a gift shop at the bottom of the mountain, and I noticed the van pulled up and parked beside us.

As we got out of our car, the van lady quickly approached with her son. She gave me a hug and said, "I am so sorry, I feel like an idiot – thank you so much for helping us out." I responded, "No problem, I was happy to help." Pikes Peak didn't get a bucket list checkmark, but I was clearly glad and relieved that the misadventure had finally and happily come to an end.

Chapter 7

The Longest Travel Days

The longest trip I ever experienced, one I would not recommend for anyone, was travelling from Dallas to Singapore on business in the early 90's. It required a 14-hour flight from Dallas to Tokyo, a 3-hour layover, and then a 7-hour flight to Singapore. That's a grand total of 24 hours. It was brutal. Back then, the entertainment options on flights were very limited. There were no cell phones or wi-fi with unlimited options. Fortunately, they did show a few movies, most of which I was not interested in watching. I tried reading a book, tried to sleep (which I found very difficult), and then writing song lyrics. None of that worked in keeping me from being restless – and that was just the flight to Tokyo.

As we landed in Tokyo, I was sure I learned what forever was like. I had never been couped up on a plane that long. After the 3-hour layover, I boarded the 7-hour flight to Singapore aboard a Singapore Airlines flight. I was already exhausted and sleep deprived. They were considered the best airline during that era, so I thought perhaps the flight would be easier and better.

Things went south pretty fast when they served my dinner shortly after takeoff. It started with a shrimp cocktail appetizer. The problem was, I am allergic to shellfish. The main course was some kind of fish and some other creature – today, I still don't know what it was. I hated fish and the other creature looked very unappetizing. I don't eat anything that swims except for cows and pigs (yes, they can swim). I had a glass of wine for dinner and ordered another one for dessert, thinking that maybe it would knock me out so I could get some sleep. Thankfully, it worked. I slept for the rest of the flight and woke up as the plane was about to land.

The reason I was travelling to Singapore was that the tech company I worked for had a huge global consulting contract with Phillip-Morris (yes, the cigarette company). My job was to manage and direct all audio-visual activities for a conference with 200 salespeople from Japan. It was an interesting challenge because everything in every conference session was in Japanese. Before the trip, we had to prepare several hundred PowerPoint slides in Japanese, and I was responsible for making sure everything went smoothly. Fortunately, prior to and during all the sessions, I had a translator that sat with me.

The sales conference was held at the Shangri-la Hotel, which at the time was one of the most prestigious hotels in the world. The hotel was absolutely gorgeous. They had a huge walk-through atrium that was breathtakingly beautiful with all kinds of exotic birds flying around. The staff of the hotel treated our team as if we were kings and queens. Everywhere we went, they greeted our team members with a smile and always addressed me as Mr. Allen. I'm not sure how they all knew my name, but everywhere I went in the hotel, all staff members knew who I was. It was amazing!

Thankfully, the 6-person A-V crew we hired in Singapore spoke very good English. At times, there were some hilarious conversations going on over the headsets. They were good at their jobs but loved to joke around. I will say, through all their verbal shenanigans, they never missed a cue and always responded to my direction during each session. I was under a lot of pressure to make sure everything went smoothly, and they didn't let me down.

The conference was full of great events during the evening. The highlight was the second night of the conference. After dinner, we loaded all the salespeople into buses and transported them to a bar called The Long Bar in Raffle's Hotel in downtown Singapore. The hotel itself is world famous, but the bar was famous for the invention of a red, fruity, gin-based drink called the Singapore Sling. I had never had one, nor did I even know what it was.

I found out it was a big deal in Japan to visit Raffle's and have a Singapore Sling. Imagine being a bartender and frantically slinging multiple Singapore Slings for 200+ thirsty people. It was an absolute circus, and the Japanese certainly liked to drink. The bar was not very large, and our 200+ person party spilled over into the lobby of this famous, ornate hotel. After about an hour and a half, things were getting pretty rowdy, and we started trying to get everyone to file out for the next act in the circus.

I'm not sure whose idea it was – perhaps the local event planner we used – but they had decided to transport all the salespeople back to our hotel in bicycle-powered rickshaws. Imagine a hundred two-person rickshaws lining up to transport all those people. It was utter chaos trying to get them all loaded into the rickshaws right in the middle of downtown Singapore. It was like herding cats – especially since many of them didn't speak any English, and not to mention many of them had more than their share of Singapore Slings. Remarkably, everyone made it back to the hotel (at least as far as we knew). It was a fun but crazy night.

The Video Challenge

Several of us team members were given Sony 8mm video cameras, and it was our job to capture interesting and funny things that happened during the conference. The plan was to put together a 20-minute highlight video to be played during the closing session. It was my job to take all the 8mm tapes (yes, video tapes), go through them (about six hours' worth), pick out the most entertaining segments, and then piece them together.

Let me remind that all of it was in Japanese, and I had no idea what Japanese people found interesting or humorous. That's where my translator came into play.

After the final conference dinner, the editing process started around 10:00pm. The next day's session was to begin at 8:00am. The video was slated to be played at 8:30. Not surprisingly, it was a hugely daunting challenge to piece through all that video and edit the highlights into twenty minutes. What made it even more difficult (besides everything being in Japanese), was that we didn't have any type of video editing machine or some fancy video editing software. We had to use three different video playback machines, and we had to copy any video we liked from one machine to the other in real time – there was no copy and paste. It was incredibly tedious to say the least. After around 3:00am, I knew it was going to be a very long night because we had not made much progress.

The clock kept ticking, and I was becoming more and more nervous that this was going to be an impossible task. I was considering how I was going to tell my boss that it wasn't possible to finish this project that could take days instead of hours, but we kept at it. When 6:00 hit, I was a mess. Coffee was not helping – everyone was getting sleepy and a little bit cranky as Steve Irwin would say. The whole thing was such a struggle, and I was on my last nerve. I was becoming delusional from all the frustration and sleep deprivation. We were getting close to finishing at around 8:00 when the session was beginning. We were in a different room, about a 5-minute walk to the main ballroom where the conference was held. I held out a sliver of hope that we would make it in time for the 8:30 cue to play the video.

At 8:25, I popped the finished tape out of the editing machine, ran out the door, down a long hallway, up two flights of stairs, down another long hallway, and then quietly entered the back of the ballroom. I sat down in the control room and popped the video tape into the playback machine. We did it – with two minutes to spare. As I gave the cue to play it, I fearfully held my breath. It played. The Japanese audience enjoyed it, my job was saved, and all was right with the world except for one thing – I was physically, mentally, and emotionally exhausted.

When the conference ended at noon, I thanked the production crew, and then all I could think about was going to my room and crashing, which is exactly what I did. After a long nap, I got up, ate dinner with our team, and all that was left was to pack my bags and get ready for a morning flight. I had trouble going to sleep – mostly because I knew I was facing another brutal 24-hour flight, but at least I was heading home.

Whole Lotta Shakin' Going On

While I served as director of marketing for Texas Instruments' Radio Frequency Identification division, part of my duties was to be the primary spokesperson and technology evangelist. RFID was still in its infancy, and there was a lot of global interest in the numerous applications of the technology. I traveled extensively speaking at conferences, training customers, doing media interviews, and even speaking at two congressional hearings on RFID.

On one of my trips to Tokyo, I was scheduled to speak in front of a large conference and attend various customer meetings. I made the 14-hour flight from DFW without incident and landed at Narita airport outside of Tokyo. It was about a two-hour bus ride because of traffic, so by the time I got to the Tokyo Hilton, it was around 7:00pm. I got settled into my room on the 33rd floor and decided to get some dinner at one of the restaurants in the hotel. After dinner, I was exhausted from the lengthy journey, so I retreated to my room. I tried watching a little TV to stay awake, but that was becoming very difficult.

I had learned from all my international travels that jetlag can be brutal, so my rule was to always stay awake until around 10:00pm and then go to bed so I could get a full night's sleep. I also learned that Ambien was my best friend in trying to adjust to different time zones – especially since there was a 15-hour time difference from Dallas to Tokyo. At precisely 10:00pm, I popped in an Ambien and laid down for a good night's rest. I was asleep about ten seconds after I turned out the light.

I was sleeping like a log until around 3:00am when I felt my bed start shaking. In my Ambien and jetlagged brain fog, I thought I had overslept and the maid was in my room trying to roust me out of bed. My eyes were still glued shut, and I was semi-consciously trying to figure out why on earth the maid was shaking my bed. I was not happy about it, and the shaking was progressively getting worse. I was getting annoyed that the maid would do that to me.

Suddenly, the entire room was catapulting back and forth and making a loud shaking noise that sounded like "jug, jug, jug, jug, jug". Even in my Ambien and exhaustion stupor, I realized something was definitely up. It was a rude awakening when it suddenly hit me – it was an earthquake – and not just a small tremor that I experienced as a kid in California, it was a full-blown kiss-your-ass-goodbye earthquake.

I jumped out of bed and was trying to get some clothes on while being jostled back and forth. It was a struggle, but I finally managed to get myself dressed. I put on my sneakers, grabbed my phone, wallet, and room key, and then headed out the door. Mind you, I'm still in a brain fog trying to figure out what to do. I ran down the hallway and as I approached the elevator, there was a loud siren going off and some kind of announcement was being broadcast over the hotel PA system. I thought, "Great, it's in Japanese, I wonder what it's saying – probably 'sayonara', which normally translates to 'good-bye', but during earthquakes, it more appropriately means kiss your ass goodbye – especially when you are on the 33rd floor." By the time I reached the elevator, an English version came on and announced, "The hotel is experiencing an earthquake, stay calm, do not use the elevator. Please exit the building by way of the stairwell."

I immediately thought, "Stay calm? Are they kidding me?" I was in full panic mode – how dare they say stay calm! I looked down the long hallway and saw the emergency exit sign and ran in that direction. The building was still shaking violently. I was running and bouncing off the walls. When I reached the stairwell, it quickly dawned on me that I was on the 33rd floor. I thought, "Seriously? I have to run down 33 flights of stairs? I'll never make it before the building completely collapses, so I might as well just die right here." I honestly started to realize that this was the end of the road for me.

As I started going down the stairs, the violent shaking began to subside. Within a few seconds, the shaking stopped. I thought, "OK, maybe I'm going to survive after all. But then again, maybe I should keep going down the stairs." I finally decided to just go back to my room – I was too tired. As I was walking down the hallway, I could feel the building swaying back and forth as if I were in a boat rocking at sea. When I got back to my room, the rocking was still occurring, and I thought, "Well, this is a lot better than the violent shaking." I immediately went to the window and opened the curtains expecting to see buildings levelled and emergency personnel trying to rescue people. I saw nothing but the normal lights of the city – no collapsed buildings, no firetrucks, and no ambulances. I thought, "Is this for real? Did I just have a bad Ambien hallucination? Was I in a Twilight Zone episode? I'm totally confused now."

The building was still rocking, and I decided to lie down and try to get back to sleep. As I was just about asleep, suddenly the thought hit me, "What about aftershocks? There are always aftershocks. What if another one happened?" I then made the executive decision that sleep was more important, so I turned over and went back to sleep.

When my alarm went off the following morning, I was relieved that I was still alive. I showered and got dressed so I could grab breakfast. I also peered out the window to see if I could see any damage. There was none. After I ordered breakfast, I asked the waiter (who spoke English) about the earthquake. I told him it was frightening and that I had never experienced anything like that before.

He shrugged and said, "It was only a 5.8 earthquake – nothing to get too worried about." I told him the hotel was shifting back and forth, and I thought the whole building was going to collapse. To me, 5.8 was pretty serious. He chuckled and told me the hotel, like most buildings in Tokyo, was built on giant rollers that were designed to absorb the energy of the earthquake and that was why it was shifting back and forth. I told him, "Well, I am relieved to know that, but I still thought I was going to die." He chuckled again and said, "We have so many that we get accustomed to it."

Fortunately, we didn't have any more quakes while I was there. I will say, however, the next time I traveled to Tokyo for another conference about a year later, I requested a room on the first floor. The young lady at the check-in counter told me they didn't have any rooms on the first or second floors – it was all conference facilities and restaurants. I then asked what the lowest floor was that they had rooms, and she told me the third floor. I said, "Perfect, I'll take a room on the third floor." She asked me if I had a fear of heights, and I said, "No, I have a fear of being on the 33rd floor when an earthquake hits which is what happened to me the last time I was in Tokyo." She smiled and said, "Oh, I understand. Here's the card for your room on the third floor – please enjoy your stay." I told her, "As long as I can quickly escape if there's another earthquake, I should be fine."

I Took the Long Way Home

It was a typical spring day in Chicago as I dropped off my rental car and boarded the courtesy bus to O'Hare airport. I was heading home after a trade show. We boarded the plane uneventfully around noon, and then we taxied out to the runway. The pilot then came on the intercom and explained that Dallas was experiencing some thunderstorms, and our flight was on hold. Two hours later, he announced that we were cleared for takeoff, and we were headed for Dallas for the usual two-hour flight.

About an hour into the flight, the pilot came on the intercom and said Dallas had been put on a ground-stop and our flight would be further delayed. I could tell we had started in a circling pattern, probably somewhere over Oklahoma. We circled, and circled, and circled for another two hours or so. The pilot kept us updated with the continuously bad news that DFW airport was still shut down. The young lady sitting in the middle seat next to me appeared to be around 20 years old, and we were kidding around that we may never make it to Dallas. We introduced ourselves and as I came to find out, we had attended the same trade show. Her name was Mary.

Another hour passed, and the pilot announced that we were landing in Oklahoma City because we were running low on fuel. I thought that was reassuring since we seemed to be in an endless loop, and I certainly did not want the plane to run out of fuel and fall out of the sky. We touched down in OKC and taxied to the gate. After refueling, we taxied back out, and we were at the end of the runway all set to take off. The engines were revving, and then suddenly, the pilot shut them down. He then announced that DFW airport had been put on a ground stop again, and we were going to park on the tarmac and wait for clearance.

We sat on the tarmac for another hour or so, and then the pilot announced that we had to head back to the gate and de-board the plane. It was now around 6:00pm and they instructed us to stay close to the gate in case we were cleared for takeoff. I was ready for a beer at that point, and fortunately, there was a bar and grill next to the gate. I asked Mary if she wanted to join me, and she said, "Sure, thank you, that would be great." I ordered a beer, and she had a Coke. She explained that this was her first business trip, and she had only been with her company for two weeks. We sat and chatted for another hour or so, and we heard an announcement that our flight had been cancelled because the flight crew was over their hourly limit. We would all have to re-book for a flight out the next day. I thought, "That's just great, now what do we do?" They announced that they would provide a dinner voucher, but we would have to pay for our own hotel room. They said they would provide bus transportation to and from a close-by Holiday Inn.

As everyone was in line to re-book the next flight, I thought, "Wait a minute, I am a three-hour drive from home – why don't I just rent a car, and I'll be home far faster than waiting until tomorrow morning. I quickly sauntered over to the Avis counter and asked to rent a car. The agent informed me that they had no cars available. I then went to Hertz and they said the same thing. I then surmised that I was stuck in OKC and would have to just suck it up and spend the night. I went back to the gate and re-booked my flight.

I noticed Mary was sitting by herself and looking a bit distraught, so I went over and asked her what was wrong. She said, "I don't know what to do because I don't have enough money for a hotel room, and I don't have a credit card." I wondered why her company sent her out without a credit card and then realized they probably didn't have time to get her one. She said, "I guess I'll have to spend the night here at the airport." I said, "Nonsense, I will pay for your hotel room and any expenses you have – no problem – I'll take care of it." She started crying and said, "I know my company will pay you back – if they don't I will." I told her not to worry about it – I had her covered.

We rode the bus to the hotel and checked in. I paid for both our rooms and then we ate our free dinner. She explained she had recently gotten married after she graduated from college. She had just moved to Dallas because her husband had also started a new job. She was a very sweet girl and thanked me profusely for taking care of her. I told her that I had three daughters and if they were ever in a situation like this, I would hope someone would step up and do the same for them. I told her it was part of paying it forward.

We met for breakfast the next morning and I paid for that as well. Again, she profusely thanked me. We then boarded the bus and went back to the airport around 10:00am. The flight was scheduled to leave around noon. We got to the gate and eventually boarded the flight.

We had the same flight crew, and everyone, including me, was anxiously anticipating finally getting to Dallas. We taxied out to the edge of the runway, and then I heard the engines revving up for takeoff. Suddenly, the engines got quiet, and the captain came on the intercom saying, "Ladies and gentlemen, you are not going to believe this, but DFW has another round of thunderstorms rolling through and is on a ground stop. We are going to sit tight here on the runway and wait for clearance to take off." There was a resounding sigh of frustration from all the passengers. I said to myself, "You have got to be kidding me – this can't be happening." Again, the thought ran through my head that I was in another episode of The Twilight Zone.

We sat there for another hour. This was getting far more ridiculous by the minute. The pilot then announced that rather than going back to the gate, he said our best bet was to sit it out and wait for clearance, so we did. Another hour passed. The pilot kept apologizing and said he was just as anxious to get back to Dallas as all of us. It was now past 2:00pm and still no progress. He promised that he was in constant contact with DFW and suggested that we all keep our seat belts fastened and remain in our seats, because as soon as he got clearance, we would take off. He explained that if we were released for takeoff and were in the air, DFW traffic control would have to let us land.

Finally, around 2:30pm he came on the intercom and said, "Ladies and gentlemen, we are cleared for takeoff and I'm letting it rip." He raced the jet to the end of the runway, turned the corner on two wheels, and put the pedal to the metal. We were finally in the air! Everyone cheered. It was only a 45-minute flight, and as we were preparing for landing, the pilot came on and said, "Ladies and gentlemen, I have good news and bad news. The bad news is that they are about to shut down the airport again." I said to myself, "There's about to be a mutiny on this plane." The pilot then said, "But the good news is that we are the last flight that is cleared for landing. Another cheer went out.

We finally touched down and taxied to the gate. When we got off the plane, Mary came up and gave me a big hug and thanked me. She said she had her boss on the phone, and she wanted to talk to me. Her boss thanked me for taking care of Mary and said she wanted me to give the receipts to Mary and she would send me a check ASAP. I told her, "It was no big deal – I was taking care of Mary and paying it forward in case my daughters ever needed help in a similar situation." Mary's boss told me she was very appreciative and again told me to give Mary the receipts so they could reimburse me. I gave Mary the receipts, and at long last, I was headed for the house.

I finally made it home – it only took me 28 hours. A few days later, I got a check in the mail along with nice thank you notes from Mary and her boss. A $100 Amex gift card was also included. I didn't expect that, but it was certainly a very nice gesture.

Chapter 8

More Mishaps and Misery

When I landed on another trip to Long Beach, it was a beautiful day in the fall of 2015, and I was looking forward to some important meetings with my company's largest customer. I previously had prepared presentations to give to various levels of management, including the product management, purchasing, and marketing departments. We were introducing a new product line, and this large information technology distributor was critical to our launch.

I had scheduled myself to have an hour to grab some lunch so I could be fully fortified for my meetings. I stopped in Santa Ana at a diner where I lunched on occasion since it was very close to our customer. I had rented a small SUV and parked the car on the side of the building in plain sight. As I walked away from the car, I made sure it was locked because I had my suitcase, my laptop bag (with my laptop), my jacket, and a box of product samples in the back of the SUV. I even laid my jacket over my suitcase and laptop bag so no one could see them.

I went inside the restaurant, sat down at a table, and then ordered my lunch. As it is with most diners, my meal was quickly brought to me, and I enjoyed my roast beef, mashed potatoes, and carrots. After I finished, I paid for my lunch on the way out and then walked to my car. I unlocked the car and was going to get my laptop bag and move it to the front seat. As the back door of the SUV popped up, much to my shock and dismay, everything was gone.

I stood there for a few seconds as I was trying to process what had just happened. I went around and opened the door to the back seat thinking maybe I had put everything there. Nope. Nothing there. My heart was racing with unmitigated anxiety as I began to realize I had no clothing, no toiletries, no laptop, no samples – nothing except the clothes I had on. Then I had this rush of anger wash over me as I realized I did not have my laptop and presentations for the meetings. More anxiety hit. I was confused, flabbergasted, irate, and unsure of what to do next.

I ran back inside the diner and asked to speak with the manager. He came over and asked, "How can I help you?" I told him my car was broken into outside his restaurant, and the thieves had stolen everything I had. He replied, "I'm so sorry, but it happens in this city all the time." I sarcastically thought that it was quite comforting to hear and then asked him if he had security cameras that covered the parking lot. He replied, "Unfortunately, we do not – and it probably wouldn't do any good anyway – crime is so bad here in Santa Ana, the police can't keep up with it all." He then advised me to call the police and report the theft.

My head was spinning like a tilt-a-whirl – so much so that I was having trouble figuring out what to do. My mind was blown. I decided to call the police. I dialed 911 and told them I did not have an emergency, but I wanted to report a theft. The operator gave me a number to call and told me they would take my report on the theft.

I called the number and reported the incident. I asked if I needed to stay at the diner so an officer could come and take down all my information. I thought they might want to dust the car for fingerprints and see if there was any other evidence they could gather. He half-laughed and explained that no one would be coming, but he would be happy to take my statement and send me a report for insurance purposes.

I didn't say it, but I thought, "Sir, my life has just been turned upside down, and all you can do is send me a report? You've got to be kidding me! These thieves should rot in hell!" He then asked if the car was damaged, and I told him it was not. He then said, "Most likely, there were probably three or four culprits. One used a jimmy bar to unlock the door, and then the other two grabbed your stuff, threw everything in their car, and then they all drove away." He then continued, "It probably took them less than fifteen or twenty seconds to do all that, and then they were gone." He then assuredly added, "Your stuff is probably halfway to Mexico by now."

Sadly, all he did was make that sick feeling in my stomach worse. I got angry once again. By then, I was so mad that I could've chewed up nails and spit out barbed wire. Then the anxiety came back. I realized I had to get back into the real world because I still had to go to my meetings. It hit me again – what was I going to do? No samples, no presentations, no nothing. I was good at musical improvisation, but I was not prepared to tap dance through these meetings with nothing but my good looks and charming personality.

I went ahead and met with everyone, and fortunately, they were sympathetic to what I had just experienced. In fact, two of them said they had experienced the same problem, except the thieves just broke the windows and stole their stuff. The meetings went as well as could be expected, and then I drove to Los Angeles and checked into my hotel room for additional meetings I scheduled for the following day.

I explained to the front desk gentleman at the hotel what had happened and asked if there was a mall or clothing store close by. He was very sympathetic and proceeded to explain it also happened to his father who once had a guitar stolen from the trunk of his car. He then said that the closest store was a Wal-Mart which was just around the corner. He told me that there was a mall about 10 miles away, but with LA traffic, it would take me somewhere between thirty minutes to an hour or more to get there. I opted for the Wal-Mart. I picked up enough clothing and toiletries to get through the next two days of meetings. As I was at the check-out counter, I realized I had to go back and buy a suitcase to take all my newly purchased stuff home with me. What a pain!

I still had that sick feeling in my stomach when I went to dinner after my shopping spree. Why me? There are more than ten million people in SoCal – why did these good-for-nothing douche-bag thieves choose me? There were so many other victims they could have chosen, but it had to be me.

While at dinner, I decided to make a list of what I was missing. Two pairs of pants, jeans, four shirts, socks, dress shoes, electric shaver, etc., etc. Then I got to my laptop bag which was also stolen. My laptop computer and charger were gone, along with my phone charger. Then I thought, "Oh crap, I have to go back to Wal-Mart to buy a phone charger."

My list of stolen items went on and it got worse. My passport was in there, so I had to call and cancel it. My car key and house key were in there, but I'll have my wife bring me my spare car key when I land in Dallas. Oops, my iPod was gone as well as my noise cancelling headphones. I thought, "I hope those thieves rot in hell for making my life a living hell."

I muddled through the rest of my trip, and before I boarded my fight, I called Linda so she could bring me the extra key. She was engaged in a local conference and couldn't get away, so I called Kat, a close friend, and begged her to please do me a favor. She agreed to bring the spare key to the airport when I landed. She met me in the baggage claim area and gave me the key. I thanked her profusely then headed to my car.

When I got there, to add insult to injury, I pushed the button on the key fob to unlock the door and suddenly, the alarm started going off. I pushed it again, but nothing happened. I was standing there dumbfounded as to what was going on. I pushed the unlock button again and again, but the alarm kept on blaring. The sound of the alarm echoed through the parking garage, and it seemed as though it was blasting out 150 decibels. I finally decided to use the actual key on the door to unlock it. Thankfully, it worked. I put the key into the slot to start the car and turned it on. The alarm stopped blaring, but the car didn't start.

I turned it off and on several times, but nothing happened except all the warning lights were flashing. I had never seen that before. I grabbed the owner's manual and found the troubleshooting section. It said if all the warning lights were flashing, then the key had been de-programmed from the anti-theft system, and a new key would have to be programmed. By this point, my hatred for the thieves was so high, not only did I want them to rot in hell, I wanted them to be waterboarded for at least a full day prior to their death.

I called Kat and told her to come back because my car key wasn't working. She turned around and headed back to the airport. In the meantime, I called a locksmith and explained what had happened, and he said there was nothing he could do for me – I had to have the car towed to a dealership so that they could re-program the key. He gave me the number for a towing company that was near the airport, so I called them. They asked where I was parked at the airport and I told them terminal C, level three. He then explained that they did not have a wrecker that would fit, so I had to call another company that had a short-crane towing mechanism. He gave me the phone number of someone who could hopefully assist, but he wasn't sure if they could.

At this point, my anger at the thieves went to a whole new level. I not only hoped they were waterboarded for a full day before their death; I wanted them to be boiled like a lobster for at least 48 hours.

After about an hour, I finally was able to speak with the tow-truck driver who could haul my car to a dealer. He said he would come as soon as he finished his dinner. I tried not to let my anger seep through the phone and choke him, although that might have been an emotional release for me and my predicament. I would have had a life sentence for strangulation, but surely, I could have pled guilty by reason of insanity and been acquitted. Instead, I told him I would patiently wait for him.

By the time he showed up, it had been more than three hours since I landed. I was thinking that the waterboarding and boiling in water would quite possibly be less painful than all I had been through on my trip. As the tow truck driver pulled away to take my car to a Cadillac dealership, I told Kat to be very careful driving us home because my run of bad luck might just get worse. I was expecting another shoe to drop. Luckily, we made it home without any further incidents.

The following morning, I got a call from the car dealership, and they said my car was ready to be picked up. He said he had never heard of the kind of problem I had, and that is was very unlucky for that to happen – especially at the airport. I told him he had no idea what I had been through the prior few days, and that it would take the rest of the day to explain.

I picked up my car, and fortunately, my company paid the tab for this part of the trip's fiasco. Mercifully, my loss of everything was covered by my homeowner's insurance, so I filed an insurance claim. Since I was on business travel, my company also picked up the $500 insurance deductible which was also a very nice gesture. After all, they thought I had suffered enough. The end of this travel nightmare had finally come to an end, but I still hoped those thieves are waterboarded, boiled, and then they rot in hell. No mercy!

The China Experience

While serving as director of marketing for Texas Instruments' RFID division, I came up with the idea of developing a trade show and conference featuring RFID technology. The industry was growing rapidly, and yet there wasn't a national gathering that featured and promoted the technology. I happened to meet an enterprising entrepreneur named Tim Downs at a security trade show. Tim introduced himself as president of a small trade show company that developed and organized shows for burgeoning technologies. He said he had read several articles I had written and read some interviews I had done. He asked if he could take me to dinner to pick my brain, and I accepted.

At dinner, we discussed RFID technology, and then I broached the idea of establishing an annual RFID conference. Tim stated that the reason he came to the conference that day was to look me up and suggest we work together to launch an RFID trade show. He said he loved the idea, and he was all in. We worked together to bring it to fruition in 2003.

After two successful annual conferences in the US and one in Europe, I approached Tim about taking the show to Beijing, China. Again, he was all in. In 2006, Texas Instruments was the lead sponsor of the show, and I was one of the keynote speakers at the inaugural conference in China.

Having never been to China and always intrigued with visiting there, I was excited to make the trip. The one thing I wasn't looking forward to was another 14-hour flight. However, I had become accustomed to long flights by then, so it wasn't too bad – especially since it was a direct flight from Dallas to Beijing.

As we were descending on our approach to the Beijing airport, I peered out the window and noticed it looked like it was foggy. As the wheels touched down, visibility was not good, and I didn't think any more about it.

In order to visit, I had to get a visa, which I received a week before my departure. Going through customs in China was much the same in terms of formalities as here in the US, but I just had a different feeling about it. I was nervous and intimidated entering the country. After all, it was China. I had heard some horror stories, but fortunately, I sailed right on through with no issues.

When I went outside to take a taxi to my hotel, there was a stench in the air. It didn't take long to realize that the smell was not from the fog, it was air pollution. It was terrible. When I got to my hotel and checked into my room, I looked out the window and could barely see the neighboring buildings in downtown Beijing. I immediately thought to myself that this was far worse than the smog I experienced growing up in Long Beach. I came to find out that during certain times of the year, Beijing experiences temperature inversions when warm upper air traps cooler air near ground level and exacerbates the already bad air pollution. This was topped off with dust and sand that had blown in from the Gobi Desert, making it even worse. Trust me, it was miserable.

It was made even more miserable when I woke up the next morning with a rip-roaring sinus infection. I thought my head was going to explode. That was my welcoming gift to Beijing. I was at a loss as to what to do. After a few hours of suffering, I decided to call the front desk to see if there was a doctor on call. Sadly, there was not. I did get a call-back several minutes later and was told I could go to the Marriott hotel next door and see the doctor who was on call. I made my way to the Marriott. The doctor was very nice, but she spoke very little English, so communication was difficult. However, it didn't take much for her to figure out what my problem was.

She gave me two written prescriptions – one a decongestant along with an antibiotic and instructed me to walk two blocks down the street to a pharmacy to get them filled. I took the walk and got the prescriptions filled. I went back to the hotel and as I was about to take the medications, the thought dawned on me that I had no idea what I was taking – the info on the bottle was written in Chinese.

I thought for a minute about whether I should trust that these meds would not kill me, and then I decided that if I died from taking some strange meds in a foreign country, at least I wouldn't be miserable anymore. Down they went. I went back to bed and slept for several hours. When I woke up, I realized I wasn't dead and was feeling a little bit better. Luckily, I had planned two extra days before the conference started, so I was hoping to be recovered by then. Sure enough, whatever medications I took got me back in shape for the conference. My keynote address went well as did the rest of the conference.

One of the more interesting meetings I had at the conference was with China's Minister of Commerce, a cabinet-level government official. It was a very formal meeting that also featured a reception that Tim put together. The minister, whose name I do not recall, was very inquisitive about RFID technology, and I worked through an interpreter to explain the various applications and the potential for market growth. He had an entourage of ten people that accompanied him. It was quite a fascinating experience to share my knowledge with a high-level government official.

One of the fortunate things about visiting Beijing is that Texas Instruments had a large presence there, and I was assigned two young TI employees during my trip to serve as my interpreter, tour guide, and host. Both the guy (Thomas) and the girl (Susan) spoke very good English and were very helpful during my visit.

One night at dinner, I was asking Thomas about the political climate in China and how long it would take before the Chinese people revolt and try to win their freedom. He leaned over and whispered to me that he could not talk about such things in public. Someone might overhear what he was saying, and he would be in deep trouble if someone reported him. It was a sudden reminder to me about how different our countries were and the restrictions the Chinese people live under.

On the car ride back to the hotel, he confided in me that there were so many younger kids that yearned for the freedoms that we enjoy in the US. He told me the older folks who grew up not knowing what freedom was like did not know anything else but heavy government control. However, younger kids like him who attended college in the US knew about freedom and wished China could be like the US. He said he did not know when a revolution would happen because the government was brutal to anyone who spoke out against the government and the Communist Party. He reminded me of what happened at Tiananmen Square. I then realized how lucky we are to be citizens in the US.

On Saturday after the conference, Thomas was kind enough to take me on a visit to the Great Wall. It was only about an hour's drive, and he filled me in on a lot of Chinese history. The car ride was interesting in and of itself, because I got to see the countryside, which was far different than the modernized downtown Beijing and its suburbs. We drove through areas of dire poverty where families were barely able to eke out enough food to survive. Living conditions were abysmal. It was far worse than any poverty-stricken areas here in the US. It was eye-opening in the saddest way.

Seeing the Great Wall was absolutely amazing. It is mind-boggling that this structure extends for more than 13,000 miles, and that some sections are 3,000 years old. It was stunning to see this huge structure wind its way up and down the hills and valleys as it stretched across the landscape as far as I could see. We walked for about a mile on the top of the wall which was about 15 feet wide. We then turned around and walked back.

At times, it was physically taxing while going up and down the hills and valleys, but it was a wonderful experience. Incidentally, only a few people have ever walked the entire length of the wall, and it took them more than 18 months. Just to put it into perspective, it would be equivalent to walking from Miami to Alaska, back to Miami, and then back to Seattle. That is a lot of walking! The visit to the Great Wall was definitely a highlight during my trip to China.

The following day, I was able to walk from my hotel to Tiananmen Square. I had read about the massacre which occurred sixteen years prior to my visit. It was a sprawling, 100-acre square that had a few memorials to recent Communist leaders and not much else. As I was walking through the square, a Chinese man approached me and said, "Rolex – you buy, twenty dollars?" I had heard that fake Rolexes were sold all over Beijing. They were mostly sold to gullible American tourists.

Before I could say no thanks, four Chinese police officers armed to the tee ran over and threw the poor guy to the ground, then piled on top of him, roughing him up while they were yelling at him. They then handcuffed him and hauled him away. I was standing there with my jaw dropped wondering what had just happened. One of the officers said, "Sorry," and then walked away. I thought to myself, "Wow, if the watch seller had hit me or assaulted me in any way, they probably would have executed him right then and there." As I turned and walked away, I felt sorry for the poor guy who was just trying to make a few bucks off a lowly American. I had never seen anything like that unfolding right before my eyes.

Across the street was the Forbidden City which was constructed between 1400 and 1420 by a member of the Ming dynasty that ruled China for more than 500 years. Interestingly, with all its buildings and complexes, it has a combined 9,999.5 rooms. The reason it was not 10,000 is that only the Lord of Heaven was allowed to enjoy that many rooms. The emperors were not quite as elevated as the Lord of Heaven and were only allowed 9,999.5 rooms. As large and intimidating as Buckingham Palace is in London, it only has a paltry 775 rooms.

It was interesting to take in all the culture and ornate decorations that filled the Imperial Palace which was part of the Forbidden City. The Imperial Palace itself has 2,700 rooms and covers 7.75 million square feet. I'd say that's quite a mansion. In fact, it is the largest palace in the world. Obviously, it would take days – maybe weeks to take it all in. I didn't make a dent in visiting the whole facility with my measly three hours. In any case, it was very fascinating.

Most of the Forbidden City's 980 buildings covering 178 acres were open to the public. For more than 500 years, only the royal family was allowed to enter, which is why they called it the Forbidden City. But now everyone, including a peasant like me, is allowed to visit. To say the least, it was inspiringly impressive.

On my walk back to the hotel, I stumbled upon a large, open-air market that resembled what we would call a flea market. I strolled around for a while and found an area where 30 or 40 artists were displaying their works. Most of them were college students. One particular young lady's watercolor paintings grabbed my attention. Her work was very beautiful – so much so, that I had to buy several pieces. I spent a total of $20 and walked away with four beautiful works of art. They were probably the best gift I ever brought home to Linda from my many trips. She loved them. We got them custom-framed, and they are proudly displayed in our bedroom.

The following morning, I took a taxi to the airport and endured another 14-hour flight back to Dallas. It was a nice visit to China, but I highly prefer life here in these good ol' United States. The Chinese people are very nice, but the Commie government makes the citizens live in constant fear. I can't imagine living like that.

Wrapping it Up

Yes, there were innumerable trips I took (both business and leisure) that were uneventful. There were numerous others that included minor issues that one learns to just endure. I have outlined above several of my most memorable experiences. After my retirement, I admit that I missed going to a lot of new places and seeing new things, but I certainly do not miss the hassles and inconveniences of travel.

I have seen many fascinating places, had a lot of thrilling experiences, and met a lot of interesting people in my travels. But as I think back to the early days of travel that included riding horses or covered wagons, I can fully appreciate that travelling by jet is far better.

Also, I have slept in some of the finest hotels in the world, as well as some pretty dicey ones, but it was certainly better than sleeping outdoors like the cowboys that had the dirt for a bed, a dusty blanket for a cover, and a rock for a pillow.

I have eaten at some of the finest restaurants in the world, while also cramming down some bad fast food because that's all I had time for. But that certainly beats eating a can of beans warmed by the campfire.

During my travels, I have encountered a number of famous people (several of which I will talk about in another part of this book). I have also come across some very unhappy people, along with many others with an infectious smile and courteous nature that brightened the end of a long day of travel.

Somehow, I do believe that all the bad travel experiences I have endured are slightly outweighed by all the good times I enjoyed and the fascinating places I had the opportunity to visit.

Section III

Music is My Muse

Chapter 9

Musical and Spiritual Experiences

Music has always been a critically important part of my life. I have always used music as a healing balm to ease the pain that life sometimes has inflicted on me – whether I was singing, playing, or writing. Most people don't have that luxury of escape and expression that music has brought to my life. I am fortunate to have that outlet which has served me oh so well.

Music, or any other creative endeavor for that matter, allows us the time to reflect and then flush those toxic feelings that come swirling around trying to overtake us. Creativity gives us all a release valve that allows us to verbalize or materialize those painful or stressful feelings.

Music has also been a muse that has kept me entertained. It has given me inspiration that challenged me to hone my playing and singing skills. It has also been a vehicle to express my love and has brought untold hours of joy to my life. I am a better person because of music, and it is an integral part of who I am.

There's nothing like music that touches my soul and stirs my emotions. There have been times when I was listening to or playing music, and my emotions would well up so much that I experienced a spiritual or out-of-body sensation that overcomes my entire being. I once read an article that said less than 10% of all people are able to totally immerse themselves in music to where it becomes akin to a religious experience – I am one of those people.

There have been numerous instances when, as an old Indian said, "My spirit soars like an eagle." One such incident occurred when I was in Boston for a trade show. Attendees were invited to a concert at the famous Berklee School of Music featuring their gospel choir. I couldn't pass that up, so I walked to the school which was only a few blocks from my hotel. The Performance Center was what I expected – a beautiful venue with immaculate acoustics. Unfortunately, only about a hundred people showed up, but those of us that were there got to see an amazing show.

I sat by myself right in the middle of the venue, about 20 rows from the front so I could get the full acoustic effect. The choir was made up of college kids of every ethnicity. They were a multi-colored tapestry woven and bound together by a common thread – music. They danced. They clapped. They sang to the top of their lungs. At times, I was so overcome with emotion that tears streamed down my face. At one point, I thought the ceiling of the auditorium was going to fly off and we all were going to ascend into heaven. It was thrilling. It was magical. It was awe-inspiring. It was a night I will never forget. I still get chills to this day thinking about it.

There are many other similar instances, and I will share one more. I have always been a huge Eagles fan (not the football team, the music group). I always respected their songwriting and musicianship – both were superb. I'm a fairly skilled musician with a degree in music, so my tastes in artists and bands require real musicianship. The Eagles had it in spades, but I had never seen them live – it was on my bucket list.

On Christmas Day in 2019, my dear, sweet, beautiful daughters conspired together to get me a ticket to see the Eagles when they were scheduled to perform in Dallas on March 1. I was thrilled. I booked a hotel room downtown since we lived about an hour outside of Dallas. I wanted to fully enjoy the concert and not have to drive home. It was a good thing I did because one of my daughter's old friends was bartending at the concert and she supplied me with ample fortifications.

My seat was in an excellent location and was made even better when two seats that were about 10 rows closer were unoccupied, so I claimed one for myself. I was also motivated to move to another seat because the guy sitting to my left was so large that his body took up about half of my seat. Being uncomfortable in my seat would not be conducive to fully enjoying the concert. My new seat was the polar opposite since I was on the end of a row and had an empty seat next to me.

It was three hours of heaven. The cherry on top was that Vince Gill was a new addition to the band. Vince happens to be one of my musical heroes, and when he did the vocals on "I Can't Tell You Why" and "Take it to The Limit," it was priceless. My spirit soared like an eagle (pun intended) throughout the whole concert. More on Vince Gill in another chapter. I was fortunate, that all the succeeding concerts in 2020 (including two more dates in Dallas that week) were cancelled because that's when Covid hit and everything shut down. I lucked out on many fronts and was able to check one more thing off my bucket list thanks to my wonderful daughters.

Music in my Genes

My first recollection of music moving me was when I was around six years old. My family attended Grace Temple Baptist Church in Oak Cliff (Dallas), and my parents were faithful members who were held in high esteem by the church family. They both sang in the choir. You could always hear my dad's deep bass voice reverberating throughout the auditorium when the choir sang, and my mother's soprano voice was one that angels would be jealous of. She sang numerous solos that were classic worthy. Each Sunday morning service was broadcast live on KSKY radio and was taped for playback that night (remember, we barely had TV back then). Many of Mom's solos were archived and played back on the radio station's other religious-related programs for many years. How I wish I could get my hands on those old tapes.

It was a rite of passage and a privilege to graduate from the kid's church to the big house. It only happened when you were deemed well-behaved enough to sit through the service without creating a ruckus. Mom and Dad sat in the choir loft. They required us three boys to sit on the first or second row so they could keep an eye on us and to make sure we could see them when they gave us the "you better behave" look. If we didn't behave ourselves, the death penalty was if they had to leave the choir and come down to sit with us. I only remember that happening once, and the consequences were stiff when we got home. It involved a come-to-Jesus meeting, a long lecture and a belt to the behind. It was far from cruel and unusual punishment – just a parental reminder of expected behavior standards at church.

That reminds me of a story about a boy who was misbehaving in church. The sermon was about how God lives within us all. After the service was over, the pastor cornered the boy and asked, "Where is God?" The boy was puzzled and didn't respond. The pastor asked again, "Son, where is God?" The boy was getting nervous and didn't know how to respond. More emphatically, the pastor exclaimed with a loud voice, "WHERE IS GOD?" Scared to death, the boy ran home as fast as he could and hid in a closet. His mother found him hiding and asked what was wrong. The boy replied, "I must be in big trouble because God is missing and the pastor thinks I did it! But I digress…

It was a thrill to see my mom sing her solos. I remember getting sweaty palms before she sang because I was nervous for her. The first song I remember her singing was the classic "How Great Thou Art." That was the first time I was deeply moved by a song. She touched my soul with her rendition. Tears welled up in my eyes, and as I look back, I didn't realize what was happening. I was too young to understand that music could do that to me, but I knew something powerful washed over me. Her song touched me deeply. It moved me in a way I hadn't experienced before. That was the first time my spirit soared like an eagle. I loved that feeling, and that's when my love for music began.

I remember sitting behind the church pianist, Catherine Armstrong, and watching her play during choir rehearsals. I was fascinated by her skill and amazed that she could do what she did. She was fantastic, and I wanted to learn how to play like her. My brother Gary had started taking piano lessons from Mrs. Armstrong. I had a few lessons from her, but I was still a bit too young, not to mention, that was about the time we packed up and moved to California. But my passion for learning music was just beginning.

It Started in Tiajuana

After a few years living in California, my big brother Rick and a few of his college buddies made a trip to Tiajuana, and he came home with a very inexpensive classical guitar. He wanted to learn how to play so he bought a Mel Bay chord book and a few books with folk songs and old classic standards like 'Tom Dooley,", "She'll be Coming Around the Mountain," "This Land is Your Land," and many others. In addition, he bought a book of an up-and-coming songwriter he had seen at his college, the University of California-Riverside. That young songwriter with long messy hair and a less-than-perfect singing voice was Bob Dylan. At the time, no one really knew who Bob Dylan was, but of course, the rest is history.

All three of us boys started learning how to play guitar and sing during the summer of 1962. We learned a few chords and started strumming away while singing those old standard folk songs. I found it to be a fun activity even though it most likely was more annoying than entertaining to my parents and Grandma Bennett.

The three of us thought we might ultimately be as good as The Kingston Trio, one of the most iconic and influential folk-singing groups of that era. We also learned a lot of Peter, Paul, and Mary songs, but none of us could match the vocal virtuosity of Mary – not to mention the fact that we were males, not females. We learned most of their songs and ended up with our first gig (although it was a non-paying gig) when we sang a few songs at a church dinner. We didn't perform well enough to get a standing ovation, but it was a start.

The folk music genre grew rapidly in popularity during the same era as a burgeoning musical style known as rock and roll had hit the music scene. It is interesting that folk music and rock and roll existed in parallel universes, with rock and roll being heavily influenced by blues and boogie woogie using electrified instrumentation, while folk music relied on old-school Americana songs with vocal harmonies and acoustic accompaniment. Folk music was easier to perform for us since amplifiers were not involved, and we could play and sing most of the songs by learning a few chords.

We learned to play on that cheap Mexican classical guitar which used nylon strings. I remember going into Los Angeles with Rick during the summer of 1963 to find an upgraded steel string acoustic guitar. We ended up at a pawn shop where he bought a Stella guitar made by Harmony, a medium-sized guitar manufacturer. On the way home, I recall Rick repeating an old meme (actually, there were no memes back then – at least they were not called memes). He kept saying, "Stella got a fella." Perhaps it was more appropriate for him to say, "A fella got a Stella," but either way, we all celebrated his purchase and looked forward to playing with the new toy.

It was a bit more challenging to play a steel string guitar, but it sounded louder and cooler. It was more painful on the tips of my fingers, but my callouses built up over time – I just had to tough it out until the pain subsided – no pain, no gain.

By teaching myself how to play guitar and learning chord progressions, I developed the skill of "playing by ear." I learned the structure of a melody as it relates to chord progressions. Playing by ear is a talent that not all musicians learn – many never acquire that skill. It came naturally to me for some reason. I could hear a song and identify the chord progressions by just listening.

Becoming a Piano Man

I always had the desire to play piano since watching Mrs. Armstrong, so I started tinkering around with one of the pianos at our church. I learned the notes on the keyboard and took the knowledge of chords I had from playing guitar and adapted that to the piano. I quickly learned how to play piano chords and was able to accompany myself while I sang. My ability to play by ear helped me pick up my piano-playing skill even easier.

The only disadvantage I had in learning to play by ear is that I didn't know the fundamentals of why certain notes were played together to make a chord, I just knew what it was supposed to sound like. The whole science of the structure of music is called music theory. Initially, I really had no interest in diving deep into music theory – all I wanted to do was play and sing. I figured out some of the basics on my own, but it was mostly by osmosis.

The very first formal training I had was when I attended my first music theory class in college. I knew so very little about music theory that I was the dumbest kid in class. Most of the other students had many years of formal piano lessons and had learned music theory all their lives. It was like I was in first grade, and they were in high school – I was very intimidated. The upside was that I was exposed to a whole new way of looking at and understanding music and why it works the way it does. It was a daily dose of enlightenment that I was fully enthralled with.

I sang in the children's choir at church for many years and then eventually graduated to the adult choir when I emerged from puberty. I went from a soprano to a baritone in a span of several months. I learned to sing the bass part in all the hymns sung at church by sitting next to my dad and listening to his booming bass voice.

I loved to sing and play guitar or piano for any type of audience – I never was nervous and always found joy and self-satisfaction in performing. I suppose the audiences had some semblance of enjoyment – at least they never threw rotten tomatoes at me during any of my performances.

The Garage Band Years

When I was a freshman in high school, I dreamed of having an electric guitar and amplifier. I'm not sure if it was Mom or Dad, but one of them ordered a Silvertone electric guitar that I had been coveting after seeing it in the Sears and Roebuck catalog. For those youngsters that don't know about it, the Sears and Roebuck company pioneered the art of direct mail advertising. The catalog was first issued in 1888 and was continuously published for 105 years. Shoppers could buy everything from jewelry, to sewing machines, car tires, musical instruments, sporting goods, bicycles, and almost anything imaginable. Sears built a huge market and became the most dominant retailer for many years. The catalog itself was about three inches thick, and it was always exciting to receive it in the mail. I did feel sorry for the postal workers that had to deliver those behemoth books because they were very heavy.

I was so excited to get that electric guitar – now all I needed was an amp. Fortunately, my dad knew someone from his office that was selling an amp. A few days after my guitar arrived, Dad came rolling home with another surprise. It was a Silvertone amp that had a separate head (the electronics part) along with a speaker cabinet. It was designed as a bass amp featuring two 12-inch speakers. It sure produced a LOT of volume – I'm sure Mom and Dad had severe regrets for buying me such a powerful amp.

Now that I had an electric guitar and amp, all I needed was some guys to put a garage band together. Garage bands were all the rage back then, mostly due to the emergence of The Beatles, the Rolling Stones, the Beach Boys, and many others that brought on a golden age of rock and roll music. There was a constant onslaught of new bands that started in the garage and achieved fame and fortune.

Luckily, one of my good friends, Lonnie, played the drums, and he knew that one of our classmates, Bud, played lead guitar. All we needed was a bass player and we had a band. Fortunately, one of my neighbors named Michael, who was two years older than us, played bass. We all got together for our first practice in our basement. Mom and Dad approved it, so that became our rehearsal studio. We were fortunate to have a nice rehearsal space since playing in a garage in the middle of winter when temperatures would fall below zero would have been impossible. I'm pretty sure Mom and Dad had second thoughts about it once we started cranking up the volume, but they never complained – anything to support their budding rock star!

I played rhythm guitar and was appointed the lead singer. Actually, I was the only one with any desire to sing. Our musical tastes ranged from the Rolling Stones to the Kinks, the Yardbirds, The Who, The Hollies, and of course, The Beatles. We didn't know what to call ourselves, so in a moment of pure creative genius, I came up with our name – Nonesuch. I thought it was fitting because we had our own style of doing popular songs in our own unique way. Also, no such band could make as much unadulterated noise as we could. Thus, I thought Nonesuch was a suitable name.

Our lead guitarist was an electronic prodigy who later got an electrical engineering degree from Purdue University, a renowned engineering school. Bud made his own guitar distortion foot pedal before they were commercially available, and he made me one as well. This was before distortion was cool, and he was inspired by the edgy sound of the Yardbirds featuring two young, up-and-coming guitarists named Eric Clapton and Jeff Beck. Some audiences didn't quite know what to think when we kicked in our distortion pedals, but we thought it sounded cool. We were definitely distinctive and ahead of our time.

We played some school sock hops. I'm sure young kids have no clue what a sock hop is. These were high school dances held in the gym where no street shoes were allowed – only sneakers so that the gym floor would not be damaged. We also played some private parties, but mostly, we were good at making a lot of noise in my basement. I do recall playing at a frat party, and the thing I remember most is that we played a song probably ten times because they wanted to hear it over and over. The song was "Devil With a Blue Dress On" by Mitch Ryder and the Detroit Wheels which was a big hit at the time. The song must be permanently implanted in my memory bank because I can sing the lyrics today after not having played the song in more than fifty years!

We stayed together for more than two years. The band disbanded when Michael graduated and went off to college. We couldn't find another bass player because most guys back then wanted to play guitar not bass. It was fun while it lasted, and it helped me to further hone my musical and performance skills.

Chapter 10

The Grand US Tour of 1969

In March of 1969 (my senior year), Mom and Dad took me to hear a Christian musical group called Continental Singers. They were exceptionally good, and everyone enjoyed the concert. At the conclusion, the director said they were holding auditions for their up-coming summer tour, and anyone interested could audition. Mom and Dad encouraged me to audition, so I worked up the courage to give it a shot. I had never auditioned for anything, but the thought of being in a group like Continental Singers was very enticing – especially since a national tour was involved.

I managed to borrow a guitar from one of the performers and sang two songs for the director. He said I did a good job and liked my guitar playing abilities. He took my contact information and said they would be deciding on personnel for the summer tour in late April when they returned to Los Angeles.

A few weeks later, I received a letter and a brochure in the mail congratulating me on being selected for the summer tour. I was blown away – I couldn't believe I made it! After discussing the tour with Mom and Dad, they encouraged me to follow my dream, and they would make it happen. There was a lot of logistical planning for us to figure out. I was scheduled to graduate on June 6th and rehearsals started in Los Angeles on June 9th. Mom and Dad were thrilled for me and I was indebted to them for making it all possible.

On the morning of June 8th, my guitar and I boarded a plane headed to LA for the adventure of a lifetime. I was picked up at the airport by one of the staff members and taken to Biola College for an intensive six days of rehearsals. The tour was to be the largest group Continental Singers had ever put together that included 20 singers and a full 30-piece orchestra that included a brass section, a string section, and a full percussion section. The show included three costumes, featuring a casual outfit, a patriotic outfit, and a tuxedo. It was quite the production! Ages in the group ranged from 16 to 25.

Along with rehearsing all the songs, we had to rehearse the set-up and tear-down that included an extensive PA system with twenty mics, risers for the vocalists, stage backdrops, along with chairs and music stands for the instrumentalists. We spent an entire day practicing the set-up and tear-down. Everyone had assigned duties, and we had to get all of the equipment off the large truck and have everything set for the show in 30 minutes. Then, we had to tear it all down and re-load the truck in 30 minutes. I was filled with excitement and anticipation for the tour to start.

As an aside, we displayed our set-up skills at one of our first gigs. Our bus broke down, so we were very late getting to our next destination. When we arrived, a full house audience was waiting for our concert to start at 7:00pm. We arrived at 7:05. It was crazy, and we all were shocked by how fast we got everything set up. Everyone was running around throwing things together like a bunch of crazed animals! Miraculously, we had everything set up and were in costume to start the show by 7:30. The audience got more than a musical performance – they got to see how the show was set up at warp speed. We got a standing ovation before we even started the show!

Back to pre-tour preparations. After three more days of rehearsals, I was humbled by and fortunate enough to be appointed as the assistant musical director for the tour. I got to conduct a few songs during each show we performed, and when Ken, our director, came down with the flu during the tour, I conducted the entire show for three nights. It was a wonderful experience and quite a thrill for an 18-year-old kid to say the least. I also conducted many of our intensive rehearsals prior to our tour departure when Ken was in meetings. I was in musical heaven for me!

We set off on tour with a full busload of musicians, a large truck, and a large van. There were a few long bus rides between gigs, but most of our travelling involved two to four-hour bus rides. We rarely had a day off, and sometimes we did two shows per day – sometimes in different locations. There were two or three times when we did three shows in a day at three different venues. Needless to say, it was at times exhausting, but performing in the shows was exhilarating.

On With the Show

The lowest part of the tour was when I caught the flu from Ken. When he got well, I got sick – I mean sick as a dawg. At least we weren't ill at the same time. Being horribly sick while riding on a bus was absolutely miserable. I remember sleeping on the floor in the back of the bus so I could be close to the bathroom when it was necessary to visit it. I toughed it out as much as I could and only missed one show.

We performed around 80 shows in a little over 10 weeks. The tour started in LA, and we wound our way through the southwest, all over the Midwest, all the way to New England, and then south to Florida. We also hit all the southern states on our way back to LA. I lost count, but I think we hit 28 different states and probably around 60 different cities from large metro areas to small towns. Venues included beautiful concert halls, civic auditoriums, small arenas, churches, malls, and even a cruise ship on a trip to and from the Bahamas.

There were so many highlights during the tour, but a few were etched into my memory that I will never forget. One of those highlights was performing at St. John The Divine Cathedral in New York City, which is the largest cathedral in the world (by volume).

The church property spans 601 feet long (think about it – that's the length of two football fields!). The ceiling in the cathedral is 124 feet in height.

The acoustics where breathtaking. Hearing our voices reverberate through the vast expanse of the cathedral was the closest thing to heavenly sounds I will ever experience here on earth. We did not do an entire concert with instruments, but we did perform part of our repertoire acapella. It was magically amazing. I had never seen a church that large and that ornate – it was a performance to remember and an ultimate highlight during my summer of '69.

The Bahama Beauty

The cruise to the Bahamas was another unforgettable memory. It was quite the experience for an 18-year-old kid who had never had the opportunity to enjoy such opulence – and the food was amazing! We performed three concerts in Nassau, and on the second night, I happened to meet a young lady in our meet-and-greet after the concert. She was well-dressed and I was awed by her beauty while also being fully captivated by her British accent. She introduced herself and said, "Hello, my name is Charlotte – welcome to the Bahamas." I had never met someone with a British accent before, so I was fully entranced as she spoke. I could not believe that this drop-dead gorgeous, blond haired, blue-eyed, beamingly bubbly beauty was speaking to me.

Our conversation extended beyond the meet-and-greet. We sat by ourselves in the auditorium for more than an hour. She was 18 and I could tell she was well educated. I asked her about life in the Bahamas, and she asked me about life in the USA. As our conversation ended, she offered to take me on a tour of Nassau the following day. There was no way I could turn her down, so I jubilantly said yes. She offered to pick me up at 11:00am. I was absolutely thrilled and was filled with so much anticipation I could hardly sleep that night.

At 10:45am, I made my way to the port-side gangway of the cruise ship where we agreed to meet. I nervously paced back and forth, eagerly awaiting her arrival. At 11:00 sharp, a black Mercedes pulled up. I first saw what looked like a chauffeur driving the car, so I thought, "Well, that's certainly not her." And then the back seat window rolled down, and there she was with a big smile on her face waving for me to get in the car. Needless to say, I was a bit taken aback. My jaw dropped so much that I'm surprised it didn't hit the ground. I had never set foot in a Mercedes, let alone one driven by a chauffeur. I gathered myself enough to nervously saunter over and climb into the car.

As I came to learn, she was the daughter of the top British diplomat in the Bahamas. At that time, the Bahamas were still a British colony. Charlotte was a wonderful hostess and tour guide, filling me in on some of the history of the Bahamas and her life as the daughter of a diplomat. I continued to be hypnotized by her accent and her polished, warm demeanor. We had a very nice lunch which, as a gracious hostess, she paid for. We shared our life stories. We laughed a lot. We talked about serious things. All in all, we had a great time together. I could have stayed and listened to her all day, but unfortunately, I had to return to the ship for a 5:00 rehearsal. It was a wonderful day we spent together touring the island.

When the car pulled up to the ship, as I prepared to get out, she leaned over, and as most Europeans do, she gave me a hug and then a kiss on each cheek. Being a young, somewhat uncouth, ill-mannered American, I really didn't know what to do in response that was proper, so I erred on the side of uncouthness and gave her a long kiss on the lips. I suppose she thought it acceptable because I didn't get slapped in the face. We had another hug, and I reluctantly crawled out of the car.

As I was climbing out, I asked if she was coming to our final show that night. She said, "Of course – I'll see you tonight." My heart soared to new heights – I was on cloud nine. During my teen years, I had a few girlfriends, but Charlotte was by far the most beautiful, charming, and intriguing young lady I had ever met. We both had an immediate attraction to each other.

Sure enough, she showed up for the concert later that night. She sat on the second row, and our eyes were glued on each other most of the night. We exchanged lots of smiles and winks. I'm sure Ken, the director, was wondering why I was smiling incessantly and why my eyes were twitching so much. At the meet-and-greet after the show, Charlotte and I managed to sneak away. We found an isolated spot in a stair well and sat on the steps and talked for more than an hour. I continued to be truly entranced by her, and she must have found me worthy since she spent so much time with this young American kid.

Unfortunately, she had to leave, and I had to carry on with my teardown and pack up duties. When it came time to say good-bye, sadly, we both knew that we most likely would never see each other again. After a more lengthy and more meaningful kiss than our first one, we exchanged a long hug. We then smiled at each other, both of us with tears in our eyes, and we said our goodbyes. As she walked away, she turned around and blew me a kiss. I blew her a kiss back, and that was the last time we ever saw each other.

Although our time together was very brief, I could tell we both felt not only an attraction to each other, but a heartfelt, meaningful connection. Later that night, our ship headed back to Miami. As the ship headed out to sea, I had my own Titanic moment like Leo di Caprio. I remember standing on the bow by myself, feeling the wind and hearing the sound of the ship cutting through the water. As I stood there, I wondered what Charlotte was thinking and what she was feeling. Our goodbye was painful, perhaps because our visit was so short, but it was certainly true that we both hit it off.

We shared our addresses before we said good-bye (no, we didn't have cell phones, text messages or email back then). We corresponded with each other for several months through letters, but as most remote romances go, we eventually lost touch with each other.

We all experience what I call random intersections where we unexpectedly encounter people that we feel an undeniable connection to. We feel something different that is beyond just a casual acquaintance. It happens more often than we think – we just don't take time to recognize it. Sometimes those intersections lead to life-long friendships (or maybe even a marriage), and sometimes it's just what I call a "passing through" connection where time together is short, yet impactful. Such was the case with my random intersection with Charlotte.

Hurricane Camille

The tour's last stop in Florida was Pensacola on August 17th. When we arrived at the municipal auditorium, which was literally right on the bay of the Gulf of Mexico (now known as the Gulf of America), it was a calm, sunny afternoon. We set up for the show that night that was scheduled to start at 7:00pm. As the evening approached, it started raining lightly. Our bus driver and truck drivers had parked their vehicles on the outer edge of the parking lot at the rear of the auditorium, literally right next to a sea wall.

Around 6:00pm, the rain started picking up steam and the wind started gusting. By 7:00, it was a deluge. We delayed the concert by about 15 minutes so that everyone could make their way through the rain and get settled into their seats. We began the show, and throughout the first half, we could hear thunder outside, and the wind had picked up substantially. By about 8:00, we could hear the pounding rain, and the wind was blowing so hard the auditorium was quivering. The noise from the wind and rain was getting louder and louder.

At the end of one of our songs, a gentleman walked onstage and began conversing with Ken. The gentleman happened to be the mayor of Pensacola. The mayor then announced, "Due to public safety, the rest of the concert is cancelled. Everyone should leave the building and be careful driving home." He explained that the outer edges of hurricane Camille were hitting Pensacola. That certainly was news to us – we had no idea a hurricane was supposed to hit the Gulf Coast.

We then started our tear-down, and I remember walking to the back entrance of the stage, and when I opened the door, I couldn't believe what I saw. Our bus that was parked next to the sea wall was rocking back and forth, and sea water was splashing over the top of the bus. The wind was so strong I thought it would blow the bus and the trucks into the ocean. The sight of all this was mind-blowing.

Our bus driver ran out to the bus, opened the door, and then hopped in. He pulled the bus up next to the building to prevent it from becoming a boat rather than a bus. The truck drivers also ran out and pulled their trucks tightly up against the building so we could load our equipment. I remember watching the bus driver get off the bus – he was absolutely soaking wet, as were the truck drivers. Ken made the executive decision that we would leave our equipment in the auditorium and load everything in the morning prior to our departure.

I had been in many Texas thunderstorms which would usually come and go quickly, but this hurricane was a whole new experience. The wind and rain was ridiculously relentless. When it peaked, there was no way anyone could stand outside – they would undoubtedly have been completely blown away. Power was out for much of Pensacola, and I remember listening to news reports on my transistor radio (battery-powered, of course) of how devastating the hurricane was.

Camille was the second most powerful hurricane to ever hit the Gulf Coast (the most powerful hit in 1935). It had reached Cat-5 status with 175 mph sustained winds, sometimes gusting over 200 mph. The eye of the hurricane made landfall in Waveland, MS, about 150 miles west of Pensacola, and about 100 miles east of New Orleans. The storm surge was around 24 feet near the eye. As crazy as things were in Pensacola during the hurricane, it was mild compared to what happened in cities along the coast of Mississippi, Alabama, and Louisiana. Camille caused $1.5 billion in damage (equivalent to $11+ billion in today's dollars) and took 256 lives.

I had seen tornado damage in my early childhood from the twisters that hit the Oak Cliff area in Dallas in 1957, but the power of Camille did not really set in until the following day when we headed out for our next gig in Biloxi, MS. After loading up our equipment, we departed. I noticed Pensacola had sustained a good bit of wind and some storm surge damage near the ocean. The further we went along the Gulf Coast, the more devastation we saw.

As we approached Biloxi, we could see entire houses and other buildings completely blown away – flattened. It was a humbling sight to see how much damage was done. Most of Biloxi was in total shambles. It was becoming apparent that we would not be performing that night, and when we got to the large church, it was still standing, but the roof was gone along with all the windows blown out and debris was scattered everywhere. Indeed, it was a sad sight to behold. We all got off the bus, gathered in a circle, and said a prayer for the church, the city, and its residents.

There was no place to stay in Biloxi, so we continued to New Orleans for our next gig. Camille was originally headed straight for New Orleans, but she took a right-hand turn prior to making landfall. New Orleans was hit hard but was mostly spared compared to the rest of the cities along the coast. There were times when traffic on the highway was halted because the road was impassable due to all the debris that was strewn everywhere.

We were all awestruck and distressed to see all the devastation as we travelled along the highway. It is very difficult to paint a word-picture that accurately describes what we witnessed. It certainly was a first-hand lesson to see the horrendous wreckage, as well as highly humbling to see how destructive Mother Nature can be when she gets really angry.

Our Stop in Big D

We continued winding our way through the southwest, making stops in various cities as we headed back to LA. One of the highlight stops was when we performed at Grace Temple Baptist church in Dallas. Recall that Grace Temple was the church where I spent my younger years listening to my mother sing her beautiful solos and my dad's booming bass voice. Their voices seemed to still be echoing throughout the auditorium. I got to perform on the same stage where my parents had performed.

It had been more than ten years since I had been back to this church, so it was meaningful in many ways to get to perform there. It was an opportunity to catch up with some of my old childhood friends and family. I was the most popular guy at the meet-and-greet and I was dismissed from my usual tear-down duties because so many people wanted to talk to me. I saw Mrs. Armstrong, the pianist that I had watched so many times during choir rehearsals. She came up to me and told me how proud she was that I had pursued music. This stop on the tour was definitely one of the highlights for me.

After our performance in Dallas, our director, Ken, informed us that we were going to record an album featuring original songs and new gospel-inspired arrangements of old standard hymns by Ralph Carmichael. At that time, and for several decades, he was the most influential composer and arranger in Christian music. The fact that we were going to record his music and work with him was a huge honor. While on the road, and as the tour was coming to a close, we rehearsed the new music in preparation for the recording session.

Back to Reality

At the end of August, the tour ended. We had a successful recording session, and it was time to get back to reality and venture off into a new segment of my life. I made a quick trip back home to pack my things and head to Dallas for college.

The one thing I regret about being on tour was not the long rides on a crowded bus. It was not the hours of hard work that were required. The one thing I regret was not keeping a journal that captured all the daily events and the places we performed. Sure, I can recall many events, including the ones highlighted here, but I know there was so much more that I could have captured – maybe not for everyone to read, but for me to recall and cherish.

Oh, and there is one more thing I do regret, and that is having to say goodbye to 50+ people that became my music soulmates. We spent a lot of time together, and one would think there would be fights or disagreements since we were all crammed into an uncomfortable metal tube for hours and miles on end, but surprisingly, everyone got along so well. I don't recall any drama or personality conflicts, which is representative of the character of all my musician mates.

They became some of my closest friends. I kept up with many of them for a while, but as we all know, life goes on, and again, it was harder to maintain remote friendships back then – we only had was letters and long-distance phone calls (they were a lot more expensive back then!).

My roommate in Continental Singers, Jim Custer, was a year younger than me, and we got to be best friends during the tour. He ended up coming to Dallas Baptist University where I was attending, so we did get to spend even more time together through our college years. Jim came to DBU to study drama – he was an excellent actor along with a good singer. After we graduated, I stayed in Dallas and Jim set off to LA to make a name for himself in the television and movie business.

As is the case with nearly all hopeful actors and actresses, Jim struggled to find roles. He did get some minor parts in a few movies and appeared in several TV series episodes, but in order to survive, he took up his other passion – cooking. Jim ended up working his way to becoming the chief chef for Universal Studios (the actual studios, not the theme park). Jim was well-liked throughout the campus, and he told me he got to know Jay Leno well by making Jay's favorite sandwich every day at lunch for more than 10 years. He also met and interfaced with many famous actors and actresses.

Jim became one of my most cherished friends. However, with him living in LA, it was hard to stay close friends, but we did keep up with each other throughout the years. I would occasionally get to see him whenever I travelled to LA.

On one of those trips, Jim and I had dinner together and he told me about something I did that changed his life. When we said good-bye after our summer with Continentals, I gave him a big hug, put my hands of his shoulders, and said, "Jim, I love you." During that dinner in LA, he said those three words were so meaningful to him because he rarely heard those words, and he had never had a friend tell him that.

I told Jim that our family has always had the tradition of saying "I love you" as we are saying good-bye. It has always been part of the drill, whether we were going to run an errand or be apart from each other for a long period of time. Jim told me that because of those three words I said, he and his family started the tradition of always saying "I love you" as they said good-bye.

It was part of our DNA that our family's parting words were always "I love you." I even wrote a song about an unexpected tragic accident taking the life of a loved one who didn't get to say that last "I love you."

The title of the song is One More Time:

I'm sick and tired of this lonesome road, I've been hauling a heavy load.
I've had better days before, I'm waiting for the day it don't hurt any more.
I thought it might be easy, but nothing's ever easy for me.
I thought that time would heal the pain, I never knew how hard this could be.

Maybe things could have been different, or maybe there's no reason or rhyme.
Maybe I'll drive myself crazy, thinking maybe I should have said I love you One More Time.

I lose my mind when I start asking why, I didn't get a chance to say good-bye.
I never thought it would end this way, I miss you more and more every day.
I think I see you in your favorite chair, then I turn to look and see that you're gone.
I know it's time for me to wake up; you'd want my life to carry on.

Maybe things could have been different, or maybe there's no reason or rhyme.
Maybe I'll drive myself crazy, thinking maybe I should have said I love you One More Time.

There are some people that are not able to or willing to say those three words – even to those friends and loved ones that they are closest to. My philosophy has always been to never be afraid of telling someone you love them if they mean a lot to you. It was ingrained in me by my parents and shall forever be a part of my life.

The Summer Ends

In 1985, Bryan Adams released a song called "Summer of '69" in which he talked about buying a six-string guitar that he bought from the five and dime (a variety store like Dollar General for the youngsters that have never heard of a five and dime) and playing until his fingers bled. He then wrote about getting some friends together to form a group and how much fun he had during the summer. He also described how it was "the best days of my life." When I first heard the song, it brought me back to my summer of '69.

The old bromide says that all good things must come to an end – so it was with my summer of '69. It was a whirlwind that started with graduation, then touring, and then it ended with a new beginning in college. Like many things, it went by all too fast.

Touring with the Continental Singers ranks way up there as some of the best days of my life. I got to see a vast swath of our country. I got to meet so many wonderful people in so many cities. I got to perform for literally tens of thousands of people. I got to share my love for music with my fellow musicians. But most of all, I got to do what I loved to do back then – and what I still love to do more than sixty years later – and that is to make music. It truly is my muse.

The Soul Album

The recording session for the "Soul" album took place at RCA studios in LA when our Continental Singers tour came to an end. The album was released in early 1970 and was a great success, being the first contemporary Christian music album to reach the Billboard Top 100. It helped fuel the growth of the Continental Singers brand and contained premieres of what would become classic songs in contemporary Christian music: Pass It On, He's There Waiting, and The New 23rd. In addition, it included old hymns that Mr. Carmichael re-arranged. These arrangements put a refreshingly new Gospel twist on some old hymns.

I was anxiously awaiting the release of the album, and five months after the tour and recording session ended, the album was finally released in January of '70. I received a copy of the album in the mail while I was in college. I excitedly opened the package and saw a distinctive all-black album cover with the word "Soul" fuzzily depicted in the center. I thought, "OK, that's pretty cool." I looked at the back of the album which listed the songs and some liner notes from Cam Floria (founder of Continental Singers) and Ralph Carmichael. Again, I thought it was pretty cool.

I then noticed that the cover was a bi-fold, and I opened it up and saw several pictures of our group. As I looked closer, I said, "Hey, that's me!" Sure enough, there was a prominent picture of me singing with my guitar. "Wow! How cool is that!" I shouted to my roommate. I quickly fired up my little record player and listened to it three times that night. It was indeed thrilling to hear the final product. I was so proud of what we did. Everyone I showed it to and those that listened to the album were very impressed. It genuinely was a great collection of songs. It also felt good to know what we accomplished, and it provided us with something tangible to show for our group's hard work – not to mention the wonderfully talented musicians that contributed to a successful production.

Chapter 11

The College and Teaching Years

When I attended Dallas Baptist University, it was a very small school with about 1600 students. There were various reasons I chose DBU, among them were moving back to a city and a state that I loved, as well as having lots of aunts, uncles, and cousins in and around Dallas. Having so many family members close by was very helpful as I adapted to living away from home. All my Dallas family were so generous and kind, hosting me for weekends, while also making sure I was well taken care of. Since we moved away from Dallas at age seven, I really had never gotten to know my extended family too well, other than occasional visits back to Dallas, or when they came to visit us in California. Being able to spend a good deal of time with them was very special because they were all wonderful people.

The other important reason for me attending DBU was the quality of the staff within the music department, and as I learned later, the quality of musicians that attended the school challenged me.

Dr. Don Gillis was chairman of the music department. I was not familiar with who he was, but I came to find out his resume was very impressive. He was a very successful symphonic composer, having written seven symphonies, several operas, and many other orchestral pieces. In addition, he served as a television and radio producer. As I came to know him, I realized that he was always looking for innovative ways to express himself, and he was obsessed with making sure his creative juices that were constantly flowing were properly fed. He was also a highly ambitious and motivated person.

Dr. Gillis' credentials also included being executive producer of the nationally broadcast "NBC Concert Hour", a weekly show featuring symphonic music that eventually became a popular television series in the early 1950's with Arturo Toscanini conducting. Mr. Toscanini became the most preeminent orchestral conductor in the world and is still one of the most revered conductors to have ever picked up the baton.

Dr. Gillis shared some interesting tidbits about rehearsals with Mr. Toscanini. Stories abound regarding Mr. Toscanini's volatility. Many producers prior to Dr. Gillis taking over were unable to work with Mr. Toscanini. He would not tolerate second-class musicianship and was famous for throwing temper tantrums as well as batons when his musicians came unprepared or lacked musical perfection. Mr. Toscanini was a pivotal personality in bringing classical music to the forefront in the early days of television, and Dr. Gillis was the driving force behind the success of the show. Dr.

Gillis found a way to work effectively with Mr. Toscanini and together they made the historic television show a major success.

I was very fortunate to be able to study music composition under Dr. Gillis during a summer semester. He did not want to teach at the school during the summer break, and since I was his only student, he invited me to come to his house three days a week for the class. It was definitely a great experience. Not only was he a wonderful teacher, but he was also one of the most affable, warm-natured people I have ever met – and he had a great sense of humor!

During one of our summer sessions, he brought out a wooden case, opened it up, and I saw a well-used conductor's baton. He explained that it was Mr. Toscanini's baton that he used in his last performance before he retired because of health issues. He lifted it out of the case and handed it to me. It was truly an honor to hold that very famous and cherished baton.

We spent most of the summer composing a new style of classical music labeled "electronic music." Back in the late 1960's and early 70's, many composers, artists, and musicians were enthralled with this unique, experimental genre that utilized a new instrument called the synthesizer. Dr. Gillis was able to acquire an early model of a Moog synthesizer which we used to produce some interesting compositions.

Later that year, Dr. Gillis was able to bring one of the early pioneers in electronic music to our campus to work with a few students. I was one of the lucky ones who got to work with Walter Carlos, perhaps the most influential innovator in the new genre of synthesized music. Mr. Carlos had released a new album called "Switched-On Bach" that won a Grammy and became a top seller. On the album, Mr. Carlos took compositions by preeminent classical composer Johan Sebastian Bach and reproduced them on a Moog synthesizer. It was another amazing experience to spend time with Mr. Carlos who later wrote compositions for various movies, including *Clockwork Orange*, *The Shining*, and *Tron*.

About six years later, when I was working for MICMIX Audio Products, I was at an Audio Engineering Society trade show in New York City manning our booth. I had heard that Walter Carlos had transitioned to a female and was now using the name Wendy Carlos. A visitor entered our booth to inquire about one of our new products. I thought the person looked somewhat familiar, so I looked at this lady's badge which read "Wendy Carlos." I introduced myself and explained that we had met several years prior while she was visiting Dallas Baptist University.

Wendy remembered me and we had a very cordial conversation. She asked about Dr. Gillis, and I explained that he had unfortunately passed away the previous year. She was sad to hear that he had died and commented about what a creative and wonderful person he was. It was great to see her again because she influenced me in my early electronic music compositions.

Dr. Gillis was also a visionary and early pioneer when it came to combining music with a visual experience. He thought by using music and visual arts, he could provide the audience with an enhanced experience. After I graduated in 1973, Dr. Gillis accepted a new challenge at the University of South Carolina that played into his vision by founding the Institute for Media Arts. He also served as composer-in-residence until his death in 1978. I am very thankful for having the honor of spending a good bit of time with Dr. Gillis. He influenced me from a musical perspective, but he also set a good example of how to be a great person.

Post-Graduation

After graduating with a degree in music education, I began applying for teaching positions. I interviewed with Carrollton-Farmer's Branch school district and was offered a job as choir director at Field Junior High School. I accepted the position, and my beginning salary was a whopping $12,500. Because I signed up to coach football, basketball and track, I got a $2,000 additional stipend. Woo Hoo! I was rich! Well, maybe not...

My first year of teaching was a major eye-opening experience. I was not prepared for what I was getting into. My seventh-grade choir class included 62 kids, while my eighth-grade choir class had 78 students. Junior high school-aged kids include a cornucopia of physical and emotional development. Some were prepubescent, some were preadolescent, some were tweeners, while some were downright out-of-control hellions. Hormones were raging in the classroom and firing off like a fireworks show on the Fourth of July.

Emotional outbursts and erratic behavior are typically common among junior high kids – that's a given. It was truly like herding cats with 60 or 70 of them in a classroom. I completed my student teaching at Carter High School in Dallas the previous year; I had no trouble communicating with and capturing the attention of those students. As I quickly learned, junior high school kids were a far different breed. No one ever warned me nor did any of my education classes in college prepare me to deal with the challenges I was facing.

On the first day of school, I thought I should first gain their respect and capture their attention, so I got out my guitar and performed a mini concert for them, singing several songs that were popular at the time. It worked. They listened attentively and applauded loudly.

It was a daily struggle to manage so many kids in a classroom, but I lived through it and so did the students. I learned a lot, and so did many of the students. After two years at the junior high level, a new high school was opening in Carrollton, and I was offered and accepted the position of choir director at Newman Smith High School. It was a good opportunity because I was able to put together a curriculum that included the usual choirs (beginning and advanced), but also, the fine arts superintendent allowed me to add other classes not typically available in high school, including guitar, music history, electronic music, and history of pop music.

Since it was a new school, I was also given a nice budget and was able to acquire some state-of-the-art equipment, including a Bose PA system, some excellent mics, a four-track studio tape recorder, an Arp 2600 synthesizer, and a baby grand piano. Most of the music classes filled up, and some of them required students to be on a waiting list because classes were so full.

One other interesting opportunity came my way. Since it was a new school, an alma mater and a fight song had to be written. As many high schools often do, the band director and I settled on using a college's music. Since he was a graduate of Southern Methodist University, he pushed for using the arrangements for their alma mater and fight song. We applied for and got permission to use them, but new lyrics were needed. I wrote the new lyrics that will forever be associated with the high school. The band and the choir premiered the alma mater and fight song at the school's first football pep rally.

Twenty-five years later, I was invited back to lead the singing of the alma mater and fight song prior to the 25th anniversary homecoming game. It was quite a thrill!

I had three good years at Smith High School. The music and drama departments produced some great musicals, and in my last year there, I worked with the drama director to produce a modernized version of Alice in Wonderland. I wrote a musical soundtrack using the Arp synthesizer to produce some cutting-edge electronic music and sound effects. We entered the state competition for drama productions and ended up winning the Texas state championship. We had some outstanding cast members, and our two leading characters won the top actor and actress awards. I had the opportunity to work with and teach some great kids.

I mostly enjoyed my five years of teaching. I say mostly because there were times when students tried my patience – one even challenged me to fight him. He was having an argument with his girlfriend in the hallway and looked like he was about to hit her. I quickly intervened and stopped him. He was not happy. He reared back with his clinched fist. I told him, "You don't want to do that because it will certainly not end well for you." Thankfully, he just turned and walked away. There were also some crazy parents I had to deal with, but most of them were very supportive.

At the end of my fifth year of teaching, I was ready to move on to something new. I turned in my resignation in May and completed the semester. I rode off into the sunset seeking a new adventure.

Chapter 12

The Twists and Turns of the Music Biz

I took a few weeks off after school ended, and one day I was reading the job classified ads in the newspaper. I came across an ad from a talent agency looking for someone to manage bands, solicit bookings, and work as a producer. I immediately picked up the phone and called them. I interviewed with the owner over the phone, and he asked me to come in for an in-person interview the following day. The primary focus for the talent agency was providing models for advertising and trade shows, but the owner wanted to build a music division.

After the interview, I was offered the job. Of course, I accepted the position. Along with booking and managing bands, I wore several other hats. Among my other duties were managing the ten rehearsal studios, auditioning talent, and teaching voice lessons. That latter duty led to a few interesting experiences, along with two life-altering decisions. More on that later.

Several days after I went to work at the agency, Bill, the owner, called me into his office and said he had received an unusual request to find a mariachi band to perform at a rally for then Vice President Walter Mondale. Mondale and President Jimmy Carter were in the middle of a re-election campaign and VP Mondale was scheduled to do a rally at Fair Park in Dallas. The campaign team wanted a true Texas flavor for the rally, thus the unusual request. Bill and I eventually found a large mariachi band that was well known in the Dallas area.

One day, Bill called me into his office and told me I had to work with the Secret Service to do background checks on all the band members. I had to go through a background check as well. I spoke with the Secret Service agent and got my clearance, but I explained that there may be some difficulty in getting clearance for all the band members. He explained to me that they all had to have green cards or be US citizens, and I needed to provide him with their driver's license and social security numbers. I was hopeful that all the band members met the criteria and would be able to provide their information.

After working with the leader of the band, all but two members met the criteria. I collected all the information and submitted it to the Secret Service agent. About a week later, the agent called me and told me they all passed the background check, and we were good to go. I breathed a sigh of relief because this was a well-paying gig, not to mention the prestige associated with the event.

I had to meet with the Secret Service again the morning of the event at The Hall of State at Fair Park, and I had to have the band members there two hours ahead of the event. Everything went smoothly in the preparations except for the fact that VP Mondale was nearly an hour late arriving. The band members were getting a bit restless, and I had to keep them calm and ready to perform. The task for the band was simple – entertain the crowd for a few minutes prior to Mondale's arrival, play a mariachi song as Mondale entered, stop when he got to the stage, and then play another song when he finished his speech as he exited.

All went well at the event, although like most politicians, he spoke for a long time, and I could tell the band was again getting restless. When Mondale finished his speech, I signaled the band to start playing again and the VP turned and walked over to greet the band. There were several Secret Service agents hovering around him. I was standing onstage when Mondale came over and started shaking hands with some of the band members. He reached out and shook my hand and gave me a thumbs-up. He then exited the stage and made his way out of the building. After he was gone, the band stopped playing and I breathed a sigh of relief.

It was an honor to have participated in the event and to meet VP Mondale. It was also an interesting experience dealing with the Secret Service and all the work it took to get everything set up and organized. The band was paid well to basically perform a few songs – and I was too.

A Strange Encounter

One of my first voice students was a young lady named Kathy. The owner, Bill, called me into his office and wanted to speak with me. I entered his office, sat down, and he told me a young lady was going to be my new student. He told me to make her into a good singer, and that money was no object. He explained that she was the girlfriend of one of his friends, and that I should do a good job because it could lead to bigger and better things for me. Bill explained that his friend had considerable influence in the music business, and that he was not someone to mess with. I was a bit taken aback by all that, but I promised Bill I would do my best to make her into a good singer.

Later that afternoon, Bill brought her into my office/studio and introduced her. I proceeded to have her sing some scales and exercises and quickly realized she could barely sing in tune. I had my work cut out for me – I could tell that making this girl into a singer might be an impossible task. That old saying of making a silk purse out of a pig's ear came to mind. After the first lesson, I walked Kathy out of the front door and noticed a black limo was there waiting for her. I thought, "OK, that's pretty cool to have your own limo and chauffeur – must be nice."

The rear door popped open and out came a short guy with a rounded body wearing what appeared to be an expensive black suit, black boots, and a black beret. He stuck his hand out and said, "You must be Bill. I'm Tony. The other Bill told me you were a talented guy, and you were going to make my girl Kathy into a singing star."

I made the wise choice and did not tell him what I thought – which was, "Sorry, buddy, but this girl couldn't carry a tune in a bucket – you're wasting your time and money." Instead, I said, "I will do everything I can, sir." He then said, "How much do I owe you?" Before I could tell him I charged $35 per hour, he then reached in his pocket and pulled out a wad of hundred-dollar bills then peeled one off and said, "Here, that ought to cover a couple of lessons." I said, "Yes sir, that certainly will." Tony and Kathy got back into the limo and off they went.

I stood there for a few minutes trying to digest what had just happened and then went back to my office. Based on what Bill had told me and then actually meeting Tony, I started to wonder who he was. I couldn't just Google him to find out because Google and the internet did not exist, so I just decided to go with the flow. I'm not using his full name – more on that later.

Kathy kept coming to voice lessons twice a week, and she always brought cash – and never asked for change. She had made a little progress, but it was a struggle – both on my part and hers too!

A couple of weeks later, we held a talent showcase at the agency and the owner Bill invited several music dignitaries and club owners from the Dallas area that he knew. Kathy wasn't quite ready for prime time, but several bands and performers were ready – including myself. I noticed Tony was in the audience. After everyone had performed, we had a meet-and-greet with the attendees and the performers.

Tony came right up to me and told me, "I like you, Bill. I'm gonna make you famous. I'll get you a band together, I'll buy you all your equipment, I'll pay for studio time, and I'll book you in some great places."

Wow. That offer sounded too good to be true. I was single, I wanted to advance my music career, and this looked like a great opportunity. Tony then said, "We'll talk about it next week when Kathy has her next lesson." I said, "OK, thanks Tony!"

As the meet-and-greet was wrapping up, Paul, the lead singer of one of the bands that had played at the showcase came up to me. I had booked his band and had gotten to know him pretty well and he asked, "Do you know who that guy is?" as he pointed to Tony. I said, "Yeah, I give his girlfriend voice lessons." Then he repeated, "Do you know who that guy is?" I said, "No, not really other than his name is Tony and it looks like he's got a lot of money."

Paul then said, "Tony is one of the biggest mob bosses in Dallas." I then responded and said, "Ah, now stuff is starting to make sense, and that must be why Bill told me to do whatever Tony asks and not to piss him off." Paul said, "He is a bad dude, and you should stay away from him – speaking from personal history." I was further intrigued and asked him to explain because I was naive.

Paul then told me the way mobsters work is to give you money or do something for you to get you in a position where you owe them money and/or favors. By doing this, they end up owning you and your career. Paul then explained that he knew a singer that got involved with Tony and things didn't work out too well. Paul explained, "Tony put a bounty on this guy's head because he didn't toe the line, and they butted heads several times." He continued, "Luckily, the guy found out about it and moved out of town. I heard that he moved to Montana and was living in the middle of nowhere hiding from the mob."

I had never met or come across any gangsters (and I have never met any since), but I had seen *The Godfather* and enough mob movies to know that getting involved with them was very rarely a good career move, even if you were one of the bosses. Life expectancy for mobsters is typically far below the average citizen, and very few of those that get entangled in the web of organized crime are able to extricate themselves and lead a normal life afterwards – it's the nature of the beast.

About a week after the showcase, Tony invited me to one of his clubs to see one of his performers (she shall remain nameless). She was very good and had a few songs that charted on Billboard's top 100. I came to find out that she was one of Tony's girlfriends and she had given birth to a son fathered by him.

I sat with Tony and his wife at a table as one of his "special guests." After learning about Tony, I was not very comfortable being there. The thought went through my mind that at any minute a bunch of gangsters were going to bust into the club and mow down Tony and any other poor souls sitting at the table. Fortunately, that didn't happen, but I was still very nervous the whole night.

Tony asked me if I had thought about his offer (which I was afraid he was going to bring up). I gathered all the courage I could and reluctantly explained to him that I was recently divorced with a very young daughter, and that I didn't think it was an appropriate time for me to take him up on his offer, but I told him I did appreciate it very much. I thought to myself, "I hope he's not upset with me." He said, "Come back to see me when you think the time is right." I breathed a huge sigh of relief and desperately hoped he meant what he said.

He also told me that night that Kathy would not be continuing her voice lessons. He said, "She and I have parted ways, so she won't be around anymore." I said to myself, "That poor girl's body is probably laying in a ditch somewhere." Tony then added, "She decided to move back home and go to college." I thought, "Yeah, right."

I did get a call from Kathy a few days later telling me she was indeed moving back home and going to college. I was relieved to hear her voice and that she was still alive. She thanked me for my time and told me she would continue to work on her voice. I wished her well and then we hung up.

After processing all the information about Tony and my suspicions about his involvement with the mob, I began to wonder about my boss, Bill, because he was good friends with Tony. At that time, I had also recently learned that Bill had served prison time for tax evasion and other charges. I began feeling uncomfortable working at the talent agency and thought I should probably start looking for another job, because there were just too many weird things going on.

As I was writing this book, I was wondering about Tony's background, so I did a Google search. There were lots of references to the fact that Tony led the life of a mobster, and I found an FBI report that outlined some of his illicit activities, including an FBI raid at one of Tony's clubs that recovered a roulette wheel, loaded dice, and 20 decks of marked cards (along with special glasses to read the cards). He was also found to be associated with a prostitution ring, a bookmaking ring, laundering money for friends who robbed banks, and he also dealt in the distribution of narcotics.

According to the same FBI report, Tony was "loosely connected" to the La Cosa Nostra crime syndicate (otherwise known as the mafia) out of New Orleans. However, the FBI could not directly connect him even though the investigative reports state that Tony was "a known associate" of the mafia kingpin in New Orleans.

Another tidbit of information I found was that Tony was part of the FBI investigation of the JFK assassination. He originally came on the radar of the FBI because of his close association with Jack Ruby, the killer of Lee Harvey Oswald. Jack Ruby was alleged to have had mafia ties, although it will probably never be fully known. The fact that Tony and Ruby were fellow club owners in Dallas and had some sort of association, along with the fact that Tony was undoubtedly involved in organized crime only adds to the conjecture about Ruby's mafia ties. Another FBI report stated that Tony was a "known associate of Jack Ruby."

Many researchers and theorists have long believed that JFK's assassination was a mob hit. There are a lot of facts and connections that hint at that theory, but most likely, we will never know the truth. Innumerable books have been written about the JFK assassination, and countless theories have been published. There is no need for me to go further with any speculation, but I thought it was an interesting intersection in my life of a momentous historical event and someone I had interfaced with on several occasions.

In my research, I also found that there were many unexplained deaths of people in and around the JFK assassination which are well documented, and many of them had mob ties. I continued my research of Tony and found out he died in 1983 at the age of 47, four years after I left the agency. I searched for what the cause of death was, but I could not find anything. I tried to find an obituary, but there wasn't one. Those facts were both interesting and intriguing.

I'm not putting forth any conspiracy theories, but reading about Tony and his background certainly got me thinking about and recalling this portion of my life.

Beyond my crossing paths with Tony, my tenure at the talent agency was very significant and life-changing, in that, I happened to meet Linda, my beautiful future wife, who was working as a model at the agency. We ended up getting married about six months after meeting each other. I outline additional details on our chance meeting and marriage in another chapter of this book.

Shortly after Linda and I met, she and I both left the agency to find greener pastures that weren't filled with piles of hazardous materials we could step in which could possibly lead to catastrophic contamination – or a mob hit.

The Middle Years

Over the next several years, my main focus moved from developing a music career to building a marriage and a family. That's not to say I discontinued playing music, I just had a lot of other things that took priority, like raising three young and beautiful daughters and trying to keep up with my spunky new wife.

I did learn to take some time for what I loved, which was creating music. After my wife and kids went to bed, it was my time for making music in my own solitude. I made a habit of taking an hour or two each night to go to my music happy place. This era was one of my most productive times as a songwriter – I wrote many of my best songs during those hours of solitude.

Linda and I developed a close friendship with a couple, Kat and Ken, and ended up spending a lot of time together. We were all trying to keep our heads above water financially and couldn't afford to go to a lot of places, so we just hung out together and sang – mostly at our house.

Ultimately, our two families became fully intertwined in a life-long friendship. Their kids and our kids forged a close friendship as well that is akin to a brother/sister relationship. They are all a part of our extended family to this day.

The story of how we got together was interesting in and of itself. Linda worked in the emergency room at a local hospital, and one evening, a call came in from a young lady named Kat who said that she and her husband had a car wreck, and they probably needed medical care. The young lady explained that they did not have insurance and couldn't afford an ER visit. Linda quietly told her that if they showed up in the ER, the hospital was required to see them. Consequently, they drove a wrecked car to the ER and got the care they needed.

Linda and Kat hit it off right away, and they exchanged phone numbers. One day the following week, Linda got off work and decided to go skating around Bachman Lake. There was a nice concrete pathway that skaters used to traverse the lake and get in some exercise. Linda was a very skilled skater, but as she was happily breezing along, there was a crack in the concrete that had separated, and she didn't see it coming. Her skate hit the crack at full speed and down she went. She reached out her left hand (she's left-handed) to break her fall, but instead of breaking her fall, she broke her wrist.

She got to a pay phone and called me while I was at work. Fortunately, I was only a few minutes away and picked her up. We walked into the ER where she worked, and she got the royal treatment. They X-rayed her wrist and saw it was a pretty good break. The doctor (who was a good friend of ours) re-set her wrist and then put a cast on it.

The following Saturday we had planned to have a party with a bunch of our friends to celebrate our anniversary. On Friday night, Kat called to say hi and Linda told her about her broken wrist. Linda told Kat that she was so upset because she wouldn't be able to clean the house before the party. Kat immediately said, "Honey, I'll come clean your house – what time do you want me to be there?" Linda burst into tears. I asked her what was wrong, and she said her new friend was coming over to help us clean the house for the party. The next morning, Kat and I got the house tidied up and we had a new, life-long friend. It was a great party, and Kat and Ken stayed after the party to help clean up the mess (and it was quite a mess!).

Our friendship blossomed and we came to find out that Kat loved to sing and had a beautiful voice. We spent a lot of time singing together and developed some very tight three-part harmonies. Ultimately, we ended up recording an album of my original songs. We called ourselves Trinity. We did a few gigs, but we mostly just sang together for the mere enjoyment.

Two of the songs off my first album, "Good Friends" and "Love Your Life Away", became life-long favorites around the Allen family and among our close friends. Those songs have been performed at all of our daughters' weddings, along with the weddings of many other friends and family members.

It became a tradition that every time we had a party, it always ended with a sing-along that usually lasted until late into the night. Of course, I was the one that always ended up with sore fingers from playing the guitar all night – but it was worth it – we had some great times!

The Band Years

For more than twelve years, I played in a band called AKA. The name came from our drummer when we were in deep discussions about what to call ourselves. We went through various names, but we just could not come up with anything that we liked. Terry, our drummer, just blurted out, "Let's just call ourselves AKA. We all looked at each other with a pure puzzled look on our faces that said, "Is he crazy? What is he thinking?"

Terry could tell we were all somewhat amused, baffled, and befuddled. He then chimed in, "It's better than nothing at all!" We all laughed and agreed to his point. John, our lead guitarist said, "But what does it stand for, Also Known As?" "No," said Terry. "It stands for Always Kicking Ass." We had another big laugh, and since we were all at a loss for a name, we voted to adopt AKA.

The band consisted of Terry, the drummer, John the lead guitarist, and JT the bass player. I was the lead singer, rhythm guitarist, harmonica player, and on several songs, I played keyboards. We took pride in being able to play various genres, including country, R&B, blues, 50's music, disco, and some of my originals. Our core genre, however, was classic rock.

Our first real gig was at a bar near DFW airport called Café 121 (it was located on highway 121 – thus the name). I had heard about the place but had never been there. It was more akin to a large old house that was about to be condemned than a cafe. I had heard that it was a biker bar that would occasionally get a wee bit rowdy, but we had to get our feet wet and get our first gig under our belts.

When we pulled up to set up for the gig, sure enough, there were about a dozen Harleys parked out front. As we got out of our cars, I immediately told the guys, "Be careful and don't knock any bikes over. Remember what happened to Pee Wee Herman!" For those youngsters who don't know anything about Pee Wee Herman, he starred in what came to be a cultish movie called *Pee Wee's Big Adventure*. In the movie's most memorable scene, Pee Wee stopped at a biker bar with about fifty bikes parked out front. Pee Wee accidentally knocked one Harley over, and that led to a long line of bikes toppling over like dominos. Needless to say, it caused quite the scene, and Pee Wee fortunately made a hilarious escape.

We carefully avoided the bikes as we entered the dumpy building to set up for the gig. As we got inside, there were a bunch of bikers lined up at the bar, all decked out in their leather gear. It looked like quite a motley crew, and the thought went through my head that if they didn't like us, we might have to pull an escape like Pee Wee Herman.

After setting up, I sauntered up to the bar to buy a beer before we started playing. I ordered my beer and thought I'd start up a conversation with some of the hooligans seated at the bar. They asked what kind of music we played, and I explained mostly classic rock and blues. One of them asked, "You don't play any disco, do you?" I didn't quite know how to respond, except to say, "No!" He then said in a gruff voice, "Then I ain't staying if you can't play any disco!" Again, I didn't know how to respond. There was an uncomfortable silence, and then all the bikers at the bar started laughing. It finally sank in that he was kidding.

I sat and had a chat with a few more of them. I was curious as to what they did for a living. The guy to my immediate left looked like he could have been a hitman for the Hells Angels – he looked like he could be pretty mean. I asked what he did for a living. He replied, "I own three beauty salons." I don't know if he noticed my mouth drop so far it hit the bar. It didn't make any sense, and I thought he was pranking me again. This time there was no laughter, and I dared not laugh.

Instead, I turned to the guy on my right and asked what he did for a living. He was a little more docile looking and said, "I am an airline pilot for American." I said, "OK, if you can fly a plane, I suppose you are pretty good at driving a Harley." He laughed and said, "Yeah, but there's a lot more crazy drivers on the road than there is in the skies."

Another biker standing behind me was listening to the riveting conversation going on, and I turned to him and asked, "What do you do for a living?" He answered, "I am a divorce attorney." Again, I was amused, and I asked him, "Have you ever had to use your own services?" He replied, "No, not yet, but if my wife doesn't straighten up, I might have to." We all chuckled.

I was amused that all these tough looking biker guys were actually normal people. Because of Hell's Angels and some of the other rough biker groups, the reputation of bikers precedes them. Having never hung around with them before, I was getting an education as to who most bikers really are.

We started playing at 8:00pm, and by 9:00 the place was absolutely packed tighter than a woman's suitcase on a three-week trip. The gig went well – we had a good time, and my biker friends seemed to enjoy our music. We played there a few more times in the following months. We actually played there the last night Café 121 was open. The owner said the city told him to tear down the building and either build a new facility or sell the place that was destined to be destroyed. He opted for selling the land. He made out like a bandit since the location was adjacent to a new highway that was under construction.

I asked him what the poor bikers are going to do after their favorite hang-out was gone. He replied, "I ain't gonna worry about it 'cause I'll be kickin' back and enjoying my retirement." I said to him, "Good for you! Maybe someday I'll get to enjoy my retirement."

Great Gigs Almighty

AKA played some cool gigs all over Dallas and we even had some groupies that followed us around. They were from the school for the deaf, but any groupie is better than none at all. Just kidding. We played gigs in East Texas and all the way to a grand opening at a Harley-Davidson dealership in Little Rock, AR.

We also played regularly at Stroker's Icehouse, a famous biker bar in Dallas. It was an interesting place to play because there were real, dyed-in-the-leather bikers there, along with biker-wannabe's. We shot a music video there for one of my songs called "Everybody's on Something." A video production company was wanting to get into the music video production business, and they had approached me at one of our gigs at Stroker's to see if we were interested in allowing them to do a full music production at no charge. They wanted to use the video of us as a demo. Of course, we said yes. They brought a whole camera crew and production people to our next gig at Stroker's. It was good fun—and note that this was long before every band and performer on the planet had a full-blown music video.

We also got a lot of private party biker gigs from playing at Stroker's. They were always a fun and sometimes entertaining group to play for. They were a bit rowdy at times, but it was all in good, clean fun. As they are sometimes wont to do, a few biker chicks flashed us while they were dancing. The highlight of every biker gig was when we played Steppenwolf's "Born to Be Wild." It always got a rousing response.

Another one of our favorite places to play was Edgar's Bar and Grill in Lewisville. We usually played there at least every six weeks or so. It was a large bar that had a nice stage and always had a good crowd.

One day, my home phone rang (yes, before cell phones) and it was Robbie, the manager and part owner of Edgar's. He said he had a special opportunity for AKA. He told me that Lynyrd Skynyrd was re-forming (this was several years after the deadly plane crash), and they were going to play at Edgar's since they were getting their act together to go on tour. Robbie asked if we wanted to be the warm-up band, and of course, I said yes.

Lynyrd Skynyrd did not want it to be a heavily promoted affair since they were refining their show. It didn't turn out that way. The place was absolutely packed when we started our set, and the place was rockin'. We did our thing, and by the time Lynyrd Skynyrd showed up in their white limo, the crowd had spilled over into the parking lot. Robbie propped the double door entrance open so that everyone in the parking lot could at least hear them play. It was mayhem.

Everyone had a great time, and it was a great experience for our lowly little band. We got to hang out with the band and have a few beers with them after their show.

The Fiddler on the Stage

Another interesting night at Edgar's happened when we least expected it. It was a normal night, and we had just completed our second set. I was at the bar ordering a beer when Robbie came up to me and asked if his friend who plays fiddle could sit in with us. I told Robbie that we had a rule that we did not let anyone sit in with us unless we knew them or had played with them. We had been burned before by letting someone on stage with us that literally not only embarrassed themselves, but it also embarrassed us.

Robbie looked at me and said, "Bill, I absolutely guarantee this guy can play, so please let him sit in." I said, "OK, but if he embarrasses us, I'm going to kick your butt." He said, "If he doesn't blow you away, I will let you kick my butt." I said, "We got a deal."

After playing a few songs to start the next set, I invited Robbie's friend to come on up – sorry, I don't recall his name, we'll call him Jim. He tuned his fiddle and climbed onstage. I thought we would take it easy on Jim, so we started playing Buffalo Springfield's "For What It's Worth" which is an easy song for a good musician to play, but not necessarily written for a fiddle player. The song was going well, and Jim was fitting right in.

It was time for him to take a solo. He ripped off into a solo that left every one of us in the band with our jaws dropped – it was magical. He definitely knew what he was doing. Needless to say, he played with us for the rest of the night, and everyone in the crowd recognized that Jim was quite a fiddle player. No matter what song we threw at him, whether it was classic rock, blues, or country, he nailed it.

After the gig was over, I went to the bar for a beer and Robbie smiled sarcastically and said, "So, are you gonna kick my butt?" I laughed and said, "No need for that – he can play with us any time!"

I started up a conversation with Jim and he seemed to be a really nice guy. I sang his praises and asked him if he played with a band. He replied, "I've been on tour and just got off the road. I wanted to come by and say hi to Robbie." I said, "Well, I'm glad you came tonight, and you are welcome to sit in with us any time." I then asked, "So, who were you touring with?" Jim said, "I just completed a six-month tour with George Strait."

My jaw dropped again. I said, "Are you kidding me?" He said, "Nope, our last show was in Fort Worth last night." Now, it all made sense as to how great a player he was. I was in awe. I told him that it was an honor to have played with him. He said, "Hey, I had a great time playing with you guys."

We continued our conversation, and he told me that George Strait was the nicest guy anyone could ever meet. He then said, "Come outside and I'll show you how nice he is." When we walked out, Jim took me over to a gorgeous new fully decked out Chevy Silverado and said, "George bought all the band members a new truck – check it out."

It was certainly a beautiful truck, and I said, "Well, I'll trade you my ten-year-old Chevy Astro van (which was my gig van) straight up – what do you think?" He said, "Naw, I'll stick with this one." I had heard that George Strait was a great guy, and that new truck certainly verified what I had heard. Unfortunately, I didn't get his phone number, but we sure had a great time playing with Jim.

Disaster Strikes the Band

No band is exempt from some adversity, and we faced a few problems ourselves. Our biggest adversity came three years in. Our bass player, JT, was a very key contributor to the band. He always played solid bass, as well as helping with background vocals, while also taking lead vocals on several songs so I could take a little break.

A strange thing happened during one of our rehearsals at my house. We got everything set up and began going through a few new songs. After about thirty minutes into the rehearsal, JT took his guitar off and started packing up to leave. We all looked at each other, and I asked, "Hey JT, what's up?" He replied, "It's time for me to go home and get some dinner." I said, "JT, we just started the rehearsal – you've only been here for thirty minutes – why are you leaving? Did we do something to piss you off?" He said, "No, it's just time for me to go home and get some dinner."

Sure enough, JT was adamant about leaving so he packed up his guitar and amp and headed to the house. Mack, John, and I were very perplexed. We looked at each other and didn't quite know what to think. JT didn't say anything else – he just left. The three of us just thought it was very strange, and we decided to stay and work on some more songs. It truly was baffling because JT was always the first one to the gig and was always a very conscientious member of the band. We blew it off and didn't think much else about it, other than it was very strange. We thought maybe he was just having a bad day.

JT showed up early for the next gig as he usually did. I asked him if he was OK, and he said he was doing great and he was looking forward to playing and having some fun. We started playing and everything was just fine. JT showed no signs of anything being wrong.

After the first set, we took a break. We all went to the bar and ordered a beer, and then I began talking to some of our friends and regular customers. After our usual fifteen-minute break, it was time to hit the stage again. John and I got on stage and started tuning, and Mack sat down behind his drums. After we got tuned up, I turned to John and said, "Where's JT?" John said, "Maybe he's in the bathroom – let me go check." John came back and said, "JT is nowhere to be found, what should we do?" I said,

"Did you check outside to see if he went out to smoke a cigarette?" John said, "Yes, he was not outside."

We were starting to get worried and had no idea what was going on. JT's car was still in the parking lot – things just weren't making sense. The bar where we were playing was in a retail strip center and there was a Mervyn's department store. Everything else was closed, so we all strolled over to see if JT might be in there. Sure enough, John found JT. I asked him, "What are you doing? We are supposed to be playing our gig?" JT replied, "I was just doing a little shopping." I said, "OK, we've got to get back and finish our gig, let's go."

We did finish the gig, but Mack, John, and I were becoming more and more bewildered and worried about what was going on with JT. After he left the gig, the three of us sat down and discussed the situation. We ended up deciding that I should call his wife Kathy the next day to see if she had any insight as to what was going on with him.

Several weeks earlier, JT had said he was excited about his retirement after putting in thirty years with AT&T. He said he and Kathy were planning on doing some traveling and spending more time with their grandkids. It had been about 2 weeks since he retired, and he said he was loving life as a retiree. I told him I was totally jealous and that I said I would probably never get to retire. I said, "You're a lucky man, JT!"

I called Kathy and relayed to her what had happened the previous night. She then said, "Yes, I had to drive to South Dallas after the gig to pick him up because he called and said he was lost and couldn't find his way home. She told me he had been acting very strangely as well and that she had taken him to the doctor the previous week. She said, "JT has had memory problems for a few months and has undergone some testing for Alzheimer's disease. We should hear back from the doctor next week." At their next visit to the doctor, the doctor explained to Kathy that JT had Alzheimer's disease.

Kathy also told me about an incident when they went to Walmart to do some shopping. As they entered the store, JT said he was going to shop for some CD's, and that he would meet her at the front of the store. Kathy went on to do her shopping and after she checked out and paid for her groceries, she started looking for JT. She spotted him speaking with a police officer at one of the exits. Kathy went up and asked what was going on.

The officer said that JT was under arrest for stealing four CD's. Kathy was mortified. JT would never try to steal something, and she explained to the officer that JT had recently been diagnosed with Alzheimer's disease. The officer said, "I'm sorry, but I have to take him in and book him. He was found exiting the store and heading for his car with four stolen CD's." Kathy then told me she started getting angry with the officer because JT was not even aware of what was going on – he didn't understand what he had done.

At his arraignment, Kathy explained to the judge what was going on with JT. The judge asked JT a few questions which he could not answer. The judge then turned to the district attorney and said, "Don't you ever bring a case like this to my court again. It's obvious this man has a medical problem. Case dismissed."

On our phone call, Kathy also told me that JT had started getting very angry at the silliest things and was starting to get physical with her. JT was always the nicest, calmest, most laid-back guy anyone could ever meet. I felt horrible for Kathy – she was such a sweet person and didn't deserve all this.

It all started making more sense. Kathy told me JT was not going to be able to continue playing with the band, but she would drive JT to and from our gigs until we could find a replacement. The crazy thing is, JT could remember all the songs and would never miss a note. But sadly, the disease left him unable to cope with daily life.

I called up one of my old friends who was an excellent bass player and asked if he was interested in joining the band. Brantley came over for a few practices and decided to join the band.

I kept in touch with Kathy to check on JT. Each time I spoke with her, she said things were getting worse and worse. On a subsequent call about a month later, she told me that JT had to be put into an Alzheimer's facility. He was diagnosed with a very aggressive, fast-moving type of Alzheimer's called Creutzfeldt-Jakob's disease. Things were very bleak.

About a week later, I got a call from Kathy, and she told me JT had passed away. Like her, I was shocked, devastated, and heartbroken. She explained that JT's mother had also died from the same type of Alzheimer's disease. It was so horribly sad that JT had no time to enjoy his retirement, and poor Kathy endured a horrific four months that ended in JT's sudden death.

The funeral was very sad as might be expected. Kathy came up to Mack, John, and me to tell us how much JT loved playing in the band – it was always the highlight of his life. We all chimed in to tell her what a great guy JT was and how we regretted that she had to go through so much pain and agony for the last several months. We all were dejected, not only for her, but for JT as well.

But The Band Played On

We recovered from the loss of JT and continued playing. AKA stayed together for another 8 years. We gigged nearly every Friday and Saturday night. As I look back, I am amazed that I was able to work a full-time job that required a good bit of travel, raise a family, and keep up with all that is needed in owning a house.

At the end, I think we were all exhausted, so we decided to take a break from playing. Linda and I had moved to a new place about twenty miles outside of Dallas, so the commute to and from gigs became increasingly more difficult. A few months prior to our break-up, I produced an album called "A Piece of Forever" featuring ten of my original songs. We had a great time recording the album and played several of the songs off the album during some of our final gigs.

After we called it quits, we did get back together for a several gigs over the next few years – it was our own version of a reunion tour. It was a fun part of my life, and it made me a much better performer and musician. We had lots of great times together, and we were Always Kicking Ass!

Chapter 13

Combining Business and Pleasure

During my entire business career, I always tried to take time for myself while travelling – I called it "my time." Quite often, my time involved sightseeing. I always tried to visit famous or interesting places, and I tried to experience local culture, whether it be from seeing monuments, visiting museums, taking a drive through mountains, or eating local food. I also loved to go hiking and take in whatever nature sights were available.

Of course, I also made sure music was a part of my adventures. I would always research if there were opportunities to play and sing in each city I visited. By my estimate, I performed in more than a hundred blues jams all over the country and even jammed in my travels to Europe and China.

As a harmonica player, blues jams were easy to find in almost every city, and travelling with harmonicas was far more transportable than trying to drag a guitar from coast to coast and north to south. That's not to mention taking a chance on getting one of my guitars irreparably damaged by the gorillas that handle baggage as previously outlined earlier in this book. Obviously, the harmonica also fits well in a blues environment.

There were some amazing jams I took part in, but there were also a few duds. In a blues jam, various musicians are called to the stage not ever having played with each other. The beauty of the blues as it pertains to jams is that chord progressions are well defined and easy to replicate for even non-professional players. Also, most players are familiar with blues songs, or they can easily follow the singer. As I said, some of my experiences with playing with players I had never met were mostly memorable, but sometimes there were a few that were definitely forgettable. I'll tell a few tales of some of my experiences.

Blues in Berlin

During a visit to Berlin, I found a blues jam on a Wednesday night that was next door to my hotel. I walked in and introduced myself to the young black guy named Sam who was running the jam. We had a nice conversation, and he was excited to meet someone from Texas since he was born and raised in Houston. After the jam started, he invited me up to the stage. I played and sang a few songs with him and his band, and evidently, he was impressed enough to invite me to sit in with them for the rest of the night.

After the gig was over, we had one of those great German beers together. I asked him what he was doing in Berlin, and he said he came there for a blues tour of Europe more than five years earlier, and he loved it so much, he stayed. He told me he originally had a six-month visa, but he obviously had overstayed it. He said, "I lay low and stay out of trouble because I'm sure they would deport me immediately if they ever found out my visa had expired four years ago. I always get paid in cash and no one has ever asked me for an ID." As I came to find out, he was known all over Germany as one of the best blues piano players.

As we were finishing up our beers, he told me he really enjoyed my playing and singing and said, "Man, I've got a big gig coming up on Saturday night, and I would love for you to play with us." I told him, "I would really love to play with you guys, but I am flying home Saturday morning." He came back and asked, "Can you change your flight to Sunday? I'll pay you 200 Euros if you can make the gig." I said, "I am honored that you asked me, but it'll cost a lot more than 200 Euros to change my flight – if I could do it, I would do it in a heartbeat!" He gave me his phone number and said, "I understand, but if you are ever in Berlin give me a call – I'd love to play with you again." I told him "Of course I will." I never made it back to Berlin, but I had a great time playing with his band – even though it was one night only.

One other incident that stands out on my visit to Berlin has nothing to do with music, but it is worthy of mentioning because it made an impression on me. When I was in 7th grade, I was assigned to do a report on the Berlin Wall. I came to learn that it was built in 1961 with the primary purpose of keeping people from leaving East Germany and relocating to West Germany.

I found it hard to believe that the East German Communist government would actually build a wall to keep people in – it didn't make any sense to me since walls are primarily erected to keep people out. It was very bothersome to me that the East German people were, in essence, being imprisoned in their own country. I found it to be cruel that families and friends that lived on opposite sides of the wall could not visit each other. It was truly hard for me to imagine. Learning about the Berlin Wall was one of the first lessons that taught me about what it's like to live in a free country versus one where freedom does not exist. It was eye-opening.

I came to understand exactly why the East German Communist leaders built the wall. After World War II and up until 1961, more than 2.5 million citizens moved from East Germany to West Germany to escape Communist rule. Had they not built the wall, perhaps there would have been no one left in East Germany. After the wall was built in 1961, more than 5,000 people successfully escaped, while around 5,000 were unsuccessful, with many of them being shot and killed during their escape attempt.

Because of the report I wrote, I was always interested in following the events surrounding the wall in subsequent years. I always felt so bad for the East German people. I was elated when Ronald Reagan gave his history-making speech in West

Berlin in 1989 when he famously implored, "Mr. Gorbachev, tear down this wall." According to some historians, those powerful and consequential words were actually removed from the original speech because it could have potentially upset the Soviet leader, Mr. Gorbachev. President Reagan felt so compelled to use those words that he added them back into the speech against his advisors' wishes. The wall ultimately came down, the people from East Germany were freed, and the rest is history.

I had always wanted to visit the Berlin Wall because of its historic nature. In my only trip to Berlin, I took the opportunity to visit Checkpoint Charlie and see what remains of the wall. I took a few minutes to stand next to and touch the wall I had learned about in the 7th grade. It was a moving experience.

Visiting Dachau

Speaking of moving experiences, let me also briefly diverge to describe a visit to another historic place in Germany, although it is famous for the wrong reasons. I had an afternoon off during one of my trips to Munich, and I decided to take a 30-minute drive to the infamous concentration camp called Dachau. I had read about Hitler's concentration camps and had seen the brutal effects of Jewish extermination when my wife Linda and I visited Anne Frank's house in Amsterdam several years earlier. Seeing the museum at Anne Frank's house had been unsettling but strolling around Dachau and seeing where more than 40,000 Jews and political figures had been executed was on a completely different level. It was so disturbing that I became sick to my stomach.

As I somberly walked the grounds, I could feel the pain and suffering lingering in the air. It deeply touched me to the point of tears. It was as if the thousands of tortured souls were still swirling around the camp. I could only imagine the terror and utter cruelty that took place there. It was terribly difficult to grasp how humans could be so filled with hate towards other humans. The next feeling that washed over me was anger toward those that inflicted unfathomable and horrific deeds on innocent people just because they were of a different race. Trying to make any sense of it was a fruitless endeavor – it was incomprehensible.

Dachau was the first concentration camp built by Hitler in 1933. In the beginning, it was primarily used to house and execute political dissidents and criminals. There was a daily roundup of prisoners that were lined up and summarily shot by firing squads. Mass graves were dug just outside of the camp. Later, a mass crematorium was built to dispose of the bodies more efficiently.

Historians estimate that more than 200,000 prisoners were held at Dachau, and an estimated 41,500 prisoners, mostly Jews, were executed by firing squad or in a gas chamber. There was also a section of the camp involved with "medical experiments", although they would be more accurately described as torture experiments. Fortunately, in April of 1945, American troops liberated an estimated 30,000 prisoners in Dachau and other area camps – including political prisoners, but mostly Jews.

After the liberation, fittingly, American troops rounded up around 18,000 German SS members who were responsible for the horrific deeds and imprisoned them in Dachau for a period of time. Additionally, many of the SS officers were tried and convicted of war crimes in trials that were held on the grounds of Dachau.

The brutality and inhumanity that occurred in the various concentration camps throughout Germany was not only despicable, but it was also truly the epitome of evil. It was hard for me to comprehend and impossible for me to understand how it all happened – but it did. On the one hand, my visit to Dachau was enlightening, while on the other hand, it was completely distressing and extremely disgusting. Needless to say, it left a long-lasting and unforgettable impression.

Marcus is the King

Back to more pleasant musical experiences. I travelled frequently to Greenville, SC for business. I always enjoyed my time there, and all the people made me feel at home – southern hospitality at its best. Greenville's population is around 75,000 and has undergone a growth spurt. Their downtown area, which used to be a mess, is now a beautiful place with lots of hotels, restaurants, and shopping. I had some wonderful meals there and it's a pleasant place to take a nice walk.

As mentioned earlier, I always researched to find out if there were any blues jams wherever I travelled, and quite fortunately, a restaurant/bar called Smiley's Acoustic Café was within two blocks of where I usually stayed downtown. They always had some sort of live music, and a blues jam was held on Thursday nights. It was usually a good group of musicians that came to the jam, and I always enjoyed singing and playing my harmonica there. On one occasion in January of 2013, I ventured over to Smiley's and had an amazing experience.

The house band played a few songs, and then I was called up to play, along with two guitar players. One of them was an older guy (like me), and one of them was a young kid who looked to be around 16 or 17 years old. Usually, younger kids are just learning how to play the blues, so my expectations were low. I thought we'd start with an easy blues standard called "You Got Me Runnin'". I sang the first three verses, and it was time for the guitarists to take their solos. The older guy lit into his solo and was exceptionally good. It was then time for the young kid to take his solo.

I was a bit apprehensive, but a few seconds into his solo, my jaw almost dropped to the floor. This kid played licks that were unbelievably difficult and very tasty. I was shocked at his skills, so much so, that when it came time for my harmonica solo, I missed the first few measures because I had to get my jaw off the floor. I was inspired by the high level of musicianship and ripped off a really good solo of my own.

The next song I called out for us to play was another great blues classic called "Stormy Monday." It's a slow, complex song with abnormal chord changes built around a standard blues progression, but I knew these great players could manage it. Again, it came time for the old guy to play a solo and he tore it up – he was phenomenal. Then came time for the kid. Once again, I was awed by his uncanny virtuosity which again pushed me to pick up my game on my harp solo (FYI—the word harp is used interchangeably for harmonica).

Next, we played two of my original blues songs which reached new heights given the superior talent that was playing them. The whole experience of playing with these virtuosos was a surreal moment for me. I had played in about a hundred blues jams, but this one topped the charts – it was truly thrilling. My biggest regret was that I did not record it on my phone – not doing that was a big mistake because our 4-song set was magical, and the audience went crazy.

When the set ended, I thanked the drummer, the bass player, and of course, I profusely thanked the two guitar wizzes. They both complimented me on my singing and harp playing and said it was a pleasure playing with me. I said, "Thank you, but the pleasure was all mine."

I went back to the table where I was sitting with John who worked for the major customer I was visiting in Greenville. He turned to me and said, "Bill, that was absolutely awesome! You guys kicked some serious ass!" I replied, "John, those two guitar players are the best I have ever played with. Do you know who they are?"

John said, "The old guy is Marvin King who is well known in this area as one of the best blues guitarists around." He continued, "The young guy is Marcus King, Marvin's son, who is also well known in the area." I then told John, "I've got to go over and talk to them."

I made my way over to their table, and they invited me to sit down. We had a good chat about music, and we shared our backgrounds. I told Marcus that I was thoroughly impressed with his knack for doing guitar licks that I had never heard before and that his artistry was beyond anything I had ever heard. Marvin gave a chuckle and said, "Yes, he's certainly a better player than I am!" I then said, "Marvin, you are an amazing guitarist yourself, and you have nothing to be ashamed of."

There are some guitar geniuses like Stevie Ray Vaughan (my favorite), Eric Clapton, Jeff Beck, or Carlos Santana where music just flows out of them. They are able to tap into an ethereal level where the notes stream straight from their soul. It's a rare and unusual talent, and I could tell Marcus was one of those guitarists that had that extra-special ability that doesn't come around very often.

I asked Marvin what was on the horizon for him and his son. He replied, "All I want right now is to keep my 16-year-old uber-talented son on the straight and narrow and get him to the finish line to graduate from high school. That's all I'm worried about right now – the rest will take care of itself – he turns 17 in a couple of months." John joined us at the table, and we continued to have a great conversation with Marvin and Marcus for the rest of the night.

I learned a few years later that Marcus didn't make it to the finish line. He dropped out of school in his junior year, but he did get his GED. Marcus was more interested in making music than he was making grades, although he seemed like a well-spoken and very smart kid. I'm sure Marvin was at least happy that Marcus got his GED.

On a subsequent trip to Greenville the following summer, I happened to notice that Marcus and his newly formed band was playing at a venue in downtown Greenville. I made my way over to the venue and enjoyed hearing Marcus with his new band. During one of their breaks, I went over to say hello to Marcus. As I walked up to him, he said, "Hey, it's Bill the harp player! Good to see you, man." We had a nice chat, and I congratulated him on his new band. He told me they were working on an album that would be out the following year. As he played that night, I was reminded of how special this young kid was.

After several years passed, I was curious to see what Marcus was up to. I Googled him and found out that he had released his first album in 2014 and that he had also released one in 2016 and 2018. His fourth album was nominated for a Grammy in 2021. He has since put out two more albums, one in 2022, and one in 2024.

I came to find out that Marcus has frequently toured as a warm-up act for Chris Stapleton. Those two have become good buddies, and according to one interview, Chris labeled Marcus as "One of my favorite guitar players ever." That is indeed a rather substantial endorsement from an iconic artist on the skill of Marcus King.

The next time he popped up in my sphere was when I noticed a PBS music special being broadcast that featured none other than Marcus King. I recorded it and watched it twice, always taking note of his extraordinary talent. Shortly thereafter, I was watching the CMA Awards show, and there was Marcus jamming with the Zach Brown Band. I was surprised, but not shocked.

Marcus has become a bonafide star whose guitar-playing skill has taken him to heights I'm sure he nor Marvin ever thought was possible. But as they say in the music business, the cream always rises to the top. I knew he was destined for greatness. It was a real pleasure and honor to have taken the stage and jammed with Marcus and Marvin. It was a rare experience, and one of the best of many highlights of my life in music.

Mozart And Me

On one of my business trips to Munich to meet with my Texas Instruments team, and because I had to stay over until Sunday to get a less expensive airfare, I decided to drive to Salzburg, Austria. It was only an hour and a half from Munich. Since German corporations shut down at noon on Friday, I got an early start and headed for Salzburg. It's an interestingly quaint city nestled in the Alps mountains with an ancient history.

The area surrounding Salzburg was taken over by the Romans in the year 15 AD, and a formalized city was established in 696. The key asset that put Salzburg on the map was its rich deposits of salt in the mountains surrounding the city. The German word "salz" means salt in English, and "burg" means "a fortified settlement city" – thus the name Salzburg.

Passing through the center of the city is a river named the Salzach. Salz, again meaning "salt", and "ach" is German for running water. The river, which eventually feeds into the Danube, was the primary means of transportation for shipping salt to other parts of Europe.

Salzburg was a small yet bustling city in the Middle Ages. There is a large hill (or a small mountain) that sits just outside the city center, measuring around 1500 feet in height. It was a perfect place to build a fortress, and construction was initiated by the local archbishop in 1077. It was expanded and reinforced several times over the next four hundred years or so. It became one of the largest fortresses in Europe. It's called Hohensalzburg Fortress. The word "hohen" means "high" – yep, it was named the "high fortress of Salzburg". Because of its position on the hill (or mountain), it is always visible from anywhere in the city.

The downtown area was very walkable, and since I was staying at a centrally located hotel, I decided to stroll through the ancient city streets and take in the beautiful Baroque architecture after I arrived on Friday afternoon. I stumbled onto the Abbey of St. Peter, which is the oldest continuously operating church and monastery in the German-speaking world, having been built in 696 when the city was first established. Its library is home to more than 100,000 books and manuscripts, many of them being of ancient origin. The Basilica (church sanctuary) was not a gargantuan place like St. Peter's at the Vatican in Rome, but it was exceedingly ornate and stunningly beautiful.

I did have one destination on my walk that I was looking forward to – the birthplace of Wolfgang Amadeus Mozart. I found the location on my pocket map that I picked up at the visitor's center and headed for my next destination.

Having studied and listened to a lot of classical music while in college, I always thought Mozart was the most creative composer – not to mention one of the most prolific. Music flowed like an endless effervescent spring from the mind of Mozart. He was penultimately brilliant – truly, a rare creative genius – yet sometimes he displayed eccentric and erratic behavior. Stories abound about his escapades. Being eccentric and erratic certainly runs in the family of creative souls even today.

The amount of music he composed was amazing, numbering more than 600 pieces, including symphonies, operas, piano and harpsichord sonatas, string quartets, choral cantatas, and just about any other musical form. I can only wonder what this creative genius would have accomplished if he were unleashed with the tools available to today's composers.

Sadly, Mozart left this earth far too soon at 35 years of age on December 5th in 1791. His cause of death has been debated by doctors for centuries with 156 different diagnoses that include tuberculosis, mercury poisoning, kidney failure, a streptococcal infection, scarlet fever, trichinosis (from under-cooked pork), and on and on. No one really knows. In any case, he was composing music at age five and one can only imagine how prolific he could have been had he lived for another twenty or thirty years.

The movie *Amadeus* is a must-see, not only for music lovers, but for everyone. The movie is fairly accurate historically except for the fact that his rival, albeit one of Mozart's closest friends, Antonio Salieri, was depicted as an assassin who poisoned Mozart. Nearly all historians doubt it ever happened, but it did make for an interesting plot twist for a Hollywood movie.

As I got to the address of Mozart's birthplace and first residence, I paused before I went in and just imagined him walking into this house. It is a three-story building and now a museum. Mozart and his family lived on the third floor. It was very much like a full-scale apartment with several rooms. Many of the furnishings and artifacts displayed were originally owned by the family. It was very fascinating to see how and where they lived, including Mozart's bed, the table where he ate with his family, and the kitchen where his mother prepared their food.

Wolfgang's father was an excellent violin player who performed in an orchestra and gave lessons to his son from an early age. Wolfgang was also encouraged to learn how to play a keyboard instrument, so his father bought him a harpsichord when he was four years old. By the age of five, Mozart began composing his own songs and his talents for playing violin and harpsichord flourished. His savant-like talents were set free.

As I made it to the music room in Mozart's house, I saw a harpsichord sitting behind a roped off area – it was the one his father bought. I was standing there imagining Wolfgang sitting at that harpsichord playing and writing musical scores. It was just a thrill for me to be a few feet away from such a historic instrument. As I was standing there, a voice from behind me said something in German. I didn't understand what he said since my German vocabulary was rather limited. I turned and said, "Sprechen Sie Englisch?" He replied, "Yes, I speak English." I noticed he was a security guard, and he asked me in English if I was a big fan of Mozart. I said, "Yes, I am a musician, and I studied or played many of his compositions. He is my favorite composer."

The security guard began walking toward me and said he was sorry, but it was time for the museum to close. There wasn't anyone else left in the museum but the security guard and me. I turned around to look at the harpsichord and I said, "It is such a thrill to see this instrument – it gives me chills." The guard then reached down and unhooked the rope and said, "Would you like to have a closer look?" I replied, "Of course."

We walked over and I was standing right next to this historic instrument. I said to the guard, "It's like I can hear him playing it right now – this is so cool." He then asked, "Can you play something from Mozart?" I then said, "It's been a very long time, but I would be honored to try and play one of his sonatas I learned in college. Are you serious, can I play it?" I sat down and ran my fingers along the keyboard and let them rest on the keys. I closed my eyes and again imagined Mozart sitting there. In the silence, I could hear him playing. I then began playing as much of the song as I could remember. I did make it through the first part, but after about 8 measures, my brain locked up as I fully realized I was actually playing a Mozart song on his first harpsichord. It was an electric experience – even a spiritual moment that was absolutely the thrill of a lifetime for me.

It was not an ornately crafted instrument, but to me, the beauty was in its simplicity and historic significance. After a minute or so of taking in the moment, the guard said it was time to close the museum. I said, "No problem, I understand, but I could stay here all night!" He laughed.

As we walked down the stairs, I thanked him profusely for allowing me to experience something that I would never forget as long as I lived. Perhaps to many people, an experience like this was no big deal. But even today, more than forty years later, I can still close my eyes, relive those few moments, and remember feeling the electricity I had in my fingers as I touched the keys of that harpsichord. As I was walking back to my hotel, I was still completely in shock and astonished about what I had just experienced.

The Hills Come Alive

The following day, I planned on driving through the Alps overlooking Salzburg. On the local map, I saw the hillside where scenes from *The Sound of Music* were famously filmed. I had to go see it. It was even more beautiful than in the movie. It was private property, and although I wanted to, I couldn't go rollicking through the hillside singing:

> The hills are alive, with the Sound of Music.
> The songs they have sung for a thousand years.
> The hills fill my heart with the sound of music
> My heart wants to sing every song it hears

After fantasizing about Julie Andrews singing and dancing through the hills, I decided to just take off and drive through the mountains as I love to do. I had no special destination, just randomly exploring to see what I could stumble across.

After about 30 minutes of driving, I came across an absolutely gorgeous lake that was deep in a valley surrounded by snow-filled mountains and surrounded by huge pine and spruce trees. I came to find out it was called Koenigsee (translated to mean King's Lake). I could see a small island off in the distance along with some sort of building. I noticed there was a boathouse next to the parking lot where I parked and wandered over to check it out.

There was a group of about ten people getting ready to board a small ferry and I saw a ticket window. I asked where the ferry was headed, and the lady in the ticket booth said the ferry would ride around the lake and make a stop at the church on a small island. I decided to spend the five Euros and bought a ticket for the two-hour tour. The trip was definitely well worth it – the lake was pristinely beautiful, and the surrounding mountain scenery was utterly exquisite.

The lake was a remnant of a large glacier that occupied the landscape inside what I would describe as a canyon. It was a long, narrow lake that wound around the mountainsides and extended for almost five miles. Some narrow portions of the lake were maybe two hundred yards wide, and the widest portion was almost a mile wide. The water was almost perfectly calm, and it was so clear I could see fish swimming 10 or fifteen feet deep.

When we pulled up to the small island, I could see a few buildings and what looked like a church. The ferry pulled up to the dock, and we gathered in a group for a tour of the island and buildings. It is called St. Batholomew's church, and it is only accessible by boat. Originally, it required hiking through very mountainous terrain that would challenge even the most experienced hikers and then taking a boat to the island. The church was originally constructed in 1134 and is known as a "pilgrimage church", meaning it took a lot to even get to the church. I suppose that the Roman Catholic provosts who originally built the church wanted a very remote yet beautifully located place to worship. Indeed, it was both.

After we re-boarded the ferry to continue our tour of the lake, we passed near a small but beautiful waterfall. When we got to the far end of the lake, the ferry stopped. The captain turned off the motor and we sat in silence for about a minute just taking in the beautiful scenery. I was curious as to what was happening. Suddenly, I heard what sounded like a trumpet playing (it was actually a flugelhorn). Sure enough, there was one of the boat's crew members playing some beautiful music. The sound was echoing throughout the steep canyon walls. He stopped for a minute and then played four short bursts of sound. I counted seven echoes as the sound bounced back and forth between the canyon walls. He then played a melody and then played it in harmony. Because of the echo effect, it sounded like multiple people were playing. It was truly exhilarating.

As we headed back to the dock, the tour guide pointed to a house that was nestled at the top of an adjoining mountain. I could see it was up there but couldn't make out much of it since it was perched so high. The guide then explained it was a chalet called Kehlsteinhaus (translated as Eagle's Nest), and it was famous for being a vacation house for Hitler. He built several other barracks and buildings around the chalet. It was used for government and military meetings during WWII, and it is purported that Hitler and his generals mapped out the invasion of Poland and France there.

I was somewhat fascinated and thought about driving up there, but the steep mountainous road was closed due to heavy snow at higher elevations. Oh well, I already know more about Hitler than I care to know.

It was time for me to make the 90-mile trip back to Munich so I could catch my flight out the following morning. It was an eventful two days in Salzburg that created wonderful memories for me. The real highlight was being in the presence of where Mozart grew up, and of course, playing the instrument of a rare musical genius.

The Party and the Piano

During my first tenure with Minuteman Power Technologies as director of marketing, I was responsible for purchasing a lot of advertising in nationally distributed publications such as PC Magazine, Byte Magazine, PC World, and PC Computing. These were all very large subscription-based magazines, most of them having circulations of more than 500,000, with PC Magazine topping out at 1.2 million subscribers. And I might mention, magazine ads back then could exceed more than $20,000 per page.

These magazines had an enormous amount of money being thrown at them by advertisers. There were times when these magazines were more than ½ inch thick because the PC market was exploding. It was big business!

Whenever ad reps would come into town to sell ad space, they showed up with large expense accounts. I was treated to very nice lunches and extravagant dinners at top steak houses. I was taken to see my Texas Rangers and Dallas Mavericks play on numerous occasions. At various trade shows which we attended and where we had an exhibit, the magazines were notorious for throwing big parties and elaborate events – sometimes featuring big-name entertainers.

The biggest trade show at that time was called Comdex which was held in Las Vegas. It peaked at 225,000 attendees in 1996. Exhibiting companies would literally spend multiple millions of dollars on their exhibits. Again, the PC industry was just flowing with money – it was the high-tech boom era. The trade show was so large, it encompassed the entire Las Vegas Convention Center (which is massive), the Sands Expo Center (which was huge in itself), as well as two hotel ballrooms.

Along with being the largest trade show in the US at the time, Comdex was also known for its parties. They were always extravagant. Some of the groups and entertainers I saw at various parties at Comdex included Fleetwood Mac, Willie Nelson, Chaka Kahn, The Pointer Sisters, and many others. As an advertiser, I was fortunate to get invitations to more parties than I could attend.

One particular instance that stands out for me was an exclusive party thrown by PC Magazine that was held at Liberace's mansion. For those that have no idea who Liberace (pronounced Lib-er-a-chee) was, just Google him. In short, he was a hugely famous, world-renowned piano player who was the highest-paid entertainer in the world during his peak. He was the Elton John of the 60's, 70's, and even into the 80's. He was the first big performer-in-residence in Las Vegas and was known for his flamboyance both on and offstage.

Liberace passed away in 1987, and his estate turned his house into somewhat of a shrine and museum. Companies could rent out the mansion for corporate parties, and I was invited to PC Magazine's private event there. I was scheduled to go to dinner with an ad rep named Donna who worked for a competitive magazine, but I could not pass up the chance to see Liberace's mansion. She was a very sweet person and ended up being a good friend. I told her I was invited to a party and that we should go to Liberace's mansion instead of dinner. She thought it was a good idea, so we hopped in a taxi and went to the mansion.

I purposely didn't tell her who was throwing the party. As we were getting out of the taxi, she asked me who was sponsoring the event. I fessed up and told her PC Magazine. She stopped dead in her tracks, looked at me like I was crazy, and then said, "I can't go in there, they are my arch-competitor – they will throw me out." I said, "Aw, don't worry about it, no one will ever know." She then said, "What if Steve (her boss) finds out? He might fire me." I said, "Don't worry, he'll never know unless you tell him." As a side note – Donna and I told Steve (who was also a good friend of mine) about the party the next day and he thought it was absolutely hilarious. She didn't get fired.

I was finally able to drag Donna into the party. There was a guide that took us on a tour of the mansion. It wasn't a huge mansion compared to what entertainers live in today, but it was certainly far bigger than my little 1400 square foot house. It was beautifully decorated – well, a better word would be gaudily decorated. Again, Liberace was known for his flamboyant extravagance.

The two things I remember about the house was that the bedroom was very large, and I looked up at the ceiling and saw it was artistically painted. Upon closer look, I then realized it was a duplicated painting of Michelangelo's masterpiece on the ceiling of the Sistine Chapel in the Vatican. I asked Donna, "Why in the world would he have that painted in his bedroom? – it seems strangely gauche and out of place for a bedroom." She laughed and said, "I totally agree! That's Liberace being Liberace."

The other thing I vividly remember was an enormous living room that featured his trademark white concert grand piano ornately trimmed in gold. It was the piano he used in his Vegas performances. The piano was beautiful and was the centerpiece of the very large room.

After making the rounds and speaking with some of my friends in the industry, Donna and I circled back, and I wanted to take a closer look at the piano. The manager of the facility was standing at the piano and we spoke about the history around Liberace, the house, and the piano. I asked him if I could sit down at the piano and touch the keys. He said, "Of course!"

After I sat there admiring the keys and imagining Liberace playing it, Donna knew I played piano, so she chimed in and asked, "Can he play something?" The manager then asked, "Do you play piano?" I sheepishly said, "Yes, but certainly not like Liberace." He then invited me to play something. I reached back into my deep memory banks and played a piece I learned in college. Miraculously, because of all the times I played and practiced it in college, I remembered the whole thing. The piano sounded beautiful echoing through the large living room that was at least as big as my entire house.

As I got to the end of the song, the room that was filled with people talking suddenly went silent. A group had gathered around the piano watching me. Someone in the crowd encouraged me to play something else, so I played and sang "Knockin' on Heaven's Door." Many in the crowd joined in singing with me – some even singing harmony.

In the meantime, Donna had gone to the bar and brought me a huge glass of tequila and a beer. I took a large shot of the tequila and then started playing and singing Billy Joel's "Piano Man." That got the crowd singing along even louder, and the group grew larger around the piano. I started taking requests and suddenly I was giving a concert. I took another shot of tequila and sang some more. You see, the more tequila I drink, the more songs I remember and the better I play (at least that's what my mind thinks).

Several other members of the crowd started bringing me tequila. I sat there for more than an hour and a half singing and playing, trying to perform anything they requested. Donna had gotten an empty water pitcher and sat it on the piano. She threw in a few dollars, and then others in the crowd started throwing money in the pitcher.

The event manager came over and complimented me on my playing and singing and said, "Even though we are supposed to close down the event, you can keep playing as long as you want." I told him, "Thank you so much for letting me play this amazing piano – it truly is a thrill of a lifetime."

I performed three more songs, and then I could tell the tequila was getting to me, and my fingers and voice were getting tired. The crowd had started to disburse, so I decided it was time to quit. I got lots of compliments, handshakes, and hugs from those that were still hanging around the piano. The publisher of PC Magazine came up to me and said, "Bill, you were the life of the party, and I can't thank you enough for making it a great night."

Donna and I left the mansion and took a taxi back to our respective hotels. She had grabbed the money out of the pitcher and counted it for me. She said, "Wow, Bill, you made $94 tonight! You've got some gambling money now." I thanked her for her brilliant idea of the pitcher and said she should take half of it. She said, "Nonsense, you're the one that earned it."

The taxi driver dropped Donna off at her hotel and then took me to mine. Despite the excessive amount of tequila, I was able to find my way back to my hotel room. I climbed into bed, and as I laid my weary head down, I thought, "What a great night – I got to play Liberace's world famous piano, AND I made 94 bucks. Life is good." And then I was out like a light.

Harry Caray's Piano

I attended many trade shows and conventions in Chicago and attended lots of parties, but one stands out in my memory. The publishing company that Steve and Donna worked for threw an advertiser party at Harry Caray's Italian Steakhouse, a high-end restaurant. They had rented out the second floor which served as a medium-sized banquet area.

Harry Caray was an iconic figure in Chicago. He was a TV broadcaster for the Chicago Cubs. His distinctive voice and notable accent became synonymous with Chicago. He spent 51 years as a baseball broadcaster, his last 12 with the Cubs. Harry gained national prominence and was enshrined in the broadcaster's wing of the Baseball Hall of Fame in 1989.

At each home game, Harry was famous for leading the crowd with his sometimes-off-key rendition of "Take Me Out to the Ball Game." He was also known for his jokingly mispronunciations of player's names as well as being an unabashed critic of the Cubs when they weren't playing well (which back then was pretty often). He was also the Cubs' biggest cheerleader.

Harry's restaurant became a hotspot in downtown Chicago. Not only was the food first-class, but patrons could also enjoy the vast collection of baseball memorabilia that was displayed throughout the restaurant.

There were probably around fifty people that attended the event. The appetizers, steak, all the sides, along with dessert were delicious and thoroughly enjoyed by all that partook.

As the waitstaff was removing all the plates, Steve came over to my table and asked if I wanted to play the piano and put a little life into the party. I said, "Sure, why not." He then went to the restaurant manager and asked if they had a piano. I overheard the manager say, "Yes, I think we have one in the closet, let me check." He and Steve left the room, and in a couple of minutes, they came around the corner and into the room pushing an old, ragged-looking upright piano. They placed the piano in the middle of the room and Steve motioned me over.

I went to the piano, and as I sat down, I noticed the keys were well-worn, with some highly discolored and it looked as though some were likely semi-functional. This piano (to be kind) had obviously seen its better days to say the least. I played a few chords, and the tuning was barely passable. Despite all my first impressions, I started playing and singing.

Before I could even finish the first song, Donna brought over a huge shot of tequila and a pitcher for tips. Needless to say, she knew the drill. Shortly thereafter, Steve sat another glass of tequila on top of the piano. I knew I was in trouble again and a long night was ahead. The piano was probably THE worst instrument I have ever played. Some of the keys didn't work and it was very difficult to play because of the rough action of the keys.

I tried to make do with what I had to work with. The crowd gathered around the piano and those that could carry a tune – and even some that couldn't sing a lick were doing the best they could. Like the Liberace event, I was taking requests, and both Steve and Donna kept me well-fortified with tequila and beer. After more than an hour of brutal punishment to my fingers, I was still going strong, and the party was getting more and more rowdy. By this time, patrons from the restaurant were climbing the stairs to join in on the fun.

After another thirty minutes or so (and a few more painkilling shots of tequila), my fingers were screaming at me to mercifully stop. After the next song, I looked down at my fingers and several of my beat-up digits were bleeding around the sides of my fingernails. Mind you, they were not dripping blood, but had I played much longer, they probably would have been. I closed the lid on the piano, then stood and said, "The tequila says 'go', but my bloody fingers say 'no.'" There were groans of disappointment, but I could no longer submit my poor fingers to any additional punishment – that was it!

The party soon dispersed, and Steve came over to me and said, "Bill, you made the party a huge success and I want to do something nice for your company." I said, "Hey, that's not necessary because I had a great time, but don't ask my fingers." I showed him the bloody nubs, and he said, "Now I really want to do something nice." I said, "No, it's really not necessary."

Steve, who had been keeping up with me on tequila shots said, "I am giving Minuteman the back cover in the next issue for free." I gave him a surprised but puzzled look because I knew that the cost of the back cover was $16,000. I asked, "Are you sure?" He said, "Hell yeah, I'm the publisher, I can do anything I want – I'll send you a no-charge contract as soon as I get back to the office." Donna was standing behind Steve and was just as shocked as I was. She smiled and gave me a thumbs up. Having an ad on the back cover, the most expensive ad placement was huge.

Sure enough, a few days later after I returned to the office, the contract came through on our fax machine. I took the contract into Rick, my boss, and said, "We're doing the back cover in the next issue of PC Computing." He said, "Bill, are you crazy? We don't have the budget for that!" I said, "How does no-charge sound to you?" He said, "What? How's that possible?" I told him about playing at the party until my fingers bled, and Steve, the publisher, wanted to thank me for providing the entertainment at their party. Rick was shocked.

The following month, the magazine issue was published. There was our ad on the back cover. I took it in to show it to Rick and said, "See, Steve really did do it!" Rick gave me a high five and congratulated me.

A few minutes later, Rick came into my office and said, "Bill, Rod (our president) wants to do something really nice for you and Linda. How does a vacation in Puerto Rico for you and Linda sound?" I told him it sounded pretty good to me, but it wasn't necessary. He said, "That's what we want to do, so make your plans and pack your bags."

While we were in Puerto Rico, I did perform sales training and went on sales calls with our distributor so it could be written off as a business expense. It was a rich reward for me for enduring a bruising bout with too much tequila and a piano that drew blood.

German Sing-along

Here's another escapade involving tequila and a piano. This one took place in Freising, Germany, outside of Munich. This was when I worked for Texas Instruments and travelled frequently to our German office where I had six members of my team.

After a long day at the office, I decided that my team deserved dinner and a few delicious German beers. I told them it was quitting time, and everyone should meet me at the bar in the lobby of the hotel where I was staying. Word spread quickly, and the group ended up including several engineers, some salespeople, and a few of the admin staff. What was supposed to be five or six people turned into eighteen.

The bar was right in the middle of a large atrium. All the hotel rooms in this ten-story hotel overlooked the atrium. I ordered a round of beers for everyone (with the approval of our division VP, of course, who was also there). I ended up opening a tab with the waitress, and she kept the beers coming, along with a wide array of appetizers.

There happened to be an unoccupied piano in the middle of the bar. My better senses said, "Danger! Danger!" As much as I didn't want to do it, I was shamed into playing a few songs. I asked the bartender if it would be OK, and he said, "Sure, no problem, as long as you can play." I told him I'd do my best.

After a few songs, one of my team members brought over a shot of tequila. I am sure there's a pattern developing here that readers have picked up on. After the next song, a person at the bar brought over another. And then a lady at the bar brought over another. I eventually had four shots of tequila lined up on the piano. Whew.

As the night went on, everyone in the bar was singing along. See, Germans love to drink, and they love to sing when they drink. If you go to any beer garden, there are always two things present – beer and music.

As an aside, I had the opportunity to go to Oktoberfest in Munich on one of my trips to witness this beer drinking and singing phenomenon. I was amazed to see these enormous circus tents jam packed with people sitting on benches at picnic tables, and of course everyone was drinking beer.

In the middle of these tents was always a stage with musicians playing German beer-drinking songs as well as American classics. The American songs that I heard the Germans singing to the top of their voices were "Country Roads," "Hey, Hey Baby," and "Sweet Caroline." They were played several times throughout the night in all the circus tents. It was a sight to behold to hear these Germans belting out the classics from the US while raising their liters of beer.

Interestingly, the beer for Oktoberfest is freshly brewed specifically for this 16-day event. And it was truly an amazing spectacle of an event unlike anything I had ever seen. I also learned that there are strict laws that govern the brewing of beer. There are around 700 breweries in Bavaria, which is the largest state in Germany, with Munich being the capital. Those 700 breweries make up more than half of the breweries in all of Germany. As might be expected, beer is king in Bavaria, and they take their beer very seriously. The Germans have a purity law for beer that dates back 500 years! The law dictates only four ingredients are allowed in beer: water, malt, hops, and yeast. No preservatives are allowed, no artificial flavors, and no nonsense ingredients.

Sorry for the diversion. Back to the hotel bar and the piano. The night wore on, and as usual, the more tequila I had, the more songs I remembered. Around 10 o'clock, the hotel manager came to the piano and said, "Sir, we appreciate your entertainment, everyone has enjoyed it, but I think it's time to stop." The crowd of probably twenty beer-filled Germans around the piano thought differently. They protested loudly. He then said, "OK, a few more songs," and then hustled away before the rioting started. I guess he realized the better part of valor was to not get between the Germans and their love for beer and music.

After about fifteen minutes later, the manager, along with a security guard (I guess he thought he needed protection), sheepishly came up to the piano and said, "Sir, you must stop playing, we have guests complaining about the noise coming from the bar." One of our German team members emphatically chimed in and said, "Maybe they just need to come down and join us!" Another loudly said, "NOISE? This is not noise—it's called having a good time!"

The manager then whispered in my ear, "Sir, I would really appreciate it if you stopped." After imbibing in lots of beer and tequila, I was feeling a bit cantankerous, so I asked the crowd, "Do you want me to stop playing?" There was a resoundingly loud, "NO!" I could tell the manager was getting more and more nervous. I then blurted out, "I've been thrown out of a lot better places than this!"

I could tell the manager was moving from nervous to annoyed, so I stood up and said, "OK, I quit!" There were boos from the crowd, but I certainly didn't want to be responsible for a hotel riot, and I undoubtedly did not want to see what the inside of a German jail cell looked like.

The Price of Keeping up With the Big Boys

As the crowd disbursed, I finished off my beer and headed for my room along with Lloyd, our international sales manager who lived in England, and Kelly, one of my team members from the US office. Lloyd and I had become good friends, and Kelly was, if not the best, definitely one of the best people I ever hired and managed. In addition to being a great employee, she was a triathlete as well as a beautiful young lady who had an effervescent personality.

Throughout the night, Kelly was adamant about keeping up with the German crowd in the consumption of beer. She always loved taking on challenges. I must say, she held her own, but it was obvious that she had over-imbibed. As we were walking down the hallway to our rooms, Lloyd and I stopped outside his room to shake hands and say goodnight. Kelly continued walking to her room, and then she turned around and ran at full speed toward me. I wasn't sure what was happening, and then she literally jumped on me, wrapping her legs around me. I held her up so she wouldn't just crash, and then she gave me a big hug and planted a giant kiss on the cheek with a loud mmmmmmwah, and then loudly exclaimed, "Thanks for being the best boss ever!" Kelly then turned and skipped down the hallway to her room, although she was weaving rather badly and bouncing off the walls.

Texas Instruments had strict rules about the proper conduct of managers and how they interact with employees. Male/female interactions were always under scrutiny. I was mortified with what just happened. I turned to Lloyd and said, "You didn't see that!" He paused for a moment, and then in his distinctive British accent said, "I saw nothing." He then started laughing hysterically. I was not laughing. He said, "The look on your face was absolutely priceless – your eyes were as big as saucers." He continued to laugh while I was still stunned. And then I started laughing. We stood there for a minute or two uncontrollably laughing. It was another one of those infectious laughs where neither of us could stop. We finally caught our breath and made our way to our rooms.

The Morning After

The next morning was no laughing matter for Kelly. We were supposed to meet for breakfast at eight o'clock. At eight-thirty, Kelly was a no-show. I called her room on the house phone, and no one answered. I waited for fifteen minutes and then called again. She picked up the phone and said hello with a mumbled voice that was barely audible. I immediately knew what was going on. I said, "Kelly, are you OK? We were supposed to meet for breakfast, are you coming down?" There was a long pause of the other end. She then said, "I don't feel so great." I said, "OK, what can I do to help?" Another long pause. I then asked her, "Are you going to be able to give your presentation to the management team this morning?"

Understand that Kelly was the team lead on a new marketing program we were beginning, and she was supposed to present it to all the management VIP's. There was another long pause, and then she screamed, "Oh shit! I'll take a shower and be down there in ten minutes!" I knew better, and said, "OK just take your time, we can still make the ten o'clock meeting." I heard some rustling in the background which sounded like she was struggling to get out of bed. She must have forgotten to hang up the phone because after a few seconds, I heard her say, "Oh shit! Ohhhhhhh shit! Bill's gonna fire me." I hung up the phone and had another good laugh. Poor Kelly.

When she finally appeared, she looked like death warmed over. Her hair was still wet, she had no make-up on, and she was weaving as she walked. I knew she was struggling, and she was still tipsy from the night before. I asked her if I could get her some coffee and something from the breakfast buffet. She snarled and said, "No thank you, I'll be OK." I said, "Kelly, the best thing to do is get something in your stomach." She said, "I can't eat anything, I'll puke." I said, "Let me get you some toast and fruit – maybe that will make you feel better." She just hung her head and said, "OK."

I went over to the buffet and made her a piece of toast and got her some fruit. As I was headed back to the table, I noticed she was standing up by where the coffee and tea were, just kind of staring. I walked over and said, "Do you want some coffee or tea?" She said, "Yes, I'm getting me some tea – that sounds better than coffee."

I stood there to make sure she was able to manage getting her tea. She put two tea bags in the little white tea pitcher and then poured in some hot water. All was going well until she turned around to walk back to our table. As she turned around, there was a tall, finely dressed German businessman standing behind her waiting to get coffee. Kelly was somewhat unsteady, and as she turned, she tipped the tea pitcher, and hot water came pouring out – right down the front of the gentleman's suit pants and into his Gucci shoes. The guy let out a primal scream and began a hot-foot dance. Everyone in the restaurant was taken aback, and all eyes were on Kelly and this screaming gentleman.

Kelly was mortified and began profusely apologizing. The gentleman was not paying attention to Kelly – he was more concerned about getting his expensive shoes and socks off. Luckily, the gentleman was not burned. I then guided Kelly back to our table and sat her down. I put her plate of toast and fruit down and filled her cup with tea and then said, "Try to eat something." She looked up with tears in her eyes and said, "Bill, you don't have to fire me, I'll just turn in my resignation." I said, "Kelly, I'm not going to fire you – all I'm concerned about right now is getting you sobered up so you can do your presentation. Now please eat something and you'll feel better."

Through her tears, Kelly did manage to eat some of the toast and fruit, and she was able to drink a little tea which seemed to settle her stomach. After breakfast, she was feeling a bit better, so we headed out the door and drove to the Texas Instruments campus.

As the meeting started, I told the management team, "Kelly is not feeling well this morning, but she's going to power through, and I'm sure she will do a good job." Kelly was obviously not her effervescent self, but she made it through the presentation. Sure enough, all went well, and the management team OK'd the new program.

Lunch was served after the meeting, and Kelly scarfed down a sandwich and some soup. She was on her way back to normalcy. After we worked the rest of the afternoon, Kelly and I headed back to the hotel. During the drive, I told her, "Well, you accomplished your goal last night in keeping up with the big boys." She then said, "I guess I did, but I sure paid the price this morning. That German beer tasted so good, and it went down so smoothly." She added, "Bill, thanks for being so good to me, I really appreciate it – and thanks for not firing me." I said, "Don't worry about it. You're a great team member that I would hate to lose."

I curiously asked her, "Do you remember anything that happened last night when you, Lloyd, and I were walking back to our rooms? She said, "Oh no, did I do something wrong? Why do you ask? What did I do?" I then said, "No, you didn't do anything wrong, I was just glad Lloyd and I didn't have to carry you back to your room."

As we pulled into the parking lot of the hotel, I asked her if she wanted to go to happy hour at the hotel bar, to which she vigorously replied, "Hell no! I am never drinking again!"

About a year later, Kelly and I were having dinner after a trade show, and I finally told her what happened. She said, "I am so sorry, I am so embarrassed." I said, "It was very sweet, and was the best compliment I ever had from an employee. The only thing I was worried about is if HR found out about it we'd both be in trouble!"

Knickerbocker Hotel Tragedy

OK, I promise, just one more story about a piano and tequila.

During my tenure with Texas Instruments, I spoke at numerous conferences regarding RFID technology. As mentioned elsewhere, I was the key spokesperson and evangelist promoting TI's products. One such conference was held at the Knickerbocker Hotel in Chicago.

As one of the premier hotels, The Knickerbocker is an iconic location that features a lavish lobby filled with beautiful antiques, classical furnishings, and ornate decor. When entering the lobby, it was like taking a journey back in time. The hotel was built in 1927, and the lobby perfectly represented a bygone era. In addition, the hotel featured an exquisitely beautiful ballroom, fittingly called the Crystal Ballroom. The vaulted and rounded ceiling is bejeweled with enormous crystal chandeliers, thus befitting its name.

The history of the hotel includes being the location of a speakeasy and secret casino in the penthouse that was operated by Al Capone's older brother Ralph in the early 1930's. Al Capone and other famous (or should I say infamous) gangsters frequented the hotel bar, and obviously the elicit casino. Prohibition was still in effect, but that didn't prevent gangsters from running their businesses. A later renovation revealed secret passageways that were associated with the elicit activity that took place within the hotel walls.

The original name was The Davis Hotel. In the early 70's, Hugh Hefner purchased the hotel and renamed it The Playboy Towers Hotel, which lasted around a decade.

The hotel was then purchased by the Millenium Group and renamed The Knickerbocker Hotel. A long list of celebrities and politicians have stayed at the hotel, including The Rolling Stones and John F. Kennedy.

The Lobby Bar was very spacious and beautifully decorated. Tucked away among the ornate antiques was a baby grand piano. I had gone to dinner with a friend of mine who was a fellow guitar player and editor that worked for one the magazines in which we advertised. Tom asked if I wanted to grab a drink at the bar before we went to our rooms. I couldn't pass it up.

We settled in at the bar and ordered a drink. In our conversation with the bartender, the topic migrated to music. Tom explained that we were both musicians and told the bartender that I sang and played the piano. Tom was at the party at Harry Carey's a few months earlier. The bartender said their usual piano player did not show up that night, and I was welcome to play and sing.

I sat down at the piano and noticed it was a Steinway, which is an outstanding brand of piano. As I started playing, I told Tom, who was sitting at a table near the piano, "This is certainly a far cry from that rickety old thing I played at Harry Carey's!" Tom laughed and said, "No bleeding fingers tonight!" I said, "Thank God. It took my fingers a week to get over that night."

A bar patron came over and requested I play "Piano Man," and so I did. He then came over and dropped ten bucks into the tip jar and asked if he could buy me a shot or a drink. Tom chimed in and said, "He loves tequila." Shortly, the guy came back over with what looked like a double shot of tequila. I thought, "Oh no, here we go again!" The bartender came over with another shot of tequila and said, "One of the customers bought you a shot." I said, "Gee thanks."

After playing several more songs, a gentleman came over to the piano and said, "Hi, I am James, the night manager at the hotel." I immediately thought, "OK, I'm about to get shut down and asked to leave the bar – just like in Germany." James then said, "I am really enjoying your playing and singing, and it looks like everyone else is too – thanks for your entertainment." I said, "Thanks James, I appreciate it – I'm just having a good time."

James said he was taking piano lessons and asked if it would be OK to watch me play. I said, "Of course you can, but I'm not a great player and I encourage you to not pick up bad habits when watching me."

When I first sat down at the piano, I noticed there was a beautiful credenza right behind me. I remember it had a gorgeous brown marble top and was made with dark mahogany wood. It had very intricate wood carvings adorning the sides and top, along with very unique decorative curved legs. I noticed how beautiful it was when I originally sat down to play. I thought to myself, "Man, that credenza is probably worth a small fortune." Tom and I both had noticed it.

James, the hotel manager, had perched himself behind me, and I happened to see he was half leaning on and half sitting on one end of the credenza. I didn't think anything of it until I finished my next song and turned around. James was clapping, and suddenly, I heard a loud "Crack!" And then there was a thud. James fell to the floor as the credenza front left leg snapped. His eyes were wide open, and he had a look of terror on his face. I jumped up from the piano bench and helped him up.

We both looked at the now three-legged credenza – it was pitifully damaged. My first reaction was, "Oh my gosh, that poor guy is going to be fired." I asked if he was OK. He said, "Yes, I'm OK, but the credenza is not! Oh crap, how am I going to explain this to my boss?" I thought for a few seconds and said, "I did it! Tell them I did it – it was my fault!" I continued, "What are they going to do to me? I'm a customer – they can't fire me!"

James and the bellman quickly picked up the wounded credenza and took it away – I'm not sure where it ended up. James came back a few minutes later and I told him how sorry I was that it had happened. I said, "Tell your boss I took full responsibility for the accident." He then said, "It'll be OK, I'm sure we can get it fixed."

The broken credenza certainly put a damper on the mood, so I decided to retire to my room. As I was walking away from the piano, Tom said, "Hey, don't forget your tips." Tom handed me the money and said, "55 dollars, not bad!" I told him, "Thanks for remembering!" I'm not sure what ever happened to James, but I hope the best for him because it seemed like he was a very good guy.

OK, I Lied – One More Piano Tale but no Tequila

While working at MICMIX Audio Products, we exhibited at the National Association of Music Merchants trade show which was held in Atlanta, GA in 1978. While manning the booth, an attendee walked in and said, "Man, we love your reverb units, they are so cool!" I looked down at his badge and saw his name was Bobby, and he was the lead sound engineer from a local recording studio in Atlanta (I don't recall the name of the studio, and after all it was 40+ years ago – at least that's my excuse).

Bobby and I had a very nice chat about how he used our reverb units, and he provided some insight and feedback, always praising the performance and sound our equipment produced. We hit it off pretty well, and he invited me to visit the studio. He said, "Hey if you want to come to the studio tonight, we are having an album release party at 7:00pm for a local band, and If you come a little earlier, I can give you a tour." I told him I'd be glad to take him up on his offer.

When the trade show was over, I went to my hotel, changed clothes, and then took a short taxi ride to the studio. I arrived around 6:15 and walked into the studio. A receptionist welcomed me, and I asked to see Bobby. She called for him over the intercom, and after a few minutes, Bobby showed up and greeted me.

We began the tour in their large Studio A. Bobby mentioned that it had recently been redesigned, and a lot of new equipment had been added. We walked into the control room, and he showed me the rack where two of our reverb units were mounted. He again reiterated how much he liked their sound.

We then walked into Studio B which was slightly smaller that Studio A. Sitting in the middle of the room was a baby grand piano. As I walked over to look at it, Bobby got a page over the intercom. The receptionist said, "Bobby, you've got a call about the party tonight." He excused himself and exited the studio to take the call. I said, "No problem, I'll just hang out here."

I noticed the piano had a bit of wear and tear, and that it definitely looked like an older piano. I decided to sit down on the bench and check it out. It was a Steinway, so I assumed it was going to sound nice. I started playing it and sure enough, it sounded warm and beautiful. I could tell it was older and seasoned because of its warm sound. I continued to just tinker around.

Bobby came back into the studio and asked, "How do you like that piano?" I said, "It plays very nicely and sounds really warm and beautiful." He then replied, "You are playing Carol King's piano." I was stunned and said, "You've got to be kidding me!" He said, "Nope, it really is her piano. She had it shipped to us – she'll be doing some recording here."

I sat there for a minute or two paying homage and thinking about all the great music that was written on that piano. I was in awe. As I came to find out later, her Steinway piano was originally built in 1923. It was gifted to her by her in-laws who had inherited it from her husband's grandmother who had bought it new in 1923.

For those that do not know who Carol King is, she was one of the most prolific songwriters during the 60's and 70's. The list of performers that sang her songs is far too lengthy to list here. She essentially penned the soundtrack of a whole generation. Her songs sold more than 75 million copies, and she released her solo album called *Tapestry* that sold 25 million copies worldwide. It stayed on the Billboard charts for SIX YEARS! In 1972, the year it was released, it won Grammy's for Album of the Year, Song of the Year, Record of the year, and Best Female Vocal Performance. Unlike many flash-in-the-pan songwriters, Carol King wrote American standards that will be covered and performed 100 years from now. While I was sitting at the piano, I decided to take time to sing and play "Fire and Rain", one of her most iconic songs and one of my favorites.

Bobby and I finished the tour of the studio, and I hung out for a while at the album release party. I don't recall who the band was. In fact, it didn't really matter. Playing Carole King's piano was another unbelievable experience and touching the keys of a world-famous piano that helped in birthing some of the greatest songs ever written was quite memorable. It was another spiritual experience for me. It was certainly a moment I'll never forget.

The Sound of Music

I have often thought about the origins of music. Who was the first person to realize they could make beautiful (or not so beautiful) sounds with their voice? Imagine cavemen and women sitting around a campfire hanging out and chillin', and then someone just breaks out and starts singing – then everyone starts clapping and joining in on the jam session. Well, maybe it didn't happen that way, but it had to start somewhere and somehow.

Researchers have theorized that singing possibly started after we humans developed the u-shaped hyoid bone in the upper part of our throats – they say it happened around 500,000 years ago. Evidently, that gave us the ability to manipulate our vocal cords and make beautiful sounds. I can imagine our early ancestors enjoying the vocal sounds that the early rock stars were producing at the parties around the campfire.

The earliest musical instruments were flutes using hollowed-out bones or tree branches. It is believed that the first flute-like instruments were used around 60,000 years ago. The earliest drums appeared around 5,500BC, and the earliest string instruments were first used around 4,000BC. It took thousands of years to get the first band together, but the rest is history.

I wonder how fast the first song ever written went viral and how many copies it sold. Come to find out, the earliest song was recorded around 1,400BC. No, it was not recorded in a studio, it was written down on cuneiform tablets in Syria. The song was in praise of the goddess Nikkal – she was the Hurian goddess of orchards, and it is said to be dedicated to promoting fertility. I wonder if it had the same effect as Marvin Gaye's "Let's Get It On," or perhaps Rod Stewart's "Do You Think I'm Sexy?". I guess we'll never know…

I bring all this music history up to make a point. Music has become a fundamental part of our existence on this planet. I have never met anyone that didn't enjoy music – either listening or playing. Perhaps there are a few people who don't like music, but they are few and far between.

The physical properties of music are on display not only in our world, but also throughout the universe. There is a physics lesson to be learned from the sound of a hollowed-out bone that is played; or the plucking of a guitar string; or the beating of a drum; or the sound of a trumpet. Musical waves echo throughout the entire universe.

A recent report said the average person spends 900 hours per year listening to music in some form or fashion, and a total of 1.3 million songs are listened to in a lifetime. The number of songs written have grown exponentially over the last 100 years and will continue to do so. As we all know, music is big business.

For musicians, music is an opportunity to express themselves and their emotions. For listeners, it is an opportunity to vicariously live through and relate to the lives of the songwriters and tap into emotions they feel. Music helps to cleanse the soul by allowing us to extricate ourselves from pain and suffering. It also allows us to immerse ourselves in the exuberance of pure joy. It resurrects meaningful memories and takes our mind to other places. Music helps us navigate the steep hills and bumpy roads, as well as the smooth byways in the beautiful valleys of our lives.

There was a time when I wanted to be a rock star and a famous songwriter. Obviously, that didn't happen for various reasons and circumstances. Eventually, I concluded that it was acceptable to just enjoy playing and creating music – even if was only for myself. I have been fortunate to be endowed with natural musical talent, but it still takes hard work to refine and improve musicianship – for which the rewards have been immeasurable.

The bottom line is that music plays an irreplaceable part in our human experience. I am honored to be both an avid consumer and an enthusiastic participant in the creation and enjoyment of music. I have used music as a healing balm in my darkest days. Music has taken me to the top of the mountain of joy where my spirit soared like an eagle.

I have been privileged to have more than my fair share of extraordinary musical memories, and I shall be forever indebted to music for what it has meant to me in my life. I am a better person, and the world – yes, even the universe – is a better place because of music.

Section IV

My Sometimes Wacky World of Business

Chapter 14

German-American Cultural Relations

As mentioned, my business trips have taken me to many different countries and have led to some fascinating encounters and interesting situations. My business trips mostly involved customer meetings, trade shows, and speaking at or attending conferences. Some included encounters with well-known people and famous (or infamous) places. My business trips were mostly uneventful (except those described elsewhere in this book), but there are a few more that stand out to me as outlined in this section.

Aa previously mentioned, good deal of my international travel involved going to Munich, Germany during my stint with the RFID division of Texas Instruments. Six members of my team worked at a Texas Instruments plant outside of Munich in a small town called Freising. A total of around thirty members of the overall RFID team worked at the Freising facility.

Germany and America share many cultural traits, but we do differ in certain areas. It was interesting to work with and manage employees from Germany and learn about their culture, work habits, and inter-personal relationships. As I learned, Germans were conscientious about their job performance and were open to coaching. I had two engineers on my team and had frequently heard about German engineering – think

Mercedes-Benz, BMW, etc. They would tediously tackle an assignment and would generally do an outstanding job. The only issue I ever had was that they were sometimes so meticulous that it would take them forever to complete a task.

Here in the US, we are more accustomed to a high volume of output and fixing any mistakes at the end. As they say in the recording industry, "Don't worry about small mistakes, we'll fix it in the mix." Not so much for the Germans, and it would sometimes drive me crazy that they took so long to finish a project.

One particular engineer on my team, Reinhard, spent a six-month stint working for me at the Dallas facility. He was a great guy, and we became close friends over the years. He always did an outstanding job, but I would challenge him to speed up his output because we were too busy to make sure every tiny little detail was excruciatingly reviewed to the point where it slowed down progress. He understood and eventually adapted to the work environment here in the US, although it did go against his German heritage.

When he returned to the German facility, he would call out the other engineers for taking so long to complete a project. In one meeting while I was in Freising, I asked one of Reinhard's fellow engineers how long it would take to finish a proposed project. He said it would take him about three months to complete it. Reinhard spoke up and said, "Stephan, that's crazy, you should be able to finish it in less than a month – forget about perfection – just get it done!" Stephan looked at Reinhard as if he had lost his mind and said, "Reinhard, you've obviously been brainwashed by the Americans – you know that's not how we do things here." Reinhard turned and looked at me and laughed. Everyone else in the meeting then joined in the laughter.

I inserted myself into the conversation and said, "Stephan, I apologize for brainwashing Reinhard, but can you possibly do the job in a month?" He said, "Yes, it's possible." Reinhard then spoke up and said, "Then just do it!" I turned to him and said, "Congratulations, Reinhard, you are now an official member of the American Brainwashed Workers Club of Germany." We all had another good laugh.

Those Hostile Americans

Each year, the entire RFID group would have an annual meeting in Germany where we would do a review and make plans for the year ahead. Between 30 and 40 people from Germany and the US usually attended the event. We had various workshop sessions and team-building events. Sometimes, the cultural differences would clash, but everyone got along famously with each other.

In one session, an outside consultant was brought in to do a cultural intermingling workshop. The goal was to help us better understand our differences and similarities, and to help support a harmonious working environment. I never understood why we needed this workshop because we all got along very well. I suppose the consultant just had to do something to earn his money.

We all lined up sitting in two rows facing each other, Germans on one side, Americans on the other. The exercise was for each person to share what they liked about the other's country or culture. I was the first person to lead off, and I said, "The best thing I like about Germany is you guys have the best beer in the world!" That set off a good laugh and was a nice icebreaker. All the other Americans agreed.

As mentioned elsewhere, it is true that the Germans take their beer very seriously. Their "purity laws", believe it or not, were established in 1516 and are still in effect today!

Another interesting added tidbit – Freising is home to the world's oldest continuously-operating brewery established in 1040. It's called Weihenstephan. German monks started the brewery to maintain peace and tranquility and insure their own survival over the centuries. They kindly provided beer and food to invading Mongols, Saxons, Poles, Hungarians, Romans, and various roaming tribes. I was able to visit the brewery on many occasions, and like the invading tribes, I gladly enjoyed imbibing in their very tasty beer and delicious German cuisine.

Back to the cultural session. The first German to share her comments on what she liked most about Americans was a middle-aged woman who managed the logistics department. She was very smart, always well-dressed, spoke excellent English, and was a very kind and considerate lady.

When asked about her thoughts, she pondered for a minute on what she loved most about Americans and couldn't think of anything right off the bat. She continued trying to come up with something, and then she blurted out, "I love the Americans for their HOSTILITY!" The room went deadly quiet – everyone froze. The consultant was horrified, dumbfounded, and he didn't know what to do or say.

One of the German engineers quickly leaned over and whispered in her ear – making sure she was using the right English word. I could tell he was explaining what the word hostility meant. She turned red-faced, stood up, and then embarrassingly shouted, "No, no, no – I meant HOSPITALITY! I am so sorry!" Everyone burst into hysterical laughter.

Her misapplied comment remains one of the best, if not the best moment of any conference I ever attended. I am still laughing as I write this. One thing for sure – laughter crosses the great cultural divide no matter the circumstances or the environment.

The extensive time I spent in Germany was always enjoyable. I gained a good deal of their respect, not only their engineering prowess, but also their tenacity, high level of job performance, and conscientious work ethic. I was also fascinated in learning about their culture and history. The whole experience taught me that Germans and Americans are far more alike than we are different.

Chapter 15

Trade Show Tales

One year during Comdex, the huge computer trade show in Las Vegas, I was scheduled to go to dinner with an ad rep named John who had become a good friend of mine. We frequently hung out together and we were both big sports fans. Consequently, most of our conversations centered around sports.

John wanted to go to dinner at Lawry's Prime Rib restaurant, and since he was buying, there was certainly no argument from me. Before dinner, he suggested we first stop by what had become a famous bar in Las Vegas called The Drink. It wasn't just a bar, it was a huge facility that had a vodka bar, a whiskey bar, a gin bar, a scotch bar, a tequila bar (yay!), and a bar just for beers. It was built in a circle, so you could literally make the rounds and easily become fully inebriated by sampling a plethora of adult beverages. I thought it sounded like an interesting concept, so we decided to go have a few drinks at The Drink. John picked me up in a taxi and we headed to our destination.

As the taxi pulled up to The Drink, I climbed out of the car and saw a Comdex exhibitor badge laying on the ground. I picked it up and saw that it belonged to someone from Microsoft, so I put it in my pocket.

When we got to the entrance, there was a table with two young ladies sitting there who worked at The Drink. They explained that the venue was closed for a private party for Microsoft employees only. John and I looked at each other and then I realized I had a Microsoft employee's badge. I pulled it out of my pocket and showed it to one of the ladies and she said, "Oh, well let me give you both a wristband and you guys are welcome to go in. Enjoy!"

As we started walking in the door, my guilty conscience overtook me, so I turned around and said, "John, I can't do this." He looked at me like I was crazy. I walked back to the table and said to the young ladies, "I found this badge laying on the ground outside, and we are not really employees of Microsoft. Sorry. I'd like to leave this with you in case someone comes looking for it." The young ladies looked at each other, and one of them said, "We can hold on to the badge to see if anyone claims it. Thanks for telling us." As John and I were headed back to catch a taxi, the other young lady said, "Since you've already got a wristband, you might as well go in and have fun – we don't care."

Being completely shameless, and because we thought Microsoft (and Bill Gates) could afford for us to have a few drinks on them, that was the only thing she needed to say.

After all, I did the right thing in turning in the badge. A drink or two was an apt reward – at least that's what my conscience said. We then headed into the party.

Our first stop was the whiskey bar. There were 30 or 40 different types of whisky to sample. We could choose between a half-shot sample tasting, or we could opt for a full shot. John and I sampled several interesting-sounding whiskies, and then we moved on to the next bar which featured gin. Since neither John nor I liked gin, we bypassed it and moved to the scotch bar. Once again, we tried a few samples.

There were also food stations featuring various types of cuisine. I told John it was probably a good idea to sample some of the food because we still had several more bars to visit. As we all know, drinking on an empty stomach can be hazardous to one's health – not to mention the ability to function and walk upright. Next up was the vodka bar. I never knew there were so many different flavors of vodka. We sampled watermelon, peach, and even blueberry flavored vodka. I wasn't a big fan of vodka in the first place, but the various flavors were more interesting than straight vodka.

The next stop was my obvious favorite – the tequila bar. We sat down and chose some tequilas to sample. Since the bartender was an expert in tequila, we got an interesting lesson and learned probably a lot more than we needed or could ever remember, given our more than already slightly inebriated state. We did partake from the fajita bar, hoping the food would provide at least some buffer between full inebriation and being completely comatose.

John and I were sitting at the bar having a nice chat when a lovely, well-dressed, middle-aged lady sat down next to me. It appeared she had visited and sampled quite a few alcoholic beverages as well, although she probably still had a ways to go to catch up to John and me. She asked what type of tequila she should sample. Since I had become an expert in tequila thanks to the bartender's expertise, and having drunk more than my fair share in my drinking career, I suggested an oak barrel aged 100% blue agave tequila. The bartender served us all, and down they went.

She then turned to me and asked, "So what do you do for Microsoft?" I suddenly recalled that this party was for Microsoft staff only, so I had to do some quick thinking to come up with a viable answer. I then said confidently and unabashedly, "I am a special assistant to Bill Gates – I'm his righthand man." She looked at me with a puzzled look and then let out a huge laugh and said, "No you're not – he doesn't have a special assistant!" In trying to further convince her, I said, "Very few people in Microsoft know who I am, and if I tell you any more information, I might have to fire you."

I'm not sure if it was the tequila or that fact that she thought I was out of my mind, she let out another huge belly laugh and said, "You're full of shit, you know it?" I said, "Well, ma'am I must admit that you are correct." She had another laugh and asked, "OK, who are you and why are you here at this party?" I decided to come clean and tell her the truth about how John and I made it into the party. I asked, "So, are you going to call security and have us thrown out? She replied, "Of course not, I think it's hilarious that you crashed our party."

I then asked her, "I take it you purport that you really do work for Microsoft, what's your name and what do you do?" She replied, "My name is Sarah." She continued, "I really do work for Microsoft, and I am the senior vice president of sales for one of our divisions." I said, "Wow, you must be filthy rich! Can I be your special assistant?" She replied, "Uhhhhh, no! But whenever I need a party crasher, I'll know who to call."

John and I sat there for a while longer talking to Sarah. She loved sports, so at least we had some good conversation – along with a few more samples of tequila. John and I traded telling her jokes. By her laughter, she obviously enjoyed our comedy show. John and I then decided we had our money's worth and decided to head back to our hotels while we were still able to do so. As we excused ourselves, Sarah gave us both a hug and said, "Thanks for making my night – I really needed some good laughs."

As we departed The Drink, the two young ladies at the entrance stopped us and said the person who lost their badge came by and claimed it. I was glad it all turned out well, and I want to take this opportunity to publicly thank Microsoft for the drinks and the good food - it was a fun and memorable night – but about that hangover...

The DC Storm and the Big Russian Deal

Throughout my career in marketing and sales, I have attended about 100 trade shows – primarily as an exhibitor. There have been memorable and exciting ones, while others have been forgettable and boring. During my tenure with Minuteman Power Technologies, one particular trade show that was held in Washington DC was a combination of memorable and forgettable, as well as boring and exciting.

After arriving in DC with one of our salesmen, Gerald, we headed to the convention center to set up our booth. It was a typical mild winter day in DC, and after completing the booth set-up, we walked back to our hotel which was only two blocks away. We had a quiet evening that included dinner and a few drinks, and then we both went to our respective rooms. We decided to meet for breakfast at 8:00am and then we would head over to the convention center after breakfast before the show opened at 10:00am.

The next morning, after my alarm went off, I woke up and got showered and dressed. I was about to walk out the door, and since the curtains were closed, I decided to open them to see what the weather looked like. When I opened the curtains, to my utter surprise, there was a blizzard that was dumping snow at a rapid pace. I had heard the day before that there was a slight chance of snow with little accumulation. The weather forecasters obviously missed this one badly.

Gerald and I ate breakfast, and the waitress told us that the city was shutting down – all government offices and businesses were told to close. Gerald and I were unsure whether we should go to the trade show or just hang out in the hotel. I had no idea if they would even have the show because of the storm. We decided to wade through the snow and take the two-block walk and venture off to see if the trade show was going to open. Sure enough, as they say, the show must go on. After all, we exhibitors had paid a lot of money for our booths along with travel expenses, so the organizers decided to open the show.

About half of the other exhibitors' personnel showed up, and I'm sure all of them were staying in nearby hotels because no taxis or buses were operating. The number of potential customers that roamed the aisles throughout the day could be counted on two hands. Every one of the exhibitors that made it to the show was bored to tears. We were all so bored that watching grass grow in slow motion would have been more exciting. The organizers made an announcement that the show would close at 2:00pm which was a relief for us all. When 2:00 rolled around, Gerald and I were shutting down our booth and gathering our things to leave when a tall gentleman walked into our booth. He was the only potential customer we had seen all day.

I asked if I could help him, and he replied in a distinctive Russian accent, "I know of your products, and I am here to ask a few questions." I said, "No problem, how can I assist?" He then asked for some technical information about several of our products and he seemed to be pleased with all the answers I provided. The guy then explained that he was the buyer for a large distributor of electronics in Russia, and he wanted to purchase thousands of our products. I was taken aback and said, "Did you say thousands?" He said, "Yes, I would like to split the shipments over the next six months."

I was getting a bit skeptical because no one had ever walked into our booth and asked to buy thousands of anything. He was mostly interested in our consumer-level surge suppressors which sold for about $20 each, along with our low-end battery backup systems that sold for around $100 each. I was mentally doing the math and thinking that if this guy was serious, we could be talking about a $1 million.

I was still skeptical until he said, "I will give you a scheduled order to be shipped over the next six months." He then wrote out a list of products and quantities for the initial shipment which totaled around $50,000. He then added, "I will pay cash for the first shipment and will set up letters of credit for the remaining shipments. I was becoming more convinced that he was serious about doing this large-scale deal. In all my years in sales and marketing, I had never had anything like this come up.

The Russian gentleman then asked if he could visit our office the following week and inquired if we would be able to accept the cash payment. Still in shock, I told him, "Of course we can take a cash payment." My answer was assumptive, even though our company was not really set up to do a cash transaction. Like most manufacturers, we accepted purchase orders, shipped our products, sent out invoices, and then got paid by check. I was pretty sure that if some guy showed up with $50,000 in cash, we would find a way to account for it and ship his products.

We then set up a time and date for him to meet with us at our office. We shook hands and I told him how much I appreciated him battling the weather to visit the show and stop by our booth. He said, "This is nothing compared to where I come from – this is just like another usual winter day."

Gerald and I packed up and went back to the hotel. We only had one customer, but despite the snowstorm and lack of booth traffic, it was a very profitable day. When I called and spoke with our VP of Sales to tell him about our day at the show, I started the conversation out with, "Les, I've got good news and bad news." He then said, "Give me the bad news first." I then explained that DC had a foot of snow, and the trade show was a disaster – we only had one booth visitor all day. He said, "That's horrible – what a waste of thousands of dollars of our money." I then asked, "So, should I just go ahead and skip the good news part?" He replied, "No, but it better be good!"

I then asked him if it was possible for us to accept cash as a form of payment. He asked, "How much are we talking about?" I then said, "Are you sitting down?" He replied, "Come on, just get to it." I then explained that a gentleman from Russia was going to visit our office the following week and was going to pay cash for his opening order. Les asked, "How much?" Les and I were good friends, so I wanted to jack with him some more and repeated, "Are you still sitting down?" I added, "It might take more than one person to count all the cash." He was getting aggravated (which was my goal) and said, "If you don't get on with it, I'm going to kick your ass when you get back!"

Les was a West Texas red neck, so I knew how far I could jerk his chain. I then said, "OK, OK, he'll be paying $50,000 in cash." Les then said, "Get the f… out of here – if you're lying, I'm going to be really pissed." I then replied, "He hasn't shown up with the money yet, but he seemed like a pretty serious guy who works for one of the largest Russian distributors of electronics." Les didn't say anything for about 15 seconds, and then he said, "You better not be sh……ing me, Bill." I then replied, "We'll see if he shows up, and oh, by the way, he wants to buy about a million dollars of our products over the next six months." Les then said, "Now I know you are sh……ing me!" I then reiterated that the guy said what he said, and that we'll see if he meant what he said. Les then let out a big "woo-hoo" and abruptly hung up the phone.

The Big Blowout

The rest of the 2-day show was a disaster because of the blizzard. I could have shot a canon down any aisle, and no one would have been hit. At the end of the last day,

Gerald and I packed up the booth and went back to the hotel. We decided that since our one sale was so big that we would go out and celebrate. We found a sports bar nearby so we could have a few beers, eat some dinner, and watch whatever sports were on TV.

Gerald was a big fan of exceedingly spicey hot wings, so we ordered some. I am not a glutton for punishment, but I decided to accommodate him. The bartender recommended a local wheat beer to go with the wings, so we agreed to try it.

The bartender served the beer which we both found to be quite tasty. I had tried wheat beer before and it gave me gas and a brief case of diarrhea, but I was hoping that it was a one-off incident. The barkeep served up our wings. We both were quite hungry, so we dove right in. After the first wing, I thought my mouth was on fire. I chugged down some beer to help put out the flames. The wings were nice and meaty, and I was so hungry I couldn't stop eating them. My lips were hotter than Hot Lips Houlihan (for the youngsters, that's a reference to a female character in the TV series M.A.S.H.). It seemed like the more I ate, the more the pain subsided. I suppose it was because my whole mouth and lips were burned beyond recognition and completely numb – or perhaps it was because of the multiple rounds of beer.

In any case, Gerald and I did away with several orders of hot wings and more than our share of alcoholic beverages – that wheat beer was certainly going down smoothly. After almost three hours of punishment, I told Gerald I had enough wings and it was time to go because I had a breakfast meeting with an ad rep at our hotel the following morning. I paid the tab, and we managed to saunter safely through the snow back to our hotel.

I would be remiss if I didn't tell "the rest of the story" as Paul Harvey used to say. It is a bit embarrassing for me, but I find it to be memorably funny so I will continue (with apologies to those reading this book). As one will see, the other protagonist in this story did not find it too amusing.

I woke up the next morning with a little bit of a hangover, but nothing too serious – I've had a lot worse! I took a shower, got dressed, and went down to the lobby to meet my ad rep for our breakfast appointment. As is usual for me, I got down there about ten minutes early. I was sitting on a couch in the hotel lobby when suddenly, I felt a rumbling in my stomach and on down into my intestines. I started cramping and decided I had better head for the nearest restroom because it felt like all hell was about to break loose. I made it to the restroom, sat down on the toilet, and the big blow-out began.

The wings and wheat beer were a near lethal combination. I should have known better than to eat hot wings and drink wheat beer, but it was far too late for regretting my poor decisions. Unfortunately, the wings burned as much coming out as they did going in. It was a small two-stall, two urinal rest room located in the lobby area, and although I had made several courtesy flushes, the smell was devastatingly raunchy.

I was hoping no one would come in until after I had finished and fled the scene of the crime. No such luck for an unsuspecting fella that walked into the firestorm (or should I say the odor storm). As soon as he entered and the door closed behind him, I heard him say, "Oh my God what has died in here?" I recognized that voice and peered between the crack of the stall door and realized that lucky guy was Ben, my ad rep friend.

As he continued to use the urinal, he kept saying over and over, "Oh my God, this is terrible – oh my God." I couldn't help but start laughing silently. The quiet chuckle turned into a full-blown laughing fit. I was laughing so hard I was crying, yet I dared not make a sound, otherwise I would give myself away. I can vouch for the fact that laughing hysterically and trying to stay silent is certainly one of the biggest challenges I have ever had. I was undaunted in my laugh suppression, and I heard the urinal flush.

Ben didn't pass go or collect two hundred dollars – nor did he pause to wash his hands – he wanted out there as fast as he could fly. I heard the door open and as he walked out, he said to himself, "That was the worst smell ever!"

I was finally relieved that I could finally laugh out loud – and it was hard to stop. The blow-out had subsided, and I exited the stall while still in hysterics. I washed my hands, dried them, and I thought to myself, "You have got to get it together and stop laughing." I stood there for a few more minutes and tried to calm myself down, but every time I got myself under control, I'd start laughing again – we've all been there.

After taking numerous deep breaths, I finally calmed down enough to depart from the crime scene. As I opened the door, I peeked out to see if Ben was watching me exit the restroom – he would have known I was the guilty culprit. Fortunately, he had his back turned so I stealthily exited and walked over and greeted him.

We ate breakfast and discussed our business. He casually mentioned that when he went to the restroom, it smelled like someone had dropped an atomic stink-bomb. I successfully fought the urge to break out laughing hysterically throughout our meeting. However, when I got back to my hotel room, it started all over again – another uncontrollable laughing spell hit me. Even as I write this story, I am laughing heartily as I recount it. If you found this episode disgusting, I apologize. If you found it funny, thank me for the laugh and for embarrassing myself

Now back to the Russian businessman. Sure enough, I got a call from him confirming our appointment the morning of our meeting. When he showed up, I noticed he had a large briefcase with him. I introduced him to Les, and we sat down to discuss the business deal. We all agreed on the products and the discount we could offer for a cash sale. After the terms were agreed upon, he sat his briefcase on Les's desk, opened it, and I had never seen so many $100 bills in my life – neither had Les. It was certainly a sight to behold.

As Patrick, our CFO, was counting the money, my mind began to wonder if this guy was with the Russian mob. Then I thought maybe it was drug money. I started to get nervous that we were doing something illicit. His business card seemed legit, and I saw a Russian passport in his briefcase. As it turned out, he and his company were legit, and they ultimately became a very large customer. Who would have ever thought that a great sales lead would come from such a disastrous trade show?

Teaming Against the Teamsters

For me, perhaps the most stressful trade show happened in Chicago at McCormick Place Convention Center when I was president of MICMIX Audio Products (more on that later). We were exhibiting at the National Association of Music Merchants trade show. The three officers of the company, including Bobby the VP of Engineering, David, the VP of Operations, and I arrived in Chicago on Sunday, the day before the show was to start. We allowed ourselves plenty of time to set up our booth since it was a somewhat complicated set-up with demo stations featuring our products.

When we arrived at McCormick Place, we went to our booth location. To our shock and horror, our shipment had not arrived, even though it was shipped in plenty of time. I started to panic. I went to the exhibitor's desk thinking maybe our shipment was delivered to the wrong booth location. My heart sank when they assured me that they had not received any shipment from our company. Fortunately, we had ordered a landline phone which was the only thing sitting on the floor in our booth besides three chairs. I immediately called Yellow Freight, who we had chosen to ship our booth equipment. Of course, it was rather difficult to get anyone on the phone because it was Sunday, but I finally was able to speak with a human when I called an 800 number.

I provided the tracking number and was informed that our shipment was in St. Louis. I was about to have a stroke – our trade show would be disastrous if we didn't have our booth. I imagined the three of us guys sitting in chairs twiddling our thumbs with nothing but our good looks to show off. I explained to the lady on the phone that I wanted to speak with the highest-ranking person I could talk to. She said she doubted she would be able to contact anyone in authority because it was Sunday. She put me on hold for several minutes and then came back and gave me a gentleman's name and number to call.

I immediately called him and was pleased to learn that he was expecting my call. The lady I had spoken to called him and informed him of the situation. I was surprised when he told me he was the regional vice president, and he was speaking to me from his home phone. I explained that we were a small company that invested $10,000 in the booth space along with all the booth-building costs and travel expenses. We could NOT afford to absorb this disaster. I was madder than a mosquito in a mannequin factory, but I pled my case in a professional manner as calmly as I could. He said he completely understood and apologized that Yellow Freight had put us in this position. He then told me that he would investigate what happened and would call me back. I then said, "I really don't care why we don't have our shipment, all I want is for you to get it here as soon as it is humanly possible." He then said he would call me back shortly.

The three of us were still panic-stricken. We were running into each other as we paced back and forth in our empty booth space. After a long 30 minutes, the phone rang. He told me, "I have good news and bad news," and he then explained that they had found out the shipment had been misplaced and was sitting in their warehouse in St. Louis – that was the good news. He then said, "The bad news is that our next shipment to Chicago doesn't leave until mid-day tomorrow and won't arrive until tomorrow night."

My patience was at a boiling point because the trade show started the next morning. I said, "Sir, that is unacceptable. Do I need to rent a truck and drive myself to St. Louis (4 hours away), pick up the shipment, and then drive back to Chicago tonight? We must have our booth before the show starts at 10:00 in the morning?" He apologized again and I said, "Sir, I would truly appreciate it if you could kindly figure something out – we desperately need your help." He paused for a moment and said, "Let me call you back – I'll see what I can do."

After another long 30 minutes, he called back and said, "Mr. Allen, here's the best I can do for you." I held my breath, and he explained, "I need to transfer a cargo van to our Chicago location, and I found one of our drivers who can leave at 4:00am tomorrow morning. We can load your freight in the cargo van and have it to you around 8:30am – that's the best I can do." I knew that he had jumped through some hoops to make it happen, so I said, "Your help and accommodation is greatly appreciated – we'll make it work if you can make it work."

We then went back to our hotel, and I called all of our manufacturer's reps and any friends I knew who were attending the show to ask for their help in setting up our booth the following morning. It was a long and nervous night.

We three officers arrived at McCormick Place at around 7:30am the following morning, anxiously anticipating the arrival of our shipment. I went to the show's freight desk to update them on our situation. I explained that we need the shipment delivered to our booth as soon as it arrives at the dock. The supervisor said, "Sir, we've got a lot going on this morning, and I have no idea when we will be able to get your shipment delivered to your booth." It's important to note that the supervisor and all the freight delivery workers are Teamsters. Recall that we were in Chicago where unions pretty much run everything – plus, they move at their own pace and no one tells them what to do, how to do it, or when to do it.

I knew I was probably in for a battle, but I had gotten Yellow Freight to do us a solid, so I was prepared for the fight. I walked back to the booth and gathered up my two partners and eight others who had shown up to help us set up the booth. Our group assembled on the receiving dock awaiting that Yellow Freight cargo van.

The dock foreman was not happy that we were standing around in the unloading area. He insisted that we leave immediately. I explained the situation to him, but he was not in the mood to cooperate. He not-so-kindly told us to "Get the f… off my dock!" I did my best to convince him that we would unload the cargo van ourselves when it arrived and would not bother him or any of his workers. Being the warm, caring person that he was, he said, "You ain't touching anything on this f….ing dock unless you're a union worker – I run things around here." I didn't want to rile him up any more than he already was, so I gathered our group together and went back just inside the convention center where I had a view of the dock. Eight o'clock rolled around. Then 8:10. At 8:15, evidently it was breaktime for the union guys, so everybody went on their break.

At around 8:20, as luck would have it, I saw a Yellow Freight van pull up to the dock. I ran outside to make sure it was our shipment, and sure enough, it was. I motioned to my crew, and we unloaded everything in a matter of minutes (which would have probably taken the union folks at least an hour). I told my crew to put everything inside the convention center doors just past the loading dock so that when the dock Nazi came back from his break, he couldn't do anything about it.

At 8:30 when break time was over, Mr. Warmth showed up as I was carrying the last few items from the van. He stopped me and said, "What the f… are you doing back on my dock?" I said, "Sorry, sir, we have to go set up our booth." He then affectionately asked, "Did you turn in a f…ing job order at the freight desk?" I said, "Sorry, but there's no need for that since we already unloaded everything." He then shouted, "I'm going to report you to my supervisor and show management!" I said, "That's fine, do what you need to do, but I've got a booth to set up."

My crew carried everything to our booth location, and we started setting everything up. We were all throwing things together as fast as we could, and when 10:00 rolled around, I breathed a huge sigh of relief because the booth was ready for customers. I shouted to the crew, "Woo hoo – we did it!"

Shortly after 10:00 as I was wiping sweat off my face, a NAMM show management person that I knew approached me. He said, "Bill, the Teamster's rep filed a complaint against you – you do know what you did broke all the rules." I proceeded to explain what happened, filling him in on what it took to get our shipment delivered. I told him, "Jim, I am sorry, but we did what we had to do." He paused for a moment and then replied, "I understand – I probably would have done the same thing if I were in your shoes." He then shook my hand and as he walked away, he said, "Hope you guys have a great show!"

Later in the day, I was speaking with a fellow exhibitor. I retold the whole sad saga of our shipment getting lost, but we finally were able to set up earlier that day – despite the pushback from the teamster bully. I explained that the foreman was not going to let us unload the van, but we went ahead and unloaded while they were on a break.

My friend said, "Bill, messing with the unions at a trade show can be dangerous." He continued, "I have a buddy who was an exhibitor here at McCormick Place that got crossways with the Teamsters. When he showed up the next morning, evidently one of the union workers had driven a forklift into their booth and destroyed the whole structure the night before."

I lost sleep over thinking we might suffer the same fate. As I anxiously made my way to the booth the following morning, I was relieved that everything was still intact. Perhaps the only reason our booth survived is because the foreman bully didn't know our booth number. I felt like we dodged a bullet – or perhaps a forklift. The entire trade show industry is replete with union workers, and for the rest of my career, I went out of my way to be nice to them, but I never let them push me around.

The show went off smoothly. We had a successful exhibition of our products and gained many new customers. When we got back to our office the following week, I called the Yellow Freight regional VP and thanked him for coming through for us, and despite their screw-up, I would continue to be a customer because he did what he said he would do.

Meeting Two Guitar Gods

Two more interesting tidbits regarding that NAMM show. First, one day during the show, I looked down the aisle and saw Eddie van Halen (great guitarist for his band called Van Halen) walking with Valerie Bertinelli (his TV star wife). They made their way into our booth and Eddie said, "Hey, I know who you guys are – you make some really nice reverb units." I said, "Thanks Eddie, I'm thrilled that you use some of our products." We had a nice chat, then we shook hands, and I gave him my business card. I also told him to let me know if I could be of any further assistance in the future. Vallerie had started wandering off, so Eddie followed her like a good husband.

At the end of the second day of the show, I had another interesting encounter. I was walking down one of the aisles and I saw a guy sitting alone on a stool in a booth playing a guitar. He had headphones on and was grooving out. I stopped in my tracks and thought he looked familiar. The exhibitor sign in the booth said Power-soak. It then dawned on me that the guy playing guitar was Tom Scholz, the lead guitarist and genius behind the band Boston. I was a huge fan of the group, and I always wondered how he achieved the unique sound of his guitar. The magic was contained in his patented guitar effects device called the Power-soak.

I wandered into the booth, and he took off his headphones. He then introduced himself. I told him I was a big fan and was thrilled to meet him. I also told him I was mystified how he achieved his unique guitar sound. Tom was an engineering graduate from MIT, and when he started explaining how the Power-soak worked, my eyes were crossed, and I had no idea what he was saying – it was engineer-speak that was completely over my head.

He then let me put the headphones on and he started ripping through some of his famous riffs off Boston's first album. He was adjusting the Power-soak and explaining what was happening electronically – again, it was way beyond my comprehension. I was thoroughly enamored with the sound he was able to get out of his famous 1968 Les Paul gold-top guitar. I spent about 15 minutes chatting with him – it was certainly another great experience for me to have met such a musical and engineering genius behind the iconic band Boston, whose debut album sold an incredible 20 million copies.

Meeting Eddie Van Halen, Valerie Bertinelli, and Tom Scholz was certainly not on my bucket list – those were experiences that were nice to add to my list of unexpected encounters.

Section V

Close Encounters of the Famous Kind

Chapter 16

A Night With Les Paul

As mentioned earlier, I have had my unfair share of crazy travel stories. Perhaps the same is true for my encounters with famous people. I have had the pleasure of meeting some very famous people, and I am happy to say none of them were jerks. In fact, they all were very congenial, and they provided me with good stories that I can share, along with substantial memories that I cherish.

I was in New York City on business when I got a call from a magazine ad rep named Mike who asked me if I had dinner plans. I said I didn't have any plans, so I told him I would be happy to meet him for dinner. He lived in Manhattan, and we met at Mickey Mantle's restaurant and bar near Central Park. We had a very nice dinner, and I enjoyed speaking with Mike. We talked about how much we both loved music. As he was paying for the meal, he casually asked, "Would you like to go see Les Paul play tonight?" I looked at him like he was crazy and said, "You've got to be kidding me, right?" Mike said, "No, I'm not kidding. Les plays every Monday night at a small club called Fat Tuesday in The Village." I said, "Of course, I'd love to see Les Paul play." We hopped in a taxi and headed to the bar.

For those that do not know who Les Paul is, suffice it to say that he was one of the most accomplished and revered guitar players to ever live. He is also acclaimed as the

"Godfather of the Modern Recording Studio," having invented multitrack recording, sound on sound recording, along with a wide variety of electronic gadgets that transformed the world of studio recording. Les Paul was arguably the most important and most influential individual in the history of modern recorded music. He had a highly advanced inventive mind that was always pursuing the next innovation. He was an icon's icon.

Les Paul also advanced the guitar world to new heights when he worked with Gibson Guitar company in 1952 in designing a new style of guitar. Together, they developed and released a solid body model that has become one of the most widely purchased styles of guitars ever built. Nearly every great guitar player owns a Les Paul model. Any guitar player worth their salt has also studied and copied his playing style. He had an unmatched impact on guitar playing techniques and guitar design.

Beyond all his exploits in recording and being a great guitar player, Les Paul was a prolific songwriter, an engaging live performer, along with being a seasoned singer that at one time had eight songs on the charts with his wife and singing partner Mary Ford. They became the top-selling artists of their era and continued topping the charts for more than ten years. Les Paul was also the prime driving force in establishing and building Capital Records into the dominant record company that it is today.

To further add to his unprecedented resume, Les Paul and Mary Ford starred in a television musical show that ran for seven years with 170 episodes. In my humble opinion, there will never be another person in the music industry that will ever be more influential and impactful in so many ways than Les Paul. He was a superstar whose light will forever shine in the world of music.

Now that I have established his unmatched and impeccable credentials, hopefully, it's not hard to understand how excited I was to have the opportunity to hear him play.

Meeting The Man

The taxi stopped in front of the Fat Tuesday bar. Mike paid for the taxi ride, and we walked through the front door. We headed down a short hallway and then down a flight of stairs. At the bottom, we took a right turn and entered the bar. It wasn't what I expected. I thought he'd be playing in a large, fancy venue and there would be a huge crowd – after all, it was Les Paul. Instead, I saw that it was a rather small venue with a bar along one wall and probably ten or twelve 4-top tables. It was a bit dark and dank.

I looked over at the bar area and saw 8 or 9 people standing in a line, and they were all carrying Les Paul guitars. I then realized that the man himself was sitting at the bar signing his autograph on each guitar and engagingly talking to each person. I was blown away and totally jealous that I didn't have a guitar for him to autograph. What a thrill it was for all those people to have a signed Les Paul guitar – not to mention the fact that the value of the guitar after it was signed increased dramatically. I was thoroughly impressed that he would do that.

Mike and I sat down at a table directly in front of the stage to have a ringside seat to watch the master play. There were only about 20 or 25 people in the bar. Again, I was confused that there wasn't a huge crowd, but then I thought to myself, "This is far better to see him play in such an intimate setting." The thought then ran through my head that everyone in the city of New York must be out of their minds for not taking the opportunity to see Les Paul perform.

After autographing all the guitars, Les got up and sauntered to the stage to join his bass player and drummer. The bass player picked up his upright acoustic bass. The drummer sat down behind a drum set that included a bass drum, a snare drum, one tom-tom, one cymbal, and a high hat. I thought, "Wow, that certainly is different than many rock drummers that are surrounded by a dozen drums and ten cymbals." Les then picked up his custom Gibson Les Paul guitar – which itself was worth a small fortune – and tuned it up without the need for a tuner. He then said, "Ok boys, let's go," and counted off the first song.

What then transpired was pure musical magic. The bass player and the drummer gave an understated yet tasteful performance, and Les Paul showed off his magnificent skills that featured his unique execution of unmatched artistry. Not a word was sung the whole night. It was purely an instrumental musical experience painted on a colorful canvas by artists that were undoubtedly on top of their game, even though the three performers were in their 80's. It was also a lesson I learned – it's not the amount of expensive, intricate gear and gadgets that makes a musician, it's the artistry that emerges when simple instruments are played to perfection.

Mike and I were both mesmerized in listening to the sonic tapestry that was woven by these three musicians. Les was very charming as he bantered back and forth with Mike and me. He joked around, told stories between songs, and was affably engaging throughout the show. After about an hour of playing, Les said they were going to take a break because they were old and needed the rest. Les put his guitar down and headed off the stage.

To my utter shock, he walked over to our table and asked if he could sit down and join us. I said, "Of course you can join us! Can I buy you a drink? He replied, "No, I gave up alcohol many years ago when my doctor threatened to fire me as a patient if I didn't stop drinking. I live a boring life and have left all my vices for everyone else to enjoy."

He sat there during the entire break and talked with us. He told story after story and had us laughing hysterically with his colorful narration of his many adventures. I told him I was from Dallas and was honored to meet him and hear him play.

He told one story that was meaningful in its own way. He explained, "I was driving in Manhattan one day when I went through an intersection and some stupid SOB ran a red light and broadsided me on the driver's side. My left elbow (his guitar-playing elbow) was crushed when the door caved in, and that bastard just drove away. I was trapped in the car, otherwise I would have chased that SOB down." He continued, "They took me to the hospital in an ambulance and when I got to there, the doctor said my elbow was in bad shape and they had to be surgically repaired and set it into one position. The doctor said I would never have full motion of my elbow." He then told the doctor to set it in an "L" shape so he could still play the guitar. The doctor knew who he was and gladly obliged.

I could only imagine the anxiety he experienced, learning that he might never be able to play guitar again. He finished his story by saying, "That m…..f….er who ran into me tried to put me out of business, but the doctor was able to set it in a way that I could still play." I said, "Well, thank God it all worked out OK." He then replied, "I'd still like to find that SOB and put him down like a sick dog."

After several more stories, Les then said, "As much as I like talking to you guys, it's time for me to do a little more playing – is that all right with you guys?" We both chimed in and said, "Of course!" As he was getting up, I asked him if he would autograph something for me. He replied, "Yeah, sure, no problem."

Unfortunately for me, I didn't have anything for him to write with or any paper. Our waiter was close by, and I asked if he had a pen and a piece of paper. Fortunately, he had both. I tore the paper in half and handed the pen and papers to Les. I had explained that I was the lead singer and guitar player in my band back in Dallas.

I told him one of the autographs was for my lead guitarist who owned a Gibson Les Paul guitar, and his name was Carl. Les kindly wrote, "To Carl – keep on rocking! Les Paul." I told him Carl would be ecstatic (which he was). I handed the second piece of paper to Les and told him that one was for me. He then wrote, "To Bill, Howdy Tex! Les Paul" and he dated it 1-95.

He then got up and said, "You guys are great – thanks for letting me hang out with you." I said, "No, No, thank you – it was a thrill of a lifetime to meet you and talk to you." I stood up to shake his hand, then he reached out, grabbed my hand, and then pulled me in and gave me a big hug.

Mike and I sat there and listened until the end. Les continued to banter with Mike and me between songs. After they got through playing, Les brought over the other two members of the trio and introduced them to us. I told them what a wonderful experience that night was and how much I loved their music. Les then said, "Come back and see us, Tex!"

As Mike and I were riding back in the taxi to my hotel, I told him how much that night meant to me and thanked him profusely for making it happen.

I put the autograph in a safe place and intended to frame it sometime in the future. The following Christmas, my wife Linda handed me a present and told me it was a special gift. When I opened it up, I saw the Les Paul autograph that was beautifully framed. To this day, it is one of my most cherished possessions. Whenever I look at it, I am transported back to a time and place when I enjoyed a once-in-a lifetime experience. It was one of my most memorable musical highlights.

Chapter 17

Bigwigs in Buffalo

When I worked at Minuteman Power Technologies, I travelled frequently to Buffalo, NY because we had a major customer there. I had some interesting experiences, and as you might imagine, some of them involved very large amounts of snow and frigidly cold temperatures. It was not bad travelling there during the warm half of the year, but when it came to the winter months, it was so unpleasant for me. Since I despised cold weather, my fellow team members had to drag me kicking and screaming and force me onto the airplane.

There were a few times when I would travel to Buffalo only to be held hostage in my hotel room because it snowed so much that everything shut down. Roads would become impassable, restaurants would be closed, and appointments would be cancelled. In the winter, I always stayed in a hotel that had its own restaurant because if everything shut down, at least I would be able to break into the kitchen and find some sustenance.

Buffalo is a very old city, having been settled around 1770 by a few brave souls who had the temerity (or stupidity) to put their roots down there. Don't get me wrong, I like Buffalo – I just hate the winters (and most people from Buffalo would agree with me). The people are very nice, and they gave the world a wonderful new food group – Buffalo style chicken wings. There are various versions of how Buffalo wings came to be, but there's little doubt that the owners of the Anchor Bar in Buffalo were the originators. Yes, I have had my share of wings at this humble establishment, and they were always a treat, but I never again drank wheat beer with wings! Lesson learned.

Buffalo is also famous for its close proximity to its most famous global tourist attraction, Niagara Falls. On my first trip to Buffalo, I took an afternoon to go see this amazing natural wonder. I made several subsequent trips to see Niagara, but the most interesting time was in the middle of winter. Much of the falls were iced over and it truly was a sight to behold – despite the fact that I almost froze to death.

I was always awed by both the beauty and power of the falls. Speaking of power, Buffalo also has the distinction of being the first city to be electrified, thanks to the falls and one of the most brilliant inventors of the late 19th and early 20th centuries, Nickolai Tesla. In 1896, the first hydroelectric power plant developed by Tesla delivered power to Buffalo.

I found the people of Buffalo to be very cordial. They are also a hearty bunch as one can imagine. Many of them have a unique accent as well. I recall checking into my hotel on one trip and the front desk clerk was an older lady who was a Buffalo native. She gave me the usual hotel instructions and then said, "Oh, and don't forget our happy hour with two-for-one drinks and we are serving free tack-o's."

With an inquisitive look on my face I asked, "What are tack-o's?" She looked at me like I was crazy and said, "You've never had tack-o's before? And you're from Texas?" I was still puzzled, then she chimed in and said, "You know, the crispy corn shells that are filled with meat and cheese?" It suddenly dawned on me that something was being lost in the translation, and I said, "Oh, you mean Mexican tacos?" She then smiled and said, "Yes, Mexican tack-o's." We both had a good laugh. I grabbed my bags and headed to my room, and I was looking forward to eating some of those Buffalo tack-o's.

Sabre Rattling and Razzing

Whenever someone from Buffalo asked where I was from, they would always get a scowl on their face and say, "Ooooo, you're from Dallas." Buffalo and Dallas have a history when it comes to NFL football and NHL hockey.

Buffalo has two professional sports teams, the NFL Buffalo Bills and the NHL Buffalo Sabers. The people are full-on crazy for the Bills and the Sabers – they are all die-hard fans. The Bills have the distinction of being the only team to ever go to four straight Super Bowls and lose them all – two of those to the Dallas Cowboys and both were blow-outs. The Sabers have been to two Stanley Cup playoffs and lost both. One of those defeats was handed to them by the Dallas Stars. As one can imagine, there's not a lot of love for Dallas among Buffalo sports fans.

I happened to have scheduled a special dinner for the top 25 salespeople at our large customer in Buffalo during game five of the Stars and Sabers Stanley Cup playoffs in 1999. I had the hosting facility bring in TVs so we could watch the game while having dinner. To show them some love, I went out and bought numerous Sabers jerseys, hockey sticks, and other goodies to raffle off to the salespeople. The giveaways were a big hit, but unfortunately for them (and me), the Sabers lost the game 2 to 0.

The next game (game six in the series) was a hard-fought battle which I was watching at home. At the end of regulation, the score was tied 1 to 1. The first overtime ended with the score still tied as did the second overtime period. Late in the third overtime, the Stars' Brett Hull managed to sneak in a very controversial goal to win the Stanley

Cup for the Dallas Stars. The Buffalo players and coaches vehemently protested, but the goal was eventually ruled valid. It was a bitter pill to swallow for Buffalo fans. It was another loss to a Dallas team, and it put the final nail in the coffin for my reputation and well-being in Buffalo. But the story doesn't end there.

On my subsequent visits to see our large customer in Buffalo, I was always greeted with the customary scowls and the chants of "No goal!" from the salespeople – of course it was all in good-natured fun, but it still made me uncomfortable. I had to figure out a way to resurrect my reputation and show them some love. I had another sales event coming up in the following summer, and I wanted to do something special.

I had the idea to bring in a Buffalo sports celebrity for my event – maybe that would make them happy and win me some points. The most famous Bills player was hall of fame quarterback Jim Kelly. I reached out to his agent to see what it would cost to bring him in to meet the sales team, take pictures, and sign autographs. The agent said he would talk to Jim about it. I got a phone call a few days later, and the agent said Jim would do the event if we donated $10,000 to his Hunter's Hope foundation.

I had read that Jim's son, Hunter, was born in 1997 and had a very rare nervous system disease called Krabbe Leukodystrophy that was fatal. Jim worked tirelessly to help his newborn son and raise money for research. I sought approval from my company's president to make the donation, and he enthusiastically gave me a yes.

From Zero to Hero

I was happy to announce Jim Kelly's appearance at my upcoming event, hoping it would get me out of the doghouse with my Buffalo salespeople. When the day of the event came, Jim showed up around 10:00am. Again, I had a large shopping spree at the local sporting goods store and bought a bunch of Buffalo Bills goodies for Jim to sign and give away. We hung out in a conference room while groups of 4 to 6 people came in to meet Jim. I also hired a photographer to take Polaroid pictures of Jim with every salesperson as well as our customer's management team and administrative staff. Jim signed each picture and all the giveaway goodies I had purchased.

We took a break to have lunch in the company cafeteria, and then we returned to the conference room so more groups could meet Jim. He stayed until after 2:00pm, making sure everyone who wanted a picture or autograph was taken care of. He was the nicest guy anyone could ever meet, and I enjoyed hanging out with him and hearing lots of NFL stories. The entire event was far beyond my expectations – he made it a very extraordinary day for all those Buffalo fans – and me.

I was honored to be in the presence of a hall of famer and such a wonderful man. As he was leaving, he thanked me profusely for making the donation. I told him it was the best $10,000 we had ever spent, and I wished all the best for him, his family, and most of all, Hunter. Unfortunately, Hunter was not expected to live more than three years. He eventually succumbed to the disease six months after his eighth birthday.

As I made my way out the door at the end of the day, everyone was high fiving me, hugging me, and applauding. It felt good to make lifelong memories for those long-suffering fans. I'm sure they all still remember that day. Because of Jim Kelly, I went from zero to hero in just a few short hours. The ever-present scowls were replaced with smiles. It was a good day.

Another Encounter with a Legend

I boarded the plane to take another business trip to Buffalo and sat down in my seat. I was fortunate enough to be upgraded to first class because of my platinum status on American Airlines. I settled in and started reading my newspaper and the pilot announced the door was about to be closed prior to departure. I saw there was still an empty seat next to me. I was engrossed in my newspaper, and I felt someone sit down in that seat. I noticed out of the corner of my eye the gentleman had very large, muscular legs (he was wearing shorts).

After completing the article I was reading, I glanced over and made eye contact with the gentleman. He said, "Hi, how are you doing?" I said, "I am doing great, how are you?" He responded with a big smile and said, "I am great." He probably thought I was a bit crazy because I stared at him. My mind was trying to process who he was, and then it suddenly hit me that I was sitting next to Herschel Walker. I reached out to shake his hand and introduced myself. I told him what an honor it was to meet him. He continued his big smile and said, "Well, I'm happy to meet you, Bill."

I explained that I was a huge football fan and that I had watched him play while he was on his way to winning the Heisman Trophy at University of Georgia and then playing for the Dallas Cowboys and Minnesota Vikings. I came to learn he was more than just a great football player. He was a track star in high school and at the University of Georgia, along with being an avid student of martial arts.

We talked incessantly for the 2 ½ hour flight, and as we spoke, he continuously autographed pictures of himself. He had a briefcase full of letters requesting a signed picture, mostly from Georgia fans. He personalized each one. I should have requested a signed picture, but I foolishly did not.

As the plane was about to land, I was curious as to why he was going to Buffalo. I thought it was an unusual destination – not everyone beats a pathway to Buffalo in the middle of winter. I asked him why he was punishing himself for going to Buffalo in the middle of winter. He explained that he participated in an anti-drug program called "Just Say No." He was scheduled to speak to high school kids at the Niagara Falls Convention Center the following day with Olympic gymnast Cathy Rigby, several Buffalo Bills football players, and some TV celebrities. As we deboarded the plane, Herschel invited me to come and check out their program. I told him if I got through with my business meetings in time, I would be glad to attend. We shook hands and he asked me if I made it out to make sure to track him down. I assured him I would.

Sure enough, I finished my meetings and then headed for the Niagara Falls Convention Center which was only a 20-minute drive from Buffalo. I made my way into the auditorium and was able to see most of the program. After it was over, I headed to where I saw Herschel and the other celebrities exiting the stage. When I got there, several security personnel were standing guard. I explained to one of them that I knew Herschel and he told me to look him up. The guard scowled at me; evidently, he thought my story was highly dubious. However, one of the event organizers overheard our conversation. She told me to sit tight, and she would see if she could find Herschel and then asked for my name.

A few minutes later, I saw Herschel walking down the hallway. When he saw me, he said, "Bill, I am so glad you made it out!" He came up to me and gave me a big hug and then said, "Let me introduce you to everybody. As I began walking backstage, I couldn't help but cast a slight sneer at the security guard and then walked off with Herschel. He introduced me to all the celebrities and we had another nice long chat.

After about 30 minutes, I explained that I had to get back to Buffalo for a late afternoon meeting and thanked him for introducing me to everybody. He reached into his pocket and pulled out a business card and said, "Here's my card – that's my home phone number – let's get together when we both get back to Dallas." We then said our goodbyes and I headed out to my meeting. I kept his card in my wallet, but somehow, it mysteriously disappeared – I suppose I lost it. In any case, I must say that Herschel was one of the nicest people you'd ever want to meet – always smiling and congenial. It was a pleasure and an honor to have crossed paths and briefly hang out with a football legend and an all-around nice guy.

Chapter 18

Hangin' With a Hall of Famer

One day while I was working at Texas Instruments in the Radio Frequency Identification (RFID) division, I got an unusual phone call. As mentioned elsewhere in this book, I was the key spokesperson and evangelist for RFID technology, and I was interviewed and quoted in several nationally distributed publications.

One day, I answered my phone, and a woman said, "Hello Mr. Allen, my name is Mary, and I am one of Emmitt Smith's business managers. Mr. Smith has read several articles where you were quoted, and he would like to meet with you to discuss and learn more about RFID technology." My first inclination was to say, "Yeah, right, who is this calling to prank me?" and then hang up. Instead, I said, "Are you talking about the REAL Emmitt Smith?" She said, "Yes sir, I am. He'd like to set up a time when you can meet with him in the next few days." I was becoming convinced that she was for real, and I said, "I'd be happy to meet with him on Friday, how does right after lunch sound?" Mary said, "Let's do two o'clock." I replied, "Works for me. I'll look forward to it." She replied, "Perfect. Thank you very much."

After I hung up the phone, I sat there for a few seconds wondering if I had been hallucinating or pranked. I then got up and went into our division VP's office and told him about the upcoming meeting. Dave, who was from England said, "That's really great, who is Emmitt Smith?" I chuckled and said, "He's a hall of fame football player who played for the Dallas Cowboys!" Dave replied, "Oh, you must mean American football, not our kind of football." I answered, "Dave, he is one of the most famous people in the US. Are you kidding me?" Dave said, "Yes, I'm kidding, I have heard of him. When is the meeting?" I told him it was at two o'clock on Friday. Dave then told me I had to contact TI's security team to let them know a celebrity was visiting our campus – it was policy. He said the security team would accompany us throughout his visit for Emmitt's protection.

I then informed my team that we would be having a famous visitor on Friday and explained to them they had to be on their best behavior during the visit. When they asked who it was, I told them, "It's someone who is Dallas Cowboy and NFL royalty – the one and only Emmitt Smith." Everyone was excited.

Friday rolled around and my team and I were anxiously anticipating Emmitt's visit. Sure enough, precisely at two o'clock, I got a call from the receptionist saying that I had a visitor at the front whose name was Emmitt Smith. I told her I would be right there. I then called security and let them know of his arrival. I walked out to the lobby and there he was chatting with the receptionist and the security team. I introduced myself and welcomed him.

I took him back to where my team was located and introduced Emmitt to everyone. He was very cordial and friendly. My team was thrilled to meet him. We toured the facility and then he and I went into a conference room for our discussion. The security guard who accompanied us stood diligently outside the door. I had gathered some brochures and samples for Emmitt.

He explained to me that he had a small investment in a local RFID company and was looking at expanding his investments in other companies in the industry. I spoke to him about market size and what the future might hold for the technology. He asked a lot of questions, and our meeting ended up lasting 2 ½ hours.

When we concluded the meeting, I accompanied him back to the lobby (along with the ever-vigilant security guard). I gave him my business card and my cell phone number. He them gave me his cell phone number and said, "Bill, I enjoyed meeting you, and thanks for all the info you provided – it was very helpful." I said, "No problem, it was an honor meeting and talking with you – let me know if I can be of any more service." He then replied, "I'll call you next week – let's get together for lunch." I said, "Sure, I'd love that!" He then left the building and drove off in his Porsche. I walked back to my office thinking, "He is really a very nice guy." I was thoroughly impressed as were all my team members.

On Wednesday the following week, my cell phone rang, and it was Emmitt. He said, "Hey Brother Bill, let's do lunch on Friday – does that work for you?" I answered, "Sure, that would be great." He said, "Let's do noon at the Addison Point restaurant." I replied, "Sounds great – see you then."

After I hung up, I sauntered over to where my team members were gathered. I stuck out my chest and proudly exclaimed, "My new best friend Emmitt is taking me to lunch on Friday!" One of my smart-alecky team members said, "Emmitt who?" I said, "The football hall of famer that you met last week, you fool." He then said, "Oh, THAT Emmitt." We all had a good laugh.

Friday rolled around and I arrived at the restaurant about fifteen minutes early – I certainly didn't want to be late for my very important date! I walked into the restaurant and told the Matre'd that I was having lunch with Emmitt Smith and requested a quiet spot for us to sit. As we walked to the table, the Matre'd said, "We love having Mr. Smith – he's a regular customer here." I sat down and a few minutes later, Emmitt came strutting up to the table, shook my hand, and then sat down. We exchanged usual pleasantries and then talked about our families, football, and more about RFID technology. Throughout our lunch, I could see several customers in the restaurant pointing to Emmitt. He was obviously very famous and very recognizable.

When we walked out of the restaurant, three very lovely young ladies were standing there waiting for us to emerge. They had their papers and pens ready and asked Emmitt for his autograph. They all said how their husbands were going to be so jealous that they got to meet Emmitt Smith. Again, he was very cordial and accommodating and posed for pictures with them.

As we walked to our cars, I said, "I thought they were waiting for me and wanted my autograph and picture – I'm so disappointed." Emmitt laughed and replied, "It gets old, but it's OK, it comes with the territory." Emmitt then gave me a hug and told me how much he enjoyed our lunch and that we had to do it again soon. I said. "No problem, any time, any place." He said he was going to be out of town for a week or so, but he'd call me when he got back because he was working on some ideas for RFID technology.

The Jersey Idea

Emmitt was soaking up as much info on RFID technology that he could find. I emailed him several more articles as well as info on various applications for RFID. About two weeks after our lunch meeting, my cell phone rang. It was Emmitt. He said, "Hey Brother Bill, I'm back in town, can we get together for lunch tomorrow? I have a great idea for an RFID application." I told him that it would be great, and we decided to meet at the same restaurant at noon.

When I arrived, Emmitt was already seated at a table. I sat down and we exchanged the usual pleasantries. He told me he was considering going on *Dancing with The Stars*. It was a very popular and highly rated TV show. I told him he should do it and that I was sure he would do well since he used so many elusive moves in avoiding would-be tacklers while becoming the all-time leading rusher in the NFL.

The conversation then turned to RFID. For those that do not know, RFID is obviously an identification technology that uses radio frequency. An RFID label is similar to a barcode, but instead of using printed bars, RFID uses a microchip to store data and an antenna to communicate with a wireless reader. The chip also carries a serial number that serves as a unique identifier. Common things that use RFID include toll tags and "tap and go" credit cards. There are hundreds of different applications that use RFID. Some of those applications utilize RFID as an authentication mechanism to prevent counterfeiting since the RFID chip carries a unique identifier. One other widely used application that uses RFID is the key or key fob in virtually every car. It is an anti-theft mechanism that is very effective.

As an interesting aside, the adoption of RFID technology as an anti-theft device for cars was brought on by a historic event. When the Berlin wall fell, and the Soviet Union was subsequently dismantled, Eastern Europeans were free to travel to Western Europe. Unfortunately for the westerners, the easterners decided to take souvenirs home with them, including cars. Auto theft skyrocketed during the first few years, and insurance companies got together with automobile manufacturers to find an anti-theft mechanism. RFID technology was the answer. RFID chips are now used by every auto manufacturer to prevent theft.

As our lunch was served, Emmitt told me that he wanted to use RFID to authenticate sports memorabilia. I thought it was a great idea, and I had some vague knowledge that counterfeiting sports memorabilia was a major problem. Game-worn jerseys are worth a lot of money, especially for future NFL hall of famers like Emmitt. He then told me what inspired the idea.

Emmitt said that when he broke the all-time rushing record, he wore four jerseys that day. After the first quarter, he took off his jersey and said, "This one's for Jerry Jones [owner of the Dallas Cowboys]." After the second quarter, he said he took his jersey off and donated that one to his own charitable foundation. He explained that the jersey he wore for the third quarter was one he would keep for himself. He then said, "After I broke the record in the fourth quarter, an NFL Hall of Fame representative was waiting on the sideline after the game. That one went straight to the Hall of Fame."

I was wondering where Emmitt was going with this. He then explained that the week following the game, there was an "authentic game worn jersey worn by Emmitt Smith during his record-breaking run" that was posted on eBay. He explained that other sports memorabilia websites boasted the same claim. Emmitt said, "Bill, I know where those four jerseys are, and if someone bought those fake jerseys, they got ripped off – that's terrible, and somebody needs to do something to prevent it." Emmitt even got the FBI involved to investigate. He told me that he researched the subject, and some studies found that 50% of sports memorabilia is counterfeit, with other estimates up to 80 or 90%.

Emmitt reached into his pants pocket and pulled out one of the sample RFID tags that I had given him. The tag was designed to be used to identify and track commercially used uniforms. The tag was waterproof, was a little smaller than a quarter, and it could be sewn into the hem of a garment. It was designed for a large industrial uniform company that wanted better tracking of their uniform rental inventory. He said, "Bill, this is it! This is huge!" He continued, "These tags can be sewn into game worn jerseys, and they can be tracked and authenticated." I said, "Emmitt, that's a brilliant solution to a big problem – you're a genius!"

He told me he was going to reach out to the NFL and propose the idea to them. He then asked, "If I can get a meeting with the NFL, will you go to New York with me so we can pitch the idea?" I said, "Of course!" He told me he would work on it and get back to me. We then finished up our lunch. I went back to work, and he went back to being Emmitt Smith in retirement – whatever that involved.

Emmitt did reach out to the NFL bigwigs, but sadly, they did not show any interest. The RFID start-up company that he invested in began pursuing the concept and developed a software application that used RFID tags for authentication. They had some success at sports memorabilia shows. Surprisingly to me, the application of RFID technology in sports memorabilia never took off like I thought it would – or like Emmitt had hoped for since he had invested money into the RFID company. It seemed like a no-brainer application and the NFL was remiss in not adopting Emmitt's idea.

One of the most interesting pieces in my small sports memorabilia collection is an autographed picture of Emmitt that he gave me containing an RFID label for authentication. It was one of only a few samples that were made, and probably the only existing autographed copy. I got the picture professionally framed and it is hanging proudly in my office.

Emmitt and I in Denver

The second annual RFID World trade show that I helped develop in conjunction with Shorecliff Communications and their president, Tim Downs, was scheduled to take place in Denver in March of 2004. I was director of marketing for the RFID division at the time. TI-RFID was the signature sponsor of the event, and several weeks prior to the show, I had the brilliant idea of having Emmitt Smith come to speak at the conference. I was sure that having him there would be a boon for the burgeoning conference.

I picked up the phone and called Tim. I said, "Hey Tim, what would you think if I could get Emmitt Smith to come be a keynote speaker at RFID World?" Tim replied, "What? Are you kidding me?" I told him about my relationship with Emmitt and that I would be happy to make the call and ask him. Tim said, "Hell YES! If you can make it happen, I'll pay his expenses and pay him whatever he wants." I then told Tim I would give Emmitt a call and broach the offer.

I called Emmitt that afternoon trying my best to sell him on the offer. Evidently, I did a good job because he immediately said, "I'd love to do it! That sounds like it would be a lot of fun. If you guys pay my expenses, I'll do it for free." I gave him the dates and he said, "I'm all in – let's go."

I immediately called Tim back and said, "Hey, I got Emmitt to speak at the show. He told me if we paid his expenses, he'd do it for free." Tim replied, "Are you kidding me? That's unbelievable. Man, I owe you big time – that's going to make the conference great!" I called Emmit back and told him to pack his bags because he was going to Denver. He thanked me and said he was excited about the opportunity. I said, "No, thank you! – we'll have a lot of fun there!" I told him that Tim would book the airfare (first class, of course), and that he would get Emmitt a nice suite at the hotel, pay for all his meals and other expenses, and get him a limo to and from the airports in Dallas and in Denver. I was so excited that it all worked out well.

I flew to Denver two days prior to the conference to oversee all the set-up and make all the pre-show preparations. Emmitt flew in the following day. I had scheduled a dinner with Emmitt that evening.

At six o'clock that day, all the TI-RFID personnel met in the hotel bar for a pre-show happy hour at the Marriott in downtown Denver where we were staying. I called Emmitt and asked him to join us before he and I went to dinner.

The bar was located on a lower level below the main lobby of the hotel. There was a long escalator that led down to the bar. There were ten of us from TI gathered at the bar, and at about 6:30pm, I looked toward the escalator and saw Emmitt coming down. He was dressed in a beautiful burnt orange silk suit with a bright yellow shirt. I waved to him, and he came walking over. Emmitt is 5 feet, 9 inches tall, and weighs about 225 lbs. He was very stocky and solid as a rock. I thought to myself, "He looks like a pumpkin coming down the escalator," but I dared not tell him that.

I stepped over to greet him and he had a big smile on his face and gave me a big hug (which thoroughly impressed all my TI-RFID team members and everyone else in the bar). I ordered a Margarita for him, and I introduced him to everybody. He was completely friendly and was his usual affable self. We spent about an hour hanging out at the bar – everyone had a great time talking to him and they were totally impressed with how nice and humble he was.

I had made reservations at Ruth's Cris Steakhouse for him and me, and we walked to the restaurant. We were quickly seated, and we had a very nice dinner which TI paid for. The waiter was gushing praise for Emmitt and was very attentive in his service, even though the waiter was a huge Broncos fan.

Emmitt and the Blues

I had discussed my love for music and told Emmitt I loved singing the blues and playing harmonica. He said he really enjoyed listening to the blues. I explained I always carried a few harmonicas in case the opportunity to play and sing ever came up, which he thought was cool. I had them stashed in my coat pocket.

When the waiter brought the bill, Emmitt asked him if there was a blues bar anywhere close. The waiter said, "Yes, actually, there is one about ten blocks from here that is a famous blues bar here in Denver – it's called El Chapultepec – you'll love it because they always have good blues music." Emmitt said, "Hey, thanks!" He then turned to me and said, "We are going there because I want to hear you play." Of course, I agreed to go.

We hopped into a taxi an headed for the bar. As we walked in, everyone was pointing fingers and saying, "Look, that's Emmitt Smith!" Of course, Emmitt stood out like a sore thumb – or should I say a very large pumpkin with his burnt orange suit and bright yellow shirt. The place was packed, and Emmitt managed to break through the crowd like he was running through a defensive line, and we made our way to the bar. Emmitt ordered two beers for us and tipped the bartender handsomely.

We listened to several songs and then the band took a break. As they were leaving the stage, Emmitt grabbed my arm and dragged me toward the stage and said, "Come on, Bill, I'm going to get you up there to play." I said, "Emmitt that's OK, they probably won't let me sit in." He said, "Shush, I'm getting you up there."

Emmitt approached the lead singer and said, "What's it going to take to get my brother Bill up there to play with you guys?" The lead singer said, "Mr. Smith, it's nice to meet you, but we don't allow anyone to play with us unless we know them and have played with them before." I said, "Emmitt, it's really OK – my band has the same rule." Emmitt then said, "Bill, shut up."

Emmitt then turned back to the singer and said, "Maybe you didn't understand my question, so I'll ask it again." He continued, "What's it going to take to get my brother Bill up there to play with you guys?" The singer said, "Mr. Smith, I'm so sorry, but we can't do it." Emmitt undauntingly reached in his pocket, pulled out a $100 bill and asked, "Will this get it done?" The singer asked me, "Can you really play the blues?" I said, "Yes, sir, I've been playing harp for many years, and I have my own band back in Dallas." The singer then grabbed the $100 bill and said, "Hell yes, he can play with us for the rest of the night!" Emmitt laughed and gave me a high five.

After the band's break, the lead singer called me up to the stage and I ended up playing five songs with them. By then, it was getting late, and I had an early morning meeting at the exhibition area, so I thanked the band and went back to sit with Emmitt. After a couple more songs, I told Emmitt I had an early meeting, and we had to leave. We then took a taxi back to our hotel. As we arrived, Emmitt said, "That was the most expensive five songs I've ever paid for." I replied, "You're the fool who paid that much – he probably would have done it for 20 bucks. I guess you don't have as much pull in Denver as you do in Dallas." We had a good laugh and headed off to our rooms.

After my meeting the next morning, I called Emmitt to see if he wanted to check out the exhibit area. He said, "Yes, that sounds great and then I'll buy your lunch." We grabbed a quick lunch and made our way to the exhibit floor. There were about 100 exhibiting companies who were setting up their trade show booths, and as we walked down the aisles, I introduced him to a lot of my industry friends. Of course, they were very excited to meet him, and I certainly made a good impression with my buddies. Emmitt was his usual sociable self and made everyone feel comfortable.

Emmitt was scheduled to speak later that evening at the opening session of the conference. I had helped him put together his speech and presentation, but he said he was somewhat nervous because he had not been a keynote speaker before. I reassured him he would do fine – just his presence was a thrill for everybody.

After the usual welcoming speech by Tim Downs, the organizer, he brought me up on stage to introduce Emmitt. As I got on the stage and walked up to the podium, I noticed the huge ballroom was packed – it was standing room only. Everyone had turned out to see Emmitt. After my introduction, he was greeted with a standing ovation. Most conference opening sessions don't have standing room only crowds, and I could tell Emmitt was a little nervous as he started his speech.

Speaking of RFID

All the RFID industry geeks and other attendees were treated to a sometimes funny, sometimes serious speech from Emmitt. He told the crowd interesting stories about his playing days in Dallas which everyone enjoyed. He explained how excited he was about RFID technology and its many applications. His speech went well, and everyone enjoyed hearing from him. He got another standing ovation after the speech.

The following day, I escorted Emmitt around the exhibit floor. He spent time watching demonstrations, asking lots of questions, and learning about applications of RFID technology. We also attended some of the conference sessions.

VIP Dinner With Emmitt

That evening, Tim had organized a dinner for about 30 industry VIPs that were attending the conference. After the meal, I did an informal interview with Emmitt that everyone enjoyed. I asked him various questions about his time in the NFL as well as some personal questions.

The one question and answer I thought was most interesting, and perhaps most telling, was when I asked Emmitt who he feared most that he played against in the NFL. After all, he did play against some very mean defensive linemen, linebackers and secondary players, including many of his fellow hall of famers. Emmitt turned and looked at me and said, "I was never afraid of any of them. The only person I was ever afraid of was my momma." I, along with everybody else in the audience, laughed loudly. He then said, "I'm not kidding!"

Emmitt went on to tell a story of when he was about 12 or 13 years old. He explained that one night he was a few doors down at a friend's house – they were watching a movie. It was 9:00pm when his friend's mother said, "Emmitt, your momma is on the phone and wants to talk to you." Emmitt went to the phone and his momma said, "Emmitt, it's a school night and it's time for you to come home and get to bed." He then said, "Oh, Momma, we are watching a movie and it'll be finished in 15 or 20 minutes – can I stay to finish the movie?" Momma replied, "No Emmitt, you better get on home right now!" He hung up the phone and sat down to finish the movie, which as one might guess was a bad mistake.

After finishing the movie, Emmitt ran home. When he got there, all the lights were turned off and the front door was locked. He went around to the back door, and it was locked. He went back to the front door and knocked. Then he knocked some more. Momma didn't answer. When he knocked again, the front porch light came on and the door opened. Emmitt said he knew he was in trouble when his momma was holding that special belt in her hands that was reserved for very special occasions.

Emmitt explained that his momma snatched him inside and administered a good whipping that he still remembered. He told us, "Even today, when my momma tells me to do something, I don't hesitate to do whatever she says – I'm still afraid of her because she could still whip my butt!" The audience and I had a rousing laugh. Emmitt then concluded by saying, "Trust me, it's no laughing matter!"

We ended the night with Emmitt shaking hands with every attendee and patiently posing for pictures with everyone. It was a fun night – we all had a great time.

Dancing With the Stars

The conference concluded two days later, and everyone who came into contact with me said they were thoroughly impressed with my friend, Emmitt Smith. They all commented on how nice and accommodating he was and how he was the highlight of the conference.

Emmitt then went back to Dallas to get ready to travel to Hollywood for his stint on *Dancing With The Stars*. I called Emmitt and wished him luck. I knew he would do well because he is extremely competitive and a very hard worker. My wife Linda and I watched religiously as Emmitt made it through on a week-to-week basis and into the finals of the competition. We were thrilled to see him get better and better as each week passed, I knew he was destined to win – and he did.

I called him a few days after the show to congratulate him. I asked him, "Which was better – winning *Dancing with the Stars* or winning your 1993 NFL MVP award?" He laughed and said, "I'll take the MVP award, but DWTS was a lot of hard work. It took a lot of practice, and I am really proud I won." I then told him, "There was never any doubt in my mind you were going to win."

A few months later, Emmitt called and invited me to a sports memorabilia show. He was scheduled to make an appearance and sign autographs. He also explained that the RFID company in which he had invested was a Texas Instruments RFID customer and they were going to be touting their sports memorabilia authentication application at the event. I went down to the Dallas Convention Center – I had never been to a show like that, so I thought it would be interesting. Sure enough, it was. I had a lot of fun and saw a wide variety of interesting sports memorabilia.

When I arrived at the show, I tracked down Emmitt and he came up to me and gave me a big hug. We had a nice chat, and then he said, "Come with me, I want to introduce you to someone." He then took me backstage where I saw Troy Aikman standing there. Emmitt introduced me to Troy, and we had a nice chat for a few minutes. Emmitt told Troy about the RFID conference where he spoke and filled Troy in on the RFID authentication application.

Both the CEO and sales manager from Emmit's RFID company came over and Emmitt said, "OK, we need a group picture." I stood between Emmitt and Troy and the others got into the picture. One of Emmitt's business managers took the picture. Since I had my small digital camera with me, I asked him to take a picture of Emmitt and me since I didn't have a picture with him. As I handed the camera to the business manager, my little finger got hung up on the small strap. He lost grip on the camera, and then it went crashing to the ground. Sadly, it shattered into several pieces.

Strangely, after all the time Emmitt and I spent together, I never took the opportunity to get a picture with him. The only chance I had just ended up disastrously. Therefore, I have no physical proof of our friendship – all I have are good stories to tell.

Over the next several months, Emmitt and I spoke on the phone occasionally, but we gradually drifted apart because he was busy with other projects and investments he was involved in, and I was busy travelling the world promoting RFID technology. I had a wonderful time meeting and getting to know Emmitt – it was a once-in-a-lifetime experience, and I shall forever treasure the time I spent with him and the memories I am able to write about.

Chapter 19

A Hero's Welcome

I have several musical heroes, but one person stands out is a very special way that goes beyond talent. His name is Vince Gill. I have closely followed his highly decorated career and admired his rare instrumental proficiency on guitar. He is in rarified air when it comes to playing the guitar – he's a master. On top of that, he plays banjo, mandolin, dobro, fiddle, and bass. As a very young performer, he made a name for himself with his guitar and mandolin virtuosity playing blue grass music which he was raised on. He rubbed elbows with and traded licks with the likes of Ricky Skaggs, Marty Stuart, and many other blue grass notables. His reputation as an instrumentalist continued to grow.

And then there's Vince's unmistakably unique voice. In the late 70's, few music lovers outside of blue grass aficionados knew who he was. His march to the top as a vocalist soon began. Although he was known for his multi-instrumental abilities, he was a bit insecure with his vocal talents, but he had a pure, pitch-perfect tenor voice. One of Vince's friends convinced him to audition as lead singer and guitarist for an up-and-coming new group called Pure Prairie League. The group had a top 10 hit with a memorable song called "Amie." PPL's lead singer decided to leave the group, and Vince won the job. The first release featuring Vince was "Let Me Love You Tonight." It was the group's biggest hit, reaching #1 on Billboard's Adult Contemporary charts.

Vince later left PPL to pursue other interests. Mark Knopfler, a highly respected guitarist himself, knew of Vince's virtuosity and tried to convince him to join a group he was putting together called Dire Straits. Instead, Vince went with his heart and moved to Nashville to further pursue a career in country music. It was important for him to get back to his roots. It was a good decision. That beautiful tenor voice carried him to heights no one has ever reached, winning five consecutive Academy of Country Music Male Vocalist of the Year awards, seven Country Music Association Male Vocalist of the Year awards, and ten Grammy's for Best Country Vocal Performance. Needless to say, no other vocalist, male or female, has won more country music awards than Vince. And then there's his songwriting accomplishments.

Vince was also a prolific and highly successful songwriter. Add fifteen Song of the Year wins to his already impressive list of awards. His song "When I Call Your Name" was released in 1990 and swept Song of the Year awards for ACM, Grammy, and CMA. One country music survey later listed it as the best country song ever written. That one song supercharged Vince's already successful career in country music.

If we total up all his awards that include other categories such as Entertainer of the Year, Single of the Year, Album of the Year, Best Collaboration, Video of the Year, Lifetime Achievement, and all other categories, he has won an unmatched 48 times. That's an astoundingly impressive resume. In fact, according to my research while writing this, he is the most widely decorated performer in the history of country music.

In 2017, Vince was then invited to join The Eagles after founding member Glenn Frey passed away. He had an additive effect on the group with his unmatched vocals and guitar playing chops. Vince said it was a great opportunity to join The Eagles, but he regretted he had to make that decision because he would have far preferred to not have to replace Glenn Frey. He would have preferred Glenn to continue contributing to The Eagles, but sadly, Mr. Fry had passed away. In any case, he was honored to join the group.

When we pile on all the awards and accolades for Vince Gill, they are certainly extraordinary. But what sets him apart from so many other performers is that he is a warm, wonderful person. He is widely considered "the nicest person in Nashville." I can personally vouch for that with stories about the kind of man he is.

Vince and Amy Visit

One of my old friends I toured with in 1969 ended up living in Nashville. On one of my trips there, I had lunch with Jim. We had a good time catching up. Jim told me a story that touched my heart. He married a contemporary Christian singer – I will call her Susan for privacy reasons. Susan was good a good friend of Amy Grant, wife of Vince Gill. Amy, of course, was a famous singer in her own right. Amy and Susan often performed together around Nashville and were close friends.

During my lunch meeting with Jim, I was sad to hear that Susan was stricken with breast cancer and was undergoing chemotherapy. As most cancer patients will testify, Jim said it was not an easy thing to endure, but Susan was battling hard. Jim told me a story about when Amy and Susan were scheduled to perform together at the Bluebird Café, but Susan had to call Amy and tell her she would be unable to perform that night because she was so sick from the chemo. Of course, Amy understood and felt bad for Susan. The show went on without Susan.

Jim told me that the following night, he and Susan had just finished eating dinner when they heard the doorbell ring. Jim went to the door and when he opened it, there stood Amy and Vince with their guitars in tow. Jim was thoroughly surprised and invited them in. Vince explained to Jim that he and Amy felt so bad that Susan was struggling, and they wanted to come over to just hang out and sing some songs with her. Jim said he was blown away by their kind gesture. He said Susan was also shocked but thrilled that they would take the time to visit her.

Jim said they had a wonderful evening, and that Amy and Vince lifted Susan's spirit. He said it had been a long time since she had smiled and laughed so much (along with being very talented, Vince also has a great sense of humor). Jim said, "Bill, they are such good people – I just can't tell you how much that night meant to Susan." Sadly, a few months later, Jim told me Susan had passed away.

The Time Jumpers

On another trip to Nashville, I was there to record some of my original country songs. Working with a Nashville producer and top session musicians was a bucket list item for me. My dream came true by recording six songs at a leading Nashville studio. The musicians were supremely talented.

The drummer, Wayne Killius, is a great player who has recorded with Big and Rich, Toby Keith, Kenny Rogers, and many others. The bass player, Jim Hyatt, had great credentials as well having toured with Allison Krauss. The lead guitar player, James Mitchell, has credits on albums by Brooks and Dunn, Alan Jackson, Ronnie Milsap, Allison Krauss, and many others.

The keyboard player, Paul Hollowell, had worked extensively with Dolly Parton, Reba McEntire, Ray Stevens, Lee Ann Womack, and a long list of other stars. Renowned session player and Grammy award winner Glen Duncan played fiddle, dobro, and acoustic guitar on my recordings. His list of artists ranges from George Strait, Randy Travis, and Tammy Wynette to Vince Gill, Merle Haggard, Loretta Lynn, and the list goes on and on. It was a thrill for me to spend the day with these guys, and they made my music come alive! I got to check that off my bucket list.

While we were wrapping up, Tim, the studio engineer, asked me if I was going to see any live music that evening. I told him, "Yes, I think I might be able to find some live music somewhere here in Nashville." Tim laughed and then gave me a tip. He asked if I liked Western Swing music, and I said yes. He said, "Then you've got to go to a place called Third and Lindsley because a group called the Time Jumpers is playing there tonight." He continued, "The group is made up of great studio musicians that have recorded with everybody in Nashville, and sometimes Vince Gill plays with them."

I asked Tim where this place was located. He sarcastically replied, "It's on the corner of Third and Lindsley streets." I said, "Oh, I got it. I didn't know the name of the place was also the location." He said, "Yeah, I guess it's confusing, but at least you don't have to know the address because the address is the name of the place."

Meeting The Man

I went back to my hotel, changed clothes, and headed toward Third and Lindsley. As I was driving to the location, I noticed it was in an industrial district and the closer I got to the facility, the more cars were parked on the streets. I drove by and saw the reason why so many cars were on the streets – there was a huge line outside waiting to get into the venue. I drove around for several minutes trying to find a parking space. I then saw a couple walking to their car and asked if they were leaving. The guy said, "Yes, we couldn't get in because it was a sellout, and they were at full capacity." I was a bit discouraged, but I decided to park in their space and see if I could get in.

When I walked up to the entrance, an older lady standing in the doorway told me the event was closed due to capacity restrictions. I thought to myself, "Well, it's time to test my sweet-talking skills to see if I can talk my way in." I told the lady, "I am from Dallas, and I was so looking forward to hearing the Time Jumpers." She smiled and said, "Hey, I'm from Dallas also." We exchanged other pleasantries and then she said, "I'm not supposed to do this, but I'll give you a standing room only ticket for $20 – you'll have to stand at the bar." I whipped out a $20 bill, grabbed the ticket, and thanked her for being so sweet. As I walked in, she said, "Enjoy! Have a good time!" I thought to myself, "Boy, that was easy," and then made my way to the bar area.

I grabbed a beer and noticed the performers were taking the stage and tuning up. On the right side of the stage, there sat the one and only Vince Gill. As the band started playing, he was kind of sitting in the background on a stool. I thought that was rather strange – he should have been the star of the show because he was obviously the most famous person, not only in the building, but in Nashville.

As the evening went on, these great instrumentalists were tearing it up – I was in awe. Vince continued to sit in the background and when it was time for him to play a solo, he would step up to the front of the stage, play his solo, and then sit back down on his stool behind the other musicians.

As I later found out, the concept of the Time Jumpers was Vince's idea. All the players in the group had played on many of Vince's recordings and contributed to making him a superstar. He wanted to give something back to these guys, so he convinced them to form a band. He produced and paid for the recording of an album of old Western Swing classics featuring the new band. All this was to show appreciation for these great players and to recognize them for their talents and contributions to not only Vince, but to country music. It's another example of the kind of person Vince Gill is.

I remained enthralled with the outstanding musicianship of the Time Jumpers. Vince did step forward and sing two of his greatest hits during the first set, which was great to hear. After Vince's songs, the band announced they were going to take a quick break, and they left the stage. They all assembled in the green room just off the stage. After about 15 minutes, they started to saunter back on stage, and I noticed that Vince was standing just outside of the green room and in front of the stage while talking to someone. I had the impulse to walk up to the stage to see if I could meet him.

When I got to the front of the stage, he was still talking to the gentleman. I stood back several feet waiting a few minutes for them to conclude their conversation. When they finished their conversation, however, I did not know what to do or how to approach him since I was so starstruck. Suddenly, he took a few steps toward me, reached out his hand, and then said, "Hi, I'm Vince. Welcome to Nashville. What's your name and where are you from?" I nervously managed to tell him my name and that I was from Dallas. He then asked if I was enjoying the show and having fun in Nashville. I said, "Of course I'm having fun watching you guys tear it up – all the musicians on stage are great – and I am a huge fan of yours!"

I explained that I was in town recording some of my original songs and got to work with Glen Duncan, Paul Holloway, and some other great players. Vince said, "Hey, those guys are great – I've worked with them and have known them both for a long time." We chatted for a few more minutes. He continued, "Hey Bill, I wish you all the best with your songs and I hope you enjoy the rest of your time in Nashville." I then told him that he was one of my musical heroes, and I admired him so much for being a great person. He then said, "Well, thanks, I'm glad you enjoy my music. I'd love to stay and chat some more, but it looks like I better get back on stage." He reached out and shook my hand again. I told him I was honored to meet him, and it was a very special moment for me. Vince then smiled and replied, "Bill, it was a pleasure meeting you, and I hope we see each other again sometime."

After I thanked him, I floated back to my place at the bar to enjoy another hour of some great music. He was so nice, so friendly, and so humble. I was beyond thrilled to have the chance to meet him. I personally could see why he's known as "the nicest guy in Nashville."

Chapter 19

Other Notable Chance Meetings

I attended yet another trade show in Chicago during my years working at Minuteman Power Technologies. Yes, it seems like a lot of my escapades happened there – and they did.

After the first day of the show, Erik, one of our salespeople and I ventured out to have a few beers and grab some dinner. I had heard about a famous bar owned by blues icon Buddy Guy. I asked the bellman at our hotel where Buddy Guy's Legends bar was located. The bellman explained it was only three blocks away – one block up and two blocks right.

Erik and I took the short walk and when we got to the entrance, there was a line to get in. We got in line and when we got to the front, a young lady asked for our tickets because it was a private party. I asked what company was sponsoring the party and she told me the name of the software company. I said, "I work for Minuteman Power Technologies, and they are a large customer of ours," which they were. I knew their sales manager and asked if he was around. She said, "I don't know if he is, but I can't let you in without a ticket." I knew that if I could talk to the sales manager, I could get us in. I pleaded with the young lady one more time. She finally relented.

For those that do not know who Buddy Guy is, he is a blues singer and guitar player that has achieved legendary status. He grew up in Louisiana picking cotton and started playing guitar at a very young age. When he was twenty-one years old, he had heard about the blues scene that was popular in Chicago, so off he went. After arriving in Chicago, he had a tough time making it in the music scene until Muddy Waters, another iconic blues legend, gave Buddy a chance to play with his band. Buddy quickly established himself as an excellent guitar player with a distinctively aggressive sound. He later recorded several songs that became regional hits, and he even had penetrated the British music scene with his recordings.

Among the British musicians that held Buddy in the highest regard and were greatly influenced by him were Eric Clapton, Jimmy Page, Keith Richards, and Jeff Beck. In the US, guitarists such as Jimi Hendrix, Stevie Ray Vaughan, John Mayer, and Gary Clark, Jr. considered Buddy a huge influence. When those guitarists call someone a legend, enough said.

Erik and I found a table on the second row right in front of the stage and sat down. There was an open bar which we unashamedly took advantage of, and there was lots of Cajun food served buffet-style which was delicious. There were quite a few guitars displayed on the walls that were autographed by most of the players mentioned above.

A band took the stage and started jamming out some blues. They were obviously seasoned players who knew what they were doing. After several songs, the leader of the band said, "Ladies and gentlemen, please welcome to the stage the legendary Mr. Buddy Guy." He made his way to the stage. I had no idea we would be fortunate enough to actually see Buddy Guy play and sing – it made the night extra special.

Buddy came out wailing and quickly worked up a heavy sweat. After four or five songs, he shouted out, "Boy, am I thirsty! Somebody buy me a drink!" Recall that we were sitting within ten feet of Buddy. I immediately stood up and said, "I'll buy you a drink, what do you want?" He said, "They know what I want – just ask the bartender." I thought, of course they know what he wants – it's his bar!"

I weaved my way through the crowd and fought my way to the bar. It took a few minutes, but finally the bartender asked what I wanted. I said I was buying Buddy Guy a drink, and he told me that you knew what he wanted." The bartender didn't hesitate and poured up a shot. He then said, "That'll be $25." I thought to myself, "Hold on. It's an open bar, and the owner of the bar wants a drink, and this guy is asking me to pay $25?" I said, "I thought this was an open bar tonight." The bartender said, "It is for beer, wine, and well liquors, but Buddy drinks a special Courvoisier."

Back then, $25 was like $50 today, so I was a bit hesitant. I then asked myself, "OK, how many times in my life will I have the chance to buy Buddy Guy a drink? It's a once-in-a-lifetime opportunity – just do it!" I threw $30 on the bar, grabbed the drink, and walked back to my seat.

At the end of the next song, I stood up and said, "Buddy, here's your drink!" He said, "Come on, bring it up here." I went to the front of the stage, and he pulled me up and asked me, "What's your name and where are you from?" I said, "I'm Bill Allen from Dallas." Buddy said, "Ah, Dallas, home of my friend Stevie Ray, God rest his soul."

Buddy then slammed down his $25 drink in one big gulp. He gave me a big hug and said, "Give it up for Bill from Dallas for buying me a drink!" I then sat back down in my seat. Erik said, "Bill, that was the coolest thing ever! Way to go." Little did Erik and I know that more memorable moments were coming.

After a few more songs, Buddy said, "I'm going to bring up one of my best friends to play with us. Please welcome Mr. Steve Cropper." I thought, "Steve Cropper – where have I heard that name?" Buddy then says, "Steve is a great guitarist, songwriter, and producer, and he is responsible for playing one of the most signature guitar licks ever played – hit it, Steve." As soon as Steve started playing the first few notes, everyone in the place knew exactly what song it was – "Soul Man."

It then dawned on me who Steve Cropper was. He was from Memphis, and he co-wrote, played on, and produced some of the greatest songs ever, including "Soul Man," "Dock of the Bay," "Midnight Hour," and "Knock on Wood." He also was the lead guitarist in a funny little band called The Blues Brothers featuring John Belushi and Dan Aykroyd. Steve even had a role in the movie *Blues Brothers*. His accomplishments were iconic in their own way.

Buddy and Steve continued to tear it up in song after song – it was pure magic. After the show closed, I got to meet and chat with both Buddy and Steve for a few minutes. I never would have guessed that I would buy Buddy Guy a drink and be pulled on stage with him, nor would I have guessed that I would meet and hang out with Steve Cropper. Meeting two music icons in one night? Are you kidding me? What a wonderful, magical evening it was, and I'm glad I was able to sweet-talk our way into the party. I owed that young lady a big thank you for letting us in! Listening to and meeting those two great musicians was not on my bucket list, but it sure was another memorable experience.

A Not So Famous Icon

There are a slew of famous singers across many genres of music, and I have had the pleasure of seeing many of them in concert. They work hard to bring music to the masses, and they get all the glory. There are countless unsung heroes in the production of live music that anonymously reside in the background and get little to no recognition for making the stars sound great. They range from roadies, to technicians, to bus drivers, and most importantly, sound engineers. As we have seen from Taylor Swift, Beyonce, and others, there is a cast of hundreds that make a music tour successful.

Concert attendees pay big bucks to enjoy an evening with their favorite performer. The sound engineer's job is to make sure the stars sound like stars during their live performances – their job is perhaps the most critical of all. Without their skills, the final product could be wrecked by poor sound that could distract from the singer's performance and ruin the audience's experience.

While working in the equipment manufacturing side of the professional audio industry at MICMIX Audio Products, I met many members of the critical, yet unknown team who make contributions in producing the sounds that we all ultimately enjoy. I got a call one day from a sound production engineer named David Morgan. I met David briefly at one of the Audio Engineering Society's annual conventions in Los Angeles and I had given him my business card. His phone call was a cry for help. David was an avid fan of our reverb systems, and he explained that he was desperate to locate one of our reverbs for a major upcoming tour. He explained that his usual equipment dealer was out of stock on one of our most popular reverbs.

David asked if I could do him a favor and supply the reverb for the tour – and he needed it ASAP. I told him we could make it happen and asked what group he was going on tour with. He told me it was for the Doobie Brothers. I was and still am a big fan, so getting him the reverb took on even more meaning. We were able to get the reverb overnighted, and David said he would make sure we would get the appropriate recognition for doing him a huge favor. We would be able to promote the Doobie Brothers as users of our reverb. Off the unit went, and I got a call the following day from David thanking us for coming through for him.

The Doobies Do Dallas

David called me about a month later and he said, "Hey Bill, we will be at Reunion Arena in Dallas next week on the tour and I want to invite you and your wife to attend the concert on me." Of course, I was thrilled to accept his invitation and responded, "David, that is so cool – I can't wait to see you!" He explained that there would be two concert passes waiting for me at the VIP reception desk.

What made this invitation so much more exciting was being able to tell my wife that we were going to see the Doobie Brothers. Like me, Linda was a big fan. She had a huge crush on Michael McDonald who was the lead singer and keyboardist. Along with being a "hunk", he had one of the most iconic voices in rock 'n roll music. When I got home from work, I nearly broke the door down in anticipation of telling her we were going to be VIPs at the Doobie Brothers concert. She was very excited and asked me if we were going to meet Michael McDonald. I said, "Well, I'm not sure, but maybe David could make that happen."

When the day arrived, I took Linda out for a nice early dinner, and then we headed for Reunion Arena in downtown Dallas. Linda wore a strapless dress, and as usual, she looked like a million bucks. I had no doubts she would be the most beautiful woman at the concert. We arrived at the VIP desk and then I gave them my name. The lady gave us each a lanyard and a badge with our names on them. I looked at the badge and it read "All Access." Since I had never been to a concert as a VIP, I didn't fully realize what that meant. I was also concerned that we didn't get tickets with a seat assignment.

We walked into the arena, and I saw David sitting at the main mixing board that was on a riser about twenty rows from the stage dead center. As we approached the mixing console and the lighting control riser, I said, "Hey David, we made it!" He turned and waved and then said, "Come on up." Four security guys were guarding all the equipment, and when Linda and I approached the riser, one of them stopped us. I showed him my badge and David said, "They're cool, let them up." We climbed the stairs and David had two chairs for us sitting right beside him. I introduced Linda and we sat down. We both were blown away and the concert hadn't even started yet. I asked David if we were sitting with him during the concert, and he said, "Absolutely – you've got the best seat in the house."

David then showed me our reverb unit and took us on a mini tour of the mixing console and all the associated equipment. For me, it was heaven – for Linda, maybe not so much. I told David that getting to watch the concert from this vantage point was the coolest thing ever. After a few minutes, David said, "OK it's time for me to get to work." The house lights were dimmed, and David was ready. The iconic guitar riff at the beginning of the Doobie Brothers mega hit "China Grove" started, the lights came up, the crowd erupted, and the concert began. I got goosebumps all over my body.

Linda's eyes were mostly focused on Michael McDonald, while I was intently watching David's masterful work and trying not to get too distracted from the concert. The sound was great, and since we were elevated above the audience, the unobstructed view was phenomenal. The Doobies cranked out hit after hit – it was exhilarating. After about 15 songs, they announced they were taking a short intermission.

During the break, Linda and I started having a nice chat with David about the show and I told David that Linda was crazy about Michael McDonald. He then got up from his chair and said, "Well, let's go backstage and meet him." Linda's eyes got big and quickly said, "Let's go!" I said, "Is it OK? Are you going to get in trouble for that?" He said, "Hell, no – those badges allow you to go backstage and go wherever you want." I then learned that's what "All Access" meant. He then said, "Come on, I'll introduce you to everybody." We climbed down the stairs and headed backstage.

When we got backstage, the band members along with some of the crew members were milling around and hanging out. David introduced us to Tom Johnston, who was a guitarist, lead singer, and one of the original founding members of the band. We had a brief chat with him, and then David introduced us to Patrick Simmons, the other guitarist and founding member. Again, we had a brief chat. Linda then excitedly said,

"Oh my gosh, there he is – it's Michael McDonald!" David said, "Come on, I'll introduce you." We walked over and he introduced us.

I recall shaking Michael's hand and noticing how small it was. Michael is an excellent keyboard player, and most keyboardists have at least decently-sized hands. I commented to him, "Wow, you've got small hands – how do you make it work playing keys?" He laughed and said, "Yes, I can barely reach an octave. It's sometimes challenging but I have learned to get by with tiny hands." I then complimented him and said, "You've done a great job, and I admire your keyboard playing abilities – you've obviously made it work. And that's not to mention you have an iconic voice!"

As we continued our chat, Linda was starstruck, as was I. He was very nice, and David then explained that I worked for the company that made the MICMIX reverb unit. Michael said, "Wow, I love the sound of your reverbs – I have one in my studio." I was psyched to hear that. I then asked if Linda could have his autograph and explained that she was a huge fan. He reached in his pocket and pulled out a Sharpie. He said, "What do you want me to sign?" Linda, with her strapless dress, then pointed to her left shoulder above her breast and said, "Just sign right here." Michael paused, looked at me and said, "Uh, Uh, Uh, really?" We all laughed, and then Michael said, "How about I sign your badge?" He obviously felt far more comfortable autographing her badge than her shoulder.

Michael was very magnanimous in spending more than ten minutes talking to us about music and other things like family. He offered an apology for the first set of songs not sounding as good as they could have. I was a bit puzzled because I thought they sounded great. He explained, "Patrick [Simmons] and me are not getting along too well because of the differences in our musical tastes." He continued, "We are still not as cohesive as we should be – he and I have a personality conflict that we still have to work out – I hate that there's so much tension on stage." He concluded, "I am sorry that it is affecting our performance." I said to him, "You guys sound great, I haven't noticed anything wrong." He then replied, "I'm glad you haven't noticed, but it's a real problem for us that we need to work out."

The intermission was concluding, and Michael said, "It's been fun meeting and chatting with you guys – thanks for coming." I told him, "It's an honor to have met you, and thanks for spending so much time with us." We shook hands again, and then he gave Linda a hug. I thought she was going to melt into a puddle right then and there. Fortunately, she didn't, and we headed back to our ringside seats with David to enjoy the rest of the concert.

I later read that Patrick and Michael did indeed have a feud going on. Patrick was an original founding member, and Michael was the new kid on the block. The challenge the Doobie Brothers faced was melding the original band's sound with what Michael brought to the party. Michael has a soulful R&B type voice and piano style, while Patrick was more interested in a harder rock 'n roll sound. They evidently worked out their differences because they stayed together for seven years before parting ways so Michael could work on a solo career that was very successful. After a five-year hiatus apart, they all got back together again and continued cranking out their hit songs on tour.

Two More Great Concerts

Our night with David and the Doobie Brothers was very memorable. But our story about hanging out with David doesn't end there. A few months after the Doobie Brothers tour ended, I got a call from David. He said he had a new gig and was working as Neil Diamond's tour engineer. He told me the tour would be in Dallas in a few weeks and said he'd hook us up again. I have always been a Neil Diamond fan, so I was excited. David also added that Neil Diamond was an avid user of our reverbs.

For those youngsters that don't know who Neil Diamond is, he has sold more than 130 million records (yes, we used to have actual vinyl records before they made a recent comeback). That does not include no telling how many digital downloads. He was a mega worldwide star performer for more than 40 years, starting in the early 70's. He wrote and recorded one of the most iconic songs of all time, "Sweet Caroline." If people don't know that song or haven't heard it, they've been living under a rock for the last 50 years. It has become a global phenomenon. He was a prolific songwriter, churning out 38 top 40 hits.

The day of the concert in Dallas, David called me and asked if I wanted to come down to the arena and hang out for a while. Of course, I said yes. I drove down to Reunion Arena and met David outside. He walked us into the arena, and I stayed for about two hours watching all the roadies and technicians set up for the show. David took me through all his set-up chores. It was very interesting to see how it all comes together.

David explained that when the sound check started, I was going to have to leave because Neil did not allow anybody inside the arena during the sound check. When Neil came out on stage, it was time to go. I did manage to find a hiding place (which is not too hard in a huge arena) and stayed for about twenty minutes listening to the sound check.

When Linda and I arrived for the concert later that night, we were not allowed to sit with David at the mixing console for the concert, but he did get us excellent tickets near him. It was an amazing show performed by a truly iconic singer and songwriter. We did get to hang out with David before, during intermission, and after the show. It was another great experience David made happen.

David and I lost touch with each other for a good while – after all, he was quite busy touring the world with Neil Diamond. Nearly two years later, my phone rang at the office, and it was David reaching out. It was great to hear from him. He explained he had been touring with Neil, and as soon as that tour ended, he went out on the road for Barry Manilow's worldwide tour. Barry Manilow was another huge global star that sold more than 85 million records. He cranked out hit after hit in the 70's, 80's, and on into the 90's. He toured constantly and he always put on a great show. He was a hugely successful singer and songwriter.

Once again, David told me Barry Manilow's tour was coming to Dallas, and he would hook us up – which he did. We had great tickets which David provided, and we got to hang out with him and catch up after the show.

After my tenure with MICMIX ended, I moved on to other endeavors, and David didn't know how to reach me – not to mention he was constantly touring – so we lost touch. Back then, we didn't have cell phones and phone numbers that stayed with us for the rest of our lives. When people changed jobs or moved to another residence, they always got a new phone number.

David has become an icon in the live music engineering industry. He has made quite a career as a road and recording studio engineer. Along with The Doobie Brothers, Neil Diamond, and Barry Manilow, David has worked on tours with Witney Houston, Paul Simon, Fleetwood Mac, Kenny Loggins, Steely Dan, Stevie Nicks, James Taylor (multiple tours), and countless others. He is a not-so-well-known critical contributor to live music who spent his career making the stars sound great and has been a mentor to many young engineers.

David is now retired from constant road work, and now he can finally call home a real home. It was interesting that a single favor I did for David turned into three memorable events for Linda and me. For Linda, meeting Michael McDonald certainly ranked number one on her list. For me, as an audio geek, it was a rare opportunity to witness what went on behind the scenes and see an artist of a different kind work his magic.

Crossing Paths with Christopher Cross

I attended a trade show and was staying at Harrah's in Reno (which was later turned into an apartment complex). I had some time to kill, so I ventured off to the hotel's pool to get some exercise and sun. I was lying by the pool doing some work on my laptop, when a group of five guys sat down beside me. As we exchanged pleasantries, I noticed one of them looked very familiar, but I couldn't quite place him.

One of the guys asked me what I was doing in Reno, and I explained I was there for the trade show that was being held in the hotel ballroom. I asked him what he was doing in Reno, and he said, "We are just hanging out by the pool and killing time before the show tonight." I asked him what show they were going to see, and he said, "We are not just going to see the show, we are playing in the show." I said, "OK, that's cool, who are you with and what kind of show is it?" He said, "I'm the bass player, that's the drummer, there's the keyboard player, and that's Christopher Cross." I said, "No way! I thought he looked familiar."

He said, "My name is Andy, what's your name?" I introduced myself and told him I was from Dallas. He told me they often played in Dallas. Christopher came over and sat next to me after his dip in the pool and Andy introduced us. I told Christopher I was a big fan and loved his music. I explained that I was the lead singer and played guitar, harmonica, and keyboards in a band in Dallas and that we played every weekend. He then said, "Andy, hook him up with a ticket and a backstage pass for the show tonight." I said, "Wow, I appreciate it, thank you Christopher."

We then continued our chat for about 30 minutes, mostly talking about music and sports. He then told his team it was time to get cleaned up for the show and they all headed out. Andy told me my ticket and VIP pass would be at the will call window and then said, "We look forward to seeing you tonight!" I told him, "I am thrilled to meet you guys and look forward to the show." I went back to my room, got cleaned up, and then grabbed some dinner at one of the hotel's restaurants.

For those that do not know who Christopher Cross is, he was born in San Antonio, and his band started performing live shows in Austin, TX. In the early years, he and his band recorded commercials and demos for other performers. Christopher was later signed to a solo artist contract with Warner Brothers Records in 1979. Along with his high tenor voice, he is a very accomplished guitarist – he even subbed for a while with Deep Purple since Ritchie Blackmore fell ill during their tour.

He released his first album in late 1979 that turned into a five-time platinum seller (5 million albums) and featured singles "Sailing", "Ride Like the Wind," and "Never Be the Same". All of those reached #1 on Billboard's Top 100 list in 1980. Chris did something no other Grammy artist had ever done at that time – he won Record of the Year, Album of the Year, Song of the Year, and best New Artist. "Sailing" also won a Grammy for Best Vocal Arrangement. It was a historic haul. He then went on to win the same trophies at the Golden Globe awards show as well as landing an Academy Award as co-writer of the theme song for the movie *Arthur*. I don't think any other performer has ever had quite the freshman year that Christopher had.

When I made my way to the concert, my seat was at a table, front-row center. The band ripped through all the songs from his award-winning album, and then they played some of his newer music along with a few cover songs. It was a great show.

When it was over, I made my way backstage and was invited into the green room with the band. Fortunately for me, it was stocked with beers and snacks. Cha-ching! It was great hanging out with them. I asked Christopher if he was surprised that his album was so successful. He told me, "Never in a million years did I ever dream I would even be nominated for a Grammy – let alone winning five in one year." He continued, "It all went by so fast – it was crazy. I still can't believe it happened as we sit here ten years later."

Christopher and the band members were very congenial – it was so much fun hanging out with them. After about an hour in the green room, we all went our separate ways. I would never have thought I'd be lucky enough to meet and hang out with Christopher Cross and his band. It was another random and highly memorable evening for me.

Happy Happenstances

Over the years, I have been more than fortunate to enjoy so many fluke encounters with music icons. I would never have thought that I would have encounters with Les Paul, Vince Gill, Buddy Guy, Steve Cropper, David Morgan, the Doobie Brothers, or Christopher Cross. I also would never have dreamed I would become friends with Emmitt Smith, nor get to know other great athletes like Jim Kelly and Herschel Walker.

One of the real coincidences is that I greatly admired all the musicians and athletes listed above, and to get to meet them and hang out with them was certainly serendipitous. Or perhaps it was just plain blind luck.

I also had several other interesting encounters that I will briefly describe. The first was meeting astronaut Buzz Aldrin. I was at a conference, and he was one of the keynote speakers. It was an entertaining speech that included behind-the-scenes stories of his life as an astronaut and the history-making flight on Apollo 11. He was the second person to walk on the moon after Neil Armstrong.

Many people do not know that a pen designed to write in zero gravity allowed the Apollo 11 lunar module to return to earth. Buzz explained that someone had accidentally broken the manual circuit breaker switch that controlled the engine on the lunar landing module. Without that switch being enabled, there was no way the engines would fire so that the moon landing module could return to the main spacecraft for the trip back to Earth. Buzz had the brilliant idea of jamming the tip of the pen into the circuit breaker slot to activate it. Fortunately for Neil and Buzz, it worked. The lunar landing module was then able to lift off the moon's surface and rejoin the main spacecraft for its return to earth. A pen saved their lives and the rest is history.

After his speech, he sat at a table and greeted those that wanted to meet him. In addition, he was signing and giving away his famous book entitled *Reaching for the Moon*. I was fortunate enough to shake his hand and receive a signed copy of his book. As I was speaking to him, I commented, "Mr. Aldrin, I have seen that Apollo space capsule and lunar landing module at the Air and Space Museum in Washington, DC. I must say that you are one brave soul to have climbed into that tin can of a space capsule and be shot to the moon by a giant rocket." I continued, "You must have been out of your mind to let them do that to you." He laughed out loud and said, "You know, you are right in more ways than one." I concluded our short conversation, saying, "I greatly admire you and all of the astronauts that put their life on the line for our country's space exploration, but I still think you must be crazy!" He laughed again and I wished him well.

The second somewhat brief encounter occurred when I was a freshman at Dallas Baptist University in 1969. Sitting in the desk behind me in my music theory class (we sat in alphabetical order) was a beautiful young lady named Bonnie Bowden. We also were in the same choir. We got to know each other throughout the semester. She had a very distinctive singing voice and would often sing to me one of the popular songs at the time called "Wedding Bell Blues" by a popular group named The 5th Dimension. The featured singer was Marilyn McCoo.

The song is about a hopeful bride pleading for her boyfriend to marry her – his name happened to be Bill. The first line of the song says, "Bill, I love you so, I always will…" The closing line is, "Please marry me Bill, I've got the Wedding Bell Blues."

Bonnie, who was a local Dallas girl, used to kiddingly sing that song to me whenever we would see each other in class. I took it as a compliment, but in no way did I think she was pleading for me to marry her – it was all in good fun. We did end up going out on several dates and hung out with each other after class periodically, but at that point, it was a budding but not serious relationship.

When the semester came to an end, we said our good-byes for the Christmas break, and I went home to spend the holidays with my parents. When the next semester began in January, I was looking forward to seeing Bonnie once again to rekindle our relationship. The day I got back to Dallas, I called her house to check in with her. I had been to her house once to meet her parents who were very nice.

Bonnie's father answered the phone, and I said, "Hello Mr. Bowden, it's Bill Allen calling – I hope you are doing well, and hope you had a great Christmas." He paused for a moment and said, "Hi, Bill, we did have a good Christmas." I then asked if I could speak to Bonnie. He paused again and said, "Bill, I hate to tell you this, and I'm not happy about it, but Bonnie has up and moved to Los Angeles to pursue a singing career. We were shocked at her decision, but she was determined to make the move." It was then my turn to pause for a moment, and I said, "Wow, I had no idea she was going to leave and go to LA." He said, "We certainly didn't know it either until she broke the news to us right after Christmas."

Although I wasn't completely heartbroken, I did feel like our relationship was on a good track and was shocked at the news. I told Mr. Bowden to please tell Bonnie I called and wish her the best. He said he would.

Nearly three years passed, and my first wife and I visited my oldest brother Rick and his family in California. We took a day to visit Disneyland. We were walking through the park and heard music playing from a stage about fifty yards away. I stopped in my tracks because I heard a familiar voice singing. As we got closer, I realized it was Bonnie who was singing. My jaw dropped. We stayed and listened to the rest of her show, and afterwards, I decided that I was going to say hello to her. When we got to the stage, Bonnie smiled and started singing, "Bill, I love you so, I always will." I was rather uncomfortable since Karel, my new wife, was standing right beside me.

Bonnie came down from the stage and gave me a hug which made me even more uncomfortable. I then introduced my wife, and then we had a brief chat. Bonnie said she couldn't hang around but told me it was good to see me and congratulated us on our marriage. I did have to explain to my wife the history behind Bonnie and me. All was well after that.

The next time I saw Bonnie, she was singing with a globally popular group at the time called Sergio Mendez and Brasil 77 on the *Tonight Show with Johnny Carson*. She traveled the world while touring with them and had a very nice career as a lead vocalist. She was one of the rare individuals who successfully dove into the pool to pursue her dream and achieve greatness. I never had the guts to do something like she did, which is probably why I never achieved greatness. I am truly happy for her.

Twisting the Night Away

Lastly, a quick story, mostly involving my wife Linda. When I worked at I-Concepts (an IT consulting company), we were exhibitors at a trade show called NetWorld in Dallas. Linda and I attended a large party sponsored by Novell, a now defunct computer networking company. The theme of that party was the 50's, and everyone was supposed to wear appropriate 50's attire. I wore the powder blue tuxedo jacket – the same one I wore when touring with the Continental Singers some twenty years earlier – and yes, I could still fit into it. I also wore black slacks, a white tuxedo shirt, and a black bow tie. Linda had bought a petroleum-based product called Pomade so I could slick my hair back (more on that later). Linda wore a strapless bright red hoop skirt. Of course, she looked like a supermodel or a movie star straight out of the 50's. She was stunningly beautiful.

The party was probably the best corporate event I ever attended. Whoever was the event planner really knew what they were doing. The music headliner was appropriately Chubby Checker. For those that don't know, Chubby was an iconic singer back in the late 50's and early 60's who had a series of hit songs. He was most famous for a song and dance called "The Twist." Saying it was a huge hit is an understatement – it was a worldwide phenomenon and was far less annoying than the Macarena.

When Chubby lit into his hit song, "The Twist," Linda and I were positioned right in front of the stage. Like everyone else at the party, we were doing the twist. Linda was showing off her substantial dance skills when Chubby reached out and pulled her up on stage. She and Chubby were killing it! After the song was over, he gave Linda a big hug and the crowd went crazy.

Later in the evening, we won the best dressed couple contest. My company was awarded free booth space (worth $6,000) for the next annual NetWorld trade show. Of course, I had little to do with winning the award because all credit had to go to my beautiful wife.

The Slicked Hair Saga

When we got home that night, I hit the shower to wash out the Pomade in my hair. After several tries with more than ample shampoo, my hair was a gummy mess. The shampoo was worthless. I got out of the shower and told Linda she was in deep trouble for buying the Pomade for me to slick back my hair. Back in those dark ages, simple hair gel that washes out easily was non-existent.

Linda suggested that I try Dawn dish soap, so I went into the kitchen, put my head in the sink, and scrubbed my hair with Dawn. Nope, it didn't do anything. My hair was still a gummy mess. She then called one of our neighbors who was a beautician (that's what we called them back then). The hairdresser suggested using laundry detergent and/or peroxide. I tried the laundry detergent to no avail. Next was the peroxide. I bent my head over into the sink and Linda poured the peroxide onto my hair. After a few seconds, I felt my scalp start to sting, and within a few more seconds, I thought my hair and scalp was on fire. It was as if someone had literally lit a flame on my hair. The pain was agonizing. I truly learned the meaning of the phrase "hair on fire."

Evidently, the combination of all the shampoos, soaps, and peroxide generated a chemical reaction that felt like my head was an exploding volcano. I ducked my head back under the faucet trying to alleviate the tortuous pain. After several minutes, the agony was easing, but the stinging aftermath was still there when I tried to go to sleep.

The following morning, I looked in the mirror and my hair was still a greasy mess. Another shower and even more shampoos made a small dent, but the Pomade was still gumming up my hair. I had to get dressed to return to our exhibit booth at the show. I tried styling my hair, but the only alternative was to slick it back like it was the prior evening.

The first customer who stopped by our booth recognized me from the party and said, "Congratulations on you and your wife winning the best dressed couple. You guys looked great. Your wife is beautiful, and she looked great dancing with Chubby Checker." He added, "And your hair still looks great slicked back like that." I didn't know if I should punch him or thank him, so I decided that it was more expedient to thank him since he was a potential customer. Throughout the day, several other attendees had similar comments. I was not happy about it, but the better part of valor was to just smile and thank them.

Although it was a great party and we had a most excellent time, I'm still not sure it was worth the pain and suffering. Fortunately, my oily hair finally got back to normal after numerous shampoos over a three or four-day period. I eventually did let Linda out of the doghouse for putting me through so much torture. It's funny now, but it wasn't so funny when my hair was on fire.

Other Notable Encounters

Additional famous people I have had more casual and brief encounters include hall of fame football player and former Dallas Cowboys assistant coach Ernie Stautner, NBA legends Akeem Olajuwan, Rolando Blackman, and Bill Russell, boxer Evander Holyfield (after Mike Tyson bit off part of his ear), German Chancellor Angela Merkle (at a trade show in Germany), along with musicians Kenny Loggins and Pat Benatar.

There are probably a few others I have forgotten, but in any case, I have been blessed with so many wonderful memories that are fun to recall, and I am happy to share them. I will forever cherish those sometimes random yet meaningful encounters with famous people.

Section VI

Close Encounters of the Animal Kind

Chapter 21

The Dog Days

As covered in the previous section, I have had many memorable encounters with famous people. The same is true with several stories I'll tell about interesting happenstances with animals. None of them were planned, and each one was unique.

I love animals and have enjoyed living with dogs my entire life. Growing up, my first animal encounter was with our family dog Taffy. As described earlier, she was a sweet cocker spaniel that left us far too soon in a tragic accident.

When we moved to California, our first dog was a mut named Duke. I'm not sure where Dad found him; at least I don't recall Duke's origins. He seemed like a good, playful puppy, but as he grew older, he became more and more cantankerous. He had a short fuse, and whenever someone pissed him off, he would growl and/or snap. He probably weighed about 40 or 50 pounds, and he was always a bit of a rebel. I recall seeing him run in a circle around the perimeter of the backyard, so much so, that he wore out a pathway in the grass. That was our first clue that he was not the brightest bulb in the box. We all tried to love him, but Duke just marched to the beat of a different drummer. The older he got, the more we realized that he definitely was several French fries short of a Happy Meal.

Duke ruled over his backyard, and he was suspicious of anyone who entered. I recall playing with him one day, and our playtime ended with his jaw wrapped around my wrist. I thought we were playing but he obviously was not in the mood. I walked away with a few scrapes and bite marks while wondering what I did to piss him off. A week or two later, he attacked my best friend while we were playing catch with a football. He left no marks, but my friend's jeans were torn at the bottom.

Duke's final act of senseless violence was when he attacked a little girl who had come over to play with me. I had to pull him off her and Duke left a few broken skin marks. Understandably, the girl's father was none too happy about it and called the dog catcher (which is what we called Animal Control back then). They came out and quarantined Duke to see if he had rabies and put a sign on the backyard gate that said, "Dog in quarantine – do not enter." Duke was held prisoner in our back yard (deservedly so since he was charged with assaulting kids).

After the two-week period, the dog catcher came for another visit. Duke was not happy about it and tried to assault him, which was not a good idea. That's when it was obvious that Duke suffered from some kind of malady and was not fit to be a family dog. Maybe he was better suited to be a prize fighter, but his eviction notice from the family was tendered. We said goodbye to Duke as he did the perp walk with the dog catcher. I was sure he was going to a better place where he could find peace.

The Frisky Chihuahua

Our next family dog arrived one day when my dad came home from work. It was a rainy day, and he was wearing a long raincoat. After he entered the house, he greeted Mom with a kiss and then reached into his pocket and pulled out a tiny little chihuahua puppy. The little thing was so adorable and the whole family went nuts. She was appropriately given the name Chiquita (which means little girl in Spanish). She was mostly white with tan coloring around her neck and face. Dad's choice of a small dog was certainly safer for the family and the neighborhood after the Duke fiasco.

Chiquita became an integral part of the family, but she did have a few quirks of her own. One idiosyncrasy was her utter dislike of my oldest brother Rick. Perhaps that's because Rick used to tease and torment her. It was all in good fun, but Chiquita didn't feel that way. My middle brother Gary was Chiquita's favorite brother – perhaps because he would rescue her from Rick's intimidation tactics. It was interesting to see Chiquita develop a hierarchy of who she liked, who she tolerated, and who she disliked. That is a usual trait for Chihuahuas.

Through observation and experience, this was the hierarchy: Mom (like everyone else, she loved my mother); Grandma Bennett (Mom's mother who was very sweet); Gary (her favorite brother); me (she more or less tolerated me); Dad (who she also tolerated); and then bringing up the rear, there was Rick (enough said).

Chiquita had a quick temper and could go from sweet little chihuahua to a vicious attack dog in less than a second. However, calling her vicious is a far reach since she could never bite anyone because her mouth was so small. I suppose she thought she was as intimidating as a pit bull when she showed her teeth and gave her screechy little growl. It was more comical than terrifying.

I recall that we had some guests who were visiting us, and they were sleeping in Rick and Gary's bedroom. Gary and Rick were to sleep on a pull-out couch in the living room. Chiquita always slept with Gary (her favorite brother). This one night, Rick had been out on a date and came home after Gary and Chiquita were already asleep. As Rick was trying to climb into bed, Chiquita was not having it. She was standing on the edge of the bed snarling, growling, and barking. She was obviously defending her turf from her primary antagonist. Rick tried to calm her down, but it didn't work.

He finally had to wake up Mom, saying, "Mom, Chiquita won't let me in bed." Mom got out of bed, picked up the terror dog so Rick could go to bed, and then took Chiquita to bed with her. We've always thought it was rather amusing that a little six-pound dog could keep a scrappy 16-year-old tough football player from climbing into bed. Obviously, Chiquita held an unwavering grudge against Rick, and she was not hesitant about showing it.

One of her other quirks was her disdain for the mailman. Whenever he approached the house to deliver our mail, Chiquita would make a beeline to the front door. Our mail was dropped through a covered slot in the door which sent Chiquita into a crazed frenzy. She was triggered by the sound of the mailman opening that slot. As the mail dropped through the door, she would commence a vicious attack on every article that came through. The daily ordeal was akin to a shark's feeding frenzy with Chiquita ripping into her prey. We often had to rescue the mail because if we didn't, she would proceed to rip each article to shreds, including letters, bills, and even magazines were not immune from the wrath of this crazed little monster.

Occasionally, the mail would get stuck in the slot, but that didn't prevent Chiquita from carrying out her intended mission. There were times when she would jump up to try and extract her vengeance on the stuck mail. It was hilarious to see her latching her teeth onto the mail to try and pry the articles loose. Sometimes when the mail would not come loose and fall, she would lock her tiny teeth onto the mail while wiggling and squirming with her feet off the ground, all the while growling and snarling. She was relentless. If there were phone cameras back then, the video of her waging war on the mail would certainly have gone viral. She truly lived up to her billing as a terror dog when it came to the mail and the mailman.

Chiquita lived through relocations from Long Beach to Chicago, from Chicago to Philadelphia, and from Philly back to Long Beach. I believe she was 17 years old when her reign of terror ended. Despite her sometimes-roiled temperament, she was a pretty good dog. She finally had to be put down because of several medical issues. It was a painful moment for Mom and Dad – especially for Mom. Her three boys had moved away to various parts of the country, and Chiquita was her constant companion.

Chapter 22

Birds of a Feather

As they say, everything is bigger in Texas, and so it is with the Texas State Fair – it's a huge, must-attend two-week event that sprawls across 277 acres. With more than two million attendees each year, it is the largest state fair in the country. It generates more than $600 million in economic impact and employs about 4,500 people. One cannot go to the Texas State Fair without eating world famous Fletcher's corny dogs. They sell more than 500,000 of them each year. Hundreds of vendors and crafters display their goods for sale. Car manufacturers display more than 200 models. The livestock contest portion of the fair has more than 13,000 animal entries.

The food pavilion features an endless display of cookware, cooking classes, and food samples. In addition, a canned food drive is held to benefit the North Texas Food bank. Each year more than 200,000 pounds of canned goods are donated. The fair hosts various cook-offs, perhaps the most famous of which is the Chile Cookoff. That particular contest hits close to home because my step-grandmother, Laura, had to retire her recipe after winning the contest five years in a row. I would provide her recipe, but it remains a secret that is only shared with close family members. Sorry. To make her recipe is a long, tedious process, but the result is a legendary flavor experience.

One year during the fair, Linda and I gathered up my mom, dad, plus our three girls and ventured out for a day at the fair. It happened to be on the day of the annual Texas-OU football rivalry game that is held each year at the Cotton Bowl which is on the fairgrounds.

Confab With a California Condor

As we entered the fair, there was a bird pavilion that featured many exotic species from all parts of the world. The bird keepers put on a show for the audience that included many of those beautiful and interesting birds. There were colorful parrots, macaws, peacocks, toucans, eagles, and even a rare gray California condor that was huge, even though it was fairly young. Many of the birds were perched on stands in the open air but were restrained by short leather straps. The condor was the most impressive bird. They typically stand about 3 ½ feet tall, their wingspan can be more than 9 feet, and they can weigh up to 25 pounds. Suffice it to say, they may not be as large as Big Bird, but they are truly impressive animals.

We were able to get close to the birds, and the girls really enjoyed seeing and watching them. We left the bird show and visited the various other pavilions, ate some corny dogs, and the girls enjoyed several carnival rides. The area where the rides were located was right next to the Cotton Bowl.

Since the girls were riding the tilt-awhirl, Linda and Dad had gone to the restroom while Mom and I stood nearby waiting for the ride to conclude. Watching them on the tilt-awhirl brought back unfond memories of me getting sick after riding one when I was a youngster. I swore off those kinds of rides ever since my day at the fair was ruined by motion sickness.

I heard a roar from the crowd in the Cotton Bowl and looked at the scoreboard and saw Texas had scored a touchdown. I just happened to notice a very large bird circling above the scoreboard and then cruising high over the crowd. I watched it for a few minutes and pointed the bird out to my mom. I commented that seeing a bird of that size hovering over the crowd was rather unusual – we just don't have big birds like that hanging out in Dallas. We both kept watching it. The bird descended near the scoreboard and then dove down at a rapid pace as he was about 50 yards away. When he got about 20 feet off the ground, he leveled off and was flying fast and furious heading straight toward us. I then said, "Mom, that has to be the California condor – he must have escaped."

The condor continued at a blazing pace heading right at us. He was now about 10 feet off the ground. He then started flapping his wings as he was putting on the brakes and then landed literally 3 feet from me. He was so close I felt the air of his wings swoosh. Mom and I just stood there in amazement. We were both shocked. I thought to myself, "This big bird had escaped, flew around, and out of probably 150,000 people on the fairgrounds that day, he decided to land right beside us." It was crazy.

We both just stood there and stared at the bird. He looked up at us as if he were saying "Hello there, humans." People began crowding around, and I saw a police officer, so I called out to him for help. When he came over, he was a bit surprised as well. I told him the condor had evidently escaped from the bird exhibit, and I advised the officer to contact someone to come get him. He then got on the radio and was told to try and keep the bird there while the bird keepers made their way over to recapture it. Neither the officer nor I were about to mess with the bird because his talons looked very intimidating, and his beak was huge. I certainly didn't want to make him mad.

The officer was at a loss as to how to keep the bird occupied, and I happened to notice there was a food truck right next to us that was selling fajitas. I slowly walked over and told one of the cooks that we had a little emergency and could he spare some meat to try and keep the big bird occupied. The cook gave me some meat, and I tossed a few pieces of beef on the ground in front of the condor. He went into a feeding frenzy and quickly gobbled up the meat as if he hadn't eaten for days. I could hear him chomping away. He seemed to like it and looked at me as if to say, "That was delicious, can I please have more?" I didn't want him to attack me, so I quickly obliged and tossed him some more meat. Again, it was gone in seconds.

I was out of meat and was beginning to think the condor was not going to be happy about it. I thought at this rate the bird was going to eat the entire inventory of the food truck before the keepers arrived. I got several more pieces – this time it was chicken meat. I tossed him a few more pieces and he gobbled those up. I later read that condors are not typically aggressive, but when it comes to eating, they are fully capable of fighting off other animals that might want to share in the spoils.

It was now about five minutes since the officer made his call for help. I asked him if he had heard anything, and he said the keepers were on their way. While hoping to assuage his voracious appetite and keep him occupied, I started feeding the condor one piece at a time. A guy in the crowd decided he was going to try and capture the bird, so he took off his jacket, went around behind the bird and tried to sneak up on him. When the guy came closer, the condor turned around. Then Big Bird unfolded his wings and snapped at the guy several times with his huge beak and made a hissing and squawking noise. The guy stopped in his tracks and quickly retreated…advisedly so, because the bird was obviously not in the mood to be messed with. I tossed the condor another piece of meat to keep him busy and calm his temper.

Finally, the keeper showed up with a net and carefully recaptured the wayward escapee. I told the keeper that the bird had enjoyed a nice gourmet lunch that included beef and chicken fajita meat. The keeper thanked me profusely for keeping the condor occupied until he got there and said that the meat was a great idea. I said I was happy to help and bade the condor a fond farewell. It was a brief but meaningful friendship that the condor and I shared. I am still baffled as to why he chose to hang out for lunch with me instead of one of the other 150,000 people that were there. I guess I was just lucky – or perhaps he remembered me telling him how beautiful and impressive he was when we met at the bird pavilion earlier in the day.

The Beach and the Brown Hawk

I had just finished a breakfast meeting with a customer at a restaurant on the beach in San Diego. I noticed a guy walking along the beach close to the restaurant with a large bird on his shoulder. I was intrigued, so I walked over to him. I approached him slowly and asked if I could see the bird up close. He said, "Of course, he's very friendly." I asked him what kind of bird it was, and he told me it was a red-shouldered hawk.

As I stood next to him, I was amazed at how stunning the bird was. His feathers were all different colors of brown with white tips, and his body was a beautiful reddish brown and orange. His tail was brown with white stripes. His back had a checkerboard pattern. He was an impressively large bird and seemed to be well-mannered. The guy said that red-shouldered hawks are commonly found along the coast in California.

The hawk was not nearly as big as my California condor friend, but he was still nearly two feet tall, and when he spread his wings, his wingspan was probably 4 feet in width. He was definitely big enough to intimidate me.

I asked the guy how he acquired his fine feathered friend, and he explained that he had rescued him. He told me he stumbled across the hawk in his neighborhood when it was a small nestling. He theorized that the hawk had somehow got separated from his mother. He nursed the bird back to health and they became fast friends. I thought that it was a strange and unique kind of pet. The man explained that he had constructed a nice nest for the hawk in his back yard and the bird comes and goes as he pleases.

As we continued our chat, I asked if the bird might let me hold him. The owner said, "Since you've got a jacket on, it should be OK – his talons probably won't hurt you." Those talons were certainly intimidating so I was a little leery, but the idea of getting to hold that beautiful animal was probably a once-in-a-lifetime opportunity. He told me to slowly raise my arm, and he would lean forward to see if the hawk would step onto my arm. I did as he told me, and sure enough, the gorgeous bird cooperated. He only weighed about 3 pounds.

I was a little nervous with the bird sitting on my arm, but I tried hard not to show it – I didn't want the hawk to freak out. I slowly lowered my arm and just admired this beautiful animal. He stared into my eyes intently. His piercing eyes had black pupils surrounded by a light brown outline. They were beautifully intimidating yet reassuringly comforting that everything was OK. I told him how beautiful he was and how nice he was behaving. After a couple of minutes of admiring and talking to the bird, he opened his wings and flapped them a few times as if to say, "OK, buddy, enough of that sweet talk; I'm done with you." I slowly raised my arm, and he climbed back on the owner's shoulders.

It was time for me to get on the road for another meeting, so I thanked the man for allowing me to do something I had never experienced before. It was certainly another memorable encounter with a magnificent animal.

Chapter 23

Uninvited Guests

It was a usual Friday night in the Allen household. We had dinner, watched TV, and when it was time for Linda to go to bed, I retreated to my office to work on some songs. Around midnight, it was time for me to hit the sack. I made sure the front and back doors were locked and then settled into bed.

Our house was built on an acre of land, and we were surrounded by large oak trees. It was a beautiful place that was in the country surroundings enough to have an assortment of wild animals that occasionally occupied our neighborhood with us, including deer, bobcats, roadrunners, large spiders, coyotes, foxes, snakes, opossums, racoons, owls, hawks, and even a mountain lion (more on that later). At times, it was like living in our own zoo habitat.

Our bedroom entrance was adjacent to the door to the garage. After a few minutes in bed, I heard a slight click that sounded like the door to the garage had opened. I hesitated to get up because I was snuggly tucked into bed. I lay there for a while and then decided I needed to get up and close the door…so I begrudgingly did. I noticed the large outside garage door had been left open, so I closed it. I recalled Linda going to her car parked out back to retrieve something. Evidently, she not only forgot to close the garage door, she also did not fully close the door to the house.

After closing both doors, I then hopped back into bed. I was almost asleep when I heard dishes rattling in the kitchen. I thought that was rather strange, but maybe some good Samaritan or perhaps an angel had descended upon the kitchen and decided to clean the dishes. It then dawned on me that it might be an ill-intentioned thief who had entered the house. I grabbed my pistol and made my way to the kitchen. I didn't see anyone in the darkness, so I turned on the light. Much to my utter surprise, there was indeed an unexpected visitor. Rocky Racoon had stepped into the room and found more than a Gideon's Bible. That's a Beatles song reference for those not familiar with it.

I looked at Rocky; Rocky looked at me. I was armed, but I didn't want to make a mess in the kitchen, nor did I want to scare the crap out of Linda by shooting him. So, Rocky and I just stared at each other, both of us wondering what to do. Rocky had plopped himself on the kitchen counter and had been licking the plates left over from dinner. He didn't get any leftovers because Linda and I were members of the clean plate club (a family childhood reference).

I had no idea how to extricate Rocky from our humble abode. He didn't seem like he was at all intimidated by my presence, but I was certainly intimidated by his. I had never encountered a predicament like this and was struggling to come up with an idea of how to get rid of Rocky without murderous violence.

I first opened the sliding glass door that was leading to the back patio near the kitchen. I was thinking maybe he would just voluntarily mosey out the door and I could get back to bed. My problem was how to convince him that this was his best option (and mine). I approached him slowly to try and shoo him out the door. He wasn't having it. He hissed, showed his teeth, and displayed his rather dangerous looking claws. I did recall that racoons were not prone to attacking, but that they did have enough self-defense weaponry to do-damage…so I backed off.

I then had the brilliant idea that I could force him into a box and then take him outside. I recalled that we had purchased a new dryer and still had the large box in the garage. I retrieved it and then got a piece of bamboo to help prod my uninvited guest into the box so that I could haul him out the sliding glass door. I was not completely sold that the plan would work, but I had to do something.

When I made my way back to the kitchen with box and stick in hand, Rocky was still perched on the countertop and surrounded by plates, pots, and pans. I scooted the box next to the counter and wielded my stick. I poked at him, but Rocky was not scared – however, I was. He merely responded with a blank stare, not showing any fear or intimidation. I'm sure he thought, "Is that ALL this guy has?" I concluded that more affirmative action was needed, so I gave him a few good whacks with the stick. Again, I'm sure he thought, "This guy is really lame if he expects me to just fall into the box – I ain't gonna go that easy." Rocky then hissed, snarled, and showed his nasty teeth; they looked like he had received dental care in the UK where many people have bad teeth.

I decided to try my old home run swing; I pretended I was hitting a Nolen Ryan fastball and hauled off with as much power as I could muster. I connected soundly and it really pissed him off. He then made a quick escape as he climbed straight up the wall and sat down on top of the upper kitchen cabinets. Linda had placed some nice antique bottles and other beautiful dishes on top of the cabinets as decorations. I could only imagine him raking off all those antiques and leaving me to explain what happened. Rocky knocked over a few of them, but fortunately, they did not tumble down.

Plan A was obviously a failure, so I needed a plan B. I went to my office, fired up my computer, and searched for "how to get rid of a racoon in your house." The first thing that came up was "Racoons can be very dangerous animals to humans – do not approach them or engage with them." I thought to myself, "Now, that was helpful." The web page advised calling an animal control person to assist. Unfortunately for me, it was now after 1:00am and I was pretty sure no one was on duty at that time of night. I was at a loss as to what to do.

Calling the Cops

I went back into the kitchen to check on Rocky, and he was still sitting on top of the cabinet. I decided to call 911 to see if they might have any suggestions.

When the operator answered the call, I explained that I did not have an emergency but that I needed help. I told her about the situation; she appeared to be a bit amused yet sympathetic. She told me that she could call an animal control officer to assist, and I thought, "Great – I can finally evict this uninvited squatter." The operator said, "Sir, it usually costs $200 for an animal control officer to come out and assist you, but since it is after 1:00am, it will be $400." I was distraught that I was going to have to pay $400 just to get Rocky removed.

Then she said, "Mr. Allen, let me put you on hold and see if I can reach a police officer who might be able to help." I then waited on hold for a few minutes. She came back on the line and said that an officer was going to stop by to see if he could be of assistance. I thanked her and she said, "Good luck!"

After about ten minutes, a car drove up our driveway. I went outside and greeted the officer. He got out of his police cruiser and told me he would try to help get rid of Rocky. He opened his trunk and said, "I stopped by my house and got this fish gaff…maybe it'll help." For those that don't know, a fish gaff is a long pole with a large sharp hook on the end. It's used to spear fish and haul them into the boat. I started imagining the officer attacking Rocky with this fish gaff and me having to clean up a bloody mess. However, I concluded it was better than living with this crazed invader. I told the officer that I truly appreciated his help.

We then proceeded into the kitchen, and when the officer saw Rocky perched on top of the cabinet, he commented, "Boy, that's a big fat racoon; how'd he get up there?" I explained that my plan A did not work, and Rocky climbed straight up the wall and sat on top of the cabinets. We could see little indentations in the sheetrock from his sharp claws. He then said, "Yeah, those guys can climb just about anything." The officer then continued to assess the situation.

After a brief strategic planning session, we decided that the officer would stand on one side of the kitchen, knock him down from on top of the cabinet, and then try to force him out the sliding glass door which was the closest exit point. We placed obstacles in the pathway, hoping he would guide himself in the right direction and scoot out the back door. We certainly did not want him to escape into another part of the house to wreak more havoc. I laid a chair on its side blocking a door to a hallway and used my infamous box to block another escape pathway. We were set to execute plan B.

We assumed our positions on the battlefield and the officer began his attack with the fish gaff. Rocky didn't seem to want to cooperate as he travelled further away on top of the cabinets, knocking over more of Linda's beautiful antiques. I thought to myself, "Rocky, if you break any of those antiques, there will be hell to pay – Linda will come after you with a vengeance." Again, fortunately, he didn't break anything.

After several attempts, the officer finally hooked the gaff around Rocky's neck and pulled him down. Rocky hit the countertop with a thud and fell to the floor. He then got up, looked around, and headed out of the kitchen. Instead of following the path we created, Rocky was undaunted and just jumped over the chair and headed down the hallway toward our bedroom. I had left the door to the garage open, and fortunately, our bedroom door was closed. Instead of heading down the hallway and out the door to his freedom, he decided to take a right-hand turn into the laundry room. I suppose he decided that he wasn't quite through tormenting me.

He then climbed straight up the wall and perched himself on top of the upper cabinet in the laundry room. It became increasingly clear that he was also fond of sitting on top of upper cabinets. Luckily, there were no antiques to destroy on top of those cabinets. It was time to develop plan C.

Extricating Rocky

The officer and I were determined to get Rocky out of my house, and we were so close to doing it. All we had to do was get him down from the cabinet, out the laundry room door, and then take a hard right turn and exit out to the garage. The victory was within our grasp, and we were determined that Rocky was NOT going to win and become a permanent resident in my house.

The officer went into the laundry room with his gaff. I placed my box accordingly to block the hallway and had my trusty stick in hand ready to let Rocky know that the better part of valor was to exit peacefully and find someone else to torture.

We began executing our battle plan. The officer raised his gaff. Rocky was hissing and showing his teeth. Once again, the officer got the gaff around his neck and pulled Rocky down from the cabinet. Rocky hit the washer with a thud and flopped to the floor. He quickly got on his feet and headed out the laundry room door. Rocky then turned and looked left toward me and the box. I said, "Don't even think about it."

Rocky then looked to his right, saw the open door, and dashed out. My happy dance was interrupted when the officer said, "Let's check to make sure he's out of the garage." I got a flashlight, and we began looking in all the nooks and crannies. Suddenly, I saw Rocky hiding behind a box underneath my workbench and said, "You've got to be kidding me!" Dejected and angry, I had had about enough of Rocky's antics. It occurred to me that the officer could easily take out his firearm and quickly terminate this endless saga; however, then he'd have to fill out a bunch of paperwork for discharging his weapon and justify the killing of a racoon. I thought maybe I could go back in the house and get my gun to shoot Rocky, but the officer would probably not approve of that either. Most likely, it would be even more paperwork and possibly a trip to the police station for me.

Plan D had to be developed, so we got our heads together. How ironic was it that a police officer and his trusty sidekick were actually trying to encourage and assist the escape of a known criminal who was guilty of criminal trespass without a reasonable doubt. Once more, we constructed a pathway, and then both of us started poking and prodding Rocky. Again, he was hissing and fighting back against our sticks. Finally, Rocky was convinced that these two super-powered humans were not going to give up, and he ran out from underneath the workbench and raced out the garage door to his freedom. I quickly closed the garage door, gave the officer a high five, and said, "Thank God that nightmare is over – I thought it would never end!"

We both had a good laugh, and I thanked the officer for his help. As he drove away, I wondered about what he wrote in his incident report. It was nearly 2:30am when I laid my weary head down after a long and arduous night doing battle with my nemesis, Rocky Racoon. Linda had slept through the whole ordeal. When I went to bed, she said, "Are you just now coming to bed? It's awfully late." Rather than going through the entire story, I said, "Go back to sleep – I'll tell you all about it in the morning." Gladly, I never saw Rocky again, but I often wonder if he gave up his life of crime or became a repeat offender. Knowing this ornery and brazen critter, probably the latter.

A Cougar Comes Calling

As mentioned earlier, our house in the country was akin to an animal farm at times. Most of the animals were welcomed, but we could do without the coyotes, bobcats, snakes, and spiders.

In the front of the house, I had designed and built some exceptionally large flower beds. I love gardening and seeing all the flowers and greenery in bloom, especially the dozen large, beautiful azaleas, which are hard to grow in Texas. I took immense pride in planting a wide variety of flowers and bulbs every spring. However, the older I got, the harder I had to work, and I realized that I was a tad bit overzealous in my design. I questioned the pain-to-gain ratio.

When driving up to our circular driveway, there was a fork in the road, and right as the driveway divided, there was a huge oak tree that was more than two feet in diameter. The center island was a large bed filled with Japanese Jasmine.

One beautiful spring morning, as I was casually watering the flowers in the front of the house, I saw something strange out of the corner of my eye; the huge oak tree did not look the same. I looked more closely and saw what looked like a large animal perched on the tree about four feet off the ground. I was about 60 or 70 feet away from the tree, so I couldn't quite make out what kind of animal it was – but I could see it was big.

I closed the nozzle and laid the hose down. As I approached the tree, I noticed it was some kind of very large-looking cat. It was a light brown or tan in color, and it had a white underbelly. We had frequent visits by bobcats, so I knew it definitely was not a bobcat. Then I saw a large tail with a brown tip move. I stood there for a minute trying to figure out exactly what it was. I slowly approached the animal, and I realized it was a cougar, also known as a mountain lion or puma. I had never seen one outside of a zoo, but it was easily identifiable.

The cougar looked at me and I stopped in my tracks when I was about forty feet away. I was aware that they are very solitary animals, and that they rarely attack humans. However, they were still considered an extremely dangerous animal if cornered or if they were protecting their young.

I happened to notice that our neighbor's cat was lying about ten feet away from the cougar. I am sure the cougar was thinking he was about to have a gray cat for breakfast, but my presence had distracted him from his mission. I certainly didn't want to get between him and his breakfast, and I was definitely not interested in a tussle with a wild animal that probably weighed 150 pounds.

The fact that we had two small chihuahuas, which would have been a happy hour snack for this beast, had me concerned. I thought I needed to scare this cougar away. As with most wild animals, if you scare them away, chances are they will not come back – I certainly did not want him hanging around our property.

I was standing near the crushed rock driveway and slowly reached down and picked up two handfuls of rocks. I then bravely ran right at the cougar, screamed loudly, and started throwing rocks at him. I managed to get in a few hits and fortunately for me, the cougar jumped down from the tree and made a fast exit down the driveway and across the street. The gray cat was also startled and ran in the opposite direction. He most likely did not know I saved his life.

I ran down the driveway to make sure the cougar had vacated the premises, and I could see him scooting toward the lake and into the forest in a hurry. I walked back up the driveway feeling like a bad ass that won a battle with a cougar; I picked up the hose, and then calmly continued to water my flowers. I did keep a keen eye out in case the cougar decided to come back for a second round. Thankfully, he did not. I felt good about saving a life that day, and I luckily never saw that big cat again. I am sure he thought, "I don't want any part of that guy – he's downright crazy!"

Section VII

Tales from the Hood

Chapter 24

Big, Bad Black Cat

Linda and I spent the first fourteen years of our marriage in our humble house nestled within a very typical middle-class neighborhood. The house was in a new construction development area in Carrollton, TX. The homes in our neighborhood were tract houses that were built by a large developer. The streets were lined with six or seven different floor plans, ours being one that would be categorized as medium-sized.

It was a good first house for us to begin our blended family. At that time, we had one daughter, Dusty, who lived with us full-time, along with Adrian, who lived with her mother but spent a good deal of time with us. Our youngest daughter, Ashley, was yet to be born when we moved in, but she joined the family two years later. Our blended children then consisted of yours, mine, and ours.

It was a nice, quiet neighborhood with numerous young families and lots of kids. A new elementary school had been constructed, and there was a strong feeling of community. We got to know all our neighbors, and our daughters knew and played with all the other kids on the block. Our neighborhood was close to being an idyllic place to raise our children in what felt like an All-American community.

Like most hoods, we generally had friendly neighbors; but some with no kids kept to themselves. Also, like most communities, there were only a few of those grouchy "keep off my lawn" neighbors on our block. They quickly identified themselves through their behaviors as they interfaced with kids that will be kids. We parents mostly just ignored those grumpy curmudgeons.

At one point, we decided to adopt a kitten. He was solid black, very cute, and developed a very likable personality. For some still unknown reason, Linda named him M-M-M-Melvin. She was a big country music fan and thought the stuttering country singer Mel Tillis was an appropriate namesake for the cat. OK, whatever.

Melvin grew very rapidly as the weeks passed. He kept growing, and growing, and growing. At full size, he reached 22 pounds, and he was not a fat cat; he was just big. Besides his big body-size and large, rounded head, he was tall, sleek, muscular, and strongly resembled a small black panther. When we took him to the veterinarian, the whole staff was intrigued by his size and beautiful, shiny black fur. The vet walked in to examine Melvin, stopped in his tracks, and said, "Wow, that's a big cat!" Fittingly, he said Melvin resembled a type of cat known as a "baby black panther." He was thoroughly impressed.

Cat Fight

Melvin roamed the neighborhood and established a reputation for being a sweet cat that everyone loved. The dogs in the hood showed respect for him, and the other cats in the hood were certainly intimidated by him. However, there was one smaller cat owned by the neighbor across the street whose cat evidently had a Napoleon complex. This cat was about half the size of Melvin and seemed to get a kick out of taunting and harassing Melvin. One day, I was out watering the front flowerbeds while Melvin was peacefully sprawled out on the front porch where he kept watch over the hood.

I noticed the neighbor's cat slowly sauntering up the front walkway in a semi-crouched position as if he were stalking prey. I tried to shoo the cat away; he retreated to the edge of the sidewalk and just sat there. I continued watering my flowers. After a few minutes, I turned and saw the cat stealthily sneaking up the walkway. Melvin just lay there peacefully taking it all in...he wasn't intimidated or bothered. I tried again to shoo away the menacing cat, but this time he didn't seem fazed. Evidently, he was undaunted in whatever mischief he was trying to stir up.

It seemed like a cat turf war was about to commence when Melvin took notice of the possible ill-intentions of the neighbor's cat. I was pretty sure who was going to get the worst end of the deal if a battle ensued. I once again turned my attention to watering the flower bed on the side of the house. As I was walking away, I noticed the neighbor's cat was continuing to sneak up on Melvin, and I decided to let nature take its course. The neighbor's cat was apparently dumber than dirt...if that's possible. The problem with stupidity is that it does not recognize itself.

After a few more minutes, I heard Melvin growling – he was giving the cat fair warning to stay off his turf. Seemingly, the neighbor's cat was dead set on a confrontation. I could hear the back and forth growling and snarling from both cats, and then all hell broke loose. The cat fight was on. I put down the hose and ran to the front to try and break up the fight. It didn't last long – it was a first-round knockout for Melvin that only lasted a few seconds. It was shorter than Mike Tyson's knockout of Marvin Frazier that lasted only 30 seconds.

The neighbor's cat made a rapid retreat, limping off in utter shame and defeat. I noticed one of his ears was detached and bleeding, a bit of fur was missing, and he continued his limping retreat across the street. I thought to myself, "Now, that's a stupid cat without any good sense whatsoever." Melvin calmly moseyed back to the front porch and laid himself down; he hadn't even broken a sweat, nor did he seem to be bothered by the provocation and short skirmish.

The following day, I was watering the flowers again when I saw the grumpy neighbor across the street marching toward me. In today's terminology, she was widely known as the neighborhood Karen. Nobody liked her, and she had a few run-ins with our friends who lived next door to her. She seemed to be coming in hot and bothered, and as she got to our sidewalk, she began to verbally accost me, saying our cat had mauled her cat. I thought about turning the hose on her to cool her off, but being the peaceful nice guy that I am, I decided against it…although it was very tempting.

She continued to rant and rave, complaining that she had to take her cat to the vet, and that I should be responsible for the bill. I told her that I witnessed the entire incident, and that I tried to shoo her cat away twice, but her cat was intent on harassing and aggravating Melvin. I explained that Melvin was serenely taking a nap on the front porch, and that her cat was the instigator. I also explained that had I not intervened, she would probably be burying her cat instead of taking it to the vet.

The irate Karen continued her verbal rampage and blamed me for the incident. I calmly remarked, "I'm sorry your cat got hurt, but your cat's stupidity in trying to fight with a cat twice its size is not my problem." I then turned around and continued my watering. Being the typical Karen, she said, "I'm going to sue you in small claims court for the vet expenses – my brother is an attorney." I knew Melvin would be found innocent because of the "stand your ground" laws in Texas; his turf was being invaded, and all he did was defend it. We had a strong case, and she had a cat with either no brains or no good sense – or both.

Rather than further agitate this Karen, I continued to ignore her. After a few more unkind words aimed in my direction, the thought of turning the hose on her was even more tempting – perhaps it would cool her down. But again, I begrudgingly convinced myself that the better part of valor was to just turn the water off and go back into the house. I never heard from her attorney brother, and the neighborhood Karen continued to spread her Karen-ness throughout the neighborhood while Melvin continued to be the bad-ass-cat-in-the-hood. Seems like the crazier the world gets the nuts are easier to find. Our neighborhood Karen was undoubtedly a nut-job.

Chapter 25

Annual Race Ritual

Our daughters grew up with some good kids in our neighborhood. They all got along, and it was a diverse ethnic group. I don't recall any internal strife or fights – they managed to live in peace and harmony – unlike some of us adults.

Since our girls were interested in other things besides sports, and I didn't have any sons, it was good to hang out with the boys in the hood sometimes. I spent time tossing the football around with many of the boys whose dads were either too busy, too lazy, or didn't play sports.

I'm not sure how it started, but each year in the spring, the neighborhood boys and girls held a mini track event where everybody raced in their own age group. There was a starting line and a finish line marked off in chalk in the middle of the street. I suppose the whole idea was to see who had grown and who could race faster than they did in the previous year.

I was an interested observer, and at the end of the event during the first year, the older boys started talking smack about how they could beat me in a race. I explained to them that my racing days were over when I turned 30. They then started throwing insults and accusing me of being gutless; they thought I was afraid of them beating me. I told those little harassers that I didn't want to shame them when they were beaten in a race by an old man such as me. I was also trying to protect myself because I had not run an all-out sprint in many years, and I might pull a muscle and be laid up for weeks.

The taunting grew louder and even more fierce, so I decided to race them to preserve my honor and get those menacing brats off my back. They cheered and then started lining up on the starting line. In order to give them one more opportunity to back out, I asked them if they were sure they wanted to continue. They responded with a rousing, "YES!"

The older boys and I were at the starting line, and one of the younger girls said, "On your mark! Get set." The tension was building. The kids were waiting with great anticipation, and she said, "GO!" The race was on.

There was probably no one amongst the boys that were older than 10 or 11, but a few of them darted off in the front of the pack. I kept up with them by simply jogging along. I was toying with them and halfway through the race, I decided it was time for payback since they had jeered and insulted me. My old track racing experience helped as I kicked in the afterburner and streaked to the lead. As I crossed the finish line, I turned around to see that I had badly beaten those brats. It was a humiliating defeat for them, although they were good sports about it as was I. I told them, "Better luck next year!"

During the spring of each subsequent year, the big race was held. My winning streak had stretched to three years in a row, but the kids were growing older, getting bigger, and becoming more athletic. I believe it was the fourth year when there was a knock on our front door. It was the neighborhood boys, and they were ready to take me on. They were now 14 or 15 years old. One of the boys announced, "Mr. Allen, you're going down this year – we've got a new neighbor, and he's on the track team at Newman Smith High School."

I had felt so sorry for those boys being beaten by an old man every year, but it appeared they had developed a new tactic with a new team member. The taunting and intimidation commenced from those pesky monsters. I agreed to take on the challenge and asked them, "If I win this time, can I retire as the all-time champ? After all, I am getting mighty old." After a brief discussion amongst the gang, they agreed.

As the new kid on the block and I lined up at the starting line, the jeering and harassment grew harsher and louder. The crowd of kids had grown, and now many of the parents were on their front porches anticipating a historic race. The starter said, "On your mark." He paused and said, "You're going down, Mr. Allen." I ignored him. He then continued, "Get set for your defeat!" I looked over and smiled at him. The starter then said, "GO!"

I didn't want to mess around and just jog from the start like I usually did. I didn't know this new competitor, so I hit top speed in just a few steps. The young buck kept up with me for about 15 steps into the race. I thought, "OK, he's pretty fast; let's see what he's got now." I kicked in what little afterburner I still had as an old man and zoomed out in front. As the race passed the halfway point, I was lengthening my lead. I knew I had it in the bag, and for the last 25 or so yards, I turned around and ran backwards across the finish line. The victory was mine. I was then able to retire as the undisputed and undefeated neighborhood racing champ.

As the kids gathered around to congratulate me, I couldn't help but snidely return some of their smack-talking – but it was good-natured. We all had some real fun over the years – they were all good kids – and I gladly retired as champion speedster of the hood.

Chapter 26

Home Invasion

My wife Linda had connections with an apparel representative who broached the idea of having a sample sale inside our home – similar to a garage sale only with a clothing manufacturer's sample garments. It sounded like a good idea to earn some extra cash by splitting the profits with the rep.

We prepared the house and picked up the samples along with some racks to display them. We decided to start the sale on a Friday afternoon and end it on Saturday evening. We posted signs throughout the neighborhood to promote the sale.

We had decent traffic on Friday afternoon, but Saturday's traffic was much better. All things considered, we had a successful sale while taking in a little over $2,000. We still had a lot of clothing samples strewn all over the house, but we were happy with the results. At the time, we were a typical family living from paycheck to paycheck, so an extra $1,000 was a big boon to our finances. We celebrated by having a large dinner feast at Taco Bueno that night. After a long day, we all went to bed early.

I was in a deep slumber when Dusty, our middle daughter, came into our room and started shaking me. When I woke up, she said, "Daddy, somebody is breaking into my room and coming through my window." I jumped out of bed and put on my robe. I was scared that someone knew we had a lot of cash in the house along with an abundance of valuable clothing samples. I quietly walked down the hallway and peered around the corner and into her room. There was enough light that I could see what looked like a young boy standing by Dusty's bed while another one was climbing through the open window.

Dusty had left her window unlocked and the screen was missing from an incident a week earlier when she had snuck out with a girlfriend on a sleepover. Dusty was not one who could live with a guilty conscience – so much so that after the girls had returned from their little escapade that lasted only a few minutes, she came into our bedroom, woke me up, and then informed me that she and her friend had snuck out. She went on to explain that she was very sorry, but they were back and that everything was OK.

In the fogginess of my awakened sleep, I looked up at her and said, "Thanks for being honest and telling me – we'll talk about it in the morning." I then added, "Go back to sleep and never do that again." She replied, "Yes, sir, I'm sorry."

A Hard Lesson Learned

Back to the home invaders. With the screen missing and the window not locked, it was an open invitation to a would-be burglar. As I said, it looked like these trespassers were kids, and I watched as the second kid made his way through the window. They had no idea I was watching, and I determined that they were most likely not armed and dangerous. I had no idea what would possess two kids to think it was a good idea to crawl through her window.

I reached around the corner, and as I turned on the light, I loudly screamed, "What are you doing in my house?" They were startled and looked at me with their eyes wide open. One of them quickly dashed out the window with the other one close behind. They scrambled out before I could grab them, so I climbed through the window right behind them. Off we went – the chase was on.

One of the kids turned left and the other turned right. Knowing I couldn't nab both of them, like a predator pursuing its prey, I picked out the slowest runner and began the chase. The kid darted into the street, and I am sure he was as juiced with adrenaline as I was. He had about a 20-yard head start on me. As we were running in the middle of the street, my robe was blowing in the breeze like Superman's cape. Luckily, no one was watching; otherwise, I would have been arrested for indecent exposure.

As the chase continued, I was yelling at the kid, "I'm gonna catch you, you little SOB." I kept saying, "Here I come, I'm gonna get you." Little did this kid know that I was the neighborhood speed champion, and his fate was doomed. I inched closer and closer to him. He kept looking back at me as I relentlessly closed the gap, and I continued to torment him with my trash talk that I was going to kick his ass! He started to veer to the left as I reached out to grab him. I snatched him by the collar of his shirt, and then he stumbled. As I was slowly bringing him to the ground, his face hit the curb, and I climbed on top of him. I pinned him down, got right in his face and screamed, "If I had a gun in my house, you'd be dead right now! What the hell were you thinking?" There were other appropriately phrased expletives involved as well.

We both were breathing hard from the chase, but I continued to shake him and yell at him – I wanted this incident to be as traumatic as possible to teach this kid a lesson. As much as I wanted to beat the crap out of him, I showed some semblance of restraint. And no, it was not child abuse; it was merely a teachable moment. I stood up, snatched him up, and we headed back to the house with my prisoner in tow. Of course, I continued to provide him with a very strongly worded lecture while we were on our way. I resoundingly reiterated that he was lucky he was not dead, and he was lucky I was not calling the police.

When we got back to the house, I knocked on the door. Linda had heard the initial commotion and Dusty explained to her what happened as I was tracking my prey. I yelled through the door that it was me, and she could open the door. When she did, the first thing I noticed was that in her hand she had a clothing iron as her defense weapon of choice. I took the boy inside and questioned him about who he was and where he lived. He told me his name was Jose and gave me his address. I then told Linda, Dusty and Ashley (our youngest) to get dressed because we were taking this boy home. Dusty did tell us that she knew the boy from school but didn't really call him a close friend.

I put Jose in the very back of our Chevy Astro van, and the rest of us loaded up in the front. It was around 3:00am when we arrived at his house. We all unloaded, and I knocked on the door to his house. It took a minute or two, and before he opened the door, Jose's father asked through the door, "Who is it?" I said, "My name is Bill Allen, and I have your son."

His father opened the door, and I explained to him what had transpired. I emphasized that Jose had broken into my house and I told his father, "You're lucky your son is still alive." Jose's father was obviously shocked and upset with what happened, and after apologizing, he promised that his son would be punished for his actions. Our family loaded back into our van and headed home. I then told Dusty that if Jose ever bothered her to please let me know – I would take care of it accordingly.

About ten years later, Linda and I were having dinner at a restaurant where Ashley worked as a bartender. Dusty was eating dinner with us as well. After dinner, she left our table to go talk with some friends.

A few minutes later, Dusty came back over to our table with a young man. She introduced him and said, "Dad, Mom, this is Jose – he's the guy that broke into our house." I was a bit surprised when he reached out to shake my hand. I obliged, and as we were shaking hands, he said, "Sir, I want to thank you for changing my life." He continued, "I was getting involved in things I shouldn't have been doing, but you taught me a very hard lesson. I went to college, I have a good job, and you helped me become a better person – thank you."

I was surprised by his comments and very happy that he had turned out to be a good kid after all. I gave him a hug and told him I was proud of him and that I was very happy things turned out well for him. Sometimes, it takes an unfortunate incident with a crazed madman protecting his family to scare a kid straight and turn his life around. I'm glad there was a happy ending and a hard lesson learned.

Section VIII

This is Personal

Chapter 27

Dredging up the Past

I have shared a wide variety of stories throughout this book. I have purposely avoided being a Debbie Downer, mostly because my life has been filled with events that have been fun, exhilarating, interesting, and sometimes very unusual. Perhaps it's safe to say that compared to most people, I have had my unfair share of memorable moments during my lifetime.

I have had a good life, having been born into a near idyllic family situation, and I've never been in trouble with the law (well, except for one speeding ticket). I've travelled the world and met some fascinating people. The one place I have not taken the reader of this book is to the dark, painful, and troubled times I endured. I suppose my life's stories would not be complete without going there, but reliving those moments is not nearly as fun and entertaining as telling tales about hanging out with Les Paul or Emmitt Smith, or visiting exotic places, or wild travel stories, or experiencing momentous musical moments.

I had a long and tedious internal debate about whether to expose my trials and tribulations and open those old wounds that have been gladly and carefully tucked away. I finally concluded that since the uncomfortable events I have lived through are part of the stories of my life, I might as well go there and disclose all aspects of my tenure on this earth.

In reliving and retelling these unpleasant memories, I had to dig up old feelings that I have mostly laid to rest, but as I retell them, many of those feelings of pain come flooding back. I am not a big fan of rehashing and reliving those experiences, but again, my story would not be complete without going down that road. I don't like to remember the bad times or talk about them; I am uncomfortable doing it, but I will. It's mostly because I am not one who likes to trouble others with my problems – after all, my problems are not anyone else's – they are mine to deal with. It's also about not wanting others to feel sorry for me and me not wanting to open the door so that other people can see into or share my pain. I am a private person, and those that know me will say it's true to a fault.

Call it a character flaw, stupidity, or whatever, I tend to suffer alone in silence. I'm not fully sure as to why or how I got this way, but that's just me. I make no excuses – I am who I am and that's all that I am. It's kind of ironic, because all through my life, people have sought me out to provide comfort and advice whenever a problem arose. I was always honored that people trusted me enough to confide in me, but strangely, I have always kept my troubles to myself.

I fully understand that life is not fun sometimes. There's hurt. There's pain. There are unpleasant memories. As Forrest Gump so famously told us, "My mom always said life was like a box of chocolates – you never know what you're going to get." Such is the nature of life.

I hark back to my song entitled, "The Road." It represents how we all live through hard times. We all question why things happen. But in the end, we somehow make it through those difficult events. The true measure of a person is how we emerge on the other side of pain and suffering. I call those events "character builders" that are the building blocks of who we are and what we have experienced.

The Road

When you look back through the pages of your life,
There's haunting memories that cut you like a knife.
The wounds have healed but each one left a scar.
It's to remind us that's what makes us who we are.

>   There's potholes and bumps that come along.
>   You gotta keep driving until the past is gone.
>   Why wonder why when things go wrong?
>   It's just The Road you were supposed to travel on.

There's always times when we have been betrayed.
Everybody's loved and laughed and cried the hurt away.

Sometimes we walk away with arrows in our back,
But we've got to lay to rest the troubles that we've had.

There's potholes and bumps that come along.
You gotta keep driving until the past is gone.
Why wonder why when things go wrong?
It's just The Road you were supposed to travel on.

We're better off forgetting than always regretting,
Looking back don't get us anywhere.
There's no U-turns on the bridges that have burned,
And nobody ever said that life is fair.

There's potholes and bumps that come along.
You gotta keep driving until the past is gone.
Why wonder why when things go wrong?
It's just The Road you were supposed to travel on.

© Copyright BR Allen Publishing, 2022

The First Cut is the Deepest

So, here we go. As mentioned at the beginning of this book, the first heartbreak that I recall was when our beautiful dog named Taffy was accidentally run over by my aunt. The next one was when my Grandma Bennett died. She was such a sweet lady who lived with us for many years, and I got very close to her – she was special to me for a lot of reasons. It broke my heart when she died due to heart problems. My next heartbreak, however, was a deep cut that left a massive scar.

I will not go into too many unpleasant details, but it involves my first wife, who shall remain nameless to protect both the innocent and the guilty. The preferred pronouns I shall use are she and her. I decided that the cause or backstory was less important than the subsequent effect that certain events and actions had on my life. In the end, it turns out that I can safely say it was just "the road I was supposed to travel on."

She and I met when I was a sophomore in college, and she was a senior in high school. We met at a church-sponsored coffee house in Oak Cliff, a section of Dallas where I was performing. She was there with one of her friends, and we happened to strike up a conversation. She was quite cute and seemed to be very smart, so I was both intrigued by her and attracted to her. She told me she enjoyed listening to my music – especially my original songs. We spent several minutes talking, and when it was time for her to leave, I escorted her and her friend to her car. I was performing at the coffee house the following Friday, and we agreed to meet up then.

When the next Friday rolled around, I made my way to the coffee house and was looking forward to seeing her again. Sure enough, she showed up, this time she was by herself. After my performance, we sat and talked for about an hour, and then I asked her if she would like to go get something to eat. She agreed and off we went on our first date.

I had dated several girls before, but this was different. We felt a special connection and our relationship continued to thrive. Two weeks later, she invited me to Sunday lunch with her and her family. I enjoyed meeting and talking to them, and there was one specific memory of that day that I recall.

We had a salad with lunch, and that is when I was introduced to Ranch dressing for the first time. I loved Thousand Island dressing, but out of respect for her mother, Evelyn, which was also my mother's name, I decided to try this new Ranch dressing that was taking the country by storm. Back then, it came in a dry powder pouch which had to be mixed with buttermilk and mayonnaise. When I first tasted the salad, I was immediately hooked – it was fabulous. Her mom was not the greatest cook, but I always looked forward to her Ranch dressing every Sunday.

Adventures With Her Dad

We continued to see each other regularly over the next several weeks and Sunday lunches after church became a regular event. Her father, Jerry, was a cool guy who owned a gas station. He seemed to enjoy my company since he had two daughters. It felt like he was excited to have a young buck to hang around with. Interestingly, he was building his own airplane inside his garage; I was impressed to say the least. I helped him build some of it on weekends, and when he finished building and testing, I was the second person to fly in the plane.

One Saturday, he called and told me the plane was finally finished, and that he had transported it to a hangar at Red Bird Airport in Dallas. He invited me to fly with him. As we drove to the airport where the plane was hangared, I thought maybe he had an ulterior motive by inviting me to fly with him – maybe this was a tactic to get rid of his daughter's suitor.

Yes, I was a brave soul to agree to fly in a homemade plane, but I trusted him because he was an airplane mechanic in the Navy – just like my dad. I was hoping and praying that he knew what he was doing; after all, his life was at stake as well. He was very meticulous during the construction, and he had been working on his hobby for more than two years, and he did have his pilot's license. Both of those were comforting.

As I climbed into the plane, I checked to see if there was an ejector seat, but I didn't find one. I started feeling OK, but then I was concerned because there was no parachute. I had never flown in a small two-passenger plane, let alone one built by some guy in his garage. I was nervous as we taxied onto the runway. As we accelerated for takeoff, I thought about bailing out before we got off the ground, but it was too late. Off we went into the wild blue yonder.

Again, having never flown in a small aircraft, it took some getting used to. When Jerry started doing fast maneuvers, my eyes were as big as saucers. Hard bank left, hard bank right, and then he performed a barrel roll. I was in shock and terrified, but the worst was yet to come. He put the plane in a straight up trajectory and then yelled, "Watch this, we're going to do a stall." I had no idea what that was, but I was white knuckling the sissy bars to my left and right. We were running at top speed straight up. Suddenly, he cut the engine, and our vertical climb stopped. I thought he had lost his mind, and we were doomed. We went into a free fall, and I thought for sure my stomach was going to exit my mouth. I had never felt that free falling feeling before, and I was pretty sure that I did not like it as we were spiraling out of control.

The nose of the plane tipped downward, and then we were in an all-out nosedive without the engine running. I was sure we would be splattered into a bloody puddle when we crashed. The memory of surviving the bomb scare flashed into my mind, but this was exceedingly scarier. Looking straight down at the ground from thousands of feet in the air was certainly a new experience for me; and I will add that it was something I never wanted to experience again.

After what seemed like an eternity in free fall, Jerry began pulling the plane out of a nosedive and then he re-started the engine. Fortunately, he successfully leveled the plane, and we rode around for a few more minutes before heading back to the airport. After we landed and taxied to the hangar, I quickly jumped out of the plane and tossed my cookies. I fought hard not to puke in his plane, and thankfully, I was successful. My knees were knocking, my hands were shaking, and I was traumatized. Flying in a tiny airplane and doing aero acrobatic tricks was certainly not on my bucket list of things I wanted to do, but at least the torment was over.

He asked if I was OK, and I bravely said, "Yes, I think I'll make it." He then asked if I had a good time. I responded, "Well, I had never done anything like that before." I then added, "It was certainly a once-in-a-lifetime experience!" I said that because I knew right then that I would never subject myself to such terror ever again. I was never so happy for my feet to be touching terra firma.

Despite Jerry torturing me with his aero acrobatic skills, he and I got along very well. He took me to Cowboy's games, Ranger's games, and I even worked at his gas station for part of one summer. I recall talking to him in the office of the gas station when a big, black Cadillac pulled up to a gas pump (note that this was before self-service). Jerry said, "Come with me, I want you to meet somebody, and you can pump his gas."

Of course, I followed him, and an enormous man stepped out of the car. Jerry said, "Bill, I want you to meet my best customer, Ed Jones." I reached out and shook his hand which swallowed mine. I then said, "No wonder they call you 'Too Tall' Jones." I pumped his gas while Jerry and Ed had a nice chat.

For those that don't know, Ed "Too Tall" Jones played for the Dallas Cowboys. He was 6' 9" tall and weighed a mere 280 pounds. I had never met such a massive giant of a man. It was exciting to meet a Dallas Cowboys legend who had a great career. He also had a strong affinity for Jerry and would never let anyone else work on his Cadillac. Ed was very congenial, and I always enjoyed pumping gas for him whenever he stopped by; plus, he always remembered my name.

Jerry and I continued to develop a very close relationship over the years. After he gave his daughter away at our wedding, he told me he was happy she had found a really good guy like me. I will add that whenever he invited me to go flying with him, unfortunately, I always had something else to do.

The New Arrival

Looking back, we probably should never have married so young. She was 18 and I was 20, but we were happily in love. I adored her and gave her my heart and soul. After about a year, things were not going well in our marriage. Like any new partnership, we had to figure each other out. Jerry was invested in our marriage, so he paid for us to work with a counsellor. Our relationship got better, and the counselling seemed to help put us on the right track.

Although our marriage was far from smooth sailing, we did make it to our fifth anniversary. Both of us had graduated from college and had gotten jobs. I was teaching school, and she started her nursing career. We bought a house in Carrollton where I was teaching. Life was good.

One day, she called me from her work and told me she had a doctor's appointment and would be home late. I cooked dinner, and when she got home, she said she had something important to tell me. We sat down on the couch, and my mind was swirling, thinking that a shoe was going to drop – which it did. Only this time, it was good news. She informed me that we were going to have a baby. I was surprised as one might expect, but she was never good at remembering to take her birth control pills, so I wasn't completely shocked.

We informed her parents and mine that they were going to be grandparents. For my mom and dad, it would be their fifth grandchild, but for her parents, it was going to be their first. They were thrilled.

The pregnancy went smoothly, and I was ecstatic that our marriage had blossomed. I was nervous about being a father, but I was fully prepared to welcome my baby into this world. We found out we were having a girl, so we decorated the baby's room accordingly, and we anxiously awaited the birth.

We had gone to bed one night when she woke me up and informed me that her water had broken; it was time to get to the hospital ASAP. I jumped out of bed, got dressed, helped her get dressed, and then loaded us into the car. Off we went.

When we got to the hospital, she was having light contractions. Since her water had broken and her contractions were not intensifying, the doctor said he had to further induce her labor. I called her parents and told them the day had come, so they rushed to the hospital. My parents lived in Chicago, so they could not be there on such short notice.

After her labor intensified, it was time to deliver. We rolled into the delivery room, and the nurses made their final preparations. When the doctor came in, he examined her and informed us that the baby had not turned, so he would try to manipulate the baby into the right position. His efforts were unsuccessful. He then informed us that the baby was trying to come out butt first which was not going to work. He explained that the only option was to do an emergency C-section, because the baby was in distress. I left the room and went to sit with Jerry and Evelyn.

After about thirty minutes of anxiety and anticipation, the nurse said I could see my new baby girl. I was elated to welcome and hold our precious new arrival that we named Adrian. She was beautiful. I could not hold the tears back as the nurse handed her to me – I finally got to meet my new baby girl. When Jerry and Evelyn came in shortly thereafter, they beamed with joy as they each held their first grandbaby. It was another momentous occasion in my life.

Over the next several months, life as a new father was great. I never knew how much I could love that little girl. She was a good baby, and I frequently took care of her since her mother was working intermittent shifts as a nurse. Adrian and I had developed a very close bond during her first year and a half. I sang and played my guitar for her, and she sat in my lap as we watched Dallas Mavericks games. Maybe that's why Adrian loves music and sports to this day.

The Big Shoe Drops

Two years after Adrian was born, our marriage had deteriorated. As mentioned earlier, I will not go into unpleasant details – all I will say is that I loved my wife dearly, and I gave everything I had toward building a good marriage. It is my opinion that I had gone above and beyond the call of duty.

It was becoming more and more obvious that my wife was on a different track than I was. I had spent a great deal of emotional capital trying to preserve our marriage, but the investment was not paying off. The writing on the wall was evident, but I still refused to acknowledge it and accept it. I was raised by my parents to stand strong, fight through, and persevere.

Several of the kids I was close to at the high school where I taught could tell something was going on in my personal life. My pianist for the choir was a very sweet young lady, and one day after class, she came to me and asked if everything was OK with me. I told her it was nice of her to ask and explained there were things going on in my personal life that were very painful. She then said, "I am so sorry Mr. Allen, I will be praying for you." She then gave me a hug and said, "Let me know if I can help you in any way." I said, "Donna, thank you so much – I appreciate it."

Later than afternoon during my free period, the principal of the school called me over the intercom and said he needed to see me in his office. I thought it was strange but didn't think anything more about it. When I walked into his office, there was a constable standing beside him. I had no idea what was going on and I was very confused.

The constable asked me for my driver's license. I gave it to him, and he said, "Mr. Allen, I am here to serve you with divorce papers. Can you please sign this form for me?" He then handed me the papers. My heart sank. I was in total disbelief. I was embarrassed in front of Ken, the principal I had worked with for five years, and I had a feeling of total devastation wash over me.

The constable left his office, and then Ken invited me to sit down. He said he felt horrible for me, and that I was welcome to take a few days off if necessary. I thanked him for his understanding and told him I would take him up on his offer.

I went home after the school day ended and sat down to read the divorce papers. I was reeling from this overwhelming gut-punch, especially when I read that I had 48 hours to vacate my house. To add insult to injury, the papers said my wife was assuming custody of Adrian, and I could only see her every other weekend. I cannot put into words how shattered I was – I thought I was living in a nightmare, but the realization of what was happening gradually began to set in.

To say I was distraught is an understatement. Not only was I losing my wife, but I was also, in a sense, losing my little girl. Our marriage was at times painful, but this was beyond the pale. I wanted to run away. I wanted to hide from the shame of divorce and losing my daughter. I did not want to accept what was happening to me. I truly loved my wife and was fully committed to making our marriage work. However, it seemed like a missile with a nuclear warhead had just hit its target – me. I did not want to accept the fact that it was over; it was too much for me to process.

The first person I called was Jerry. As I mentioned, he and I had grown very close. When I told him the news, he had no idea what was going on. He was shocked, although not nearly as much as I was. He reassured me that I could call on him any time if I needed something, which I greatly appreciated.

I then called my mom and dad and told them what had happened. They were obviously deeply upset about what I was going through. I told them I needed to get away from all this, and I was coming to Chicago for a few days. I called one of my friends who came to my house then drove me to the airport that night. I took the first flight to Chicago.

It seemed like the flight lasted forever. I could not think of anything other than my little girl and how I would never be able to be a full-time father. Yes, I knew I would always be her father, but that didn't assuage the hurt. Again, as I write this, I struggle to find the words to describe the darkness and pain that had completely overtaken me. My life was forever altered. At the time, I felt like my soul was seemingly forever crushed.

The Day After

When I arrived in Chicago, it felt exceedingly good to get hugs from Mom and Dad. There was some feeling of solace and comfort in being with them. We had productive talks, but there was nothing anyone could say to make me feel any better. My deep funk lasted several days. Finally, my dad sat me down and we had a good father-son talk. He told me I had to move on and get back to living my life despite what happened. I knew he was right, but I was still in the first phase of grief which is denial. I was refusing to accept what had transpired. Our talk did move me to the next phase of grief, which is anger.

I had always been taught to never hate anyone for any reason, but in that moment, I couldn't help but despise the person that would do this to me. After all, I freely admit that I am only human, and my feelings were real and raw. I have never been so angry and hurt in all my life. Perhaps it's hard for others to understand or relate to the anger and hurt that I experienced. These emotions were new to me, and gladly, I have not been put in that same position again.

The next phase of grief is bargaining, but I was in no mood for that, so I just skipped to the next phase – depression. Admittedly, I was in this phase since the beginning of this nightmare. I had never experienced the deep depths of depression, but now I had learned what it was like. My dad was trying to move me to the final step, which is acceptance, but that was something that would take me a long time to accomplish – and it did.

On my sixth day of grief, Dad finally convinced me I had to go back to Dallas, face the music, and move on with my life. I flew back on the seventh day. I had arranged to move in with my best friend, Jack, and his two young boys. Jack and I were teachers at the same school where we both coached football, basketball, and track. He had a similar experience, except he got custody of his boys. He was a great friend and helped me immensely with getting through the first few weeks as I adjusted to my new life.

I ultimately convinced myself that I would find a new wife someday – that's not what worried me. What did concern me, however, was how to deal with being a part-time father. I was not fully prepared nor able to accept that reality. I started all over again in going through the stages of grief. Admittedly, at the time, I held a staunch grudge against my now ex-wife. It seemed like each day a thief was robbing me of my life as a father. My bitterness was hard to get over.

Jack continued to help me a lot. As mentioned, we were both schoolteachers and coaches, and Jack loved to drink beer – but only on the weekends. I often tried to keep up with him, but he was a true professional, and I was a mere amateur compared to him. His two young boys were eight and ten at the time, and they enjoyed playing with Adrian on the weekends that I had her. They liked having a little sister. It was always great having her, but taking her home to her mother was something I had to force myself to get used to. It was exceedingly hard, and I never liked it. After dropping her off, my ride home was painful, and often tearful.

New Love, New Life

It had been nearly a year and a half since the divorce when my life turned around. That's when I met my future wife, Linda. As previously described, she was stunningly beautiful. She was funny, had a spunky personality, and was exactly what I needed to light up my life. The rest, as they say, is history.

I vividly recall our first encounter. We met while we both worked at the talent agency. I arrived at work one morning, and as I opened the front door, she was walking out. We literally almost collided. I stopped in my tracks and then held the door open for her. My first thought was, "Wow, she is gorgeous!"

Being the outgoing, effervescent person she is, she quickly introduced herself. I was thoroughly enamored with her wide, beautiful smile, and I managed to shyly spit out my name. She asked if I worked at the agency and I explained I was the music producer, voice teacher, and managed bands and the rehearsal studios. She then explained that she loved to sing and would be interested in taking voice lessons (which was music to my ears). I asked what she did at the agency, and she said she was one of the models. I thought to myself, "I can certainly see why!" I told her to stop by my office any time and we would sing a few songs. She said, "That sounds great. How about this afternoon?" Of course, I replied, "That sounds great to me!"

Later that afternoon, Linda showed up and we had a good time singing together. She had a beautiful voice, and little did I know we would end up making beautiful music together for many years (in more ways than one!). We agreed to go to lunch the following day. Needless to say, I was thrilled. I anxiously waited for noon to arrive. Sure enough, at precisely 12:00, she walked into my office and greeted me with, "Come on, let's go to lunch." I quickly obliged.

We decided to eat at a sandwich shop near the agency. We both ordered, and the cashier said, "Your total is $12.00." I reached into my back pocket for my wallet and immediately went into shear panic mode – I realized I had left my wallet at home. I was mortified. I embarrassingly and sheepishly said, "You're not going to believe this, but I don't have my wallet with me." She smiled and said, "No problem, I'll get this one."

I thought, "Well, I've got no shot now – I'm sure she thinks I'm a complete idiot and deadbeat." I felt even worse when during the course of our lunchtime conversation, she told me she was a single mom. I told her I would pay her back and would make it up to her. I was desperately hoping she would give me a second chance so I said I would gladly take her to dinner the following night. Thankfully, she said, "Great, I'll look forward to it." Over the next few days, we quickly became inseparable, and five months later, we were married. As of this writing, we have been together for 46 years.

At the time we met, Linda had a young daughter named Dusty, who was about 15 months old. Linda was also recently divorced and had been through a very similar marital breakup. We both needed someone, and I suppose one could say that we rescued each other.

Blending a Family Together

We both had young daughters, and having a blended family poses many challenges as all of us who were involved came to learn. It takes love and hard work to be successful. It wasn't easy at times, but we learned how to cope. After our youngest daughter Ashely was born three years into our marriage, our family consisted of yours, mine, and ours. Occasionally, as is the case with most families, a cat fight would break out, but like most sisters, it was usually settled quickly, and they moved on. They certainly all had distinctively different personalities, which is true now that they are all adults. They still enjoy a sisterhood bond and deep love for each other.

Dusty and I grew close over the years and developed a strong bond with each other. As she grew up, she needed a strong, and at times a patient father figure which I did my best to fulfill. She developed an outgoing spunky personality like her mother and has grown up to be a good sister and daughter. Adrian fulfilled the role of smart older sister, while Ashley grew up as the pretty baby sister (more on that later).

Through the years, taking Adrian home after a weekend at our house did get easier, but it was still a painful thing for me – I never did get used to it, and I still never liked it. Adrian and I had some very meaningful and in-depth talks during the 30 or 45-minute ride to and from her mother's house – it was our special time together, and we made the best of it. We formed a special connection that could never be altered – I would always be her daddy, and she would always be my baby girl – nothing could ever change that.

Both Our Exes Lived in Texas

For the sake of the kids, Linda and I were determined to make peace with our exes – and we did. The fact that we were able to get along was admirable on the part of all parties. We worked to balance time during holidays and weekend visits. It sure made things much easier, not only on the exes, but most importantly, on the kids. Poor Ashley, she did not have a means of escape from her parents. In fact, she asked us one time when she was the only one left at home, "Why don't I have someplace to go every other weekend?" I replied, "Sorry, kid, you just have to stay home with your mean old parents."

I am proud to say that we are all one big (mostly) happy family. Yes, at times it wasn't easy, but we made it work. One bit of advice to those that may have to deal with the challenges of a blended family: set aside the animosity and differences with your exes – yes, it can be really hard, but it is worth it for both the parents, and most especially, the kids. The higher goal should always be to do what's best for the kids and to keep them out of any disagreements.

The early years were at times uncomfortable, but by maintaining peace, it made everyone's life easier. Ultimately, all the exes became friends with each other. I developed a good relationship with Linda's ex, and we even sang at his next wedding. My ex and Linda became friends, and we attended many family and social events together. Yes, it was unusual, but I suppose by osmosis, we all came to agree that life is too short to hold grudges and live in the past. Live and let live, love and let love live.

A friend of mine once asked if it was weird having a blended family and an ex-wife. I answered, "Yes, it's kind of like still being a little bit married to your ex, but the good news is, you always get to go home with your new spouse, and you don't get in trouble because your ex-wife or ex-husband can't say a thing about it!"

One other closing caveat that is meaningful to me. Since I was the father of Jerry and Evelyn's first granddaughter, we were forever linked. Even after the divorce, they were supportive of me. Jerry and I would talk occasionally just to keep up with each other. Unfortunately, Jerry left us far too soon when he succumbed to lung cancer at the age of 55. I was deeply saddened to lose someone who I considered a dear friend and a part of my extended family.

Prior to the funeral, I got a call from Evelyn. She told me how much Jerry thought of me and asked if I would serve as a pall bearer. I was sincerely touched to tears by her request and told her I would be honored to do so.

Forrest Gump's mother was right. My box of chocolates included many tasty treats along with a few bitter ones that I didn't expect or want. Such is life.

Chapter 28

From Rags to Riches to Ruin

I have previously written about my time and adventures while working at MICMIX Audio Products (pronounced mike-mix) and how it was one of the best jobs I ever had. It was where I cut my chops in sales and marketing while I learned a great deal about the business world. I met many famous people, did a lot of interesting things, and for a guy with a new wife and a young family, it was an ideal situation.

The first product the company produced was a 4-channel microphone mixing board (thus the name MICMIX). Over the years, the company developed other products and carved out a small niche in the recording studio marketplace by specializing in high quality spring reverberation systems. When I went to work for MICMIX, the founder, John Saul, had applied for a patent on the reverb systems. Our reverbs were better that any other competitive products and they were used in nearly every top recording studio in the US and Europe. Some of the greatest recordings ever produced used our products, and as mentioned earlier, many of the most famous artists used our equipment.

Our competitors were baffled as to how we were able to produce our unmatched sound. They all tried to figure out how we could produce a superior sound. They even tried to reverse engineer our systems to figure out the special sauce we used. It was a company secret that was kept until the patent was officially granted. Not to get too technical, but the secret was simple – we tuned our springs in a harmonic sequence.

The original idea came about when one of the original partners, Bill, was playing around with his baby grand piano. He pushed down on the sustain pedal, and he noticed that when he shouted into the piano, a beautiful reverberation sound was produced. He then tinkered around with the reverb springs, tuning them in a specific harmonic sequence. Voila – a more perfect reverb sound was produced. John and Bill then decided to patent the concept, and the rest was history. It was an accidental but brilliant discovery of a simple concept that relied on natural acoustic properties.

John was an excellent engineer, and the reason he hired me was to bring creativity to the company's sales and marketing strategies. The company was very small; the entirety of the sales and marketing department consisted of one person – me. I learned how to create magazine ads. Just to be clear, this was in the early 1980's, and there were no computers or desktop publishing software – it was all done by hand on a drafting table. Yes, it was the dark ages and there were no marketing tools that we have today.

John had developed a reverb system featuring a new form factor. Our previous products were built in a tower configuration, but the new product was designed to be installed in a rack – much like every piece of equipment that is now used in a recording studio. When we released the product, it was a huge hit in the marketplace. Sales boomed and our company was on a roll.

A Shocking Day at Work

In the fifth year of my employment at MICMIX, we had grown from 7 employees to 15. Although still very small, the company was growing. Our reverbs were still popular, and we had introduced two lower-cost models that were also selling well. John developed other new products for the studio, including our Dynaflanger special audio effects unit. The most famous user was Stevie Wonder who was an avid fan of the Dynaflanger. I had the honor of meeting him at a trade show and he sung his praises about our unique product. Things were going great for the company until a tragic event happened.

It was a usual day at work. I went to lunch, and when I returned to the office, our production manager, David, met me at the front door and told me some heartbreaking news. He said he went into the men's restroom and found John lying on the floor. He suffered a catastrophic heart attack and had passed away. I was in shock, as was David and all the other employees. John's wife Barbara also worked in the office. She was devastated.

After the funeral, Barbara returned to the office, and we had a company meeting. She was still in shock, and she explained that she needed time to figure out what she was going to do since John was the sole proprietor, and she was now the sole owner. She asked me to take over running the company temporarily, which I was happy to do. I knew she was not interested in coming to work daily where her husband had just died – I honestly could not blame her. I assured Barbara that we would honor John and her by doing the best we could to help keep the company going. At that time, there were three key employees: David, the production manager, Bobby, the lead engineer, and me.

After the meeting was over, I asked David and Bobby to meet with me. I broached the subject of the three of us buying the company. They were both very enthusiastic, so I started putting together a proposal to submit to Barbara. I worked with an outside accountant who was also the company's corporate treasurer.

Alan, the accountant, was very supportive of the idea of us buying the company and had a discussion with Barbara who was also very receptive to the idea. He put together all the appropriate documents and the sale was consummated about a month later. Since we didn't have the cash for the purchase, we worked out a monthly payment option with Barbara. She was relieved to have it completed, and we three partners were ecstatic to be new business owners.

I assumed the position of president, while David was vice president of production, and Bobby was vice president of engineering. Alan stayed on as our accountant and corporate treasurer, although he was not an owner. MICMIX continued to have success over the next year. At 30 years old, I was flying high as president and part owner of a nice little company. Life was good, and the future was bright for us all.

Bobby and I developed a new product that was selling very well. It was a single-ended noise reduction system called Dynafex. It was designed to remove unwanted noise from previously recorded material. It became very popular in re-mastering old recordings. It was different than the Dolby and dbx noise reduction systems that were widely used in recording studios. Those systems were designed to reduce background noise during the recording process; however, they could not reduce the high-frequency hissing and other noise components after a recording was made.

It was such a unique product that could do what no other product could. I broached the idea of developing a microchip that could be incorporated into car radios, recording studio equipment, and home entertainment systems. I contacted a chip manufacturer, and they became interested in developing the chip in partnership with us. During the development process, we applied for, and we were eventually granted a patent on our invention. We were planning on selling the chip and licensing the technology to other audio manufacturers.

After two years or so, MICMIX was doing well as a company, but the reverb market started undergoing a major change. Spring reverbs were being replaced by new digital technology. The entire industry, from tape recorders to sound processing gear, was moving from analog recording technology to digital. The change was happening fast. Huge companies like Sony, AKG, Mitsubishi, Philips, and 3M were going all in on digital technology.

A wide array of digital reverb systems were rapidly hitting the market – they were the new, hot thing. Sales of MICMIX reverbs began to shrink, although we still had some loyal customers. We had begun trying to develop a digital version using our patented tuning technology, but we didn't have the money or the manpower to move quickly enough. Our bread-and-butter revenue stream was drying up while our other products were not selling fast enough due to the market upheaval as recording moved from analog to digital. That's not to mention that a recession had devastated the US economy. We could tell that trouble was on the horizon, so we had to lay off several staffers, cut our marketing budget, and tighten our belts.

The onslaught of the major players introducing less expensive digital products and the diminishing market for spring reverbs, along with the devastating recession was more than we could fight off. The audio recording equipment market was in disarray, and it hit us hard. Our cash flow was drying up and we did not have deep pockets that would allow us to weather the storm.

After almost three years, the painful decision was made to close the company down, and all three of us business partners had to file bankruptcy to eliminate our debts. It was horribly depressing to go from a thriving small company to a business that lay in ruins.

The two main patents the company owned were still of significant value. As part of our settlement with Barbara, we turned the patents over to her, and I helped arrange the sale of those assets. Making that decision was a tough one, but it was the right thing to do. The chip manufacturer bought the noise reduction patent, and one of our major competitors bought the reverb patent. Barbara made out OK, but not so much with us three partners.

It is a bit ironic that the recording industry has recently trended back to analog technology. Most recording engineers and producers have come to realize that analog recordings just have a more realistic sound than digital recordings. As a result, there is new demand on the audio resale market for old MICMIX products, especially our reverb systems. It's funny and sad how that worked out.

The Aftermath

Needless to say, because of the business closure and the personal bankruptcy filing, those were very dark days for me and my family. The financial hit we took was catastrophic, and the emotional toll was devastating. Things only got worse in both aspects. Linda and I had a little money salted away, but we drained that dry within the first two months. I thought that having a few years of experience running a small business would be beneficial on my resume. Conversely, it worked against me, not to mention that the company I was running went out of business.

To make matters worse, the US economy was coming off the President Carter years and the country continued to be mired in a deep recession with high unemployment and very high interest rates. Jobs were hard to come by, especially for someone with the title of president of a failed company on their resume. I went on unemployment and began a comprehensive search for any type of job I could find, but to no avail. No one was hiring.

As the months ticked by, our financial condition was in dire straits. Linda had been a stay-at-home mom, but she had to find a part-time job. That part-time job ended up as manager for Ashley, our three-year-old daughter. Linda was interested in getting Ashley involved in modelling, thinking they both could bring in a little extra cash. Ashley was a beautiful young girl who I can safely say got her looks from her mother – certainly not me. She sent off a bio and a photo of Ashley to four different agencies, and three of them called her back because they wanted to see Ashely in person. All three wanted to sign Ashley.

First, as was explained to us, we had to get a photographer to take some pictures for a head shot and composite sheet to send to various agency clients. It just so happened that the photographer that I had used at MICMIX for product photos owed me a favor, so I called it in. Next, Linda said she needed to pick up a few outfits for the photoshoot. We were flat broke, so I reminded her of that on her way out the door. She assured me she had a plan and not to worry – which made me worry even more!

Later that afternoon, Linda and Ashley walked in the door after the shopping trip. The first thing I noticed was that the shopping bags were from Neiman-Marcus along with Lord and Taylor. There were probably 8 bags of clothing. I started to go into panic mode and break into a cold sweat. I agitatedly said, "What are you doing buying all those clothes – we can't afford it!" I then asked, "How much did you spend?" She replied, "I think it was well over $1,000." I thought I was going to faint and said, "Are you out of your mind?" She then said, "Calm down; I put it all on our Visa card, and when we are finished with the photoshoot, I'll return it all – that's been my plan all along. I made the store clerks sign the receipt that the items were returnable." I was relieved, but still worried.

The photoshoot went well. Ashley looked great and performed well for the photographer – he was thoroughly impressed with her. We then had to get 4-color comp sheets printed, so I called in another favor from a printer I had spent a lot of money with while at MICMIX. He printed them for free. Linda chose to go with one of the agencies, and they were blown away with all the photos and the comp sheet.

A few days later, Linda got a call from the agency, and they said they needed Ashley for a photoshoot for a department store magazine advertisement the following morning. The agency informed Linda that Ashley would be getting $75 per hour, with a two-hour minimum. I thought they were joking but they weren't. That was the beginning of Ashley's four-year career as a child supermodel.

A Star is Born

She was obviously a very beautiful little girl that was highly photogenic and had a bubbly personality. Linda and I weren't sure how well she would do in modelling because she was so full of energy that her nickname was Cricket. She was always jumping around and in constant motion. As strange as it may seem, she was always very calm, cool, and collected during the photoshoots. The ad directors and photographers absolutely loved her because she was so cooperative and would sit in poses for as long as they wanted her to. Along with her beauty, her demeanor during the photoshoots was another reason why she was in high demand.

She worked consistently and was featured in magazines and in-store ads for Walmart, JC Penney, K-Mart, Sears, and ironically, Neiman-Marcus, plus other national and regional retailers. She also appeared in numerous corporate ads and brochures. She was a star! Since Linda also had worked as a model, I give her credit for artfully managing Ashley's career. My only claim for credit is that I was present during her creation – plus I did catch her when she was born because the doctor was late getting to her birth.

Not only was she a star, but she was also the primary breadwinner in our household since her dad could not find a job for more than a year. Her modelling career helped make house payments and kept food on the table while her dad was an out-of-work deadbeat – at least that's what I felt like.

Men are supposed to be the breadwinner, and when I was not able to provide for my family, it was a very tough time for me. First, I lost my company, and then, no matter how hard I tried, I could not find employment in a horrible job market. I doubted myself and even began to question my sanity. It was more dark days for me. I was ashamed and disappointed in myself. I guess it was good that our young girls did not fully grasp the severity of our year-long financial struggles. To Linda's credit, she stood by her man. I guess she was serious about the "for better or worse" part of our marriage vows because it seemed like things could not get any worse! Meanwhile, at the time, Ashley had no idea she was helping make ends meet – all she knew was that she was having fun getting her picture taken.

I finally found a part-time job with a consulting agency helping a few small businesses with their marketing efforts. Fortunately, it was something that I could put on my resume that helped me land a full-time gig with an IT consulting company as their sales and marketing manager. At long last, the financial drought had ended – I had a real job. I was finally freed from the shackles and imprisonment of unemployment. Now, I could put an end to that forgettable part of my story and move on with the rest of my life. Subsequently, I had a successful marketing career that spanned an additional 30 years.

Chapter 29

Medical Errors, Irreversible Damage

I will fast forward to August of 2022. It was a normal morning in our household. My wife Linda was in good health and led a normal life. She was taking a shower when she called out for my help. In that moment, our lives quickly and irrevocably changed.

After helping her out of the shower, Linda said she felt dizzy, so I laid her on our bed. She said she wanted to rest. She slept for an hour, and I woke her up to see how she was feeling. She could not answer any simple questions – she just blankly stared at me. Realizing something strange was going on, I called 911. Upon arrival, the paramedics decided to transport her to Texas Health Resources hospital in Denton.

I followed the ambulance to the hospital, and after providing Linda's ID and insurance information, I headed to her room. The triage nurse checked her vital signs, and everything was fine. All of Linda's blood tests showed nothing unusual. They tested for a heart attack which was negative. They performed an MRI and CT scan of her brain and found no evidence of a stroke.

After approximately two hours, Linda's status had not changed. The ER nurses and doctor were at a loss as to what Linda was experiencing. Her symptoms continued: eyes fully dilated, unable to respond, blank stare, and unable to swallow.

I broached the idea that her problem may be neurological – maybe some sort of seizure – and suggested they do an electroencephalogram (EEG). Since Linda had no history of seizures, the doctor told me a seizure was unlikely. He also explained that the hospital did not have anyone available to do an EEG. I was appalled that a level two trauma center and a 255-bed hospital could not perform a simple EEG.

Doing an EEG would have captured the cause and location if Linda was experiencing a neurological episode. Every doctor and nurse knows it is a critical diagnostic tool to detect brain injuries, seizures, tumors, or other brain-related disorders. THR-Denton was negligent for not having someone available to do an EEG, and any chance of capturing important data was forever lost.

Transferred for Overnight Observation

Linda was transferred to a hospital room for observation. After about 30 minutes, her hands began to shake, and shortly thereafter, her legs began to tremor. Another half hour had passed when she started experiencing full body convulsions with her arms and legs flailing wildly with jerky movements. It was the most horrific thing I had ever seen – it still haunts me today.

The attending nurse theorized Linda was having a panic attack, which I thought was ridiculous. The nurse then called in a nurse practitioner who determined it was a psychotic episode, which again, I thought was erroneous. By this time, Linda's blood pressure, heart rate, and respirations had skyrocketed. She was gasping for air and her eyes seemed to be screaming out to me, "Please help me – do something." That sight also still haunts me today.

I quickly Googled "symptoms of a seizure." Linda met all these criteria: fully dilated eyes, eyes locked wide open, full body convulsions with jerky movements, unable to swallow, high heart rate and blood pressure, rapid and shallow respirations, and inability to respond to commands. It was patently clear to me what was happening, but THR personnel were clueless.

I sensed that the nurses were in over their heads, so I asked that a neurologist or any type of doctor be brought in for consultation. I was then informed that there was no doctor on duty since it was well past midnight. I was in disbelief. THR was again negligent for the lack of adequate staffing and having appropriate medical personnel available.

As I found out later through another simple Google search, there is a detailed protocol for mitigating a seizure. There are numerous on-line documents that outline specific procedures and instructions that include common medications which can be quickly and easily administered. Because of a lack of training on recognizing and mitigating a seizure, things only got worse.

Transfer to ICU

I could not believe that more than two hours had passed since the convulsions started, and all the nurses and NPs were doing was standing around looking bewildered. I finally and emphatically told the nurse practitioners, "If you don't do something she's going to die – are you OK with that? Because I am NOT!" They then excused themselves and went into the hall to talk. After a few minutes, they informed me that Linda was being transferred to ICU.

Upon arrival in the ICU, a nurse practitioner informed me that to stop the seizure, they would have to administer heavy sedation medications and intubate Linda to protect her airway. I asked her, "Is there a doctor in ICU or has ANY doctor been consulted?" Her reply was, "No, but I am qualified to perform these procedures." I was becoming less and less comfortable with the situation, but I wanted the seizure episode to end. She handed me a release form and said, "Here, sign this so we can proceed."

I was hesitant to sign the form and told the NP, "Linda has a small airway as explained to me by an anesthesiologist who had lacerated her airway prior to a surgical procedure a few years earlier." I continued, "He told me that he used an intubation tube that was too large and to caution other anesthesiologists about it if she ever has other surgeries."

I requested that the NP use a small intubation tube to which she perfunctorily replied, "We'll use whatever we have available. Please sign the form." I then replied, "Respectfully ma'am, it evidently was important enough that the anesthesiologist pointed it out to me. Why is this a problem for you?" I also asked, "Aren't there other less invasive ways to protect her airway besides intubation?" She then stated, "Mr. Allen, we are trying to help your wife, and we cannot proceed until you just sign the form." I hesitatingly signed the form, and then she asked me to leave the room.

The sedation and intubation procedures were administered. After an agonizingly anxious 30 minutes in the waiting room, I was escorted back to Linda's room. It was gut-wrenching to see my wife on a respirator and in an induced coma. It was hard for me to grasp that several hours earlier, it was a usual quiet day in our household.

Mistakes Made and Damage Done

As I later found out, the NP used an 8.0 endotracheal tube (ETT) inserted to 25cm to intubate Linda. The National Institutes for Health recommend a maximum 6.5 or 7.0 ETT be inserted to a depth of 21cm for adult females and warns that some patients with smaller, difficult airways require smaller ETTs. In addition, NIH states that nasotracheal tubes (through the nose and into the trachea) are commonly used in seizure mitigation to protect an airway. NIH also states that an NTT is much safer, far less invasive, and will not cause damage to the larynx or vocal cords.

It was highly frustrating that even after I had warned the NP about Linda's small airway, she arrogantly and stubbornly didn't heed my warning. Subsequently, Linda paid a steep price. Because of the actions of an ill-informed, inexperienced, and obstinate nurse practitioner employed by THR, Linda's larynx, vocal cords, and trachea were badly damaged as we later found out.

By not having an EEG available, not recognizing the seizure, not mitigating the seizure early on, and then using an oversized ETT, THR's poor decisions team was winning 4 to 0.

Ill-advised Orders

On the first day in ICU, the attending physician ordered heavy IV fluids to be administered to flush Linda's system. He suspected that she ingested something that caused the seizure. This was despite all her bloodwork testing normal – there was no medical necessity for this decision. On the third day, it was reported on her chart that she had gained 14 pounds despite not having any nutritional intake. The weight gain was purely because of excess fluids.

When I visited the hospital that morning, Linda was so bloated that she was unrecognizable. According to her chart, she had 15.5 liters of excess fluids onboard. Now, imagine 7 ½ two-liter bottles of your favorite soda lined up on a countertop. That is a very large amount to be infused, and Linda's kidneys could not keep up in ridding her body of that amount of fluids. After I pointed it out to the ICU doctor, he ordered doses of Lasix to reduce the fluids. On day five, Linda was still 15 liters positive. This doctor's ill-advised orders likely contributed to a catastrophic event yet to come. THR's bad decisions team was now winning 5 to 0.

The Beatdown Continues

After a brief stay in ICU, Linda should have been brought off sedation and extubated (removal of the ETT). The longer a patient is intubated, the more damage is done to the airway. Instead, her stay kept getting extended for no valid medical reason. Again, indecisive and ineffective medical staff were making matters worse.

In the afternoon of the fifth day, the ICU doctor told me they were going to extubate Linda. I was excited, relieved, and hopeful that the nightmare was coming to an end. The doctor said she passed all the pre-extubation tests – he assured me that she was ready.

He removed the ETT, and immediately Linda could not breathe and was desperately gasping for air. The doctor instantly re-intubated her and placed her back under heavy sedation. The unsuccessful extubation was like a Mike Tyson gut punch. I was devastated and distraught.

I asked the doctor what happened and why it failed, and he replied, "She just wasn't ready." I immediately thought that was a rather strange and inane answer, especially after he assured me she was "ready." He offered no medical explanation for the failed extubation.

I sat down with my laptop and Googled "why extubations fail." I found laryngospasm as one of the leading causes. It is an involuntary muscular contraction of the vocal cords. In other words, the vocal cords uncontrollably close, thus preventing breathing. The primary causes of a laryngospasm include damage to the airway because of an improperly executed intubation, an extended time being intubated (beyond 36 hours), excess fluid retention, an extended time under sedation, being on a respirator (beyond 36 hours), and use of an improperly sized ETT that causes damage to the airway.

I quickly realized that all of those factors were present prior to Linda's failed extubation. I also learned that there are specific protocols for alleviating a laryngospasm that utilizes physical actions and/or commonly used medications. When I asked him if Linda suffered a laryngospasm, the doctor looked at me like he had no idea what it was. I gave him the definition and he again replied, "She just wasn't ready." Truth be told, he had no clue.

Sadly, the ICU doctor was completely unprepared for what had transpired. He should have known Linda was at high risk of extubation failure due to the reasons mentioned earlier. To Linda's detriment, he was negligent – not to mention incompetent.

I later spoke with two anesthesiologists, including one that practiced at THR-Denton, and they both told me the ICU doctor should have had an anesthesiologist present during the extubation. I also read portions of two medical textbooks that highly recommended that an anesthesiologist always be present during a high risk extubation. Another bad decision upped the score to 6 to 0.

Extended Stay is Extended

Because of additional extenuating circumstances and inept management of Linda's condition, her stay in ICU hit two weeks. The THR staff was unable to bring the nightmare to an end. Quite unfortunately, being on a respirator and intubated for so long caused even more damage to her airway as every day passed. It never should have happened, and I blame THR personnel and their ineffectiveness for extending the misery both Linda and I suffered.

I met with the Chief Quality Medical Officer at THR-Denton who had been following Linda's case and expressed my disappointment that his staff was unable to bring Linda's problems to a conclusion. I told him, "THR-Denton has failed my wife in so many ways, from inadequate training of personnel to recognizing and mitigating a seizure, as well as ill-advised decisions, poor planning, incompetent execution, and I could go on and on." I added, "Unfortunately, your team has only made matters worse on a daily basis." After trying to explain away his staff's failures, he exasperatedly admitted, "Yes, we failed your wife, we failed you, and we failed your daughter" (who was present at the meeting).

Finally, on day 15, he came to me and said, "Mr. Allen, I know when it's time for me to get off the horse and let someone else ride." He then suggested that Linda be transferred to a higher-level trauma center for better care. I was utterly flabbergasted and exceedingly frustrated that it took this long for THR to admit that they were incapable of solving the maladies they had caused. In the end, it was a further outright admission that they had failed my wife. The score was now 7 to 0 in favor of the bad decisions team.

Transfer to THR-Dallas

Linda was subsequently helicoptered to THR-Dallas. I was hopeful that this would soon lead us to awakening Linda and me from this nightmare. As it regrettably turned out, even more mistakes and poor patient management were ahead.

On her second day at THR-Dallas, an ICU doctor attempted another extubation. Tragically, she experienced another laryngospasm. Once again, the medical team did not have an anesthesiologist present, nor were they prepared for or even attempted to mitigate the laryngospasm. She had to be re-intubated. The result? More damage was done to Linda's airway.

The only recourse left was for Linda to have a tracheotomy, which was the last resort since her airway was so severely injured. That's what happens when a patient has three intubations, two failed extubations, and spends more than two weeks under sedation and on a respirator. None of that should have ever happened, but sadly, it did.

At this point, I was physically exhausted, emotionally drained, justifiably angry, but most of all, I was immeasurably disgusted with the failures and incompetence of the medical professionals I had trusted.

After several more days in ICU, it was time to bring Linda out from under sedation. When she awoke, I had the ignominious task of telling her she had a trach, and then I filled her in on the gory details that had transpired the previous three weeks. Fortunately for her, she didn't remember a thing that happened because of the heavy sedation. I, on the other hand, had to live through this excruciatingly painful ordeal. The THR bad decisions team had pitched a shutout and won 8 to 0.

The Saga Continues

After Linda was discharged, I took her to see an airway specialist. He took one look at Linda's airway and said, "This is above my pay grade – she needs to see a specialist at UT Southwestern Medical Center."

After two surgical procedures at UTSMC, the surgeon examined Linda's airway and said, "The procedures didn't work. How do you guys feel about travelling to see a surgical specialist?" He added, "I don't trust anyone in Texas to perform the airway reconstruction Linda needs." I replied, "Of course, we want to pursue anything necessary – whatever it takes."

I researched airway surgical specialists and found Dr. Alexander Gelbard at Vanderbilt Medical Center in Nashville, TN. I found his email address and wrote him a detailed email explaining what Linda had gone through. I asked if he would take Linda as a patient. Within literally five minutes of me sending the email, my phone rang – it was

Dr. Gelbard calling me. I was in shock from the quick response, and he said he would gladly do everything he could to help Linda. We were thrilled and hopeful.

Dr. Gelbard is a nationally known, highly respected pioneer in airway reconstruction surgery – not to mention that he ended up being the warmest, kindest, most caring doctor we had ever encountered. Our experience at Vanderbilt Medical Center with Dr. Gelbard and his staff was the polar opposite of our experience with THR. The culture at VMC was highly commendable, and the level of competence was impeccable.

After six trips to Nashville for various surgeries, Linda's larynx and trachea were repaired to his satisfaction. There was one drawback. Her vocal cords were damaged beyond repair. The permanent injury has left Linda with only the ability to whisper due to vocal cord paralysis. In addition, because of this whole two-year saga, her lungs were permanently damaged from the 2 ½ hours of convulsions as well as the more than two week-long stay on a respirator. She now must be on oxygen 24/7, and because of her inactivity due to her physical constraints, it's going to be a long haul to get her strength back – if she ever does.

Questions Still Remain

What I have learned from a more than two-year ordeal is that medical workers are fallible – they make mistakes just like everyone else. The difference between their profession and other lines of work, nonetheless, is that poor judgement and costly errors can result in long-term, life-changing outcomes.

Competency is critical in the medical profession. When mistakes are made, patients suffer the consequences. As much as hospitals attempt to eliminate errors and bad judgement, regrettably, they still happen. I get that, but I am still left with many questions.

Why didn't the nurse practitioners recognize that Linda was having a seizure and mitigate it immediately before things got out of control? I knew it was a seizure, why didn't they? Why was an over-sized ETT used when it was unnecessary? Why wasn't less invasive airway protection used? Why did a doctor order excessive fluids which unnecessarily contributed to the first laryngospasm? Why didn't the ICU doctors consider Linda's extubation to be at high risk of failure? Why weren't they prepared for a laryngospasm? Why didn't the ICU doctors make any attempt to mitigate the laryngospasms? Why didn't they have an anesthesiologist present to assist? Why did it take two weeks for THR-Denton to admit they failed?

Some of the answers include the following: a lack of proper training, not anticipating potential negative outcomes, not being fully prepared, not fulfilling their duty of care, and not acting in a professional manner. From my perspective, also included was a lack of common sense, stubbornness for not listening to a family member, and an overconfident or conceited attitude that they know everything. And yes, I will add to the list pure ineptitude, carelessness, and negligence.

Where's the Accountability?

The THR medical teams and administrators will defend their personnel by saying their decisions were made "within the scope of standard medical care". In response, I say that they may be absolving themselves of liability in their own minds, but there is no escaping from the ultimate reality that their actions caused irreparable harm to my wife. It's not complicated – it's the simple and unavoidable truth.

They can try to justify and explain away what happened, which the CMO attempted to do, but that does nothing to heal the permanent wounds or take away the immense pain and suffering Linda and I both experienced. We must live with the cold, hard truth, while they simply live with an empty, blameless, and nebulous excuse.

It is deeply bothersome that no one will ever be held accountable for their poor judgement and the errors made. THR's doctors and administrators will never own up to their blunders. No apology will ever be offered. No responsibility will ever be taken. What remains within us is a hollow feeling of "that's just the way it is."

A Life Forever Altered

Linda used to be an active, vibrant person. Unfortunately, her life has been forever changed because of a series of failures by medical personnel at Texas Health Resources in Denton and Dallas.

What Linda is left with is permanent physical damage and a deteriorated lifestyle. There is also the indescribably devastating mental and emotional toll it has taken on her. That is a crying shame, but no amount Linda's or my tears can wash away the pain and suffering.

All of these consequences and ultimate costs are the result of cascading mistakes and ill-advised decisions, as well as defectively executed procedures performed by THR staff. That is not to mention the out-of-pocket expenses of more than $40,000 we had to absorb that included six trips to Nashville, deductibles, medical equipment rentals, supplies, medications, and co-pays.

Thankfully, Linda did not lose a limb or her life, but then again, she did lose the life she enjoyed prior to this saga. Imagine the shock and angst when one day a healthy woman wakes up a month later to find her life had been completely and negatively transformed.

The most exasperating and crushing part is that this catastrophic yet avoidable ordeal forever changed the life of a beautiful, funny, warm-hearted, and healthy person. Now, Linda must live with the aftermath of flawed judgement at the hands of inadequately trained and ill-informed medical personnel who made highly questionable and devastatingly consequential decisions. They did not live up to their duty of care.

THR personnel will never pay any price for their failures and life-altering mistakes – only Linda will. It's sad but true. A normal day in our lives turned into a never-ending nightmare. All we are left with is accepting and dealing with a reality that never should have happened.

Every day during Linda's ordeal was stress-filled and heart-wrenching for me. Those who have experienced seeing a loved one on life support understand how hard it was to witness and process. It felt like the weight of the world was on my shoulders. I ached for her, but I was determined to do everything I could to help her. I thoroughly researched all the surgeries and procedures. I did my best to support her and ensure that she was getting the best care. Unfortunately, as described above, there were medical personnel that miserably failed Linda.

I spoke with five different attorneys to see if we had grounds for a malpractice lawsuit. They all agreed that we had a strong case, but regrettably, because there was no loss of life, no loss of a limb, or no loss of wages, there was not enough recoverable damage done. They explained that Medicare would have to be reimbursed first, expensive medical experts would have to be hired to do an extensive report, and by the time all expenses were paid, we would end up with nothing. Sad but true.

I have subsequently filed formal complaints with two hospital accreditation organizations plus the Texas Health and Human Services department against Texas Health Resources. In addition, I filed complaints with the state medical board against the nurse practitioner who botched the intubation, along with the ICU doctors – both of whom are no longer employed by the hospital.

As hard as it was on me, Linda was ultimately the one most affected. Through all the hospital stays, surgeries, agonizing pain, and rehab, she remained strong through even the most difficult times. She was a real trooper through her horrific ordeal, and I admire her for the continued bravery that she shows. Neither she nor I want to go through anything like that again. Once is plenty enough.

Section IX

It's a Wrap

Chapter 30

The Beginning of the End

I'm not sure what the future holds for me as I conclude writing this book. It has been an adventurous journey reliving various heartwarming experiences, harrowing travel adventures, heartbreaking incidents, and sharing many of my hilarious mishaps. Meeting famous people and hanging out with them has also been a true highlight. By contrast, it has been painful to return to those sad and often agonizing memories that I had safely compartmentalized and put on the shelf. But that's OK – it's all part of my history and legacy.

As mentioned at the beginning of this book, I have enjoyed my retirement. As I look back, I regret that I didn't retire far earlier, but it was not financially feasible. In addition, I was afraid of becoming bored and personally stagnated, while also having a fear of becoming a grumpy old man who screams at the neighborhood kids, "Get off my lawn!"

During my retirement years, I have rekindled my love for writing, having now completed two books. In addition, I have maintained my love for music by releasing two albums and have still been performing periodically. I also must admit that I have enjoyed those frequent naps in between writing sessions and music production. Naps are good – especially when you can get away with them and not feel guilty.

Even though time seems to pass quickly, ironically, it also seems like things have slowed down. With no kids to raise and no hustle and bustle of working at a job, life has become quieter and has allowed me to cogitate (one of my dad's favorite words) and look at life more introspectively. Although I have valued all the events throughout my life that I described in this book, they have taken on new meaning and importance upon reflection. It has been a fruitful exercise and has made me realize how blessed and fortunate I have been to experience so many wonderful things and meet so many good people, while also enduring and surviving those "character-building" trying times.

As Joe Walsh said in one of his greatest hits, "Life's been good to me so far." It is true with me. I'm sure there are other events and adventures ahead of me for however long I am on this earth looking down at the grass. Maybe this book will be turned into a blockbuster movie (LOL!). Maybe there will be a sequel book with more of my life's adventures. Maybe there will be more music to write and produce. One thing I do know is that I will always be creative because that's a part of who I am – not to mention it might keep my brain fully functional until my hard drive gives out.

I will close with some advice to all who may read this book – many of these tidbits may be trite, but they are everlastingly true.

Take time to savor life – we only have one shot at it—unless, of course, one thinks reincarnation is real. We all must enrich ourselves and expand our horizons by learning, observing, and discovering – it's in our DNA as humans. We must also value our family and other personal relationships – they are indispensable. And finally, as Tim McGraw sang, "Always be humble and kind."

One special recommendation to kids – and adults as well: get off the damn phone! There's so much more to life than what is contained in that stupid little screen. Remember, Tik-Toc is the sound of your life wasting away. Go play outside. Get dirty. Take a hike. Do things with friends. There is an amazingly wonderful world out there. Time on this earth is much too precious – don't waste it! I believe that life is the most precious thing, and perhaps the rarest thing, in the entire universe. And we are extremely fortunate to experience it!

And Now, The End is Near

One of the greatest songs ever written was sung by Frank Sinatra. Besides his iconic hit "New York, New York," he put his indelible stamp on the great song entitled "My Way." I love the song – it's one of my all-time favorites. If anyone has never heard the song or if it's been a while, it is certainly worth the three minutes spent listening to it. It's a classic. I can now fully relate to the eloquent and poignant lyrics more than any other time in my life.

Yes, I have lived my life my way. Has life gone perfectly for me? Of course not. Do I have regrets? Absolutely. Did I make mistakes? Undeniably. Would I like to go back and change a few things? Sure. But I can unequivocally say, as I find myself in the proverbial twilight years of my life that I am happy, content, and most of all, blessed and thankful.

Although I have accomplished many things in my lifetime, my bucket list still has some boxes not marked off. I must admit I am not quite ready to check into my presidential suite in Heaven. When I first checked in for my stay on this beautiful blue planet in 1950, I had complete maid service (thanks Mom!), three square meals per day, (thanks Mom!), and a comfy place to sleep (thanks Dad!). Yes, my all-inclusive resort was certainly not Buckingham Palace or a 9,999 room Imperial Palace in China, but all in all, my earthly stay has been mostly cozy and generally pleasant.

My earthly vacation adventure here has included amazing sightseeing opportunities, interesting encounters with other resort guests, ample accommodations, and mostly excellent cuisine. I would rate my stay as 4 out of 5 stars. I withheld 1 star because I did have some unpleasant experiences, having run into a few people whose primary mission at this resort was to seemingly make others miserable – I will nicely refer to them as idiots. The accommodations have mostly been excellent, although I did have to spend two semesters with an inconsiderate, smelly, and mostly rude roommate during my freshman year in college – I'm sure many can relate. Finally, the resort activities have at times exceeded my expectations, but life has not always been fun and games.

I have done my best to be a good and giving person during my earthly stay, although I am sure I let some people down. Hopefully I have racked up enough points and good reviews that God will welcome me to my new resort property and He will have stocked my presidential suite with enough goodies and pleasantries to last me for at least most of eternity. I suppose I won't really know until I walk through those pearly gates, arrive at the reception desk, and then check into my room. Maybe the presidential suite is not what He has planned for me, but there's nothing wrong with asking for an upgrade when I check in.

I am not a rich man – never have been and never will be – but all the experiences in my life, including the places I have been, the people I have met, the friends I have made, the family I love, along with the loved ones I've lost, it all has more than fully filled my cup with more riches than I probably deserve.

And so, the end is here. My current brain download is complete. Maybe there's another book or more music in me, but for now, it's time for me to take another nap.

Mom and Dad's wedding, 1943

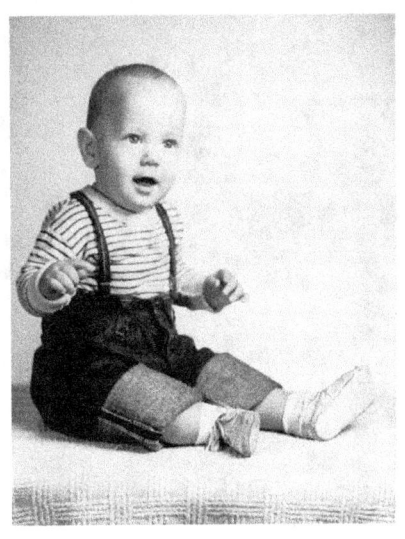
One year old me

9 years old, future LL all-star

Senior picture, 1969

Winning conference finals, 1969

Continental Singers tour, 1969

Wedding day, 1979

The family, 1989

Linda and me at Hirschhorn Castle on our belated honeymoon

Happy couple, 1994

Beauty and the beast, 1998

Linda and the punks in London, 1985

Linda and me in Venice, Italy, 1993

Adrian, Dusty, and Ashley HS graduates

The girls, their spouses, and us, 2002

Brady, JD, Gracie and Evan - Cutest grandkids ever!

Tres Hombres - Gary, me, Rick

Me at the Great Wall of China

Jamming at Buddy Guy's club in Chicago, 2002

Playing at a corporate gig in Las Vegas, 2014

Promo pic, 2022   Playing at a coffee house, 1970

Acknowledgements

Writing a book has always been on my bucket list. My first book, *I Know We Are Better Than This*, was my political commentary on various cultural issues. It allowed me to express my opinions and pontificate. This book, *The Stories of My Life*, is vastly different in that I share my personal stories about events, people, and unusual occurrences – nothing political. Now I can put two check marks on my bucket list.

I am fortunate to have experienced some hilarious incidents. I also have been lucky to have lived through several harrowing episodes. And finally, like everyone else, I have endured a number of both heart-warming and heart-breaking sagas.

I must provide a deeply sincere thank you to everyone whose stories are included in this book; without you, there would be no book. Thanks to my parents, brothers, wife, daughters, sons-in-law, sisters-in-law, brothers-in-law, nieces, nephews, ex-wife, extended family, friends, business associates, several animals, and even extraterrestrial beings (if indeed they do exist). And of course, I can't forget our grandkids. All of them are very special. Had Linda and I known how great grandkids are, we would have had them first!

A very special shoutout to my sister-in-law, Suzanne Allen, for her editing and grammar skills. Having been an English teacher for many years, she explains and makes sense out of the sometimes idiosyncratic, sometimes enigmatic, and quite often non-sensical rules in the English language that frequently befuddle someone like me. I always learn a lot from her, and I appreciate the innumerable hours she spent working with me.

One final acknowledgement to my daughter Adrian. After a night of storytelling with her, she suggested, "Dad, you should write all those stories down; they are really good ones." So, I took her advice. Thanks for issuing the challenge, Adrian – I can now say I did it!

About the Author

BR Allen is a retired Vice President of Marketing, having worked for a several tech companies throughout his business career. He has long had a passion for writing and has displayed a proclivity for creative writing in the business world, including unique advertisements, effective press releases, and informative magazine articles. In addition, he has been a contributing author for several chapters of book compilations on various tech subjects.

While directing the marketing activities for Texas Instruments' RFID division, the author served as a technology evangelist and was interviewed by and quoted in numerous national publications. He has also been a featured speaker at numerous tech conferences across the US, Asia, and Europe and has participated in committee hearings before Congress on radio frequency identification (RFID) technologies.

Mr. Allen's first book, *I Know We Are Better Than This,* was published in 2020. He was inspired to write the book to convey his insights and interpretations of cultural issues.

Mr. Allen has also shown his musical creativity by becoming a skilled multi-instrumentalist and has written more than 150 songs. He has released four albums and continues to perform his original music along with cover songs. His YouTube channel is: @DaddyBillMusic.

www.ingramcontent.com/pod-product-compliance
Lightning Source LLC
Chambersburg PA
CBHW072148070526
44585CB00015B/1051